TAKING JOURNALISM SERIOUSLY

D1157237

SAGE Publications
International Educational and Professional Publisher
Thousand Oaks ■ London ■ New Delhi

To my kids:
the kitchen table returns . . . until the next time

TAKING JOURNALISM SERIOUSLY

News and the Academy

Barbie Zelizer
University of Pennsylvania

SAGE Publications
International Educational and Professional Publisher
Thousand Oaks ▪ London ▪ New Delhi

For information:

Sage Publications, Inc.
2455 Teller Road
Thousand Oaks, California 91320
E-mail: order@sagepub.com

Sage Publications Ltd.
1 Oliver's Yard
55 City Road
London EC1Y 1SP
United Kingdom

Sage Publications India Pvt. Ltd.
B-42, Panchsheel Enclave
Post Box 4109
New Delhi 110 017 India

Printed in the United States of America on acid-free paper.

Library of Congress Cataloging-in-Publication Data

Zelizer, Barbie.
Taking journalism seriously: news and the academy / Barbie Zelizer.
    p. cm.
Includes bibliographical references and index.
ISBN 0-8039-7313-6—ISBN 0-8039-7314-4 (pbk.)
    1. Journalism. I. Title.
PN4731.Z45 2004
070—dc22   2003025694

04   05   06   07   08   09   10   9   8   7   6   5   4   3   2   1

Acquiring Editor:	Margaret H. Seawell
Editorial Assistant:	Jill Meyers
Project Editor:	Claudia A. Hoffman
Typesetter:	C&M Digitals (P) Ltd.
Indexer:	Molly Hall
Cover Designer:	Michelle Kenny

Contents

About the Author

Barbie Zelizer is the Raymond Williams Professor of Communication at the University of Pennsylvania's Annenberg School for Communication. A former journalist, Zelizer has authored or edited seven books, including the award-winning *Remembering to Forget: Holocaust Memory Through the Camera's Eye* (University of Chicago Press, 1998), *Covering the Body: The Kennedy Assassination, the Media, and the Shaping of Collective Memory* (University of Chicago Press, 1992), and *Journalism After September 11* (with Stuart Allan; Routledge, 2002). A recipient of a Guggenheim Fellowship, a Freedom Forum Center Research Fellowship, and a Fellowship from Harvard University's Joan Shorenstein Center on the Press, Politics, and Public Policy, Zelizer is also a media critic whose work has appeared in *The Nation* and *Newsday*, as well as on the Jim Lehrer News Hour and Radio National of Australia. She is presently working on a book on about-to-die photographs and journalism.

Acknowledgments

This book reflects a very personal journey. As a journalist-turned-academic, I see it as the culmination of many years of moving out of one profession and into another. That journey showed me the importance of taking journalism seriously, both for practitioners and for scholars. So it is with a long memory—and a long list of individuals—that I contemplate the sources of my gratitude.

For teaching me how rewarding journalism can be, I thank fellow reporters Howard Arenstein, Arik Bachar, Alex Berlyne, Cordelia Edvardson, the late Michael Elkins, David Landau, David Lennon, Pat Massey, Art Max, Mike Precker, Ruth Rembaum, David Rogers, Gil Sadan, and Sasha Sadan, as well as the many sources, spokespeople, and officials with whom we shared late hours. For helping me recognize and come to terms with the limitations of journalism's rewards, I thank Dan Caspi, Akiba Cohen, Daniel Dayan, Maxine and Yossi Fassberg, Linda Futterman, Elihu Katz, Richard Juran, Judy Juran, Yehiel Limor, Yosefa Loshitzky, Rafi and Yoram Shir, Itzhak Roeh, and Shosh Zilberberg, who showed me how academic and personal lives could vie with the world of a journalist. I thank Roger Abrahams, Liz Bird, Chuck Bosk, Jim Carey, David Eason, Jim Ettema, Ted Glasser, John Nerone, John Pauly, Michael Schudson, Marsha Siefert, and Linda Steiner, and especially Larry Gross for supporting my interest in journalism once the academy beckoned with its own set of priorities.

Thanks also go to various people for generously giving of their time to either comment on parts of the argument here or read manuscript drafts: Stuart Allan, Michael Bromley, Jim Carey, Herb Gans, Ted Glasser, Larry Gross, Klaus Krippendorff, Toby Miller, Michael Schudson, Linda Steiner, Howard Tumber, Keyan Tomaselli, Joe Turow, Silvio Waisbord, and three anonymous reviewers. Thanks to Sharon Black and her staff for extraordinary library help and to the many students both at Temple University and at Penn's Annenberg School for Communication who along the way helped shape these ideas while in my ever-evolving class on journalism and the academy. In that this project involved a significant amount of literature review over a long period of time, special thanks go to numerous students, present and former, for research assistance, some of whom retrieved for me copies of articles and books when it was not yet clear that they would figure in this manuscript: Carrie Brown, Julia Chang, Gus Dantas, Lauren Feldman, Ted Florea, Rachel Gans, Masaki Hadaka, Courtney Hamilton, John Huxford, Bethany Klein, Kimberly Meltzer, Oren Meyers, Susan Nasberg, Claire Wardle, Louise Woodstock, and Yuan Zhang. Kathleen Hall Jamieson, Michael Delli Carpini, and the Annenberg School gave me time off to set this project in motion. Chuck Whitney and Sophy Craze initially gave it a life, and Margaret Seawell showed remarkable patience and generosity in keeping it on the books long after most editors would have buried it. Ruth Anolik, Carol Gantman, Amy Jordan, Lisa Rosenstein, Pamela Sankar, and Juliet Spitzer pitched in at crisis moments. The immeasurable dose of thanks goes to my children—Noa, Jonathan, and Gideon Glick—who, despite their mother's best efforts, in two out of three cases still prefer reading *People* magazine to the *New York Times*. In the third, watching Jon Stewart wins out every time.

1

Regarding Journalism

Inquiry and the Academy

Any light projects shadows.

Gaston Bachelard

Journalism is most appreciated when it turns into a nonjournalistic phenomenon. When Ernest Hemingway worked as a reporter for the *Kansas City Star*, the *Toronto Star*, and other newspapers during the 1920s, his journalistic experiences were seen as an "apprenticeship" for his later work, and his writing was dismissed as "just journalism." But when he turned portions of that same material verbatim into fiction, it was heralded as literature, portions of which continue to inhabit literary canons around the world.[1]

That transformation—from "just journalism" to a phenomenon elevated and worthy of appreciation—motivated the writing of this book. Why is journalism not easily appreciated at the moment of its creation, with all of its problems, contradictions, limitations, and anomalies? For those interested in journalism's study, repeatedly facing its reticent appreciation resembles having to review basic driving procedures when all one wants to do is take the car onto the highway. It burdens much existing journalism scholarship by forcing scholars to repeatedly address the fundamental question of why journalism matters. Given that journalism has been with us in one form or another since people recognized a need to share information about themselves with others, it is bewildering that such a question persists.

Scholars of journalism are partly responsible for the fact that journalism remains at question and under fire in many collective sensibilities. Have scholars done enough to establish why journalism matters and under which circumstances it matters most? The starting point of this book is to suggest that they have not. And so this book crafts a framework for rethinking journalism, by which it might be better appreciated for what it is, not for what it might be or what it turns into. Looking anew at what we as scholars have established about journalism and aiming to get the story of journalism's study told in many of its configurations, the book borrows its title from a phrase coined by James Carey—it begins by "taking journalism seriously."[2]

Taking journalism seriously means first of all reviewing the scholarly literature, with an eye to tracking the role that scholars have played in thinking about journalism. How have scholars tended to conceptualize news, news making, journalism, journalists, and the news media? Which explanatory frames have they used to explore journalistic practice? From which fields of inquiry have they borrowed in shaping their assumptions about how journalism works? And have their studies taken journalism seriously enough?

In considering what has been stressed and understated in existing scholarly literature, the book also takes journalism seriously by raising questions about the viability of the field of journalism scholarship. Its shape today, its evolution over time, even the challenges it has drawn from elsewhere in the academy—these issues make the politics of inquiry central to the viability of journalism's study. How have negotiations over what counts as knowledge legitimated certain kinds of scholarship and marginalized others in the burgeoning scholarly literature on journalism?

Underlying this endeavor is a deep concern for the future of journalism and journalism scholarship. While some might argue that they have always taken journalism seriously, this book rests on an assumption that that is not universally the case. My own experience offers evidence. As a former journalist who gradually made her way from wire-service reporting to the academy, I am continually wrestling with how best to approach journalism from a scholarly point of view. When I arrived at the university—"freshly expert" from the world of journalism—I felt like I'd entered a parallel universe. Nothing I read as a graduate student reflected the working world I had just left. Partial, often uncompromisingly authoritative, and reflective far more of the academic environments in which they'd been tendered than the journalistic settings they described, these views failed to capture the life I knew. Where were the small but unmistakable triumphs, the unending tensions, the tedium blasted by moments of wild unpredictability, the unexplainable loyalties, the pettiness tempered by camaraderie, and the irresolvable dilemmas that comprised my time as a journalist? My discomfort was shared by many other journalists I knew, who felt uneasy with the journalism scholarship that was fervently putting their world under a microscope. Underlying this tension, of course, was journalism's fierce durability: Although many academic works separated journalists from the world around them for the purposes of academic inquiry, journalism continued to thrive in the world, regardless of what academics did or did not say about it.

The situation has been no less fraught inside the academy, where the terrain of journalism's study has looked at times like a territory at war with itself. The contemporary study of journalism has divided journalism scholars not only from each other but also from other parts of the academy. Within it are deep pockets separating groups of people who share concerns for the past, present, and future of journalism but lack a shared conversational platform for their concerns. They include journalism educators, journalism scholars in communication and media studies departments, writing teachers interested in the texts of journalism, technology scholars involved in information transfer. The list goes on, with each new visitor to the territory encountering a prompt and definitive attempt at colonization by those already there. This suggests a less than encouraging prognosis about our ability to provide a full understanding of journalism in its many dimensions. And so in attempting to take journalism seriously, this book holds constant our understanding long enough to uncover the default assumptions that have guided our thinking about journalism as a field, a profession, a practice, and a cultural phenomenon.

Though intended primarily as a review of the literature, it is hoped that the book also provides an intervention, however limited, into ongoing debates about the role of journalism. Setting the story of journalism's study in place is crucial, because without doing so journalism cannot be taken seriously. Thus this book points in the directions from which we can realign the goalposts through which journalism has been regarded. It calls for rethinking the ways in which it has traditionally been conceptualized and invites a reappraisal of what journalism is, which tools many of us use in its evaluation, and why we see it as we do.

Journalism Scholarship and the Politics of Inquiry

Taking Journalism Seriously proceeds from the assumption that if journalism matters, then journalism scholarship matters. In that it sees both as crucial to journalism's vitality, the book focuses on the broader ways of knowing through which journalism scholarship has taken shape. It assumes that no one voice in journalism's study is better or more authoritative than the others; nor is there one unitary vision of journalism to be found. Rather, different voices offer more—and more complete—ways to understand what journalism is. Accommodating a greater number of voices works to journalism's benefit for the simple reason that inquiry making is not only a cognitive act but a social one too. Undoing the givens behind journalism scholarship is thereby an exercise with foundations in a number of areas of inquiry—work in cultural criticism, the interpretive social sciences, and the sociology of knowledge, to name a few. As James Clifford observed some time ago (1986), the act of building inquiry needs to address the discursive dimensions of conceptualization alongside its cognitive ones.

A number of guiding assumptions thus arise when thinking about journalism scholarship. For in reconsidering journalism's study, we face a series of basic epistemological questions concerning how best to open ourselves up to the received view of what many of us think we know. What do we let go of in our understanding of journalism? What do we put in its place? How do we account for what we are seeing, and which frame do we use to explain it? In thinking about how many of us conceptualize journalism, we need too to think about what makes many of us decide to conceptualize it in one way or another and how we negotiate consensus across different ways of knowing. When making the choice to study journalism, for instance, do we do so because we hope to present our work at certain kinds of conferences or publish in certain kinds of journals? Or do we do so because we hope to land additional work in the popular press or on television? Our concern by definition thus needs to address who is engaged in conceptualizing and to which ends. When and from where do we work on the issue at hand and in which field? To whom do we hope to speak and under which institutional and historical constraints? And how do many of us navigate the terrain we share with others with whom we do not necessarily agree?

Interpretation is key here, and it too is subject to collective consideration. If we make a claim that all journalists are interested in public affairs without an interpretive frame that brings journalism and governance together in a way that convinces others of its viability, we fail to interpret the phenomenon at hand. In that the authority of interpretation is always partial, ruling in and ruling out certain types of knowledge, we cannot claim that historical research is better than sociological research without comparing the two. Nor can we make necessarily unitary claims about either domain. Furthermore, interpretation is always subject to considerations about how research has been conducted and with which field one is connecting oneself.

The identity of a given researcher often has bearing on the appraisals of the scholarship produced, and in journalism studies this has often centered on the question of whether or not a researcher has had personal experience as a journalist. Finally, interpretation can and need always be contrasted with the authority of other observers with other views.

Many of these assumptions can be informally traced to Emile Durkheim's interest in the forces that help maintain a social group's solidarity. Social bonds, said Durkheim (1915), emerge as individuals think of themselves as members of a social order, a process by which the collective is formed. A regard for collective ways of knowing has been advanced elsewhere too (Foucault 1972, 1980; Goodman 1978), where the successful development of cognitive categories has been seen to depend on their suitability to the larger world. Science grows, offered Thomas Kuhn (1964), by developing shared paradigms that name and characterize problems and procedures. True solidarity, observed Mary Douglas (1986: 8), "is only possible to the extent that individuals share the categories of their thought."

The decision to frame scholarship by focusing on its social dimensions has two primary effects. On the one hand, it underscores the difficulty in breaking free of established classificatory schemes. Once consensus is established for a given classification, new phenomena tend to be classified using the same scheme. On the other hand, when fields of inquiry are situated in what Kuhn (1964) called a "pre-paradigmatic" stage, they battle over competing insights that might alter existing classifications. Residuals of these battles often linger in reduced form long after disciplines seem set in place.

This focus implies three premises:

1. It implies that conceptualizing does not end with the concepts it produces. Rather, it extends into whatever gets made of these concepts, where they take us in our scholarship, and how many of us use them or not to make sense of everyday life.

2. It implies investing a certain degree of attention to the forces behind the conceptualization, whether they are individuals, organizations, professional lobbies, or informal groups. Such forces tend to be hierarchical, be politicized, and reflect an enactment of cultural power. For instance, many of us paid attention when critical linguist Roger Fowler produced a new book on language and the news because he was established in his own field (Fowler 1991), even if he had not previously targeted journalism as his focus of inquiry.

3. It implies a dislodging of certainty with which certain groups, fields, individuals can be seen as knowing all or, at the very least, knowing best.

No one agency is more capable than others to conceptualize journalism and journalistic practice. This equalization of voices is a necessary precondition to engaging in renewed inquiry into journalism, even though accepting it side-steps ongoing academic tensions over who in the academy is best qualified to make claims about knowledge.

When taken together, these points suggest that "doing journalism" is not significantly different from "doing art" or "doing religion" (Carey 1985: 41). Thinking about journalism takes shape in patterned ways, and these ways reveal not only a wealth of cognitive information but also a social map of points of commonality and difference that goes beyond journalism per se.

Existing Inquiry Into Journalism

For journalism, that social map has two valuable referent points— journalists and journalism scholars. Both groups are invested in the shape of inquiry about journalism as it persists and changes. Both play a part in shaping that inquiry, and both have much to lose if that inquiry is not made explicit to all those it touches. Conversely, the common interest of both groups necessitates a workable and ongoing awareness of what each group thinks in regards to journalism. At the same time, what it takes to be a member of both groups is neither clear nor constant.

It is fair to say that existing journalism scholarship has not produced a body of material that reflects all of journalism. Rather, much existing scholarly work reflects only a portion of that which constitutes journalism and allows it to stand in for the whole, producing what Peter Dahlgren (1992) called the scholarship's "metonymic character." In his view, journalism has been primarily defined in terms of only a small (and decreasing) dimension of news making—hard news, and this has created a bias that undermines scholars' capacity to embrace journalism in all of its different forms, venues, and practices. In other words, what many of us study accounts for only a small part of the *materiel* that is contemporary journalism.

Consider a repertoire of candidates that would not currently merit membership under the narrowed definition of journalism: *A Current Affair,* MTV's *The Week in Rock,* internet listservs, Jon Stewart, www.nakednews.com, reporters for the Weather Channel, and rap music are but a few that come to mind. This book suggests that the reigning definition of journalism may not be the most inclusive way of defining who counts as a journalist. For as the practices, forms, and technologies for news gathering and news presentation increase in variety, demeanor, and number, the existing body of scholarly material shrinks in relevance.

The metonymic bias of journalism studies is buttressed first by professional journalists themselves, who often repair to a sense of self that either draws on a romanticized, partial, and biased view of the news world or reduces news to a set of narrow, functional activities. On the one hand, many consider themselves hard-core independent news hounds, constantly on the lookout for that enormously important and life-changing story—even when most of their work time is spent in the mundane activities of waiting for meetings to end, checking quotes, paraphrasing official statements and press releases, and following the leads of others. On the other hand, journalists often find it difficult to envision their work beyond the stern boundaries of bureaucratic settings. In G. Stuart Adam's (1993: 7) view, "professional practitioners are inclined to define journalism in terms of limited newsroom conceptions and thus jettison any consideration of journalism's poetics or its ambitious forms." The recent eruption at Columbia University's School of Journalism over the teaching of journalism theory and practice is only one case attesting to the divergent expectations held by journalists and journalism scholars regarding journalism's study.

And so a glaring disconnect taints the spaces between journalistic practice and journalistic inquiry. To quote Dahlgren (1992: 7), a growing gap between "the realities of journalism and its official presentation of self," which affects both journalists and academics, lies at the core of most discussions of contemporary journalism.

To exacerbate an already complicated situation, the academy's move to professionalize journalists has made things worse. Not only has it told journalists that they are professional whether or not they want to be, but it has raised the stakes involved in being a journalist, often to the detriment of those practicing the craft. This has generated some rather bewildering responses on the part of journalists, exemplified by the claim by Ian Hargreaves, former editor of *The Independent,* that journalism requires no qualifications because everyone in a democracy is a journalist.

The metonymic bias of journalism studies also comes in part from the separation of the efforts of academics who study journalists, on the one hand, from those of journalism educators, on the other. As I have argued elsewhere (Zelizer 1998a), the largely isolated pockets of inquiry produced by these two populations have run themselves into the ground. The result is clear: As journalism has flourished in form and in content, it now seems to be no clear place in the public imagination. The "it's just journalism" rejoinder, heard too often as an insulting response to overly descriptive academic scholarship, frames and marginalizes journalism as out-of-touch, trivial, and of secondary importance. It should come as no surprise that in one opinion poll after another, journalists come out near the bottom where issues of public trust are concerned.

What does this tell us about the study of journalism? It underscores how overdue is a reexamination of journalism's received view. One given about journalism scholarship is a lack of consensus about what *is* the best way to understand journalism. Informally, or perhaps even subconsciously, many of us have tended to accept the social sciences, and particularly sociology, as the background field for conceptually considering journalism. But in adopting a sociological mode of explanation, we may have cut ourselves off from other ways of knowing (Adam 1993; Cottle 2000a). This is not a novel notion: Everette Dennis (1984) called for a revamping of journalism education in the early 1980s by wedding it more effectively to the wider university curriculum. Adam (1993) suggested reconceptualizing journalism as human expression and positioning it within the arts. Indeed, humanistic inquiry may offer us one way to offset the bias of sociological inquiry: Rather than conceptualize journalism as effect, we might find alternative forms for considering how journalism works, such as performance, narrative, ritual, and interpretive community (Zelizer 1993a, 1993b).

There is need, then, to suspend our default assumptions in journalism's study long enough to look anew at the evolving world of journalistic forms and practices. Admittedly, approaching all of journalism—as it takes on divergent shapes across national boundaries, media, interests, temporal periods, and localities—is difficult, as there is no unitary description to fit all of its evolutions. In fact, the story of how and why journalism turned into an object of scholarly inquiry in the first place has many points of origin, which follow trajectories that differ by location, discipline, and time period. No wonder, then, that even a project such as this is limited by a gravitation to that which is most familiar. But even with the natural limitations of one's perspective, engaging in a suspension of givens is valuable, in that doing so may help us evaluate new research on journalism as well as create a more welcoming home for journalism's continued study.

Organization of the Book

Based in the sociology of knowledge, this book reviews the literature on journalism by examining five fields of inquiry through which news has been studied—sociology, history, language studies, political science, and cultural analysis. These areas by no means account for all of the relevant scholarly fields invested in journalism's study; given no chapter of their own are important fields like economics, anthropology, law, and philosophy. Equally important, the two related fields of communication and media studies have no chapter here, for their explicitly interdisciplinary character renders them somewhat ahead of the heuristic exercise attempted in these pages. Indeed, many premises described here could be seen as providing a common basis for much work on journalism in communication and media studies.

Nor are the chapters offered here mutually discrete or exclusive. Each chapter claims ownership of certain scholars in ways that by definition narrow his or her work into one disciplinary envelope: Michael Schudson, for instance, appears in the chapters on sociology, history, political science, language studies, and cultural analysis, because his work employs premises directly aligned with each of those perspectives. Scholars are grouped by the premises characteristic of their work rather than the training they received: hence, Kathleen Hall Jamieson, though trained as a rhetorical scholar, is positioned primarily under political science. Each chapter also claims ownership of certain scholarship because doing so illustrates premises central to a given disciplinary perspective. Scholarship on sourcing practices is offered here as a more effective illustration of the premises of political science than of sociology, despite the fact that it has more often been aligned with the latter than the former. For a similar reason, much recent textual work on journalism is positioned more directly in the chapter on cultural analysis than in the chapter on language studies.

Thus the delineations offered here may feel forced and subjectively drawn to many readers. However, they have been strategically chosen because they help us focus on different dimensions of journalism. Each disciplinary field offers aspects of journalism that have been stressed and ignored— differently in each case—and it is hoped that by drawing the map variously its constituents may appear in an alternative light.

By tracking these fields of inquiry, *Taking Journalism Seriously* also considers a number of central debates as they pertain to journalism. Journalism scholarship has evolved into a terrain with many noncommunicative neighborhoods. Suggested here is the identification of numerous interdisciplinary threads by which journalism can be better understood, for the simple reason that they echo different existing disciplinary views. Moreover, by tracking primarily literature written in English (with an uneven attention paid to scholarship in German, French, and Spanish and even less to scholarship in other languages), the view offered here privileges those English-speaking nations where such scholarship was produced—notably the United States, Canada, the United Kingdom, Australia, and New Zealand—because they offer ground with which I am most familiar. References to U.S. and British journalism may appear more often than descriptions of journalism in Latin America or Africa. That said, no view offered here provides a complete register of the traits relevant to each perspective, but it is hoped that each takes us closer to providing a better, if still incomplete, view of what many of us call journalism.

Beyond the close consideration of journalism scholarship offered here, the book also raises questions about the politics of academic authority. While the sociological frame of inquiry has long dominated journalism scholarship, prolonging the recognition of alternative ways of understanding journalistic practice, more general patterns of establishing academic authority have transformed partial frames into general statements about news. Not only has this detached much of the existing research from that employing other perspectives, but it has postponed the building of bridges across the many relevant fields of inquiry.

The book is organized around the five aforementioned fields of inquiry. This chapter, Regarding Journalism, and the concluding chapter, Taking Journalism Seriously, provide theoretical overviews that locate the project within the larger framework provided by scholarship on the sociology of knowledge. Chapter 2, Defining Journalism, offers some observations on the variant ways in which journalism, news, and news making have been defined. Chapters 3 through 7 each review and critique the literature invoking a different theoretical perspective on journalism, in an attempt to clarify the implicit assumptions behind each. These chapters are as follows:

Chapter 3 - Sociology and Journalism

Chapter 4 - History and Journalism

Chapter 5 - Language Studies and Journalism

Chapter 6 - Political Science and Journalism

Chapter 7 - Cultural Analysis and Journalism

The final chapter, Chapter 8, raises questions drawn from the discussion of the preceding chapters, attempting to etch out a space from which the academic discourse on journalism's study might proceed.

Briefly, these chapters trace the ways in which different kinds of inquiry have promoted different ways of thinking about journalism. Positioned here largely as a heuristic device, the different kinds of inquiry are separated in a way that proposes more mutual exclusivity than exists in real practice. While most inquiry tends to blend the different explanatory modes to a greater degree than suggested here, nonetheless each kind of inquiry does appear to follow patterned and systematic lines of explanation.

Sociological inquiry by and large has examined people over documents, developing a regard for the patterned interaction of groups. The most far-reaching template for thinking about news, the sociology of news, focuses on the relationships, work routines, and other formulaic interactions across members of the community who are involved in gathering and presenting news, as well as the organizations, institutions, and structures that guide their work. Sociological inquiry has shaped journalism scholarship by favoring the study of dominant practices over deviant ones and by freezing moments within the news-making process for analysis rather than considering the whole phenomenon. It has emphasized behavior and effect over meaning and has produced a view of journalists as professionals, albeit not very successful ones in that they have not displayed the formal attributes of professionalism. This inquiry has also generated substantial work on the nature, functions, and types of news audiences.

Historical inquiry into the journalistic setting has established the longevity of journalism and journalistic practice. Largely dependent on documents rather than people, this kind of inquiry uses the past—its lessons, triumphs, and tragedies—as a legitimating impulse for understanding contemporary journalism. Within this frame, what has drawn academic attention has tended to be that which has persisted. The contemporary, then, has tended to be seen through a visor situated at some point in the past.

The study of language and journalism has emphasized the texts of journalism in several ways. Inquiry within language studies has assumed that journalists' messages are neither transparent nor simplistic but the result of constructed activity on the part of speakers. Some studies engage in close and explicit textual, linguistic, or discursive analysis of news language; others examine the pragmatics of language—patterns of language use in news as they are shaped by narrative storytelling, framing, or rhetorical conventions. This inquiry thereby stresses not only the shape of language itself but also its role in shaping larger social and cultural life.

Political scientists have long held an interest in journalism. Branching from broad considerations of the role of the media in different types of political systems to studies of political campaign behavior or research on the sourcing patterns of reporters and officials, the shape of political science inquiry into journalism has had numerous strains. Each has been invested in considering journalism's larger "political" role in the making of news. Political science inquiry tackles journalism at its highest echelons—the publishers, boards of directors, managing editors—more often than through its low-ranking individual journalists. At the same time, many studies are motivated by normative impulses and conclude on notes of recuperation, which suggest that journalism is and should be in tune with more general political impulses in the society at large.

Finally, the cultural analysis of journalism has been actively involved in querying the givens behind journalism's own sense of self. The inquiry here assumes that journalism is ultimately relative to the assumptions of the cultural groups engaged in its production. Inquiry focuses on contextual factors that shape journalistic practice, and it necessitates some consideration of the blurred lines between different kinds of news work. Much of this scholarship seeks to examine what is important to journalists themselves, by exploring the cultural symbol systems by which reporters make sense of their profession. Cultural inquiry often assumes a lack of unity within journalism—in news-gathering routines, norms, values, technologies, and assumptions about what is important, appropriate, and preferred—and in its research perspective, which uses various conceptual tools to explain journalism.

As cultural criticism, *Taking Journalism Seriously* examines what many of us know about journalism, and how we have agreed on what we know. In tracking some of the cross-disciplinary and interdisciplinary threads through which scholars have examined journalism, it offers a fuller way of reconsidering much of the existing scholarship. It is thus hoped that the book will shed light not only on our understanding of journalism but also on the more general workings of academic authority. And in so doing, it will establish that taking journalism seriously is an endeavor worth pursuing, not only for the journalists and journalism scholars of today but for those in generations to come.

2

Defining Journalism

A regard for the social aspects of inquiry has particular relevance for the study of journalism. Although one might think that academics, journalism educators, and journalists themselves talk about journalism in roughly the same manner, defining "journalism" is not in fact consensual. Rather, when invoked as a frame of reference, the term reveals much about those invoking it—their background, education, experience, placement in the academy, to name a few. Defining journalism, then, emerges from the tacit knowledge and interpretive strategies that people share when thinking about journalism as a phenomenon. And when tacit knowledge and interpretive strategies are shared by people in patterned ways, it causes them to act in the fashion of interpretive communities, offering various ways of thinking about journalism that impact in turn upon the resulting scholarship.

The Academy as a Set of Interpretive Communities

This book assumes that journalism's study emerges from and through different interpretive communities, defined by their shared strategies for interpreting evidence. The choice of interpretive community is central here. As Stanley Fish (1980) demonstrated long ago, interpretive communities determine how a phenomenon will be interpreted, and dealings with interpretive texts ultimately bring us to controversy or arguments over evidence. In that the goal becomes "not to solve problems, but to signify," there arises a need to look at controversy in the field of journalism scholarship as evidence itself.

This means that interpretive communities are seen not as preliminary to questions of value but as a way of settling and resettling questions of value. Elevating one's analysis from the level of the text to that of its readings, from the concept to the conceptualizing activity that goes on around it, locates the formal units of analysis not in the text (that is, in journalism itself) but in the person, institution, organization, or field of inquiry engaged in journalism's analysis. In this sense, recognizing that the academy offers a number of different interpretive communities provides a way of knowing that what is consensual for members of one community may not work for communities elsewhere. For the purposes of this discussion, various ways to think about, experience, and discuss journalism thereby become relevant.

While this suggests that there is no one best way to view a problematic or issue (Schutz 1982), it also underscores the need to recognize that a problematic or an issue takes shape in different ways. Following Robert Park (1940), we might ask ourselves about the conditions under which different kinds of knowledge arise. What are the functions and roles of each kind of knowledge? How do different kinds of knowledge coexist? How do they support and neutralize each other? And most important, in preferring certain kinds of knowledge, what have we done with the ones that are not preferred? Where have we hidden them, deliberately or inadvertently?

Consider the newsroom as an example. Long used as a stand-in term for the making of news, scholars have maintained an emphasis on the newsroom as the venue from which news emerges. This raises two sets of problems. On the one hand, most journalists tend to take exception to the idea that they make or construct the news, preferring to see their role as one of holding up a mirror to events rather than reflecting the acts of negotiation, power brokering, and resource management that typify newsroom practices. In that regard, a focus on the newsroom undercuts what journalists see as most relevant to journalistic work—the activities of discovery, eyewitnessing, and fact gathering that often take place beyond the newsroom's boundaries. On the other hand, the emphasis on the newsroom in much existing scholarship results primarily from sociological inquiry, which long ago identified it as the primary setting for examining the negotiations among news reporters and editors (Breed 1955). Yet due to less centralized technologies of news gathering and presentation, much contemporary news work is no longer accomplished in the newsroom. Reporters are often scattered across locales as they do their work, to the extent that many rarely encounter the home base of a news organization. And yet the emphasis on the newsroom persists.

A similar argument can be made about the lingering centrality of Fleet Street as a marker of journalism in the United Kingdom, despite the widespread move of the British newspaper industry to Wapping during the mid 1980s. Motivated by the industry's replacement of printing presses with computer technology, many journalists in London ceased to inhabit Fleet Street from that time onward. The brightly colored, open-plan settings of Wapping, combined with its security passes and fortress-like environment, were starkly different from the romanticized pubs, clubs, and other social networks of Fleet Street that had fueled much of the mythology surrounding British journalism. For this reason, Fleet Street continues to exist in memory as large and important, even if it exists in much smaller dimensions in actuality (Bailey and Williams 1997; also Tunstall 1996).

Examples like these underscore the fact that fields of inquiry work from their own interpretive assumptions. While such assumptions help researchers fashion broad statements about how journalism might work, they also facilitate an inattention to their relative and partial nature and limited applicability. Assessing the validity of claims about how journalism works thus rests with scholars themselves, who need to remember the difficulty, if not impossibility, of producing a whole and complete picture of journalism. Taking journalism seriously means that our views of its world will always be tempered by the perspectives with which we have aligned ourselves and the fields in which we work.

The Development of Interpretive Communities in Journalism's Study

For the evolving field of journalism scholarship, the choice of which interpretive community to invoke has been loosely aligned with the ways in which journalism's study has taken shape over time. In different time periods, different academic settings, and different parts of the world, the study of journalism has followed alternative pathways, each of which impacted upon the terms used in delineating its boundaries.

While most choices for defining journalism derived from the differences between long-standing fields of inquiry like history and sociology, broader distinctions also derived from distinctions separating the humanities from the social sciences, and, in turn, journalism scholarship from journalism education. In different regional and temporal settings, journalism educators and journalism scholars could borrow in varying degrees from each of the relevant fields and have much to say about the burgeoning relevance of journalism and its study, though each said it differently.

It is worth beginning with the development of journalism's study in the United States, which left its imprint on much of the inquiry on journalism around the world. U.S. journalism emerged from years of justifying its viability and positioning in the academy to contemplate the development of the social sciences during the mid-20th century. The teaching of journalism began in U.S. universities around 1900 in the humanities, with singular courses given at the Universities of Kansas, Iowa, and Wisconsin that focused on "journalistic" skills like news writing or the history of journalism. Spun off primarily from English departments, these individual courses provided a popular basis of what came to be recognized as journalism education. With time, its largely humanistic inquiry sought to expand the curriculum into ethics, history, and the law, where the teaching of a vernacular craft could be justified (Carey 2000).

In some cases, the early attempts at journalism education spurred the development of schools of journalism, which were established by 1927 at the Universities of Wisconsin and Iowa, the former headed by ex-journalist turned academic Willard Bleyer, the latter by journalism historian Frank Luther Mott (Rogers 1997). The development of the program at the University of Wisconsin was key, as Bleyer envisioned a journalism curriculum that could present itself as a systematic body of knowledge (Bronstein and Vaughn 1998). Insisting that vocational training was not sufficiently scientific and that history was a largely romantic and descriptive field that did not blend well with the rest of the academy, Bleyer set out to build a journalism curriculum with a research orientation (Purcell 1970; Dennis and Wartella 1996; Rogers 1997). His vision was to bring the new social sciences into the core of journalism's study.

A parallel interest in journalism developed in the social sciences at the same time. Spearheaded by sociologist Robert Park at the University of Chicago, who implemented different studies of journalists in the school of urban ethnography during the 1930s (e.g., Park, Burgess, and McKenzie 1925), scholars here saw journalism as a setting worthy of systematic analytical study. Following the work of John Dewey and George Herbert Mead in pragmatism, Park envisioned a periodic newspaper, *Thought News,* as a way of bringing together journalism and the new social sciences; though the paper never appeared, it nonetheless marked an attempt to address journalism's scholarly study. These primarily humanistic social science efforts, novel for their interest in journalism as a viable focus of inquiry, began to give way by the 1940s to another sort of social science once the war in Europe erupted. Positioned at the core of questions arising from the role of propaganda and the need to counter America's lack of readiness to enter the war, journalism began to draw interest as a relevant locus of social science inquiry once the creation of a bureaucratic apparatus surrounding the war effort changed the academic landscape. The Office of Facts and Figures, the Office for War Information, and eventually the Social Science Research

Council brought together academics from different disciplines in a range of activities—propaganda campaign design, training film development, monitoring Axis propaganda—each designed to incorporate the new social sciences in the wider war effort, creating a concrete foundation by which the social sciences could be differentiated from the rest of the academy. These efforts also paved the way for the beginning of journalism's development into a field of scientific inquiry (Dennis and Wartella 1996); for many of those involved, this meant using sociology, psychology, economics, and political science to position the journalist in an environment shaped by forces external to journalism (e.g., Lasswell 1941, 1948; Lazarsfeld 1962, Lazarsfeld, Sewell, and Wilensky 1967).

A number of U.S. scholars capitalized on the new interest in the social sciences so as to enhance journalism education, often within the newly developing paradigm of communication. Indirectly involved in these efforts were four of Bleyer's students—Fred Siebert, Ralph Casey, Ralph Nafziger, and Chick Bush, who independently experimented with the formal integration of the university's research mission into their journalism units. To that effect, they developed Ph.D. programs, insisted on a 25/75 rule by which only 25% of the journalism curricula could focus on skills courses, and developed seminars on academic topics such as public opinion and survey research for the edification of journalism students. A contemporaneous interest in the blending of mass communication and journalism by scholar Wilbur Schramm, who headed Iowa's program after Frank Luther Mott in 1942, facilitated blended enterprises at institutions as wide-ranging as the Universities of Iowa, Illinois, Minnesota, Wisconsin, and Stanford (Dennis and Wartella 1996). Schramm incorporated the work of Paul Lazarsfeld in sociology, Harold Lasswell in political science, and Carl Hovland in social psychology to push journalism in the direction of the social sciences, where newly formed questions of production, influence, effect, and structure became the reigning research focal points of the time: Researchers began to think about how to situate journalists in a network of motivations, agendas, and interactions, how to frame journalists as a group with systematic relations, and how to situate journalists and news making in a world replete with peer pressures, rewards, and punishments, and their effects on the public. Such questions not only complicated journalism's presentation of self but also situated journalists in the real world. The resulting scholarship demonstrated that journalism did not just reflect a world "out there" but was the outcome of collective action engaged in shaping that reflection.

At the same time, however, the draw of the social sciences was not unanimous. In certain views it "did enormous damage to the craft [of journalism], reading journalism functionally rather than intrinsically" and leveling it "down to that of a signaling system while not immeasurably increasing our understanding of journalism" (Carey 2000: 21). From those scholars who resisted journalism's adoption by the social sciences and who insisted on a more broadly defined though still humanistic curriculum for journalism education, curricular efforts were made that did not sufficiently develop journalism as a focus of inquiry, either. At first attempting "to duplicate the atmospherics of a newspaper" by offering "an old-fashioned apprenticeship carried out via extensive laboratories that dominated the program of study, supplemented and sometimes replaced by work at the student newspaper," these efforts in effect facilitated journalism's displacement to the margins of the academy (Carey 2000: 13-14). Over time they came to address the growing world of journalism by dividing it via its technologies of production, separating newspapers, magazines, television, and radio from each other as topics of inquiry, and by the time they expanded to include other areas, like advertising and public relations, journalism was marginalized within its own curriculum. The resulting curriculum thereby lacked "historical understanding, criticism, or self-consciousness" (Carey 2000: 13), and consequently failed to provide a persuasive sense of the craft or world of journalism to complement the science of journalism as set in place by social science inquiry.

In the United Kingdom, the path to journalism's study developed differently but was impacted by the U.S. example. Here too, tensions between journalism educators and journalism scholars and between the humanities and social sciences shaped the inquiry that resulted. While journalism education in the United States preceded its British counterpart at the university level by nearly a century, when it did develop in the United Kingdom it was against a long-standing tradition of learning though apprenticeship. Efforts to professionalize journalism through the efforts of the National Association of Journalists had been evident as early as the late 1800s, but they did not succeed in transporting journalism into the British academy, where concern prevailed that the "'technical elements' of journalism were too lacking in academic rigor to be included in even a sub-degree course" (Bromley 1997: 334). For that reason, practical journalism did not appear as a curricular subject until 1937. Once the course appeared at the University of London, it "gained a reputation in the working world of journalism for being 'too theoretical' and was never highly regarded," closing within 2 years (Bromley 1997: 334). Even the establishment of the first Royal Commission on the Press in 1949, which placed a premium on journalism education and training, did not boost journalism's academic inquiry, and the National Council for the Training of Journalists, which insisted on one model of "learnership" to serve all kinds of journalism (Bromley 1997: 338), remained at odds both with notions of journalism education that saw journalism as an academic sequence within a liberal arts curriculum and with notions of journalism inquiry that regarded journalism as a setting worthy of academic investigation. The United Kingdom, then, continued to favor a model of industrial training, which echoed the trade school model that had drawn uneven bursts of attention during the 1930s (Bromley 1997, in press). The picture somewhat changed when a burgeoning interest in journalism from the surrounding social sciences, primarily from the fields of sociology and political science, took flight during the late 1960s. Largely through the efforts of Jeremy Tunstall (1970, 1971, 1977), the academic study of journalism took shape as the core of the burgeoning field of media studies. Called one of the "founding fathers of British media studies" by James Curran (Tumber 2000), Tunstall singlehandedly put journalism on the map of the British social sciences and ushered in a long-standing tradition of journalism studies in the years that followed.

Elsewhere, journalism's study borrowed unevenly from both the humanities and the social sciences. In Germany, an academic interest in journalism was evident already in the early 1900s in the work of Ferdinand Toennies, Karl Knies, Karl Buecher, Albert Salomon, and Emil Loebl (Hardt 1975; Lang 1996). It was later articulated by Max Weber, who in 1918 saluted journalists' role in the political world (Weber 1948) and in a 1924 address to the German Sociological Society called for multiple studies of journalistic practice, journalistic professionalism, and the career prospects of journalists in different countries (cited in Lang 1996: 13–14). In later years, journalism's study became coopted by German communication schools, following parts of the U.S. model (Schulz 1997). Such too was the case in the Scandinavian countries, which developed communication departments over time that stressed journalism as one of their key components (Rogers 1997). In France, a strong move toward interdisciplinary study, embodied by the work of Gabriel Tarde and Roland Barthes and by literary studies and structuralism, borrowed strongly from the humanities in developing an approach to journalism, though the impact of humanistic social sciences was also evident (Neveu 1998). In Latin America, particularly Mexico and Brazil, journalism was coopted by schools of communication during the 1960s that were particularly strong in the social sciences, especially sociology (Marques de Melo 1988, Chaffee, Gomaz-Palacio, and Rogers 1990; Rogers 1997). Similar patterns of development were displayed in the Middle East (specifically Israel and Egypt), Asia (specifically Korea), and Africa, where journalism remained one of the key draws in the field of communication.

In each case, the ascent of academic inquiry into journalism, particularly as shaped by the social sciences, was by and large resisted by journalists and journalism educators, who found its theoretical impulses problematic for the continued training of journalists. Journalism educators saw the arrival of the social sciences in particular as encroaching on the long-held aim of training journalists in the trade. Bitter arguments between what were called the "Green Eye-Shades" and the "Chi Squares" produced antagonistic public statements, battles over terminology, and challenges to the espistemological basis for understanding journalistic practice (Rogers 1997: 460). Originally backed by the owners and publishers of newspapers, many journalism educators to this day remain outraged by the co-opting of journalism by communication curricula, and as recently as a few years ago, journalists continued to view the study of journalism as "Mickey Mouse studies" (Gaber and Phillips 2000; Bromley in press). Other than certain instances of effective blending of the two, as in some U.S. locations, journalism schools did not successfully manage the transition from trade school to academic institution. In Slavko Splichal and Colin Sparks's (1994) survey of journalism students around the world, institutions of journalism education were found generally to have avoided research activity, employed faculty without Ph.D.s, and failed to develop links with other university disciplines and courses of intellectual substance. At the same time, the alternative path for journalism's study, by which it might have been structurally located in humanities or literature programs, thereby hearkening back to the early days of journalism education when journalists presented themselves as bohemians with a "nose" for news, did not receive sustained attention in the academy once the social sciences arrived on the scene. Though numerous scholars lobbied calls for the humanistic study of journalism (e.g., Carey 1969; Adam 1989, 1993), even the humanities tended to classify journalism as "part of the vernacular, the vulgate," so that "the natural estrangement of journalism from the academy was compounded by the natural snobbism of the humanities" (Carey 2000: 22).

Against this conflicted and uneven development of journalism's study, it was no wonder that more than one interpretive community arose for thinking about the phenomenon at hand. Regardless of the background tensions and conflicting priorities about what to teach and study in journalism's inquiry, journalists, journalism educators, and journalism scholars all needed to find consensual terms for delineating the phenomenon at the core of their interest. In so doing, they drifted toward informal collectives whose members shared independent interpretive strategies for thinking about journalism.

Terms for Journalism

Given the background tensions between journalism educators and journalism scholars and between the humanities and the social sciences that were complicated by the durable and often articulate presence of journalism professionals, the thrust to define "journalism" unsurprisingly went in many directions. Choices for naming, labeling, evaluating, and critiquing journalism and journalistic practice belonged squarely within the interpretive communities from which journalism scholars came. The lexical choices they made were differentially related to the type of news work being referenced, the medium and technology, the historical time period in which it developed, and the scholarly setting in which each term originated. The differences that emerged suggested the degree to which all lexical terms for journalism needed to be considered in conjunction with the available alternatives for referencing the phenomenon and the interpretive communities that shaped them.

"Journalists" and "Journalism"

The most recognizable terms—"journalists" and "journalism"—are often used as generalized labels for the broadest possible range of activities associated with news making and the people who engage in them. Originating from the idea of one who "writes in a journal, or diary" (*Webster's Unabridged Dictionary* 1983: 988), the term "journalist" initially connoted someone who systematically kept a record of certain happenings within a specified time frame and who tended to make that record public. Originating from the French *Journal des Savants* during the 17th century (Mattelart 1996), the term has since broadened in usage, now referring to individuals who engage in a slew of related activities—"reporting, criticism, editorializing, and the conferral of judgment on the shape of things" (Adam 1993: 12). The journalist "in the simplest and most complex tasks expresses a judgment on the importance of an item, engages in reporting, adopts words and metaphors, solves a narrative puzzle, assesses and interprets" (Adam 1989: 73).

The list of traits necessary to be a good journalist has varied. As Nicholas Tomalin (1969/1997: 174), a former gossip columnist, diary writer, correspondent, and literary editor of the *New Statesman*, wrote in the late 1960s, journalists needed

> a knack with telephones, trains and petty officials; a good digestion and a steady head; total recall; enough idealism to inspire indignant prose (but not enough to inhibit detached professionalism); a paranoid temperament; an ability to behave passionately in second-rate projects; well-placed relatives; good luck; the willingness to betray, if not friends, acquaintances; a reluctance to understand too much too well (because *tout comprendre c'est tout pardoner* and *tout pardoner* makes dull copy); an implacable hatred of spokesmen,

administrators, lawyers, public relations men and all those who would rather purvey words than policies; and the strength of character to lead a disrupted life without going absolutely haywire.

Tensions over the boundaries of who is a journalist persist, as seen in the freelance writer currently sitting in a Texas jail for contempt of court and claiming First Amendment protection while refusing to reveal her sources. A broad sense of "who is a journalist" is implied by agencies like the United Nations, which take care in times of war to include in their definitions camera operators, field producers, and documentary makers under the rubric "journalist." Either a broader or more restricted sense of the same question is reflected in the actions of certain states and political parties, which make extensive efforts, to the advantage and detriment of journalists, to define their rights and duties in support of larger strategic aims.

While the term "journalists" signifies most directly the news workers themselves, "journalism" refers to the actions that have come to be associated with news work. Referenced in the 1700s in France by Denis Diderot as the "work of a society of scholars," the word "journalism" was later applied to "the reportage of current events in printed form, specifically newspapers" (cited in Mattelart 1996: 36). Now it more broadly references "the collection, preparation, and distribution of news and related commentary and feature materials through such media as pamphlets, newsletters, newspapers, magazines, radio, motion pictures, television and books" [*Encyclopedia Britannica* (Vol. 6) 1989: 627]. Seen as distinct from less organized modes of recounting public experience, such as rumor, gossip, or hearsay, journalism has come to refer to the organized and public relay of accounts of happenings in the world. Academic definitions have varied: Brian McNair (1998: 4) sees journalism as "any authored text in written, audio or visual form, which claims to be . . . a truthful statement about, or record of, some hitherto unknown new feature of the actual, social world." Michael Schudson (2002: 14) defines it as "information and commentary on contemporary affairs taken to be publicly important." Because journalism is "particularly responsive to social and technological change . . . [its] concrete content varies from one historic period to another and from one country to another," as Splichal and Sparks (1994: 20) noted. In the end, journalism remains "the most succinct term we have for the activity of gathering and disseminating news" (Stephens 1988: 3). No surprise, then, that it is often used as a stand-in reference for the widespread communication of current affairs information.

Implied in the term "journalism" has been a sense of the evolving crafts, routines, skills, and conventions that individuals and groups tend to employ in news making. These have varied over time, including the public posting of handwritten news sheets called Acta Diurna during the Roman Empire, the oral proclamations of German town criers during the mid 1500s about the collection of sacred relics, and the "human wireless telegraphy" system of the Zulus during the 19th century, where runners vocally mourning the death of a tribe member efficiently spread the news (Stephens 1988: 23; also Olasky 1991). Today, journalism offers "reports, story-telling and commentaries in the public media about events and ideas as they occur. Its principle elements are judgment–broadly speaking, news judgment—and reporting, language, narration, and analysis" (Adam 1989: 73). That capacity for judgment has been seen as either a learned skill or a talent with which some journalists claim they are born, exemplified in the idea of having "a nose for news." In addressing what journalists do to constitute themselves as such, "journalism" is differentiated as a lexical choice from terms referencing the institutional apparatuses of the news world, such as "media" or "news," and has at times been used to signify the more communal, collective dimensions of news work.

Yet even here we have not agreed on what constitutes journalism and journalists at any one point in time. Following work on the constitution of professional groups engaged in creative activity (Becker 1984), the differences between central and peripheral roles can be simultaneously vast and minute. There thus remains ambivalence over both questions, and professionals and scholars are divided as to how broadly these definitional lines can or should be drawn. Is a teenage girl who produces daily entries in her diary and shares them with her friend a journalist? According to the above-mentioned definition, she is. And what can be said of printers, publishers, copyeditors, proofreaders, or internet providers? Even if they are not involved in the collection of information that becomes news, they are clearly involved in the craft work of journalism. What can be said of Geraldo Rivera and Jim Romanesko? What separates them from the more quintessential journalistic personalities like Edward Murrow and Walter Cronkite? Does journalism stretch to include film reviewers or music critics? Does it include talk radio, weblogs, and reality television? As technologies of news relay broaden the field of who might be considered a journalist and what might be considered journalism, the evolving consensus over the qualities and skills belonging to the world of journalism changes: lingering discussions over Matt Drudge and his role in relaying information shifted emphasis to the uneven editorial role he played in shaping the information he gave his public. More recently, a thrust in certain quarters to classify comedy shows and reality television as journalism turned a related spotlight on whether or not to include personalities like Jon Stewart and Sharon Osbourne as members of the collective known as journalists.

"News"

A similar degree of relativity surrounds the usage of one of the more popular terms for news work—"news." "News" refers to "new information about a subject of some public interest that is shared with some portion of the public," reflecting whatever is on a culture or society's mind (Stephens 1988: 9). Roughly in use in the same way for at least the past 500 years, the term "news" derived from the word "new" and originally spelled in the Old English "newes" or "niwes" during the late 16th century and was rumored to be an acronym for the four directions in which news traveled—north, east, west, and south. The development of the printing press and the emergence of capitalism at that time rendered the then-favored term—the Old English word "tydings"—an insufficient way of signifying the commercial aura that was beginning to surround the provision of information about current events. Although during the 1500s, newsletters, personal letters, and lengthy pamphlets devoted to a single event were called "newsbooks," the substitution of the word "news" for "tydings" marked a crucial turn in how the provision of current affairs information was seen by the populace—it offered the populace a way to gain a sense of itself as a public. Using the word "news" signified that its provision resembled that of other commodities—like food or clothing—that could be used to secure profit within a larger supply-and-demand framework. News was thereby "coined to differentiate between the casual dissemination of information and the deliberate attempt to gather and process the latest intelligence" (Emery and Emery 1999: 5) and elaborated as such in later scholarship addressing the public sphere (e.g., Habermas 1989). This early linkage between journalistic and commercial viability underscored the strategic nature of the growing list of activities related to news making and brought to the forefront of analysis journalism's economic role, often alongside an understated emphasis on the other roles it played.

Implicit within the term "news" is a conflation of the distinction between the material being reported and the report itself. In that light, *Websters Unabridged Dictionary* (1983: 1209) defined news as both "reports of recent happenings" *and* "new information about anything." This popular blurring of the distinction between the report and the activity the report chronicles has helped obscure journalists' burgeoning authority. Too often, what journalists claim to see stands in for reality itself, obscuring the fact that news is no more than a report, account, chronicle, or story about an event.

Unlike the twinned association between the activity and the people who engaged in it that was implied by yoking the terms "journalism" and "journalists," there has evolved no readily identifiable term for the individuals associated with news. Some attempts have been made—"newsmen," "newswomen," and "newsworkers" come to mind (Hardt and Brennen 1995). In Europe from the 15th century onward, youth involved in the sale of ballad songs or penny papers were described as "newsboys," whereas in the 19th century, the term "news-agents" evolved to refer both to what we might now call freelancers or stringers and to sellers of newsprint products. The fact that both descriptions derived from the market status of news reflects a commodified aura that has come to be associated with the term "news," and it has been further strengthened over time by the stress in this lexical choice on what is communicated rather than on who communicates it.

Finally, definitions of "news" remain as broad as some contemporary journalists would have them be. While people are often cited for saying that they know what makes news but cannot explain it to others—"it is easier to recognize news than define it," said one journalist back in the early 1940s (cited in Johnson and Harris 1942: 19)—most journalistic guidebooks spend more effort on detailing how to write the news or get the news than on defining what news actually is. One well-known maxim, traded often and easily in editorial meetings, stipulates that the "news is what the editor says it is." Yet while news can alternately be conceptualized as a range of activities— news gathering, copy reading, production, camera and video work, archival retrieval, interviewing, feature writing, internet relay, to name a few—the reigning trait of attempts to define news has been to admit their partiality. One eight-location U.S. survey—*What Is News? Who Decides? And How?* conducted by the American Society of Newspaper Editors as part of its Newspaper Readership Project (ASNE 1982)—prefaced its report by offering the titular head and following it up with the parenthetical statement "(Do not read this report expecting to find out.)" The report noted that when journalists were asked to define news, they inevitably responded by saying it was difficult if not impossible to define, yet it justified their difficulties with the following statement:

> The diversity, the individuality, the fierce independence of American journalists insure the uniqueness of every daily newspaper and, happily, defy any generalized, research-formulated answers to the questions above.

Some answers to the question of "what is news" instead produced lists of qualities—such as proximity, timeliness, consequence, interest, and prominence—that characterize news (ASNE 1982: 1), and that definitional strategy was reflected in other efforts as well. Glasser and Ettema (1989a), for instance, delineated qualities by which news could be recognized as a type of commonsensical approach to events shared by journalists. Responses ranged from the irreverent to the pragmatic while focusing on the impact of news in shaping a definition: "news is what will sell papers," "news is what the public wants to read," and "news is what raises eyebrows." Still others, offered in a closer reading of journalistic practice, argued that "news is what newspapermen choose to make it" (Johnson 1926) and were repeated in various formulations over the years that followed (e.g., Gieber 1964).

"Media"

Yet another term commonly used for journalism—"media"—refers to the mediating agencies that allow the relay of information to take place. In its singular form, the word "medium" has been in use roughly since the late 16th century, when it referred to "the sense of an intervening or inter-mediate agency or substance" (Williams 1983b: 203). Not until the 18th century was it used in conjunction with newspapers, and only with the ascent of broadcasting in the 20th century did the plural form—"media"—come into use. The term "mass media" was coined in the late 1940s, after socially scientific-based notions of advertising, social psychology, and media influence made their way into the academy (Czitrom 1982: 126). At the same time, the word "media" took on what Raymond Williams called "a social" connotation, whereby "the practices and institutions are seen as agencies for quite other than their primary purposes" (Williams 1983b: 204). In this view, media are also seen as agents of empowerment or disempowerment, of marginalization of certain groups, and charged with upholding the status quo. In each case, "media" is used as a referent to journalism, even though the term refers to phenomena that extend beyond the scope of news making per se.

The term "media" is differentiated from the other lexical choices for news making by its implicit recognition of the industrial, institutional environment in which journalists are presumed to work. In this regard, attention is often paid here to the trappings that ensure the provision of information—such as media ownership, standardized content, and patterns of convergence—rather than to the information itself. Journalistic practices themselves reflect the altered emphasis. For instance, photographic credits in the news today often denote corporate ownership—Corbis, TimeInc, Reuters—rather than the photojournalist who actually took the photograph. Similarly, as seen with the term "news," there is no readily available word for "journalist" that derives from the invocation of "media" to refer to news making, although at times the terms "media worker" and "media professional" have been used. Thus, the focus here on industrial and institutional concerns, constitutive when using this lexical choice, highlights the large-scale processes by which the news is made rather than considering the news itself and the people who make it.

The term "media" is also differentiated from other terms by its explicit recognition of technology, or the channels in which the news is made and presented. At times the word "media" refers more to the technological apparatus than to the information it conveys, even as basic questions remain over what is a technology and over which technology can be considered a medium. This lack of clarity has direct implications for news: For instance, is Indymedia's online news service the same kind of news as Peter Jennings's reports on ABC? The emphasis on technology has also produced its own bias in considerations of news making that favor the faster, stronger, more sophisticated technologies. Not only does this bias toward sophisticated technologies reduce the potential relevance of the information of news, but it has also rendered early forms of spoken news nearly "invisible in the shadow of more advanced news media," with early or nontechnological means of providing information recast as nonviable forms of news work (Stephens 1988: 40). How might we classify the media that some journalists in certain rural areas of Africa continue to use, which are neither mass nor modern—street singers, storytellers, traveling theater? How might we classify the impromptu public postings of photographs and bits of information in New York City about individuals who were missing after September 11? Moreover, how are we to account for the larger media environment of news making? The recent individualized technologies for delivering news—such as the internet delivery of news dispatches relayed into private computers—have so enhanced the capacity to deliver news fast and far that they make mainstream news channels seem obsolete.

"Communication" and "Information"

A more recent set of terms for journalism is "communication" and "information." Gaining meaning during the second half of the 19th century, these terms particularly came into vogue during the middle of the 20th century, once communication developed as a field of study in the United States and journalism was frequently co-opted as part of its curriculum. With "communication" defined as "the act of imparting, conferring, or delivering from one to another" (*Webster's Unabridged Dictionary* 1983: 367) and "information" defined as "knowledge acquired in any manner" (*Webster's Unabridged Dictionary* 1983: 940), the ascendancy of these terms had to do with a post-World War II interest in the evolution of a certain kind of communication research (Carey 2000). Positioning journalism as part of the communication field necessitated recasting journalism in a way that was reflected in the lexical choices used in its referencing, and the term "communicator" was an obvious extension here.

The terms "communication" and "information" emphasize the process of news making—that is, the delivery of information—as well as the substance of the relay. At the time of these terms' ascendancy, the emphasis made sense. The idea of media influence was so inbred to U.S. communication scholarship during the 1940s and 1950s that virtually all study derived from some notion of media influence, and the corresponding notion—that journalism too had an effect on the public—was reflected in the suggestion to turn schools of journalism into schools of communication (Marvin 1983). In that the concern was with influence, researchers consequently needed to be looking at those who wielded the influence. These terms for news making, then, focus on the effect of journalism as much as on its making.

This set of lexical choices, however, like the terms "news" and "media," lacks any reference to the people behind the news making. While there have been attempts to label journalists "communicators," the terms have been problematic for many journalism professionals, for whom the field of communication makes it appear as if anybody can be a journalist. In the United States, their concerns generated "a kind of cold war over their shared curriculum" between journalism educators and communication researchers during the 1960s and 1970s (Marvin 1983: 28), and many journalism professionals were concerned by the reduced interest in journalists that these lexical terms reflected—either as craftspeople or as professionals. Emphasized instead has been the utilitarian role of journalists as information providers.

Relevant here have been the boundaries used to mark journalism through what it is not. For instance, the establishment of public relations as one strand of journalism studies has forced conversations about the degree of similarity between the two (Tumber 2002; Cottle 2003), drawing attention to the boundaries of journalism as a field of inquiry.

What do each of these lexical choices tell us? Each alternative has brought with it a patterned change of how we think about journalism, offering a corresponding set of values, norms, and beliefs about what matters. In some cases, the new term has dissipated consensus about what we think we know. In others, it has built upon earlier notions and complicated them in accordance with contemporary worldviews and circumstances. But no one lexical choice is value free; nor is any choice detached from larger notions associated with the type of news work, the type of medium and technology, the historical time period, and the scholarly setting in which each term originated. Even the relevant term for a "journalist" becomes implicitly if not explicitly a "newsworker," a "media professional," and a "communicator." While such evolution has been rightly applauded for freeing certain reporters from the professional mythology accompanying journalistic work in a given set of circumstances and time period (see Dahlgren 1992: 8), it has also underscored a tendency to argue for the universal nature of much of what we call news work. In other words, all lexical choices remain alternatives, and they need always to be seen against the choices not selected.

This matters because each lexical choice already renders certain premises about journalism natural while delegating others irrelevant, if not obscure. Dependent upon a frame of reference, time period, and focus on technology and medium, these terms are no better than boundary markers for conducting inquiry. They convey who a journalism scholar is, what a scholar's premises for research might be, and what kinds of questions a scholar chooses to ask about the phenomenon at hand. Thus, in choosing one term over another, scholars display much about who they are as researchers. The terms they choose reveal much about where they are coming from and with which approaches they show more and less empathy. But they almost never convey all that there is to know about journalism.

Definitional Dimensions of Journalism

Much of the discussion thus far has provided a sense that the choice of terms for journalism reveals how we think about the phenomenon. Yet semantics extend even further than the definitions appended to each term surrounding journalistic work. In fact, the varieties of lexical choice underscore an even more fundamental fact—that journalism itself is comprised of many contradictory sets of people, dimensions, practices, and functions.

How Journalists Talk About Journalism

Given the difficulties in defining journalism and news, it is no surprise that competitive verbal cues have risen to the fore of discussions among journalists about what journalism is. Beyond the obvious references to journalism as a story and journalism as a practice, which are both central to journalists' discussions and addressed by the scholarly literature, certain ways of talking about journalism reveal the underlying ways in which journalism professionals make sense of journalism. Many such cues are not typically mentioned in scholarly literature, for as Theodore L. Glasser and James Ettema (1989a: 18) argued, there remains a "widening gap between how journalists know what they know and what students are told about how journalists know what they know."

Yet journalists talk about journalism in patterned ways. Typical of what Robert Park (1940) called "synthetic knowledge"—the kind of tacit knowledge that is "embodied in habit and custom" rather than that which forms the core of formalized knowledge systems—cues to how journalists think about journalism can be found in journalistic guidebooks or "how-to" manuals and in numerous catch phrases associated with journalism's practice. Following work on metaphors (Black 1962; Lakoff and Johnson 1980; Lakoff 1987), these cues can be understood to metaphorically address potentially problematic, and not altogether revered, dimensions of journalistic practice, by which journalism professionals informally reference journalism in ways that are true to experience but not necessarily respected by the professional community.

Five such references are particularly prominent in journalists' discussions of their craft:

1. Journalism as a sixth sense—a "news sense": Here discussions of having "a nose for news" or references to journalists "smelling out news" figure prominently in journalists' discussions of what they do and how they do it. Such cues underscore a commonsensical and natural quality that characterizes the skill of recognizing news, and often journalists maintain that one is either born with a news sense or not. Lord Riddell (1932/1997: 110), a long-term newspaper editor in both the United Kingdom and Australia, wrote in 1932 that all "true journalists" possess an itch to communicate the news. Having "a nose for news" was so important for the journalism educator Curtis MacDougall that he used the expression to title a section in the many editions of his *Interpretative Reporting* (Reid and MacDougall 1987). It was also what prompted *Washington Post* editor Ben Bradlee to explain why he decided to publish Seymour Hersh's expose of the My Lai massacre: "This smells right," he was rumored to have said (quoted in Glasser and Ettema 1989a: 25).

2. Journalism as a container: This metaphor suggests that news is a phenomenon with volume, materiality, dimension, depth, and possibly complexity. Numerous associations arise here: Journalism is seen "to contain" the day's news, holding information for the public until it can appraise what has happened. The associated notion of the "news-hole" derives from a related assumption, that there exist spaces that a given day's newscast or newspaper must fill on a regular basis. One early U.S. textbook for novice practitioners put it this way: "'We're filling up,' the news editor warns. 'Boil hard.' The copy editor hears this warning often. There is almost always more news than space" (Neal 1933: 27). The journalistic "scoop," or the advantage gained by being first on an important news story, similarly references journalism's material dimensions. The title of Evelyn Waugh's (1938) book-length lampoon of England's newspaper business during the 1930s, "the

scoop" has been used to reference not only the victorious activity of filing a story before anyone else but also the news items themselves, positioning them as evidence of journalistic triumph over usually adverse circumstances. The idea of journalism as a container is also implicated in the idea of "journalistic depth," used in reference to a journalistic approach that reflects the complexities of a given news story, and the notion of an event or a certain kind of issue being "*in* the news."

3. Journalism as a mirror: In this view, journalistic practice is reduced to gazing on reality or objective happenings in the real world. News is seen as all that happens, without any filtering activity on the part of journalists. Central to professional notions of objectivity, catch phrases here include "news as a lens on the world," "newspaper copy," and the "camera as reporter." In that regard, Lincoln Steffens remembered his years on the *Saturday Evening Post* by recounting that "reporters were to report the news as it happened, like machines, without prejudice, color, or style" (Steffens 1931: 171). The names given to both newspapers and broadcast news organizations often reference journalism as a mirror. From epithets like "eyewitness news" or mottos like "all the news that's fit to print" to specific newspaper names that liken them to a sentinel, beacon, herald, tribune, or chronicle, journalism's function as one of recording the happenings of the real world remains uppermost in journalistic considerations of journalism.

4. Journalism as a child: This view positions journalists as caretakers of the news, and it identifies journalism as a phenomenon in need of nurturing, attending, supervision, and care. Implying journalism's fragility and vulnerability as well as its association with somewhat frivolous, unreasonable, and unpredictable demands, this metaphor assumes that journalists adopt a somewhat continuous parental position, by which they necessarily attend to the news at all times. Part of journalistic folklore, by which the demanding nature of news has been variously held responsible for journalists' so-called premature professional burnout, high divorce rates, and absent social lives, at times journalism's childlike nature forces on journalists a watchdog role, by which they must stridently stand guard over the shaping of news. At other times journalists need adopt a gentler role toward news making. Relevant catch phrases in this regard are telling: "Putting the paper to bed" involves closing the press for the night, while "sitting on a story" involves taking care of a story until it is time for publication. "Pampering" or "coddling" a story refers to elaborating a "thin" or unsubstantiated story line. By contrast, "breaking news" connotes the circumstances when journalism is out of a journalist's control and refers to a story that is raw and in need of finishing, refinement, or further nurturing by

journalists. "Killing a story" involves the editor-in-charge deciding that a given news item needs no further attention.

5. Journalism as a service: Referring to journalism as a service positions journalism in the public interest and in conjunction with the needs of citizenship. The notion of service permeates the language that journalists use in referencing journalism and connotes service to both the profession and the community: news service, wire services, news as being in the general interest, and the public's journalistic representative "serving" London, Washington, or Beijing. Rewards are regularly given for journalistic service in a variety of areas—including specific areas or categories of coverage and specific geographic domains. The awards named for journalistic service are numerous: the Missouri Honor Medal, G. Richard Dew Award for Journalistic Service as awarded by the Pennsylvania Newspaper Association Foundation, the William Allen White Medal, and the Maria Moors Cabot Prize Award from Columbia University are but a few.

Each of these options shows that journalists experience their craft in complicated ways. Their regard for journalism as a sixth sense, container, mirror, child, and service suggests a strong sense of responsibility for the news that is complicated by both its materiality and its continual and ever-changing nature. At the same time, journalists regard the public dimensions of what they do as critical to a definition of their own work as journalists.

How Scholars Talk About Journalism

The definitional dimensions of journalism do not end with how journalism professionals talk about journalism, however. Although they certainly figure into the informal discussions by which journalism is referenced, scholars exist in their own interpretive communities that have produced distinctive definitional sets by which journalism can be identified.

Five such sets seem to prevail in the scholarly literature on journalism: Journalism is seen as a profession, as an institution, as a text, as people, and as a set of practices. None of these perspectives is mutually exclusive, and each is invoked in accordance with broader understandings affixed to journalism.

Journalism as a Profession

Journalism refers, first of all, to a set of activities by which one qualifies as a "journalist." Implied here is a notion of the profession, a frame particularly relevant to the evolution of journalism in the United States. Though helpful in the early 1900s for organizing a basically disorganized group of writers into a consolidated group (Schudson 1978; Schiller 1981), the notion of "the profession" now promotes a sense of U.S. journalists as "unsuccessful professionals" (Tuchman 1978b: 111). The checklist of traits by which sociologists identify professions—certain levels of skill, autonomy, service orientation, licensing procedures, testing of competence, organization, codes of conduct, training and educational programs (e.g., Moore 1970)—lends status to those thought to be acting as professionals. Yet U.S. journalism and journalists display few of these traits. In David Weaver and G. Cleveland Wilhoit's (1986: 145) words, "the modern journalist is *of* a profession but not *in* one . . . the institutional forms of professionalism likely will always elude the journalist."

At the same time, "the profession" is invoked for aims other than the enumeration or listing of external traits (Hughes 1958). It provides a body of knowledge that instructs individuals what to do and avoid in any given circumstance (Larson 1977; Friedson 1986). For U.S. journalists in particular, this has provided an ideological orientation that facilitates the maintenance of journalism's collective boundaries (Johnstone, Slawski, and Bowman 1976; Weaver and Wilhoit 1986, 1996; Becker, Fruit, and Caudill 1987; Lont 1995). Already by the 1920s, U.S. journalists looked to the idea of the profession as a way to consolidate the expertise that allowed them to decide what was and was not news, and that interest was replicated years later in both the United Kingdom and Australia (e.g., Boyd-Barrett 1980; Henningham 1985). Moreover, the defining traits of professionalism have changed over time, with the definition of a professional undergoing a degree of liberalization and modification that may better reflect journalism than did earlier definitions. Elihu Katz, for instance, pondered the possibility of tracking journalistic professionalism through the lens of scientific inquiry (1989, also 1992).

While the regard for journalism as a profession has been tracked in sociological work on the media (e.g., Janowitz 1975; Tunstall 1977; Boyd-Barrett 1980; Henningham 1985), it has also generated criticism in other areas of inquiry. James Carey (1978), for instance, branded journalism's professional orientation "the great danger in modern journalism," primarily because the client-professional relationship it implied left the public no real control over information and thus dependent on journalism for knowledge about the real world. Professionalism was held responsible for journalists safeguarding their reporting, arguing that it was necessarily objective, neutral, and balanced (Schiller 1979, 1981). As an organizational and institutional firewall, professionalism was used to safeguard against change, loss of control, and possible rebellion in all domains of U.S. journalism (Soloski 1989). Discussions of the failure of journalists to energize a robust political sphere pinpointed the limitations of one of the long-standing supports for U.S. professionalism, the idea that journalists could and should be politically neutral (Patterson 1993).

In some locations, journalism's invocation as a profession was seen to undermine its recognition as a craft, an issue that has drawn particular attention in the United Kingdom. In one typical response to the then-growing sociological literature, British reporter James Cameron, a longtime correspondent with the *Daily Express, Picture Post,* the *News Chronicle,* and the *Guardian,* complained in 1967 about "the talking about the profession of journalism":

> Journalism is not and never has been a profession; it is a trade, or a calling, that can be practiced in many ways, but it can never be a profession since its practice has neither standards nor sanctions. . . . This may well be a good thing, since while this flexibility and permissiveness gives entry to a number of dubious oddballs it equally does not exclude many valuable and original people. It is fatuous, however, to compensate for our insecurity by calling ourselves members of a profession; it is both pretentious and disabling; we are at our best craftsmen, and that is by no means an ignoble thing to be. (Cameron 1967/1997: 170)

The turn toward deskilling journalists in the United Kingdom tainted the reverence for journalists' craft orientation at the same time as it recodified journalists as members of a professional community (Bromley 1997, in press). And yet, the fact that the journalistic profession imposed certain codified rules of entry and exclusion (exemplified, for instance, by the unionization of British journalists), and then found that there were not enough places to accommodate the growing numbers of Ph.D.s necessitated by such professionalization, has both worked against journalism as a whole and generated an oppositional collectivity among journalists: The antiprofessionalization position it created helped forge a collective sense of identity among journalists, who became increasingly visible and articulate about their opposition to invocations of journalism as a profession. Other problems with professionalization presented in France, where the learned status of French journalism coupled with the newly won autonomy of French journalists, as facilitated by privatization, produced numerous instances of aggressive investigative reporting that were seen by some observers as scandalous (Neveu 1998).

Yet the idea of journalism as a profession has remained uppermost in the minds of many journalists, suggesting its continued relevance for reporters, regardless of how happy they are about adopting it. For instance, concerns over professionalism provided much of the impetus for A.J. Liebling's "Wayward Press" column, begun in 1947 at the *New Yorker.* Similarly, the various chronologies of the professional unions of journalists— C.J. Bundock's *The National Union of Journalists: A Jubilee History,* published in 1957 to mark the 50th year of the journalists' union in the United Kingdom, and Clem Lloyd's *Profession: Journalist: A History of the Australian Journalists' Association,* published in 1985 to mark 75 years of professional journalism in Australia, to cite two examples—detailed the ways in which professional concerns over areas of training and the establishment of ethical standards mixed with industrial issues in maintaining standards in journalism over time. Since its foundation in 1910, the Australian Journalists' Association described journalism in professional terms (Henningham 1985).

The idea of professionalism has also remained implicit in much of the journalistic trade literature. Trade journals as wide-ranging as the *American Journalism Review, British Journalism Review, The Quill,* and *Editor and Publisher* repair to an invocation of journalistic professionalism in discussions of journalistic scandals, worries over breaches of consensual journalistic practice, and ongoing conversations about the need for stronger journalistic ethics. For instance, the *British Journalism Review*—established by a charter that, as articulated in its inaugural issue of 1989, aimed to "help journalists reflect on the changing character and problems of their job" (*British Journalism Review* 1989: 1)—within 10 odd years already lamented a shifting of "the professional goalposts that once were regarded as firmly embedded and sancrosant" (Goodman 2002: 4). Its response was to tackle what it saw as the violations of professionalism, as when a reporter used the pages of the *British Journalism Review* to query confidentiality as a workable professional standard in certain types of news stories (Martin-Clark 2003) or when a U.K. trade editorial lamented the "vast array of communicators in which professional journalists are, increasingly, a mere minority" (Goodman 2002: 3). Invocations to professionalism were similarly displayed in the U.S. trade press: In the *Columbia Journalism Review*'s overview of the last century, professionalism provided its own sub-rosa narrative of the period, invoked in contexts as diverse as the fabrications of the Spanish-American War, the media's hounding of the Lindbergh family, the responses to a 1950s *New York Times* picture editor who promoted a photo of an open-mouthed kiss between Marilyn Monroe and Joe Dimaggio, and the professional skepticism that greeted the arrival of both CNN and *USA Today*—both of which survived despite early hostility and technological difficulties (Evans 1999). And the various embarrassments of journalism—the mislabeling of the safe arrival of the Titanic's passengers, Walter Duranty's coverage of the Soviet Union, Clifford Irving's "autobiography" of Howard Hughes, and the Janet Cooke scandal—predictably invoked cries of faulty professional behavior (Leo 1999). Concerns over privacy and freedom of speech were seen as tweaking the boundaries of professional behavior among reporters over a wide range of cases (Mayes 2002; Hagerty 2003; Riddell 2003). And even the recent outcries over the Hutton Inquiry and BBC reporter Andrew Gilligan's problematic journalistic performance in the United Kingdom or over Jayson Blair and the *New York Times*' attempts to cleanse itself of his unethical behavior in the United States were shaped around invocations to professionalism.

All of this suggests that the idea of journalism as a profession lives, if unevenly so. Many quarters of the academy have long dismissed professionalism as a fertile way of thinking about journalistic authority. However, at the same time they readily include the norms, values, and practices associated with professionalism as part of their curriculum. Journalists, particularly in the United States, steadily invoke professionalism as a safeguard against the tremblings, fault lines, and misdemeanors of their collective life. And regarding journalism as a profession continues to gain mileage in scholarly arenas in which the notion of "the profession" holds a priori significance, namely sociology.

Journalism as an Institution

A second perspective on journalism assumes that it exists in or functions as an institutional setting characterized by social, political, economic, and/or cultural privilege. Largely adopted by scholars involved in critical and cultural studies, political economy, ideology studies, and some sociologists and historians, this perspective sees journalism as a large-scale phenomenon whose primary effect is wielding power, primarily to shape public opinion, and controlling the distribution of informational or symbolic resources in society.

Defined as a setting characterized by "patterns of behavior which are established, approved and usually of some permanence" (Watson and Hill 1994: 93), the institution is valuable as a way to think about journalism because it offers a way to discern journalism's relationship to public life. Often it is taken simultaneously to mean the setting, the behaviors that constitute the setting, and the values by which the setting is organized. It holds within it organizations, or formal groups that work according to collective standards of action. As the British editor C.P. Scott (1921/1997: 198) said of the *Manchester Guardian*, it is "more than a business; it is an institution. . . . It may educate, stimulate, assist, or it may do the opposite. It has, therefore, a moral as well as a material existence, and its character and influence are in the main determined by the balance of these two factors." To regard journalism as an institution is by definition to address the historical and situational contingencies against which journalism performs a range of social, cultural, economic, and political tasks or functions. That said, journalism by this view must exist institutionally, if it is to exist at all.

But regarding journalism as an institution is limited by the difficulties in identifying journalistic institutions, which are by definition invisible. The lack of formal codification or articulation of the reportorial ethos of journalistic institutions renders an analysis of the tacit rules of socialization crucial. Scholars here thereby often try to identify signs of the institution rather than the institution itself. This can involve searching for the interfaces by which news as an institution links to other institutions, facilitating connections between journalism and the government, the market, the world of culture, the educational system, and the religious establishment.

This definitional nexus has tended to draw scholars of two sorts. On the one hand have been those concerned with the intersection of journalism and economics, and the connected issues surrounding patterns of ownership and convergence, corporate influences, deregulation and privatization (Gandy 1982; Golding and Murdock 1991; McManus 1994; Mosco 1996, Bagdikian 1997). The ways in which journalism impacts upon the production and distribution of material goods and wealth have been central here. On the other hand, this nexus has drawn those concerned with the meeting point of journalism and politics. Issues such as governmentality, the linkage of public and private spheres, and the conventions of citizenship (Scannell 1989, 1996; Blumler and Gurevitch 1995; Miller 1998) have suggested wide-ranging ways in which journalism impacts upon the exercise of power in everyday life. At the same time, however, the difficulties involved in documenting this kind of institutional impact have been widespread. For instance, the notion that a newspaper owner's capitalist orientation shapes the institution in which news accounts are written, which in turn reproduces capitalist ideology, has been taken as axiomatic, despite the fact that few studies have shown how this is actually achieved.

The adoption of institutional trappings has not been limited to one time period or one geographic locus by scholars addressing the issue. For example, Richard Schwarzlose (1990) argued that the real "rush to institution" occurred in the United States with the ascent of the wire services during the post-Civil War period, when the rapid growth of intercity news gathering and distribution made journalism look beyond itself to broader technological innovations, corporate interests and growing internationalism in the public sphere. Conversely, looking at journalism as an institution has been widely adopted in journalism scholarship in the United Kingdom (Curran and Seaton 1985; Curran and Gurevitch 1991), Australia (Tiffen 1990; Schultz 1998; Curthoys and Schultz 1999), Israel (Liebes 1997; Caspi and Limor 1999), and Latin America (Waisbord 2000; Fox and Waisbord 2002).

Adopting the institutional lens has also been a relevant frame for global and comparative analyses of news, where institutional pressures vary as nation-states jockey for power with the interests of broader economic corporations and global concerns (Boyd-Barrett and Rantanen 1998; Morris and Waisbord 2001).

At the same time, however, institutional prestige does not always ensure a "better" or more effective journalistic performance. Following the Branch Davidian incident in 1993 in Waco, Texas (in which the FBI assaulted a compound inhabited by members of the Seventh-Day Adventists Movement who were suspected of child abuse, causing the deaths of scores of individuals), one survivor was expected to appear on ABC's *Nightline*. He cancelled at the last moment to appear instead on the less prestigious *A Current Affair*, from which he received a hefty financial retainer.

Journalism as a Text

A third definitional set for journalism sees "news" as a text. In most cases, the texts of journalism have agreed-upon features—a concern with certain events (a fire, a summit conference, a murder), recency or timeliness, and factuality. They also tend to display less readily articulated features, at least in the U.S. mainstream media—an anonymous third person author, a generally reasoned and unemotional accounting of events, and an uncritical gravitation to the middle of the road on issues of contested public interest. In David Halberstam's view, such features "required the journalist to be much dumber and more innocent than in fact he was" (quoted in Parenti 1986: 53). By contrast, the texts of non-U.S. journalism—particularly in parts of Europe, the Middle East, and Latin America—tend to be politically driven, opinionated, and authored (e.g., Hallin and Mancini 1984; Waisbord 2000; Benson 2002).

The emphasis on journalism as text considers the public use of words, images, and sounds in patterned ways. Key here has been the evolving notion of news stories, and the focus on "story" as a way of explaining what journalists produce when gathering and presenting news. Thus, what is news is made explicit by defining it in terms of a report, a record, or an account, and news takes on the attributes of either a written document or an oral tale. Catch phrases, employed frequently by journalists, include references to a "top or lead story," "special report," "story behind the story," or "news series." And yet, as Walter Benjamin lamented in the 1920s, the art of storytelling was reaching its end already then, "because the epic side of truth, wisdom, is dying out," to be replaced by a new form of information called "communication" (Benjamin 1970: 88).

Nonetheless, texts have offered a useful analytical entry for thinking about journalism, because texts, as objects of investigation, are to a degree finite, are identifiable, and have more or less clear beginnings and ends. Preferred by scholars in areas as wide-ranging as content analysis and framing (Krippendorff 1980; Gamson 1988), sociolinguistics and discourse analysis (van Dijk 1988; Bell 1991; Fowler 1991), and semiology and cultural analysis (Hartley 1982, 1996; Fiske 1988, 1992b), this definitional set has facilitated an exchange of ideas around identifiable stories, reports, editions, or programs. Across these options, scholars have probed texts using both quantitative and qualitative approaches, with the often-cited distinctions between content analysis, as embodied by the Glasgow University Media Group (1976), and textual analysis, as embodied by John Fiske and John Hartley (1978), marking the difference.

At the same time, scholars are not agreed about which journalistic features to analyze—words tend to take prominence over either images or sounds. Neither are they agreed about which texts to appraise—one issue of a newspaper, one segment of a broadcast, or all existing coverage of a given event. News coverage of the events of September 11, for instance, was looked at by collecting first-round responses to the events (BlueEar.com 2001), examining the central frames of coverage and the political and institutional responses (Kellner 2003), narrating recollections of the events (Denzin and Lincoln 2003), collecting and positioning global responses side by side (*Television and New Media* 2002), and examining the range of journalistic practices by which the events were covered (Zelizer and Allan 2002); each case focused on the same coverage, yet few analyzed the same texts. The same topic can thus easily be dissected in ways that do not necessarily correspond with other research in the same area.

Journalism as People

Defining journalism through the people who work as journalists has been common since much of the early work on journalism. Certain scholars meticulously defined a wide range of attributes about the people we call journalists. Particularly in the U.S. context, a number of wide-ranging surveys of journalists themselves (e.g., Johnstone et al. 1976; Weaver and Wilhoit 1986; Weaver and Wilhoit 1996) provided a comprehensive picture of who they are, where they were educated, and what kinds of experiences they have had as journalists. Weaver (1998) extended that view worldwide, while Splichal and Sparks (1994) surveyed journalism school students in 21 countries and found patterned similarities in the level of expected professionalization, degree and quality of training, and extent of journalistic apprenticeship, despite national location.

But attention has been directed primarily at a narrow and unrepresentative slice of the journalistic population, most often chronicling the practices of the powerful and famous who have offered very narrow views of what counts as journalism. Usually it focuses on high-ranking individuals who are employed by recognized and elite mainstream news institutions. Such work in the United States has tracked the lives of Benjamin Franklin, William Randolph Hearst, and James Gordon Bennett, and more recently William Paley, Edward R. Murrow, I.F. Stone, and Walter Cronkite. In Australia, biographies have abounded about Marcus Clarke, C.E.W. Bean, and John Norton (Curthoys and Schultz 1999). Some work has been written by journalists themselves (e.g., Rather 1977; Ellerbee 1986; Brokaw 2002). For instance, in the late 1990s, former *Sunday Times* correspondent turned scholar Phillip Knightley wrote *A Hack's Progress*, in which he told readers that "the influence journalists can exercise is limited and that what we achieve is not always what we intended. It is the fight that counts" (Knightley 1998: 267).

Defining journalism through people has been marked by a residual disagreement over who is a journalist. Part of the disagreement stems from the changed practices by which journalism is implemented. Although printsetters may no longer be part of the picture in many parts of the world, questions remain about individuals performing the more technical sides of journalistic work. As is the case beyond journalism (Becker 1984), an ambivalence about central and marginal practices persists: Whether to classify print setters, proofreaders, and copyeditors as journalists has simply given way to an ambivalence directed at individuals engaged in page layout, graphic design, videocam editing, and fact checking. The repository of skills and talents differently embodied by columnists like Walter Lippmann and H.L. Mencken or correspondents like Martha Gellhorn, Dorothy Thomas, and Michael Herr has never been sufficiently elucidated. That is to say little of Matthew Brady, Dorothea Lange, or Larry Burrows: Photographers have never quite become the first-class journalistic citizens they could be, and despite the long-standing prevalence of photojournalism in news, a photographer was first elected president of the Foreign Press Association only in the late 1990s.

The privileging of high-ranking members of elite organizations has also excluded the wide range of people working in journalism, particularly the people of color and marginal ethnicities who often occupy the low-status positions. In part, this has had to do with their uneven representation as journalists; as recently as 1998, Beulah Ainley reported that reporters from ethnic minorities made up a mere 1% of the British journalistic workforce (cited in Allan 1999: 181). Figures from the United States were not more encouraging; according to the American Society of Newspaper Editors, in 1996 only slightly more than 11% of U.S. journalists were members of ethnic minorities, though ethnic minorities comprised one-fourth of the population (Shipler 1998). A similar ambivalence has kept the scribes of nonmainstream political views out of the rolodex of major journalistic personalities. How many lists, for instance, regularly point to Antonio Gramsci, Andre Malraux, Victor Navasky, and John Pilger as role models for budding journalists? Moreover, we may wonder how many draw our attention to the more legendary but hard-to-emulate personalities, like Ryszard Kapucinski and John Simpson, who were paired as "journalistic wanderers" by Fred Inglis (2002: 347–351). The ensuing status wars over these questions suggest that they are far from resolved. The repeated battles by professional organizations and journalism groups often reveal that they attempt to increase prestige by limiting membership, such as one memorable example involving a woman's press group and the inclusion of Eleanor Roosevelt, who wrote a newspaper column, alongside public relations personnel (Beasley 1988).

Of late, however, the human subjects of journalism scholarship have become more diversified as an increasing number of researchers look beyond the predictable echelons of the mainstream. Kathleen Hauke wrote of the first African American to be fully employed by a New York City newspaper (Hauke 1999). Matt Drudge produced a book widely reviewed by the trade press, despite the fact that it oscillated between manifesto and biography (Drudge 2001). Fred Inglis (2002: x) produced a "parade of [journalistic] biographies" that by definition broadened the parameters of the group. A growing amount of research is tracking the trajectories of representatives of marginalized groups working in the news (e.g., Dahlgren and Sparks 1991). Issues of gender (van Zoonen 1988; Lont 1995; Lafky 1993; Carter, Branston, and Allan 1998), race (Gordon and Rosenberg 1989; Wilson and Gutierrez 1995; Dennis and Pease 1997, Gandy 1998), and ethnicity (Gabriel 1998; Cottle 2000c) are becoming part of the ongoing conversations about who is a journalist. Even the trade journals are reflecting these newly expanded boundaries of who counts. The *Columbia Journalism Review* recently ran a piece by *New York Times* reporter David Shipler, in which he decried the absence of people of color in the newsroom (Shipler 1998; also Schultz-Brooks 1984).

And yet, even these portraits of the individuals of journalism are narrow and self-limiting. New kinds of journalists and alternate models for thinking about how to "be" a journalist are left out of the picture. For instance, how much effort has been directed at clarifying the new models of journalism evolving in Asia, which cater to individuals with decidedly non-Western values?

Journalism as a Set of Practices

A fifth way of envisioning journalism is as a set of practices. How to gather, present, and disseminate the news has been a key application of this lens, which has produced a myriad of terms among journalists, such as references to "getting the news," "writing the news," "breaking news," "making news," "news-making strategies," and "newsroom practices." As journalism has expanded into new technological frames, the set of practices involved in doing news work has changed. For instance, typesetting skills of the print room have given way to a demand for computer literacy. The increasingly diverse kinds of sources from which information can be gathered into a news story have also allowed for changes in the practices of news that often have made journalism a more collective operation: Practices like fact checking, for instance, lend news making a collaborative dimension that it did not have in earlier days.

This definitional frame has been favored both by historians, who tracked the practices germane to the historical period under analysis (Dicken-Garcia 1989; Steiner 1992; Solomon and McChesney 1993; Nerone 1994; Hardt and Brennen 1995; Chalaby 1998); by sociologically oriented scholars, who provided a wide-ranging repertoire of the practices of news gathering and their larger symbolic import (Tuchman 1978a, 1978b, Fishman 1980, Gitlin 1980; Ericson, Baranek, and Chan 1987); and by culturally oriented researchers, who used the practices of journalism to interrogate the external world order (Carey 1989c; Schudson 1995; Hartley 1996; Bourdieu 1998). Scholars have used this dimensional set to examine alternative kinds of journalism: The familiar conventions of mainstream news were used as a starting point for discussions of practices in tabloids (Bird 1992; Langer 1998; Lumby 1999); similarly, so-called oppositional news practices were rendered understandable by virtue of their comparison with the practices of more centrist news organizations (Eliasoph 1988; Meyers 1994).

The value behind thinking about journalism as a set of practices is that such practices can be thought to have both practical and symbolic dimensions. Not only have they been seen to have pragmatic effects, such as information relay and agenda setting, but they have also been ascribed a crucial role in shaping consensus by relying upon tested routines, practices, and formula for gathering and presenting the news.

Also relevant here have been the alternative ways for thinking about journalistic practices. Development journalism, for instance, ranks the actions of journalists differently than does investigative journalism. Those following the tenets of muckraking would be hard-pressed to deliver their relays through wire-service briefs.

* * * * *

Why are these different definitional sets valuable to us when thinking about journalism? Like the larger disciplinary frames from which they borrow, each set suggests different ways in which to approach and understand journalism. Each has strong points and points of neglect. Most importantly, no one definitional set is capable of conveying all there is to know about journalism.

These definitional sets for understanding journalism become further complicated when they are embedded *across* other modes of inquiry, such as history, sociology, English, and political science—that is, the many disciplines where the analysis of journalism is readily located. This suggests that the basic lack of consensus over journalism is itself an artifact of its placement in the academy. When compounded by different disciplinary perspectives, means of record keeping, and appropriate standards of analysis, journalism becomes a whole of various contradictory parts.

Where to Go From Here?

In one of his classic articles on journalism and journalistic practice, James Carey tackled the state of journalism studies with a clear sense of its inadequacies. In discussing the understated role of "why" in American journalism, he argued that answers to the "why" question have often been elided into the "how" question. "Why"—even when positioned in the news—has been dismissed, misunderstood, simplified, wrongly codified, or even wrongly attributed, ensuring that audiences receive no real or satisfying explanation of what has transpired as current events. Carey suggested examining journalism either as a curriculum, whose courses took shape over different kinds of news accounts, or as a corpus, whose meaning extended across multiple treatments of an event within a news organization (Carey 1986a).

Carey's logic applies not only to journalism but to journalism scholarship as well. The study of journalism across its different courses, taking into account the various perspectives of its analysts and practitioners so as to reflect more fully all that journalism is, is a way to tackle journalism's study that underscores the degree to which journalism and journalism scholarship matter. Indeed, the growing number of venues for thinking about these questions points us in the right direction: The continued vitality of the trade press, including the *British Journalism Review, Editor and Publisher, The Quill, American Journalism Review, Columbia Journalism Review*; the long-standing appeal of academic journals like *Journalism and Mass*

Communication Quarterly, and the establishment of new journals like *Journalism: Theory, Practice and Criticism* and *Journalism Studies* all offer places in which the study of journalism can ferment.

The questions to ask regarding journalism are many. As Richard Dyer (1985) observed in the context of television, they might include versions of the following: What sense do our conceptions make of journalism? What do they emphasize and how? What is left out of the picture? What are the typical conceptualizations in any given field? What strikes us as atypical? Who is speaking, and for whom? Which media individuals, organizations, and institutions are being acted upon in generating certain notions of journalism's trappings? What does this conceptualization or frame suggest to me? What might it mean to others? Following the lead set by these questions and others, this book explores the shape of journalism scholarship in its many forms and invites others to continue the explorations begun here.

3

Sociology and Journalism

D iscussing the sociological inquiry of journalism is much like discussing journalism scholarship without a frame. This paradigm of journalism research—with its focus on people, patterned interactions, organizations, institutions, and structures—is the ongoing standard against which much inquiry into journalism has been evaluated, to the extent that the frame's existence has become largely invisible. Sociology has long existed as the background setting for evolving journalism scholarship, even if much of the recent work on journalism no longer derives necessarily from sociological inquiry.

The Shape of Sociological Inquiry

Webster's Unabridged Dictionary (1983: 1723) defines "sociology" as "the study of the history, development, organization, and problems of people living together as social groups." Once pegged as the "science of society," sociological inquiry provides an elaboration of some arena of behavior in social networks, reflecting "any general interest in social processes" (Williams 1983b: 295). The term "society" has emerged as so central to sociological inquiry that it has replaced "community" as the dominant way of conceptualizing groups (Schudson 1991).

Yet the term "society" is itself imprecise. It denotes with varying degrees of exactitude a large complex of human interactions or systems of interaction (Berger 1963). Beyond its invocation of "a common band of people," four main motifs have been thought to characterize its examination: (1) a debunking motif, by which sociology sees through the facades and backstages of social structures; (2) a fascination with society's less respectable sides, organizations, institutions, and structures; (3) an interest in cosmopolitanism; and (4) an insistence on relativization (Berger 1963). Central to each motif is a focus on people, particularly as they organize themselves into groups involving systematic patterns of interaction.

As a discipline, sociology originated in "the coming of modernity—in the dissolution of the traditional world and the consolidation of the modern" (Giddens 1987: 15). Nurtured in different directions by Karl Marx, Emile Durkheim, Max Weber, and George Simmel, sociology was long torn between functionalist and Marxist leanings, on the one hand, and by the culturalist thinking established by Robert Park, John Dewey, Margaret Mead, and Robert Cooley, on the other. Each of these trajectories shared a common aim: "stat[ing] the obvious, but with an air of discovery," qualifying an often-assumed premise that most of the time people know what their actions are (Giddens 1987: 2).

The variegated nature of the discipline's foundation generated a certain degree of dissonance over the years. In Anthony Giddens's view, sociologists

> dress up what they have to say in terminology which seems to deny to agents the freedom of action we know ourselves to have. . . . [Therefore, sociology is in a] doubly redundant position, not only telling us what we already know, but parading the familiar in a garb which conceals its proper nature. (Giddens 1987: 2–3)

Though it could be argued that such remarks remained at odds with Giddens's own practice of sociology, the degree to which laypersons felt they were able to access, gauge, and evaluate sociological phenomena was marked. No wonder, then, that Richard Rovere, by no means a typical journalist, observed that "those of us who have been educated in the twentieth century habitually think in sociological terms, whether or not we have had any training in sociology" (quoted in Schudson 1997b: 49).

Sociologists examine social conduct in a number of ways. They perform an anthropological function, showing people of one culture what it is like to live in another culture. They identify the complexity in social systems, dressing the simple and the everyday in complex frameworks, and they target the unintended, latent, and accidental consequences of everyday activities so as to make those consequences manifest. This notion—which extends the Durkheimian premise that we live inescapably under society's logic (Durkheim 1915/1965)—suggests a need to continually look for the hidden reasons for behavior. Sociologists also study the long-term patterns of institutional stability and change, with a concern for the demonstrated impact of the past on the present.

Through each focal point, the reigning function of sociological inquiry has been to provide a wide-ranging research setting that targets people and the interactions among them, the organizations and institutions in which they reside, and the structures by which their lives proceed. While sociology resembles the other social sciences in that many are concerned with "the problem of collective action, of how people manage to act together" (Becker 1986: 11), sociological inquiry positions its target of analysis squarely within the network of individuals engaged in patterned interaction in primarily complex settings.

The Sociology of Journalism

With these premises in mind, sociological inquiry has emerged as germane to the study of journalism around the world. Cueing journalists as agents of modernity, sociology found its way into journalism research in accordance with an emphasis on people, with an eye both to the patterns by which they grouped themselves into organizational and institutional settings and to the surrounding structures, functions, and effects through which they worked. Though the journalism of the United States, the United Kingdom, Germany, Latin America, and elsewhere differed markedly in form, common to all sociological inquiry into journalism was an emphasis on the systematic actions, practices, and interactions by which journalists maintained themselves as journalists. Although extensive scholarship queried the identification of journalists as professionals (e.g., Henningham 1985; Zelizer 1993a)—to the extent that Elihu Katz (1989) suggested displacing the idea of the journalism professional with that of the journalist as scientist—journalists were seen within this view as sociological beings who systematically acted in patterned ways that had bearing on the stature and shape of the journalistic collective at large.

In the United States, the sociological inquiry into journalism was born of a particularly fertile set of historical circumstances that helped shape scholarship—by example or by contrast—elsewhere in the world. It germinated both from a burgeoning interest in journalism during the 1920s, spearheaded by Robert Park at the University of Chicago, and from the widespread establishment of the social sciences during the 1930s as a preferred mode of academic inquiry and the consequent emergence of communication schools in the United States during the following decade. In the latter set of circumstances, journalism's eventual co-opting by communication schools was often solidified along the parameters of sociological research, which proved a fertile means for thinking about journalism as a phenomenon. Journalism's development as a focus of social scientific study was thus largely associated with sociology's ascent in the academy.

Early efforts moved first in the direction of a blend of social scientific and humanistic inquiry. Robert Park and others of the Chicago School were instrumental in focusing on journalism as a target of humanistic sociology, and Park's efforts at identifying journalism as a locus for sociological inquiry, spurred by his own earlier career as a reporter, helped put journalism on the analytical map of many U.S. sociologists. But the main colonization of journalism within the sociological paradigm in the United States took shape in another form during the 1940s and 1950s, largely through studies examining journalism as a political phenomenon often connected to electoral processes. Although the idea of a hypodermic needle model of media influence had been around since World War I largely as a folk belief, by which it was argued that the media, and journalism, unidimensionally affected the public in strong and direct ways, scholars offset that notion during the post World War II years. Wilbur Schramm (1949, 1954, 1959), though not trained as a sociologist, did much to establish a view of journalism as systematic activity that was shaped through the lens of communication processes. Paul Lazarsfeld, Joseph Klapper, and Charles Wright, among others, took part in the immediate postwar thrust to use administrative bureaucratic apparatuses to position journalism in the larger world, and they worked from the Bureau of Applied Social Research at Columbia University to develop a detailed picture of the intersection between journalism and the public. Klapper (1949/1960) argued that the effects of journalism and the media were minimal, showing that the most definitive effect of media exposure was the reinforcement of already existing opinions. Wright (1959) introduced a systematic template for thinking about the wide-ranging effects of media and journalism from a functional perspective. Lazarsfeld and his colleagues established in *The People's Choice* (Lazarsfeld, Berelson, and Gaudet, 1944) that journalism's influence on political attitudes during electoral campaigns was elaborated by suggestions of a two-step flow of influence, mediated by opinion leaders. That idea was further developed by Elihu Katz and Paul Lazarsfeld when they argued in *Personal Influence* (1960) that journalism played a less powerful role in shaping public attitudes than had been established by the hypodermic needle model. Paul Lazarsfeld and Robert Merton (1948) laid out a series of effects that the media, including journalism, were thought to have upon the public, including an ability to narcotize the people they addressed. While each of these efforts was instrumental in positioning journalism within a larger setting, none of them focused on the internal workings of journalism. Instead, they saw journalism as one type of media output with an effect on the public, and their analysis was less targeted to journalism per se than was the analysis exhibited in later scholarship.

These efforts introduced a mode of academic research that raised questions about the agendas to which sociological inquiry could be put. The U.S. mode of scholarship—labeled "administrative" by Lazarsfeld (1941)— denoted empirical research generally used in the service of government and mass media institutions (Rogers 1997). Over the following decades, the administrative mode of sociological research was held responsible for narrowing the target of inquiry and understandings of the larger world in which the media and journalism existed. In an important critique of the research agenda set in place by Columbia's Applied Bureau for Social Research, Todd Gitlin (1978: 207) argued that the search by Lazarsfeld and his colleagues "for specific, measurable, short-term, individual, attitudinal and behavioral 'effects' of media content and the conclusion that media are not very important in the shaping of public opinion" drained academic attention from the ongoing power of the media, consolidating and legitimizing the capitalist structures of ownership, control, and function that scholars were supposed to analyze. Although the issues were not related only to journalism, their impact on an understanding of journalism's position in the world was demonstrable nonetheless. Elsewhere in the world, sociological inquiry developed in conjunction with what came to be known as "critical" research. More European in following and derivative of the Frankfurt School, the Institute for Social Research, and the work of critical scholars from Germany like Max Horkheimer and Theodor Adorno, this research viewed scholarly endeavor as necessarily critical of the same institutions that were underwriting the administrative research so popular in the United States. Although by the 1930s many of these scholars were already in the United States, and in 1944 Leo Lowenthal produced a critical paper on the cult of celebrity in U.S. magazine journalism, their influence was nonetheless felt more strongly elsewhere, where scholars made choices about which approach to follow often in association with the kinds of academic journals available at the time and the kinds of articles sought for publication.

The path to journalism's sociological study developed more cautiously in the United Kingdom than it had in the United States. Though sociology was slower to arrive in the academy in the United Kingdom than in the United States, with only a few sociology departments in U.K. universities as late as the 1950s (Tumber 2000: 1), it was one of the first academic settings to take note of what journalism had to offer. Of interest were the ways in which journalism helped socialize individuals into upholding certain norms, values, and beliefs via institutions, and British sociologists thereby positioned journalism easily alongside education, the legal system, the family, and religious institutional settings. Although the dominant paradigm of structural functionalism persisted as a way of conducting sociological inquiry, over time dependence on it softened, particularly as sociologists in the United Kingdom experimented with new analytical settings and alternative methodological approaches. In the 1960s and 1970s, sociology became the embodiment of the social sciences across the United Kingdom, and with it came a burgeoning interest in journalism as a potential setting in which to examine sociological concerns.

Efforts in this regard were led by sociologist Jeremy Tunstall, whose book-length study of British journalists, *Journalists At Work* (1971), paved the way for thinking about journalism through a sociological lens, leading one scholar to observe that "much of Jeremy Tunstall's prolific output has concerned itself with how journalists behave" (Stephenson 2000: 84). Others, including Michael Tracey (1977) and Philip Schlesinger (1978), followed Tunstall's lead as they began to elaborate the sociological contours of the British TV newsroom. Steve Chibnall (1977) offered a detailed picture of the relations between the police and crime reporters, while Peter Golding and Philip Elliott (1979) provided a comparative examination of the newsroom in broadcasting organizations in Sweden, Ireland, and Nigeria.

Key here were evolving discussions, seen differently by journalism professionals and academics, as to whether journalism constituted a profession or a craft (Splichal and Sparks 1994; Bromley 1997, in press). Although later efforts in the United Kingdom departed from what one scholar called "the British disposition to empirical sociology" and traveled instead the path of cultural studies as a way of focusing journalism's inquiry (Bromley in press), the early endeavors in sociology nonetheless facilitated journalism's continued academic study.

Elsewhere, sociology left a different kind of imprint. In France, the work of Gabriel Tarde and Roland Barthes and the influence of structuralism turned sociological inquiry toward the humanities, as Edgar Morin urged French scholars to develop what he called a "sociology of the present" in their approach to journalism (Mattelart and Mattelart 1992: 22). A sociological interest in journalism was evident in Germany already at the turn of the century—when Ferdinand Toennies, Karl Knies, Karl Buecher, Albert Salomon, and Emil Loebl mentioned journalism's role in shaping public sentiment (Hardt 1975; Lang 1996)—but it was clearly articulated by Max Weber when in a 1924 address to the German Sociological Society he called for multiple studies of journalistic practice, journalistic professionalism, and the career prospects of journalists in different countries (cited in Lang 1996: 13–14). In the 1960s in Latin America, Scandinavia, Asia, and the Middle

East, journalism was co-opted by schools of communication that were particularly strong in sociological inquiry (Marques de Melo 1988, Chaffee et al. 1990; Rogers 1997). In each case, sociological inquiry offered a compelling way to shape journalism's study, often under the rubric of communication. In each case, too, the ascent of sociology in journalism's study was by and large resisted by journalists and journalism educators, who found its theoretical impulses problematic for the continued training of journalists.

The amount of sociological scholarship on journalism prompted scholars to attempt wrestling the material into coherent organizational schema. Schudson (1991), for instance, identified three main trends emerging from such research—mainstream sociological research, scholarship on the political economy of news, and culturological approaches to news. Yet it is primarily the first trend identified by Schudson—mainstream sociological research—that constitutes the body of research most often identified as sociological inquiry, work concerned chiefly with social organization and occupational sociology. Gaye Tuchman (2002) revisited Schudson's typology, arguing that the three types of research were more complementary than had been suggested at first. In the United Kingdom, Howard Tumber (1999) classified research on the sociology of news by the point at which it entered the news-making process—production, economics, sourcing, and ideology. Sig Hjarvard (2002) developed a four-cell grid for thinking about journalism's study: research focusing on selection or construction activities and research formed as micro-level or macro-level analysis. In each case, sociology offered a valuable way of tracking journalists' simultaneous existence in occupations, organizations, professional communities, and institutional settings, revealing how they were constrained and empowered by their interactions with others.

A more targeted track across time than those displayed by existing classifications reveals three main temporal waves of sociological inquiry on journalism. Each wave progressively broadened the setting against which journalism and journalistic practice were examined yet remained steadfast to the principles of sociological inquiry.

Early Sociological Inquiry: Journalists as Sociological Beings

The early sociological inquiry of journalism provided a gradually broadening frame through which to consider journalism as a set of interactions and patterned behaviors. Propelled by developments outside the academy that forced a closer look at journalism's workings—such as the convening in the

United Kingdom of two Royal Commissions on the Press, one in 1947 and another in 1962, which led to the establishment of press councils and a formalized training system for journalists (Bromley 1997; Bromley and O'Malley 1997)—this early research forced scholars to think about journalists as part of an environment inhabited by other people, resources, agendas, pressures, and interests. It started with a consideration of the finite and identifiable practices involved in journalistic work and gradually expanded to examine the larger settings in which journalists interacted with each other.

Gatekeeping, Social Control, and Selectivity Processes

Early journalism research focused on discrete journalistic practices, limiting analysis to a locus that could be easily examined. Gatekeeping research was one of the first academic areas to be applied to journalism in the United States during the World War II era and postwar period. Following upon Kurt Lewin's work (1947) in social psychology that examined how people went about making decisions, the gatekeeping studies saw "gates" as the codes by which people admitted or refused entry of certain information to a given system. David Manning White was first to apply the gatekeeping idea to journalism and news-making routines, and he devised a study of the story selection process among newswire editors, where he found that eight news items were rejected for every one selected as newsworthy (White 1950). He concluded that news selection operated on the basis of subjective choice, with the wire editor acting as a "Mr. Gates" who subjectively classified items in deciding what counted as news.

From this largely psychosocial explanation, "gatekeeper" became a household term in journalism scholarship. Though White himself was not a sociologist, his analysis opened doors in the sociological analysis of journalism. Gatekeepers came to be seen as capable of blocking, adding, and changing information, and as they were identified as a range of individuals or groups who determined which information an audience received, notions of journalistic practice broadened. Gatekeeping thus opened the door to considerations of what happened to a news story once it entered the channels of news making. However, the study did leave open the possibility that Mr. Gates simply possessed an idiosyncratic view of life, and it remained for other researchers to link it with the news setting itself—that is, to make the study sociological.

Such a development was not long in coming, and sociological terms of analysis helped redefine the process originally identified by White as subjective selection. Over the years that followed, White's finding was reinterpreted in ways that reflected the broadening reliance in journalism inquiry on sociological terms of reference. "Subjective selection" was redefined as evidence of a collective thought process by which journalists made their selections. Using sociological terms such as "task orientation," "employer-employee relationships," and "interpersonal relations," Walter Gieber (1964; based on his earlier work, see Gieber 1956) provided evidence of an early form of social control when he found that later wire editors used group-think to evaluate news in basically the same way as had Mr. Gates. Gatekeepers were located across the whole chain of news makers (McNelly 1959); Mr. Gates himself was reexamined and found to be unchanged (Snider 1967); and the gatekeeping findings were found to be stable across gender differences (Bleske 1991), patterned in their invocation of newspapers of record (Whitney and Becker 1982), more group oriented in local news settings (Berkowitz 1990), and a viable foundation for a broader model of journalistic practice (Janowitz 1975). In the latter case, Morris Janowitz claimed that gatekeeping was circumscribed by notions of professional journalism, including the development of technical expertise, professional responsibility, neutrality, objectivity, and the notion of balance. Pamela Shoemaker (1991: 4) elaborated the multiple gatekeepers in news making, noting that the notion might have been "well-studied" but was "hardly worn-out." Eventually, gatekeeping came to include more broadly the idea of "knowledge control" or "information control." These variations on the gatekeeping concept prompted an interest in the effect of gatekeeping more broadly—how gatekeeping controls were set in place, where in the communication process they occurred, and what were their consequences. Equally important, however, was the resonance generated by gatekeeping as a way of thinking about the workings of news. No surprise, then, that it was again invoked when thinking about online journalism (Singer 1998).

Journalistic inquiry became significantly more sociological with Warren Breed's classic study "Social Control in the Newsroom" (1955). A sociologist by training, whose Ph.D. dissertation examined the newsroom, Breed applied one of the most frequented concepts in sociological research—social control—to journalism. Recognizing that no society could exist without "social control," a term for the various means by which a society tries to bring its recalcitrant members in line with consensual behavior, he set about isolating how modes of social control were implemented in what claimed to be a democratic environment. Breed found that while ideally the newspaper should have been a "democracy," in fact the publisher set policy and the reporters followed it. Breed concluded that journalists' actions were by and large motivated by their search for a conflict-free environment and their need for reference group formation.

Breed's article helped establish that journalism's standards tended to be largely unwritten yet were willingly followed by journalists in forming a wide range of behaviors. It also offset any remaining assumptions that news making was generated on the basis of an editor's personal whim, doing so by utilizing literature on social organizations and the sociology of occupations, relying on participant observation as its method, and developing a focus on the production processes involved in news work. A classic functional analysis, the study bore both its strengths and weaknesses. Through social control, the newspaper was thought to maintain its own smooth functioning as well as that of existing power relationships in society. While this suggested that journalists directed rewards and motivations toward colleagues rather than readers, it also portrayed journalists acting only according to normative behavior and existing within a world populated exclusively by other journalists. Journalists thus had no connection with audiences, a greater external world, or history. Nonetheless, Breed's article suggested a context for journalism that involved a flexing of authority and power, directing journalism's study away from empiricist notions of reflecting reality and toward more critical ones of producing it.

Perhaps the single piece of research that most cogently advanced a general understanding of news selection processes was that of Johannes Galtung and Marie Ruge (1965). Their study of gatekeeping and selectivity remains even today one of the most influential pieces on news making, showing how what appeared to be basically a simplistic and restrictive frame for understanding journalistic practice and news production was a "process of successive selections, according to a number of news values or criteria which affect the perception of news events" (McQuail and Windahl 1982: 105). This research tackled precisely what had been left undeveloped in preceding studies—the criteria of selection and rejection. Moreover, it outlined not only what was presumed "natural" about news but also what could be seen as "cultural."

Arguing that the notion of "newsworthiness" was in fact a complex set of 12 criteria,[3] Galtung and Ruge stipulated that the more criteria an event satisfied, the more likely it would be reported. Each factor existed according to three hypotheses: an additive hypothesis, by which the more factors an event fulfilled, the greater the chance the event became and stayed as news; a complementarity hypothesis, which argued that if an event was low on one factor, it compensated by being higher on another factor; and an exclusion hypothesis, by which an event low on all factors did not become news. Though some saw the theory as too psychological, depending too much on individual selective perception, untestable, and not open to falsification (e.g., Rosengren 1974), Galtung and Ruge underscored the patterned and predictable nature of the selection process and introduced a constructed view of news making that complicated the idea of selection in journalistic work.

Over the years, extensions of Galtung and Ruge's thesis drew support for their original findings. Extended to the United Kingdom, James Halloran, Philip Elliot, and Graham Murdock (1970) applied the hypothesis to coverage of demonstrations and showed how the media framed a peaceful British demonstration against U.S. presence in Vietnam as a violent protest merely by clipping photographs to emphasize violence. Sophia Peterson (1979, 1981) interviewed reporters in different countries who supported the criteria, while attempts in Germany to replicate the study received mixed results (Schulz 1976, 1982; Wilke 1984a, 1984b; Wilke and Rosenberger 1994). As recently as 2001, Tony Harcup and Diedre O'Neill found that Galtung and Ruge's original suppositions remained relevant. They also noted that the work needed to remain open to inquiry rather than be seen as a closed set of values for journalism in all times and places.

These early studies helped set in place an entry field against which the sociological inquiry of journalism could develop. Establishing the notions of gatekeeping, social control, and selectivity processes as relevant to an understanding of news making, this scholarship pointed to a set of influences, external to the mindset of an individual journalist, which would prove to be valuable building blocks on which to construct more complex portrayals of the settings in which journalists worked. Primarily originating in the United States, the literature that developed here proved highly adaptable and easily transportable across geographic boundaries, lending an aura of universality to the sociological claims on which it rested.

Occupational Studies:
Values, Ethics, Roles, and Demographics

From sociology's early days, scholars addressed the occupational settings in which journalists worked, delineating how journalists crafted their identities through values, ethics, roles, behavior, and socialization patterns. Extensive research established the notion that primarily Western journalists, repairing to a primarily U.S. model of professionalism, set standards of action around values like responsibility, accuracy, impartiality, balance, objectivity, and truthfulness (e.g., McLeod and Hawley 1964; Johnstone, Slawski, and Bowman 1972). Although much of this literature focused on U.S. journalists (Roshco 1975; Levy 1981), discussions of news values continued to draw scholars' attention around the world as journalists were expected to accommodate new contexts, technologies, and challenges. This remained the case even though the perspectives detailed here were often found to differ from those displayed in other parts of the world (e.g., Ruotolo 1987). Alongside the examination of values was a substantial literature, particularly drawn in the United Kingdom, about journalists' occupational settings. Jeremy Tunstall almost singlehandedly developed the literature on the occupational life of journalists, where his examination of the patterns of career entry and maintenance among a variety of specialist journalists—political reporters, provincial journalists, newspaper editors, circulation managers—showed the shared attributes of occupational and professional life, regardless of specialization (Tunstall 1970, 1971, 1977). Anthony Smith (1978) tracked changes over time in the values of British journalists, while the work of others (Elliott 1972, 1980; Kumar 1977; Golding and Elliott 1979) further developed the nuances of journalists' occupational setting.

Work on ethics and ethical standards, lodged equally in philosophy and sociology, was everpresent though uneven. Prevalent before the 1930s (Crawford 1924) and after the 1960s in the United States (Gerald 1963; Christians, Fackler, Rotzoll, and McKee 1983; Starck 2001), its unevenness was attributed to the rise of positivism in discussions of journalistic practice that pushed ethical concerns for a time to the background of scholarly attention (Christians 2000). Against the discussion of values like trust, responsibility, honesty, and accountability, these studies, primarily drawn in the U.S. context, surveyed the responses of editors and publishers to ethical quandaries (Meyer 1983, 1987), discussed the ethical values implied in news work (Merrill 1974; Goldstein 1985), or addressed the practice and teaching of ethics in journalism (Elliott 1986; Klaidman and Beauchamp 1987). Theodore L. Glasser and James Ettema (1998) used the ethical standards of vice and virtue to establish their view of journalists as custodians of a moral order. Beyond the United States, Kaarle Nordenstreng and Hifzi Topuz (1989) conducted a UNESCO study that surveyed journalistic ethics in North America, Europe, the Middle East, Africa, Latin America, and Asia; their study included a collection of ten different ethical codes. John Hurst and Sally White (1994) examined ethics in Australian journalism, while Andrew Belsey and Ruth Chadwick (1992) studied the U.K. context. Clifford Christians and Michael Traber (1997) considered the application of what they called "universal values" across nation-states in different world regions, arguing that ethical standards of behavior were established in patterned ways regardless of nationality.

The demographic characteristics of the journalistic community proved to have lasting interest for journalism researchers. In the United States, in particular, large scale surveys and general overviews tracked from various perspectives who journalists were and how they entered and stayed in the workplace (e.g., Lichter, Rothman, and Lichter 1986; Becker et al. 1987). One particularly comprehensive survey conducted in the mid-1970s (Johnstone et al. 1976) was repeated over the years that followed (Weaver and Wilhoit 1986, 1996). The interest in demographics prevailed across geographical contexts. David Weaver and G. Cleveland Wilhoit's study of U.S. journalists was replicated in 21 countries and regions, yielding a picture of "the global journalist" (Weaver 1998), and in 2003, Lars Willnat and David Weaver (2003) further applied the survey to foreign correspondents stationed in the United States. Across Europe, Africa, Asia, North, Central, and South America, Slavko Splichal and Colin Sparks (1994) tracked journalism students and their occupational trajectory, while Anthony Delano and John Henningham (1995) conducted an industrywide study in the United Kingdom for the London College of Printing, and John Henningham (1993) profiled the impact of the multicultural background of Hawaiian journalists on the news they produced.

Relevant here was work on journalists' role perceptions (Cohen 1963; Janowitz 1975; Roshco 1975). A plurality of roles and role perceptions emerged, as in Wolfgang Donsbach's (1983) consideration of which roles remained uppermost among reporters of different nationalities: German reporters saw themselves taking on tasks characteristic of active players in a democratic system, while British reporters, like their American and Canadian counterparts, did not. A large literature on the professionalization of journalists simultaneously codified professionalism as a refinement of journalistic practice—with a commitment to certain values of objectivity, impartiality, nonbias, accuracy, and balance—and established it as a way to control behavior and to bestow status and prestige (e.g., Windahl and Rosengren 1978; Ettema and Whitney 1987; Soloski 1989). In Philip Elliott's words, "professionalism is when skill and competence in the performance of routine tasks become elevated to the occupational ideal" (Elliott 1972: 17). Sociological work on professionalism struck a high when interest in professionalization among journalists was also strong. Hence, it peaked in the 1960s but receded over the following 30 years (Tunstall 1996). Nonetheless, work by Hugh Stephenson as late as 2000 still tracked the professional mores among British journalists, even though discomfort over the question of whether journalism was best characterized as a profession or a craft lingered substantially beyond the early occupational studies and continued to be reflected in contemporary discussions of journalism (e.g., Henningham 1985, 1990; Bromley 1997). Its persistence suggested that at some level the earlier distinction between craft and profession did not adequately capture the full world of journalistic practice, succeeding instead in cutting part of the picture from view. The impossibility of simultaneously embracing both notions—craft *and* profession—suggested how limited the dichotomy actually was.

When combined with the early work on discrete journalistic practices, the scholarship tracking journalists' occupational settings set in place an increasingly complicated frame against which to envision the making of news. Bringing to the forefront issues like values, roles, and ethics, what emerged from this literature was a growing recognition that journalists crafted standards of action collectively with others and that those standards in turn structured journalists' approaches to news.

Normative, Ritual, and Purposive Behavior

As journalists' occupational settings became more elaborated, how to define journalistic behavior became a focal point of sociologically minded scholars intent on delineating how journalists worked. Scholarship on normative behavior was the most prevalent stream of this research, taking the implications of earlier work on journalistic practices, roles, values, and ethics and establishing that the patterned and collective nature of journalism was central to understanding it as a sociological phenomenon.

Standardized codes of action were seen as a central way of repairing to normative behavior, and many discussions were derived from the U.S. setting, particularly from issues surrounding the professionalization of U.S. journalists. Although Bernard Roshco (1975) argued early on that journalistic values were not an absolute, and Linda Steiner (1992, 1994) showed that both career manuals and textbooks often rested on an implicit sense of an "ideal" journalist, as late as 2000 U.S. journalism textbooks still employed a shared professional prism in their discussion of journalistic norms (Brennen 2000). While the norms of primarily Western, if not U.S., journalists regarding objectivity, accuracy, balance, and impartiality were not similarly followed in other countries (e.g., Hallin and Mancini 1984), they nonetheless struck a certain resonance with journalism scholars. Related here was a large literature on the sourcing practices of journalists (e.g., Sigal 1973, 1986; Tiffen 1990; Schlesinger and Tumber 1995), whereby the symbiotic relationship between source and reporter was found to take the shape of an exchange model that exchanged information for publicity. Though such literature borrowed both from sociology and political science, it is discussed here in the chapter on political science.

Not all of this early work was enthusiastic about the norms and professional mores by which journalists worked. The work of two British sociologists—Stanley Cohen and Jock Young—was ahead of its time. In a collection titled *The Manufacture of News* (Cohen and Young 1973), journalists' norms, images, practices, and conflicts surrounding the coverage of deviance and its effects on the public were comprehensively tracked. Forward looking for its recognition of the ideological positioning of journalists, the book concluded with a section called "Do-It-Yourself Media Sociology." Other work of this ilk included that of Stanley Cohen (1972) and of James Curran, Michael Gurevitch, and Janet Woollacott (1977; Curran and Gurevitch 1991), each of which positioned journalists' codes of action against prisms that complicated their reasons for acting in certain ways. The occupational practices afoot in certain kinds of journalism were also tracked, such as war and terrorism reporting (Schlesinger, Murdock, and Elliott 1983; Morrison and Tumber 1988), investigative reporting (Glasser and Ettema 1989b, 1998; Protess, Cook, Gordon, and Ettema, 1991), crime reporting (Chibnall 1977), social welfare reporting (Golding and Middleton 1982), and the work of foreign correspondents (Batscha 1975; Pedelty 1995). Each was seen to invoke strategic aims not necessarily related to codes of objectivity or impartiality.

By the late 1960s, normative explanations of journalistic behavior were no longer the only way to explain practice. One area of scholarship, primarily British in origin, followed the work of Emile Durkheim (1915/1965), Robert Bocock (1974), Victor Turner (1974), Steven Lukes (1975), and other social anthropologists to develop an address to the rituals and rites by which journalists worked (e.g., Chaney 1972). While this stream of research became increasingly attractive over time and eventually spread to U.S. scholars (e.g., Carey 1989a; Ettema 1990; Lule 1995), its first appearance drew attention due to its unusual application of rites and rituals to workers in industrialized societies. As Philip Elliott (1980: 141–142) then argued, while ritual as a concept appeared to have "little analytic value" and implied what seemed to be a unitary view of society, its durability in a "skeptical if not secular age" suggested that it functioned centrally in the exercise of power. In that sense, journalistic stories that relied on social order, by showing a nation-state stable under threat, overcoming threat, or working via consensus, were evidence of an enactment of political ritual of the highest order. Similar findings were suggested in Cohen and Young's (1973) examination of news of deviance.

Another stream of primarily U.S. sociological research began to see collective action through a social constructivist lens. Largely influenced by symbolic interactionism and social constructivism in sociology, these scholars presumed that journalists acted as agents of the social construction involved in meaning making rather than consolidating influence. The agenda became one of seeking out the purposes by which journalism created one reality instead of another.

Two salient examples here were the work of Gaye Tuchman and of Harvey Molotch and Marilyn Lester. In a groundbreaking article, "Objectivity as Strategic Ritual: An Examination of Newsmen's Notions of Objectivity," Tuchman (1972) pointed scholars in the direction of critiquing norms by suggesting that journalists engaged in objectivity for strategic reasons. Arguing that objectivity functioned primarily to help journalists avoid the consequences of their actions, Tuchman turned on its head the long-standing reverence for objectivity by reducing it to a means for achievement of strategic aims. Part of a broader quasi-revolt in sociology against the cult of value-free social science, Tuchman's work was a touchstone in pushing scholars to think more critically about journalists' values and norms.

Also central was Molotch and Lester's "News as Purposive Behavior" (1974). Ushering in the study of what Schudson called the "sociological organization of newswork" (1991), they claimed that all news production was the result of purposive behavior. Journalists worked according to a typology of news stories by which they could organize their coverage of news events, and they often organized their approach to stories in accordance with how they fit the typology. At heart here was the idea that news was a constructed reality shaped according to some underlying notion of social power; the process of news creation was seen as a kind of accounting procedure determined by the needs of those with access to media and utilizing complementary activities of promotion, assembly, and consumption. Journalism was thought to reflect not a world "out there" but the practices of those with the power to determine the experience of others. While Molotch and Lester's work complicated the "reality claims" of most journalists and placed journalists on a continuum with other kinds of workers, its overly tight explanatory scheme left unaddressed the basic question of whether or not everything in journalism was as purposive as their research proposed.

Effects Research

One long-standing consequence of the sociological interest in journalism was the appearance of studies that viewed journalistic practice through its effect on the public. Primarily originating in the United States, these studies built upon those earlier circumstances by which journalism came to be seen as a legitimate focus for sociological inquiry. Although this area of interest became the signature of mass communication curricula more than of inquiry into journalism per se, it nonetheless was shaped in part through the sociological study of journalism. Studies of journalism's effect were drawn from various areas of inquiry—the work of Herbert Blumer and the Payne Fund studies of cinema, the early interest of Paul Lazarsfeld in mass communication effects, Lazarsfeld and Stanton's work on audience research, Lazarsfeld's partnership with Robert Merton at Columbia, and the work of Leo Bogart on the newspaper industry, to name a few. From these earlier works and others, a slew of effects came to be attributed to journalism over the years that followed.

Though called "media effects" rather than "journalism effects," work on journalism followed the broader scholarly flips over what kind of effects to measure: small or large, limited or strong, short term or long term, direct or indirect, intended or unintended, latent or manifest. Examined by scholars whose disciplinary association was both within and beyond sociology, journalism was seen nonetheless to play various sociological roles.

Of primary relevance was the work of Kurt Lang and Gladys Lang (1953), whose analysis of the MacArthur Day Parade showed how a particular event was covered by the news media and thus focused attention on journalism's role in fixing the boundaries of the collective. Lang and Lang's elucidation of journalism's "unwitting bias," by which television viewers were given a more exciting event than were real viewers, showed how TV produced a mistaken impression of widespread support for MacArthur and his politics. Following in the vein of this work, British scholars James Halloran, Philip Elliott, and Graham Murdock (1970) conducted a similar close analysis of an anti-Vietnam War rally in London that was presented in ways divergent from the experience of those who took part. Years later, Daniel Dayan and Elihu Katz (1992) established a broad typology which extended the logic of media's bias to the structuring of news events marking the celebrations, conquests, and contests in different cultural settings. Examining the function of media events across settings, they broadened notions of how the media worked under such circumstances.

Also relevant was the more wide-ranging scholarship of Elihu Katz, which extended from his early study with Paul Lazarsfeld of the two-step flow of information (Katz and Lazarsfeld 1960) to consider a repository of effects shaped and nurtured by journalism. In Katz's work with Jay Blumler (Blumler and Katz 1974), journalism was seen to play a role in uses and gratifications research, where it was argued that journalism, like the media more generally, played a minimalist role in a range of private and public actions. Although the uses and gratifications tradition had been key in underscoring journalism's relevance—as seen in Bernard Berelson's (1949) classic study "What Missing the Newspaper Means," which considered the impact of a 1945 strike that halted operations at the major New York City newspapers by demonstrating a far-reaching connection between people and their newspapers—the later work in uses and gratifications set the stage for thinking about a wide range of journalism effects. It also traveled indirectly around the world, as when the electoral study conducted by Jay Blumler, Roland Cayrol, and Michel Thoveron (1978) introduced to French scholars the uses and gratifications research then popular in the United States (Neveu 1998).

Following this early work, an interest in journalism's effect on the public became a natural part of sociological inquiry on journalism. Other work showed how journalists established the public agenda under the name "agenda setting" (McCombs and Shaw 1972), shaped learning processes (Greenberg 1964; Robinson and Levy 1986), closed the knowledge gap (Blumler and McQuail 1968), structured reality (Lang and Lang 1983), created a spiral of silence in the political environment (Noelle-Neumann 1973), cultivated certain notions of reality (Gerbner and Gross 1976), and set off special times for celebration and community (Dayan and Katz 1992). The residuals of thinking about journalism through its effect on the public even turned up in some literature not usually aligned with the effects tradition; Schudson's most recent book-length discussion of the sociology of the news, for instance, considered what he called "information effects, aura effects, and framing effects" (Schudson 2002: 62).

This research established a route for thinking about the impact and positioning of journalism in the real world. Although over time it came to be known less as inquiry into journalism than into the media more generally, it nonetheless left its imprint on thinking about journalism. Equally important, this research further established sociology's role as the background lens through which to consider journalism's trappings. At the same time, however, it was roundly critiqued by a number of sociologists who felt it was insufficiently attentive to issues of power and control (e.g., Gitlin 1978; also see Rogers 1997).

* * * * *

What did all of this early sociological research on journalism suggest? Simply put, it set the stage for the sociological inquiry that followed. Inviting much of the critical work that came to the fore in later years, these works suggested a more complicated portrait of journalism, shaped at first by the questions of gatekeeping and social power and elaborated in the occupational studies conducted primarily in the United Kingdom. At the same time, however, the explanatory frames offered here were limited, largely because of what was taken to be (purposefully or not) highly indicative and generalized statements about how journalism worked.

Mid-Period Sociological Inquiry: Organizational Studies of Journalism

A second stage of sociologically motivated inquiries, from the late 1960s onward, looked toward broad organizational settings as a way to examine the patterns of interaction among journalists (e.g., Ettema and Whitney 1982; Bantz 1985). Although as early as 1937 Leo Rosten looked at the settings in which journalists worked through a sociological lens in *The Washington Correspondents*, here organizational theory, and particularly the ethnography of work places, became a favored perspective, particularly in the United States, for considering journalistic practice and journalism.

Rendering journalism more similar to than different from other social settings, these studies saw news as a manufactured organizational product like other manufactured goods. Individual preferences, values, and attitudes mattered little once journalists were socialized within the organizational setting. The basic argument, according to Schudson (1991: 143), was that "the central problem for understanding journalism in liberal societies [is] the journalist's professed autonomy and decision-making power. This perspective tries to understand how journalists' efforts on the job are constrained by organizational and occupational routines."

Here an emphasis on organizational constraints began to displace a focus on the values, ethics, roles, and norms of individuals. At the same time, the inevitablity of social constructions and their organizational function were accepted as part of most research conceptualizations.

Organizational Theory

The earliest studies in this vein used social control as a means to explain journalistic interaction within an organizational setting (Warner 1971; Sigelman 1973). The first extensive study of journalism, utilizing in part organizational theory, was Edward J. Epstein's *News From Nowhere* (1973). Begun as a paper for a political science seminar at Harvard, Epstein's analysis suggested that organizational and technical constraints managed the making of news. Staking his claim on organizational theory, Epstein argued that most of what we regard as news was derived from the organizational tensions involved in producing news. So-called news norms needed to be accomplished through organizational routines: A time bias, for instance, was resolved by dividing news pieces into types (such as spot news or delayed news), while a bias toward the unexpected depended on covering routinized events (such as press conferences). Certain composite pictures of the world thus resulted: California was seen as bizarre, curious, and unpredictable, largely because the logistic difficulties involved in transporting stories quickly to New York City rendered timeless stories "of perennial interest" the more economically and technologically feasible option for including news from the West Coast.

Debunking many of the prevailing normative explanations for journalistic practice, Epstein's work was valuable because it successfully positioned journalists as workers in a setting (Epstein 1973, 1975). At the same time, however, organizational theory introduced a somewhat lopsided view of how news worked, positioning the journalist primarily as an organizational actor and filtering a view of news work through a technologically specific lens that changed rapidly over time.

Other work followed the lead set by Edward Epstein, with research by Bernard Roshco (1975) and Charles Bantz (1985) tracking the ways in which normative, professional standards of action often needed to be accommodated to the needs of the organization. In the United Kingdom, work by Philip Elliott (1972; Golding and Elliot 1979) and Philip Schlesinger (1978) examined the organizational imperatives afoot in television production. More so than the earlier work, their organizational studies exhibited the broader differences between the administrative and critical impulses of sociological research. Roscho, working in the U.S. context, appeared to provide a more sympathetic view of news work than did Golding and Elliott, who aired concerns about the threat to the autonomy of public service broadcasting in the United Kingdom:

> We view the evidence presented here as strong support for an interpretation of broadcast news as a systematically partial account of society, an interpretation with disturbing implications for broadcasters' claims of neutrality, and not least for our understanding of how political and social opinions are formed. (Golding and Elliott 1979: 1–2)

Nonetheless, in both the U.S. and U.K. settings, this work expanded journalism's inquiry by showing how journalists worked with the values and priorities imposed upon them by the organizational setting. The basic logic of this research prevailed in more contemporary scholarship and leaked into more popular discussions of the news. For instance, journalists writing with a sociological flair offered organizational views of how journalists needed to accommodate various organizational pressures during political campaigns (e.g., Greenfield 1982; Rosenstiel 1993).

Newsroom Ethnographies

Sociological studies of journalism came into their prime, particularly in the United States and the United Kingdom, during the 1970s and early 1980s. Although valuable information continued to be compiled on journalistic work routines, work values, and organizational constraints, scholarship in the United States increasingly took the form of ethnographies, which offered a way of extending participant-observer methodology into a grounded tool for exploring journalism. Touted as providing an anthropological take on the newsroom, and borrowing largely from the techniques and conceptual vocabulary of ethnomethodology, these studies were driven by grounded questions that tried to see the world through the news worker's point of view, tracking primarily decision-making processes regarding who decided what was newsworthy, how, and why.

The development of ethnography as a valuable approach to research on journalism was not accidental. Derived in the United States from the Chicago School of urban ethnography during the 1930s, scholars like Robert Park, W.I. Thomas, and Ernest Burgess implemented different kinds of studies of journalists and established simple guidelines for ethnographers that underscored the similarity between ethnographers and journalists. Robert Park told ethnographers, just "write down what you see and hear, like a newspaper reporter" (quoted in Kirk and Miller 1986: 40). Everett C. Hughes (1958) drew attention to the conditions under which a profession could be thought to evolve, moving the focus in research on the professions away from givens for all circumstances and onto the conditions by which those givens varied, showing that ethnography could constitute a useful way to do empirical research and think about professional life. A renewed interest during the 1970s and 1980s from scholars like Joseph Gusfield, Erving Goffman, and Elliot Friedson and from anthropologists like James Clifford, George Marcus, and Clifford Geertz further underscored the view that ethnographic studies provided a different way of understanding the complexity of social life, in that they generated detailed accounts of the laws, rules, and practices by which a given group existed.

For journalism research, this had particular value. In the United Kingdom, Philip Schlesinger (1978) conducted an extensive ethnographic analysis of British news making that borrowed from a healthy tradition in British empirical media sociology to revitalize the study of news organizations. Philip Elliott (1972) spent 4 months trailing a television production team for a British documentary program, and Tom Burns engaged in lengthy participant observation at the BBC (1977). Yet the main work here came from the United States. Three main newsroom ethnographies were published during this period, by Gaye Tuchman, Herbert Gans, and Mark Fishman. They took the form of what John Van Maanen later called "realist tales," displaying a near complete absence of the author from the finished text, a documentary style that provided minute and often mundane details of the practices under study, an attempt to produce the participants' point of view, and an interpretive omnipotence (Van Maanen 1988: 47–48).

Gaye Tuchman's *Making News* (1978a) and a number of related journal articles (Tuchman 1972, 1973) resulted from a 10-year odyssey.[4] Interested in the constructedness of news and its positioning as purposive behavior, Tuchman set about demonstrating that news routines were in fact necessary accomplishments that served strategic purposes for journalists. For Tuchman, news was a frame through which the social world was routinely constructed, and her goal was to show the devices of construction used by journalists as they learned to accommodate the organizational and other constraints of their work.

Tuchman's work was critical in reconstituting academic understandings of journalistic practice. Not only did she refuse to accept the received view of journalism at face value, but she also offered a way of thinking that situated journalistic practice in the circumstances of its use. Key journalistic practices—classifying news, verifying facts, and upholding objectivity—were seen as practical contentions for journalists: Hard and soft news, for instance, were distinguishable not because they reflected inherent attributes of news but because they made scheduling more predictable and manageable. Although Tuchman's categories were not mutually exclusive, their positioning as a continuum of classifying practices was nonetheless helpful in mapping journalistic routine. Using similar logic, she argued that fact verification was simply practical activity geared to deadlines (1973, 1978a).

In each case that Tuchman analyzed, news was defined as a result of the accommodation to organizational constraints. Her detailed analysis of news work and its codification as strategic behavior left an influential imprint on the study of journalism. Its links with earlier work—both on journalists and their organizations and on the constructedness of news—made Tuchman's research a landmark study in inquiry on journalism. Cited most often for its emphasis on strategic behavior, Tuchman's introduction of the concepts of strategic rituals and organizational routines into news making was seen by scholars as valuable (e.g., Reese 1990; Lule 1995).

In an ethnography drawing from a similar long-term investment in a research setting, Herbert Gans's *Deciding What's News* (1979) adopted a commitment to pluralism that underpinned a number of themes central to news making—the organization of stories, the link between sources and journalists, problems related to values and ideology, problems related to profits and audiences, and political censorship. From a somewhat uneven 10-year research period, Gans concluded that journalists operated by adopting external preference statements about real life that he consequently labeled "news values."[5] Asserting that journalists could not do their work without these values, he claimed that they used them in deciding what made news, constituting what he termed "paraideology"—a journalistic worldview that was conservative, was reformist, and embraced Progressive movement values from early 20th-century America.

Introducing the question of ideology into sociological research on journalism, Gans's scholarship altered the focus of sociological inquiry. Not only did he fine-tune the examination of journalism as a work environment with its own values, practices, and standards of action, but he pointed other researchers toward the issue of values establishment and maintenance as well (Entman 1989: 344). His work also demonstrated the mainstream media's upper middle class bias, showing news to be reflective of the upper or upper middle class white male social order (Bird 1990: 383). However, he did not go as far as he might have in teasing out the complications involved in ideological consciousness, and he implied a pluralistic view of values that did not sufficiently consider their conflicted public status.

Another newsroom ethnography was that of Mark Fishman, a graduate school contemporary of Gaye Tuchman. Driven by many of the same issues as in Tuchman's *Making News,* Fishman's *Manufacturing the News* (1980) was motivated by a 1976 crime wave in New York City in which most reporters doubted the existence of the crime wave yet continued to report it. Embarking on a 2-year ethnography of a small California newspaper, he found that the organization of the paper's reporting staff into beats, including crime, was a bureaucratic and organizational necessity that legitimated the government sources from whom journalists received most of their news and led to a uniform way of presenting the world that operated in tandem with constraints on news making. Fishman drew a picture of a bureaucratically constructed journalistic universe, where bureaucratic needs determined how journalists moved through a beat territory, their exposure to news sources, how they made decisions about what they witnessed, the permissible times at which events could be reported, how they defined a factual or suspicious account, and how they identified errors and controversies. When in doubt, journalists presumed the smooth functioning of things, and news emerged as ideological because it was produced through procedures that kept the world consonant with implicit and explicit ideological frames. This study broadened notions of social power to typify the organizational structure of the journalistic setting. Fishman also advanced the importance of constructivism in news, underscoring the essentially complex and complicated links between journalism and other worlds.

Recent research has both echoed and questioned the tenor of the original news ethnographies. The workings of oppositional news attracted several more recent ethnographers (e.g., Meyers 1994). Nina Eliasoph (1988) showed that the same rules applied as in the early ethnographies but for different purposes. Criticism of late laid the blame more on the ethnographies' continued resonance among scholars than on the degree to which they validly represented what was going on at the time they were written. Arguing for their limited generalizability, Simon Cottle (2000a) lamented that they had set in place a number of orthodoxies in news study that were no longer characteristic of contemporary production practices; he pointed out that contemporary journalism was shaped more by corporate presence, satellite and cable delivery systems, the multiple nature of journalistic work, and the standardization of contemporary journalism than by the circumstances described by the newsroom ethnographies. He also argued that the ethnographers saw news work through a narrowed lens that did not prevail over time, failing to differentiate across types of news work and news organization; paying insufficient attention to issues like nationality, ethnicity, and gender; and detailing norms to which many if not most journalists no longer subscribed. The limitations he mentioned in effect addressed contemporary journalism researchers themselves: The fact that no one has updated the news ethnographies to address many of these changes in journalistic practice offers a curious epilogue to the centrality they have long occupied in journalism scholarship.

How representative were the findings of the newsroom ethnographies? Their similar focus was facilitated by the fundamental similarities in their structure. Employing parallel methodologies of participant observation and implementing research in roughly the same time era of the 1970s and 1980s, all examined the organizational settings of large urban centers (in two cases, New York City). All used the news organization to examine the relationship of values to practices, and all shared an emphasis—whether macrosociological or microsociological—on patterned behavior, with one focal point of analysis—usually the newsroom—frozen in order to flesh out the practices by which it was inhabited. These similarities are important because they enhance what appeared to be the generalizability of the research, yet the degree to which these studies reflect journalism more generally is questionable.

At the same time, the ethnographies set in place certain—by now—overused frames for thinking about journalistic practice. Perhaps nowhere is this as evident as in the lingering currency of "the newsroom" as a metaphor for journalistic practice, a currency largely due to the studies that used newsrooms as stand-ins for the broader picture of journalism. While emphasis on the newsroom as a research setting made sense for ethnographers, it has since been generalized far beyond its relevance to news making. Few, if any, news organizations operate with the same degree of dependence on "classic" newsrooms that they displayed in earlier decades, and decisions taken at a far more diverse set of venues—in the field, internet or telephone exchanges, social gatherings, publishing conventions—should not be left out of the picture. In so privileging certain settings over others, what counts as evidence has here been narrowed.

Methodological questions also haunt the ethnographers. Did journalists themselves define categories of news or were such categories simply an artifact of academic analysis? Why were such categories typically constructed along routine versus nonroutine dimensions, and was the routine stressed because it was so difficult to study the non-routine? Although Tuchman addressed some of these questions, the fact that two of the studies developed residual categories—Tuchman's "what a story" and Gans's "gee whiz story"—to accommodate holes in the classification schemes being offered (see also Berkowitz 1992) deserves some consideration. Furthermore, each of these studies fell short somewhat because they only considered news work from the moment at which an event was approached by a journalist.

However, the newsroom ethnographies did leave a powerful imprint on the evolution of inquiry into journalism. They masterfully interrogated many of the reigning commonsensical assumptions about news work, showing that news reality was constructed, often in the name of agendas like practical work accomplishment. In addition, the links suggested here between journalism and other structures at work in the play of news paved the way for thinking fruitfully about ideology. It is important to remember that the original aim of the news ethnographies was not to suggest a far-reaching generalizability about news making but to display precise formulations by which certain sets of circumstances came into existence. The overgeneralization of ethnographic authority beyond its original positioning, by which the concrete pictures they fashioned came to stand in for more generalizable statements about how journalism is thought to work, is as much a statement about the evolution of inquiry as it is about the ethnographies themselves. It may be that we have not yet found a way to build upon the newsroom ethnographies as an integral but limited part of the sociological inquiry on news.

Later Sociological Inquiry: Journalistic Institutions and Ideology

The frame offered by the news ethnographers provided an incomplete picture of the link between journalistic settings and their larger sociocultural surroundings, and to address that insufficiency, certain journalism researchers began to formulate their work around institutional and ideological questions. Taking a critical view on the media and journalistic practice, these studies located the force of ideological positioning outside journalism, where it worked in tandem with other institutions. Journalists thus came to be increasingly considered agents of a dominant ideological order external to the news world itself.

This scholarship's key attribute was its ability to markedly complicate the frame for analyzing news. Unlike the earliest sociological work, which targeted selection activities in newsroom settings, or the mid-period sociological studies, which considered news as a social construct largely within the frame of the news organization, here the emphasis was on linking journalistic settings, routines, practices, and texts with the institutional settings that surrounded them. While some of the mid-period studies (e.g., Gans 1979) moved sociological inquiry in this direction, later studies were critical in establishing an ongoing connection between journalism and the outside world.

The Institutions of Journalism

Although an interest in the institutions of journalism had already generated scholarly work by the mid-1960s (e.g., Gerbner 1964, 1969; Burns 1969), it was primarily on the heels of the extensive research on news organizations that sociologists began to realize a need to broaden the analytical locus in which they thought about journalism. Specifically, scholars of a critical sociological bent saw institutions and their resultant problems, such as media ownership and control, as a corrective to much of the administrative work that had been produced in sociological inquiry into journalism, particularly in the United States. In the United Kingdom, the establishment of a third Royal Commission on the Press (1974–1977) intensified pressures for reform but also fine-tuned an interest in the symbiotic relationship between journalism and its institutional settings.

Scholars focusing on the institutional domain moved interchangeably between politics and economics in attempting to target the broad ties connecting journalists with their environment. Although this work drew from other disciplines in the development of inquiry into journalism, it retained a decidedly sociological flavor. Scholarship on media ownership, advertising, and commercialism (Altschull 1984; Bagdikian 1997) was accompanied by considerations of the decline of the party press due to commercial imperatives. Hanno Hardt (1996), for example, offered a view of U.S. journalism that tracked the replacement of political independence with the interests of corporate power. The problems of media concentration across Europe were widely discussed by scholars (e.g., Picard 1988; Sanchez-Tabernero 1993; Sparks 1996). In his recent book *The Sociology of Journalism*, Brian McNair (1998) focused two of his five sections on the political and economic environments of journalism.

Work in Europe and Latin America in particular examined the political dimensions of journalistic work through sociological questions. For instance, Colin Seymour-Ure (1974) spent considerable effort investigating the intersection between British governmental circles and Fleet Street, while Paddy Scannell (1979) tracked postwar British television. French media scholar Serge Halimi (1997) discussed the emergence of "the new media watchdogs" that had developed in conjunction with the media's domination by a market mentality. Jay Blumler and Michael Gurevitch (1995) provided a comprehensive view of the institutional pressures afoot for both U.K. and U.S. political reporters. Governmental and global management of information was seen as aggressively intruding upon the very structures through which news was produced (Curran, Gurevitch, and Woollacott 1977; Curran and Gurevitch 1991; Boyd-Barrett and Rantanen 1998; Curran 2000a). Studies of news flow facilitated an understanding of the broader global context in which journalism took shape (Varis and Jokelin 1976; Gurevitch 1991; Hjarvard 1999). Armand Mattelart's systematic inquiry into the nuances of the political imperatives of journalism in Latin America (Mattelart 1980; Mattelart and Schmucler 1985) was followed by similarly politically driven work by Elizabeth Fox, Jesus Martin-Barbero, and Silvio Waisbord (Fox 1988; Martin-Barbero 1993; Waisbord 2000; Fox and Waisbord 2002). Work was also conducted along similar lines in Eastern Europe (e.g., Nordenstreng, Vartanova, and Zassoursky 2001), and the emergence of transnational news channels drew significant scholarly attention (Volkmer 1999; Robinson 2002). Significantly, work on these lines was often codified as following different disciplinary tenets: in the U.S. context much was conducted through political science rather than sociology (e.g., Bennett 1988; Entman 1989), while some work in the United Kingdom tended to be classified more directly as philosophy (e.g., Keane 1991).

Similar developments occurred surrounding journalism's economic dimensions. While the groundbreaking work of Ben Bagdikian (1997) showed that a few corporations owned much of U.S. journalism, other scholars' work elaborated an understanding of news management and corporate presence (e.g., McManus 1994). Robert Picard (1985) offered a detailed view of the economic pressures inherent in the democratic press, and Robert McChesney (1993, 1999) led a far-reaching discussion of journalism's dependence on corporate structures. In *Rich Media, Poor Democracy* (1999), he argued that journalism did not "give people what they wanted," as had been long claimed, but instead failed its missions as a public service; an organized reform of the media was necessary for the revitalization of democracy itself.

While much of this work drew directly from earlier research on the newsroom and news organizations, its unidimensionality and often highly functionalist character left many researchers in search of a term to denote a wider phenomenon that might help explain journalism's institutional setting. "Ideology" provided one such term.

Ideology as Part of Journalistic Inquiry

While some notion of ideology was implied in earlier studies of journalism (e.g., Epstein 1973; Tuchman 1978a; Gans 1979), it was primarily in later studies that ideological analysis became a motivating force in inquiry. Typically scholars define "ideology" as that which refers to the social relations of signification—knowledge and consciousness—in class societies (e.g., Thompson 1995) or the ways in which conflicting positions about reality are "produced, deployed, regulated, institutionalized, and resisted" (O'Sullivan, Hartley, Saunders, and Fiske 1983: 110), but the term "ideology" has long suffered from a lack of precision in application. A term that came into general usage around the end of the 18th century with the Enlightenment, "ideology" in German originally meant simply "the study of systems of ideas," but it was rendered more complex after Karl Mannheim examined its workings and Karl Marx and Frederick Engels used it in the mid 1800s to refer to the maintenance of ruling class interests. Tensions between its prescriptive and descriptive uses continue to characterize its invocation even today.

Raymond Williams was perhaps first to delineate the variant attributes that come to play when invoking ideology, arguing that ideology could be defined as a "general process for producing meanings and ideas," to be contrasted with ideology as belief or as false consciousness (Williams 1983b). This notion, which pushed the term beyond assumedly static mental frameworks toward continually evolving practice, proved particularly useful in inquiry into journalism, for it assumed that ideology was dynamic rather than static, that natural meanings did not exist but were always socially constructed and socially oriented (i.e., aligned with indices of identity, like race, gender, and ethnicity), and that ideology worked according to certain attributes. Other accounts of ideology—that it worked by mystifying, generalizing certain group interests over others, naturalizing all historical contexts, promoting hegemony, and making chaos seem coherent—offered a particularly fruitful way to think about ideology (LaCapra 1985). As Dominick LaCapra argued, the charter of ideological criticism was to "disclose what ideology mystifies . . . with an implication for praxis" (LaCapra 1985: 140). In contemporary eyes, ideology was seen as "meaning in the service of power" (Thompson 1990: 7).

However, as notions of ideology gave way to the alternative idea of hegemony (Gramsci 1971), ideological critique offered a fruitful way to consider journalism. The introduction of "hegemony," which was defined as the voluntary yielding to authority, positioned journalists as ideological agents who secured agreement by consensus rather than forced compliance (e.g., Gitlin 1980). This proved a compelling frame for linking journalism to its broader institutional environment. Hegemonic analysis also provided terms that could clarify journalism's ambiguous institutional parameters.

Scholarship in the United Kingdom led the way in incorporating ideology and hegemony into sociological inquiry on journalism, with British sociological scholars attributing to ideology a "common-sense awareness of social processes" (Glasgow University Media Group 1976: 13). Power was invoked as a way of defining normality and setting agendas. Thus, news developed not as a reflection of "the events in the world 'out there,' but as the manifestation of the collective cultural codes of those employed to do this selective and judgmental work for society" (Glasgow University Media Group 1976: 14).

A prime source of studies of ideology and hegemony in the late 1960s and early 1970s was the Center for Contemporary Cultural Studies at the University of Birmingham. Perhaps its best-known scholar was Stuart Hall, who attempted to make explicit how journalists recognized and crafted news. Arguing against the unexamined assumption that pluralism works, Hall maintained that as the notion of consensus began to break down and recognition increased that labels like "deviant" and "subcultural" were constructions, reality itself came to be seen not as a given set of facts but as a mode of definition (Hall 1982). That move replaced the pluralistic or administrative model of critical research with a critical one, with models of journalistic power necessarily taking into account the shaping of the whole ideological environment as a move toward winning a universal validity and legitimacy for partial and particular accounts of the world. This meant that from the 1960s onward, ideology came to be seen as ways in which certain accounts were given validity and legitimacy, despite the fact that they were not representative. A concern for how ideological processes worked, and the ability to conceive of the ideological in relation to other practices within a social formation, generated a lingering interest in this line of inquiry: How could anything but the dominant ideology be reproduced? Reality came to be seen not as a given set of facts but as the result of a particular way of defining those facts. Particularly interested in seeing how journalists used power to signify events in a particular way, Hall (1982) analyzed what he called the "reality effect," the effect of ideology to efface itself and appear natural. The ideological effect of the media was to impose an imaginary coherence on the units being represented. Hall (1973a) also argued against what appeared to be the neutral ideology of news production and showed that meaning was constructed by various levels of coding within the news photograph. Even though news values appeared to be a set of neutral, routine practices, in Hall's view, news selection emerged from an intersection of formal news values and ideological treatment. At the same time, Hall opened up a stream of research that examined the opportunities to decode in negotiated and oppositional ways (Hall 1973b). His recognition of the slippages that appeared alongside the dominant readings offered a new way to think about audiences alternately decoding news in accordance with their own identities (see, e.g., Morley 1980).

One of the foremost studies examining the ideological parameters of news was a set of research volumes produced by the Glasgow University Media Group. Called the "Bad News" project, the group's work was not sociological analysis only but instead mixed organizational theory, ideological critique, and language studies to analyze British television's verbal and visual coverage of industrial relations. Funded by the British Social Science Research Council on Television News, the group was mandated to uncover whether or not TV news projected bias in labor disputes, and it focused on one year of coverage of a British miner's strike. Different from other studies of the time, in that it utilized a team of researchers and a multiplicity of research methods, the group produced two initial volumes that reinforced the difficulties in maintaining a neutral stance in journalism (Glasgow University Media Group 1976, 1980). The group argued that a sequence of socially manufactured messages carried many of society's culturally dominant assumptions, and it claimed that in covering strikes and industrial disputes, television news makers tended to favor dominant interpretations of such strikes via a range of practices, including interviewing technique, shot length, word choice, and visual perspective. The worker's point of view was seen as less credible or was simply less seen than that of management.

The Glasgow group's influence on the sociological inquiry of journalism was manifest. To date, the collective has published numerous research volumes (Glasgow University Media Group 1976, 1980, 1982, 1986; Philo 1990, 1999; Eldridge 1993; Miller et al. 1998). While the group's early work focused on British TV news, its later work targeted the broader questions of AIDS representations, child sexual abuse, and mental health (Eldridge 2000). More recently, Brian Winston (2002) described a revisit to the group's 1975 research, where he argued that its essential findings remained the same.

Work focusing on ideology was also generated by U.S. scholars, where media theory began somewhere around the 1950s to work rather loosely with the notion of "ideology." Unlike the British academy, however, this was accepted more slowly. Perhaps the best known U.S. study of journalism's ideological setting was Todd Gitlin's *The Whole World is Watching*

(1980), which straddled a bridge between the U.S. ethnographies of the 1970s and later explicitly ideological work. Gitlin's own story as an activist became embedded within the story of the media that he chose to tell. A former lead member of Students for a Democratic Society, he analyzed CBS and the *New York Times* during the early period of the antiwar movement, combining his own recollections, interviews with key activists and reporters, and transcripts of broadcast newscasts to support the argument that he had long personally been interested in examining—that American journalism was ruled by "hegemony," a nonforceful domination by the ruling class. In examining the relationship between the media and the New Left in the 1960s, Gitlin found the mainstream media complicit with hegemonic structures in society. The coverage of anti-war movements that they provided offered only stereotypical challenges to the established order and portrayed leftist groups in a way that made them look foolish. In this way, journalism supported the ruling class by characterizing the New Left as violent, deviant, and silly. Gitlin found that hegemony worked in journalism in two main ways: through the structure of the newsroom and through the format of the news story. In other words, journalistic values were steady enough to sustain hegemony yet flexible enough to give the appearance of being open.

Connected to Gitlin's work was the emerging importance of journalism in the formation and maintenance of social movements. While Gitlin's work set the stage for this issue in regard to the peace movement and the Vietnam War, arguing that the frames used by the news media to cover the movement both propelled it into existence and then undermined it, scholars elsewhere displayed similar interests. In Canada, Robert Hackett (1991) used three case studies—the reporting of human rights in the context of the Cold War, Vancouver's annual Walk For Peace, and the 1986 American raid on Libya—as a way of discussing the Canadian media's treatment of the peace movement. In so doing, he offered a more upbeat prognosis than did Gitlin of the treatment of social movements by the news media. In France, Erik Neveu (1996) examined new forms of social movements, including the media's role in the demise of violence and other changes in activist behaviors. Others (Molotch 1979; Kielbowicz and Sherer 1986; Gamson 1988) considered the media strategies used by social movements in different cultures.

There were other scholars who also took a sociological view of journalism's ideological parameters as ideology began to be seen as a more integral part of journalistic decision making (e.g., Hackett 1984; Soloski 1989). In Canada, Richard Ericson, Patricia Baranek, and Janet Chan (1987, 1989, 1990) interwove notions of ideology in their large-scale examination of the various personnel involved in the news production process, while Stephen Reese (1990) offered a close analysis of the ideological tensions arising from socialist Kent MacDougall's long-term employment at the *Wall Street Journal*. These attempts were all aimed at moving the journalistic mind-set away from its sense of self as a reflector of reality.

Interest in journalism's ideological parameters in both the United States and United Kingdom, however, was not universally hailed. The work of both Gitlin and the Glasgow Media Group drew the attention of cultural critic Raymond Williams in 1982, who wrote somewhat scathingly that while it had become trendy to speak of "news gone bad," the very regard for news as a cultural product was a "major intellectual gain" that was being overlooked. Lamenting journalist scholars' discomfort over the entry of sociology into ideology critique, Williams argued that a disregard for what journalists called "academic whining," a sense of outraged professionalism among reporters, and journalism's own strict separation of theory and practice undermined an appreciation for sociology's strong penchant in examining ideology. At the same time, Williams criticized both Gitlin and the Glasgow group for focusing their interest in ideology away from people and toward texts, overlooking the cultural practices by which texts were made meaningful. The point Williams was making was clear—the academy had not yet developed a place in which it could comfortably analyze ideology in all of its workings, particularly not in its application to journalism— and his concern became the rallying point for much of the cultural work that was developed later by sociologists.

The ideological line of inquiry was valuable because it showed that things are not always as they seem. It opened the door for thinking about important issues regarding representation, access, and power (e.g., Cottle 2000b). It facilitated useful discussions of taken-for-granted premises like objectivity and impartiality, which were found to be responses to the changing circumstances of news production in both the United States and the United Kingdom (Allan 1997). But ongoing questions linger regarding where to locate evidence of ideology, how to agree on its presence and force, and how to stabilize it long enough for analysis. Generally, the latent rather than manifest outcomes of ideological positioning were emphasized and a functional view of ideology's workings prevailed. In addition, much ideological work on journalism offered a somewhat narrowed vision of how journalism can and should look, with insufficient attention paid to non-Western journalism. The interest in ideology as part of journalistic practice also left little room for simultaneously considering the real life events by which journalism constitutes itself. As ideology critique moved journalistic inquiry increasingly in the direction of construction, there seemed to develop an infinite regress, by which relativizing occurred to such an extent that we can longer reach "the facts" at the heart of journalism.

How to get back to reality, as one of the privileged terms of the journalistic world, remains a quandary that has yet to see resolution.

Political Economy of Journalism

A further elaboration of the sociological inquiry on journalism blended an interest in the political domain with a focus on both the sociology and the economics of journalism. Called the "political economy of news," this scholarship related news production to the economic structure of the news organization. Political economists argued that a ruling capitalist class dictated to editors and reporters what to run in their newspapers (e.g., Garnham 1979). In this regard, most news organizations were seen as simply system maintaining, with any adversarial or oppositional journalistic practices undone by the extensive intervention of ruling elites. News here was assumed to take shape at the whim of either conservative government or big business, both of which constrained it (Golding and Murdock 1991; Curran, Douglas, and Whannel 1980; Gandy 1982; Mosco 1996).

One book that appeared parallel to the rise of political economy and embraced many of its central tenets was that of Edward S. Herman and Noam Chomsky. In *Manufacturing Consent* (1988), they offered what came to be known as the "propaganda model of journalism," by which journalism was thought to mobilize support for special interests underlying both state and private activity. Herman and Chomsky claimed, in an argument that invoked a pre-Gramscian notion of ideology, that in capitalist nation-states, journalism inevitably served the established and recognized powers that be. Servicing them was inevitable because the news was produced by a concentrated industry of profit-making corporations that reflected the status quo. At the heart of Herman and Chomsky's propaganda model was the notion that wealth and power were unequally distributed and that such distribution was in need of maintenance by the news media. Identifying five filters by which the media marginalized dissent and fostered the perpetration of governmental and private interest, they argued that only material that passed through these filters ended up as news.[6]

This subset of political science, sociology, and economics, by which the media of liberal societies were painted as authoritarian, produced a unique blend of disciplinary overlap. While the political economy of journalism offered a powerful examination of journalism's "big picture," this research proved particularly valuable for its critical consideration of a normative impulse—the notion that journalism "ought" to do better by its public. While looking primarily at capitalist democracies, and in Schudson's view (1991) in effect neglecting politics by taking democracies for granted, the combination of normative and critical voices in this scholarship nonetheless underscored the value of interdisciplinary work on journalism. Yet, at the same time that political economists helped explore the broad dimensions of news, they did not account for the fuzzy territory in-between the daily routines of journalism and the larger political economy of society.

Where Is the Sociological Inquiry of Today?

Despite the auspicious beginnings of the sociological inquiry into journalism, much contemporary work on journalism no longer comes from sociology per se. While the centrality of sociological research has been contested (Gans 1972), it is fair to say that it is referenced widely as the established beginning of journalism studies, not only in the United States but around the world, and that sociology remains a large part of the default setting of journalism inquiry.

And yet the growth of sociological studies of journalism has been uneven. While the early work of Lazarsfeld and his colleagues produced a temporary institutionalization of sociological inquiry into journalism in the early years, and the 1970s and 1980s generated a flurry of primarily ethnographic sociological research surrounding the work of Tuchman, Gans, Molotch and Lester, Fishman, Schudson, and Gitlin, more recent scholarship has not produced a sustained interest in journalism. Indeed, the centrality of sociology in journalism studies is no longer certain. In one view from the United Kingdom, "media studies is to present-day social science what sociology was in the 1960s and 1970s: on the intellectual cutting edge, radical and challenging, essential to an understanding of how modern societies work" (McNair 1998: vii). Much contemporary work on the cultural dimensions of journalism vies with the status originally accorded sociological inquiry.

There have been exceptions, however, particularly of late. Within the past few years, three renowned sociologists—Herbert Gans, Todd Gitlin, and Michael Schudson—all revisited the inquiry of journalism with new books. Gans's *Democracy and the News* (2003) lamented the lowered public esteem of journalists and the degradation of contemporary democracy. Tracking the involvement of private corporations in public policy, rampant citizen mistrust, and a weakened democratic apparatus, Gans argued that the twinning of journalism's "shrinkage" and a decline in news audiences could best be offset by wide-ranging economic and political measures, including a more democratic economy and electoral process, more diverse newsrooms, and more active political lobbies. In *Media Unlimited*, Gitlin (2002), who spent much of the past few years addressing the news in public forums like *Dissent* and *Tikkun,* delivered a multipronged attack on contemporary journalism and its unending torrent of information, cautioning that the public no longer received the information needed to function as a democratic collective. Gitlin called for more thoughtful boundaries to be used in information relay in the hope of offsetting the race toward more and faster information—to media unlimited—that had become a mainstay of the contemporary age. In *The Sociology of News,* Schudson (2002) offered a wide-ranging overview of the issues in journalism that remained in need of a sociological fine-tuning. Surveying the broad intersections beyond politics by which journalism connected with the world outside—the market, history, literature—Schudson delivered a less pessimistic though equally trenchant analysis of the often internally contradictory yet always complex environment in which journalists mustered authority to convey the words and images of news. Each of these authors offered views that remained in tune with long-standing tenets of sociological inquiry; significantly, however, each also tweaked and stretched the borders of sociology to think anew about journalism and politics, journalism and the economy, journalism and technology, journalism and its publics. Even though the expansion of sociology's boundaries may not have always been articulated as such, it has been the mark of much ongoing sociological conversation about what journalists are for (see particularly Katz 1989, 1992).

Newcomers also left their mark: The work of Nina Eliasoph (1988), Joshua Gamson (1998), Ronald Jacobs (2000), and Rodney Benson (2002), to name a few, reflected an invigoration of sociological interest in journalism. Eric Klinenberg's (2003) analysis of coverage of the 1995 heat wave in Chicago showed how limited, patterned, and often intractable journalists could be in reporting events beyond their expertise. Anthropologists Mark Pedelty (1995) and Ulf Hannerz (2004) both used premises of sociological inquiry to structure their discussions of foreign correspondents, and media critic Eric Alterman (2003) offered a probing consideration of journalistic bias. In France, Pierre Bourdieu, in *On Television and Journalism* (1998), offered an extended lamentation of journalism's general "structural corruption," due to the ascendancy of television and its panderings to entertainment and talk show chatter. His argument, in large part a reversal of his earlier work extolling the value of popular taste, lambasted not only journalism's populist impulses and superficiality but also the threat posed by its new forms of discourse to science, the arts, and philosophy. A collection of his students' papers, considering his work's relation to journalism, was recently compiled for publication (Benson and Neveu, in press). However, by and large, sociologists no longer seem intrigued by the wide-ranging settings of journalism, at least not to the extent exhibited by the earlier decades of research.

And yet, sociology has taught us much about how journalism works. In the three frames of sociological study discussed here, questions about journalism were explained by linking them to the practices shaping lives in a complex society. Sociology portrayed journalism and news making as a potentially conflicted environment in which the actors strove to maintain equilibrium. This view of the organizational, institutional, and structural sides of journalism suggested that journalists sought primarily to act in tandem with others inside and beyond the news setting.

Sociological research, however, also overstated certain ways of seeing journalism. Versions of how journalism works were overgeneralized beyond their applicability in the real world of news. A regard for journalists as strategic actors who move in response to their environment distracted scholarly attention from the nonpurposive, nonstrategic sides of journalistic practice. Sociological explanations of news, moreover, offered a lopsided picture of the process of news making. News begins before journalists negotiate all the contexts—cultural, historical, political, economic—in which journalism exists. In other words, sociological inquiry reduced journalists to one kind of actor in one kind of environment. It was up to other disciplinary frames to complicate that picture.

4

History and Journalism

Historical inquiry lends temporal depth to the study of journalism. Spanning a wide range of issues related to the application of what is commonly known as "the historical perspective," history places journalism in a context by which its seemingly unexplainable dimensions come together in a frame made more sensical by evolution, chronology, and some degree of causality. Frequently portrayed as "the heroic and passionate struggle of journalists for a free press, the creation of which ennobles both their own profession and the democracy it helps sustain" (Golding and Elliott 1979: 20), historical inquiry in fact attends to much more. It locates big and small problems in context, weaving events, issues, and personalities across time into a narrative that aims to render journalism's past as a phenomenon with more stitches than holes.

Seen by its purveyors as a craft or set of skills by which the past is excavated, historical inquiry offers up the seemingly unlimited terrain of history as a reservoir from which to cull details that make sense of journalism's unresolved dimensions. Central here have been those historical studies that challenge certain orthodoxies about journalism, demonstrating the value of historical inquiry for studying the contemporary. Ranging from studies of the collective memory of Watergate (Schudson 1992) to assessments of the newspaper's role in colonial times (Clark 1994) and revisits to Whig press history (Curran and Seaton 1985), the most valuable historical inquires are those that redress the givens of old. It is no surprise, then, that historical inquiry into journalism has wrestled across time and space with many masters. Never certain of its reception, it continually crafts its stories with an eye to its neighbors—what has been labeled "journalism history," general modes of historical inquiry, and modes of nonhistorical inquiry in the field.

The Shape of Historical Perspective

Engaging in historical research on journalism does not necessarily call to mind agreed-upon parameters for inquiry. The shape of historical inquiry depends on one's definition of history, which means that ultimately historical research links up with ongoing debates about what it means to "do" history.

And yet defining historical inquiry is no easy task. Simply put, "historical inquiry" is defined as inquiry that examines events of the past; in Raymond Williams's view, it is a convergence of two ideas—"inquiry" and "account" (Williams 1983b: 146–148). Two historically contingent developments somewhat alter this definition, however. First, "history" was not always associated with factual chronicles of the past but instead referenced "accounts of imagined events" (Williams 1983b: 147). An early regard for fictitious chronicles was displaced during the 15th century by an appreciation for knowledge based on facts. Second, by the early 18th century, history began to be referenced as an abstract entity. Seen as more than just organized knowledge of the past, it came to be regarded as progressive and implicated in human self-betterment. History making began to be professionalized (Stone 1987). From that point onward, history was conceptualized as a continuous and connected abstract process, essential for the development of the collective and guarded by a group called "historians."

In Raymond Williams's (1983b) view, contemporary understandings of historical inquiry derived from the following three main premises:

1. a relatively neutral definition of a method of study that relies on facts of the past and traces the precedents of current events

2. a deliberate emphasis on variable historical conditions and contexts, through which all specific events must be interpreted (e.g., Marxist theories of history or the so-called conspiracy theories of the past)

3. a hostility to all forms of interpretation or prediction by historical necessity (e.g., scholarship that tackles general laws of historical development and rejects the notion of a probable future)

Williams argued that contemporary notions of history moved in the direction of the third premise, though they were by no means limited to it. At the same time, the 20th century premise of history as a general process borrowed from each of the other frames for understanding history in a way that rendered its precise definition unclear.

Attempts to popularize history also gained momentum over time, reincorporating aspects of history making that had been shunted aside from the 15th to 18th centuries. During the early 1930s, Carl Becker rattled his colleagues when he argued in an address to the American Historical Association that everyone was capable of being an historian. In his eyes, history was "an imaginative creation, a personal possession which each one of us, Mr. Everyman, fashions out of his individual experience, adapts to his practical or emotional needs, and adorns as well as may be to suit his aesthetic tastes" (Becker 1932, in Winks 1968: 13). For others too, being a historian was simply a question of figuring out how to "deal . . . with questions of evidence" (Winks 1968: xiii). Robin Winks (1968: xiii) argued that the "historian must collect, interpret, and then explain his evidence by methods which are not greatly different from those techniques employed by the detective."

This pull between keeping history the domain of the privileged few and opening it for popular consumption set the stage for additional complications regarding what "doing history" actually entailed. Such complications involved even the fundamental question of how one knows when something is true. As Winks asked, do they know it because they assume

> that it happened when, or how, or where the press, or a text, or a friend, or a parent, or an encyclopedia said that it did? In other words, while the professional historian frequently is engaged in judging the credibility of a witness, in attempting to gauge the bias that will be present in the account of a contemporary involved in the events he describes, the lay reader more often is concerned with assessing the credibility of a printed record, of one book's account against another's. Both levels of assessment involve the problem of evidence. (Winks 1968: xiv–xv)

On a fundamental level, then, questions have lingered over the very definition and shape of historical inquiry.

Whose Journalism History Is It?

Such questions have underlined—and often undermined—the positioning of historical inquiry in journalism's study. Complicated by a lack of clarity over the relation of historical inquiry to journalism scholarship, communication scholarship, and the history of the media, as well as to the historical inquiry of other kinds of social, cultural, economic, and political institutions, the study of journalism's past has been implemented with an eye to its scholarly neighbors both in the field and beyond.

To begin with, differences over the purposes for which history had been gathered remain at the core of historical inquiry into journalism. Generalized history was long presumed to collect evidence of the past in order to generate a more or less objective and distanced recounting of what happened (Novick 1988), a development derived from history's professionalization as a field. Begun in the 19th century when a chair in history was established at the University of Oxford in the United Kingdom, and continued with substantial effort in Germany—where, following the lead of Leopold Van Ranke, the doyen of German historicism, historians began to work in archives and developed a sophisticated set of techniques for evaluating documents about the past—there was "pioneering concern with the establishment of history as an academic discipline on a 'scientific' basis" (Scannell 2002: 192). This brought with it no small number of attempts to guard history's borders, and concerns about insiders and outsiders came to the forefront of discussions of the matter (Scannell 2002). Historians developed so-called correct ways of doing history—and boundary crossings from scholars outside of the discipline (such as journalism history) were looked at with disdain and contacts with such scholars implicitly, if not explicitly, discouraged. With time, historians came to write primarily for each other, talking "among themselves as a self-legitimating subset of a new historical genus–*homo academicus* (Scannell 2002: 192; also Stone 1987; Bourdieu 1988). Furthermore, as it divided up its own areas of interest, the historical field tended to overlook histories of the professions, leaving it up to the professional schools, like schools of journalism, to chronicle their own past. The result was that journalism's past was independently tracked in ways that collided with generalized historical accounting.

Key here was the production of journalism histories—that is, histories of journalistic practices that related specifically to journalists—that were published primarily in journalism schools with the aim of legitimating journalism as a field of inquiry. These works tended to be written with the passions and self-interest that generally accompany individuals' chronicling of their own professional lives, producing a mode of recording that was often romanticized and at odds with a presumably more neutral mode of historical record keeping. Although this gave journalism histories a mission that was different from that attached to other modes of inquiry about journalism's past—raising the question of how individuals can remain dispassionate about their own legitimation—journalism schools were not the only place in which histories of journalism were written. At their side were both histories of the media, which privileged a certain medium by which journalism had been crafted, such as radio or the press, and histories of communication, which fit journalism's past into a broader scheme about the workings of communication over time. Each of these modes of historical recounting followed often unarticulated but nonetheless distinct guidelines about examining the past (and the purposes of such examination), none of which necessarily followed generalized lines of historical recording.

All of this made it easier to cast deviations from the norm of "doing history" as suspect. For many historians, journalism history continued to be seen as "a backwater of the historical profession" (Schudson 2002: 65) that was not evenly or readily read, and the much-cited criticism of Allan Nevins, leveled in 1959, continued to ring clear: Speaking of the "thinness" and "spottiness" of journalism history, he complained that in addition to being

> marred by . . . [an] overemphasis on editorial personalities and opinion as distinguished from reporters and news, it has one still more glaring fault. Taken as a whole, it is deplorably uncritical and some of it is dishonest. (Nevins 1959: 418)

The typical newspaper historian, Nevins wrote, "is a *laudator tempus acti*, who hangs nothing but spotless linen on the line" (Nevins 1959: 419). The situation looked different to journalism historians, who chronicled the past of their professional existence for purposes that were at odds with the more distanced perspectives expected of them by historians. And because their journalism histories were crafted at a point in time when journalism education was making its way into the academic curriculum, the histories lent a much-needed depth to the collective identity of journalists and journalism and hence were written according to aims that delegitimated them when seen against the broader field of historical inquiry. Moreover, the very information culled by journalism historians, as well as by other types of journalism scholars, was often left untouched by general historians, who mined the press for data without sufficiently considering the processes by which news came to be.

Thus, disagreements over the validity and generalizability of the evidence collected about the past continued to thwart the notion of history as a disciplinary field relevant for understanding journalism. Simply put, the study of journalism's history was surrounded by an uneven interest in inquiry about the past and a lack of consensus about how best to conduct such study. Journalism historians remained somewhat isolated from their colleagues in communication and media studies, and even more separated from generalized historians. For instance, in the United States, a preference for social science research in many communications schools drew queries about the reliability of historical method, and this was accompanied by a broader ambivalence over who was "qualified" to act as an historian. Questions challenged the relevant form of historical explanation in journalism and the degree to which journalism historians lagged behind currents in both historical and ahistorical research. In sum, trends in general history, communication and media history, and the typically ahistorical fields of communication and media studies all pulled journalism history in different directions, making it a stepchild within a number of largely indifferent family set ups.

And so, questions persisted regarding what history was supposed to do, by whom, and for whom. As the 20th century gave way to new ways of historical recording—notably, the Annales School in France, started in 1929 by Marcel Bloch, Lucien Febvre, and Fernand Braudel, which established doubts as to which individuals and events actually shaped history, and the History Workshop movement in the United Kingdom from the 1950s onward, with its emphasis on "history from below" as a way of accounting for the people's view of the past—historians began to slowly diversify. But in the U.S. context it did not happen quickly or broadly enough, and there remained numerous pleas to resurrect journalism history above the tensions surrounding it.

The first call to study journalism's past differently came from James Carey, who in one of his earliest articles on the topic—"The Problem of Journalism History," published in the inaugural issue of *Journalism History* (1974)—argued for a cultural history of journalism. Noting that the present "study of journalism history remains something of an embarrassment" (Carey 1974: 3), he argued for an approach by which scholars could explore how people thought about the events in history that they were recording. Asserting that "we have defined our craft too narrowly and too modestly, and, therefore, constricted the range of problems we study and the claims we make for our knowledge" (1974: 4), Carey complained of an overabundance of institutional histories with no real tracking of the people inside them. He argued against history as a tracking of progress, by which the expansion of freedom and knowledge progressed linearly across stages of development, and called instead for a study of consciousness in the past—an address to the patterns of thought within events, including how action made sense to the actors of the time it was played out and particularly how journalists made sense of their craft. In his words, journalism provided "audiences with models for action and feeling, with ways to size up situations and it share[d] these qualities with all literary acts" (Carey 1974: 5).[7] Carey's call immediately generated other attempts to define what journalism history could be (Jowett 1975; McKerns 1977), and 14 years later, David Paul Nord (1988) stipulated that the anthropological tenor of Carey's remarks did not reflect the linkage between history and sociology that had come with the ascent of social history that Carey praised. In Nord's view, journalism history had much to gain by becoming more sociological, providing more elaborated institutional histories that could develop an understanding of the structures that motivated historical sensibilities.

Other calls continued during the following decade. One came from U.S. historian John Nerone (1993), who argued that the problem partly derived from historical inquiry's broader deficiencies. Historians did not pay enough attention to theory and tried to "tell the past in its own terms," he complained, with historians still viewing themselves "as blue collar workers who mine archives and craft narratives," whose professional development depended on accepting critical and apolitical distance and rejecting theory and deductive method (Nerone 1993: 148). Nerone argued that by adopting grand narratives of the past and producing atheoretical stories that were true only for a specific instance, historians sealed the boundaries of historyland to outsiders, barring entry to both the public and other scholars.[8] Yet another call came from Michael Schudson (1997a), who urged journalism historians to become less insulated from other areas of historical research. Calling on them to abandon their mediacentricity, their insistence that commercial forces corrupted journalism, their preference for technological and economic explanations of complex events, and their assumption that journalism served a popular need, Schudson argued that journalism history needed to ask larger questions than "what has happened in the past in this noble profession" (Schudson 1997a: 474). By the end of the 1990s, the numerous calls had exhausted many journalism historians, who felt that journalism history was all but ossified:

> Journalism historians may feel that no matter what they do, the action will be criticized by someone. Consequently, our tendency is to ossify our positions—to stand immobile, to go with what we understand, to further limit our horizons by rigid definitions of what scholarship is and indeed, of what history is. (Blanchard 1999: 107)

In Margaret Blanchard's view, the constant calls to resurrect journalism history were data; they called on the field to open itself to new definitions, methodologies, and standards of evaluation so as to stay current with the academy.

Although these conversations took place in the U.S. context, they were reflective of a larger universe of ongoing conversations about what journalism history could be. It was thus no surprise that the accounts of the past produced by journalism historians remained suspect among their colleagues in communication history. By and large, communication history evolved from either primarily humanist, nonsynthetic accounts of particular media institutions, such as newspapers or radio, or more synoptic accounts of the large systemic forces of the past. In Germany, for instance, the history of journalism remained focused on journalism's political dimensions (Schulz 1997). Communication historians were faulted too for being ungenerous, territorial, and limited in scope—with Hardt and Brennen (1993: 131) arguing that "traditional communication history generally involves empirically based, chronological explanations of events, crises, ruptures, and catastrophes, measured and explained as aberrations from the norm of continuity." Historians were criticized for holding onto grand narrative versions of history that displayed a near absolute lack of cross-narrative controversy (Nerone 1993). These circumstances were at odds with those of journalism historians, whose chronicles were often seen as out-of-date and "less interested in the social process of communication than in the detailed stories of individuals and institutions that have, at some time in the past, communicated" (Nord 1989: 308). In the U.S. context, much scholarship produced as journalism history was derided by communication historians as tailored to what journalists wanted to hear, supporting the "reigning historical model of institutions cast in splendid and improving isolation" (Marvin 1983: 25).

Similar responses surrounded textbooks on journalism history: In the United States, the much-used *The Press and America* continued to utilize a dated and mythological definition of how the news worked, arguing somewhat optimistically and with a marked disregard for research suggesting otherwise that "newspapers did not create news; news created newspapers" (Emery and Emery 1999: 7). U.S. journalism historians were seen as remaining stubbornly humanistic and atheoretical, wedded to a Progressive or Whiggish view of the past primarily because it had been the foremost interpretive model among historians during the 1920s and 1930s when many U.S. journalism schools were established (Carey 1974; Marvin 1983; Nord 1989). Journalism historians, many of whom were not trained as historians, were also critiqued for being solipsistic, insufficiently consulting general historical work and providing exaggerated interpretations of media influence as historical explanation (Schudson 1997a). They were criticized too for showing little interest in communication, per se, or in communication theory, in particular. While journalism history of late has drawn more attention from other historical scholars (e.g., Schudson 2002), it still has remained something of a second-class citizen.

Given these circumstances, it is no surprise that the efforts of journalism historians drew not recognition but criticism from general communication scholars, whose own work was critiqued for an "absence of history, linked to an absence of self-reflection, [that] reinforces the status-quo of theory and practice as ahistorical and acritical" (Hardt and Brennen 1993: 130). Although the situation improved over time, journalism history still remained a sideshow of communication research, persisting primarily in the margins of professional organizations, journals, and conferences where research articles or conference presentations on "history" claimed as much in their titles—"A Historical Look at . . . ," "A Historical Survey of . . . ," or "Reporting in the Colonial Period." The unevenness was further deepened by an institutional separation between most journalism historians and scholars in communication and media studies: Journalism historians were often situated in journalism schools or departments of American studies or English and affiliated with organizations like the American Journalism Historians' Association (AJHA) or the history division of the Association for Education in Journalism and Mass Communication (AEJMC), while communication historians and scholars in media studies tended to be employed by communication departments and affiliate with communication organizations, such as the International Communication Association (ICA), National Communication Association (NCA), and International Association for Mass Communication Research (IAMCR). This, however, was an uneven affiliation; there is still no communication history section within the ICA. In addition, the distance facilitated different ways of tracking the same scholarly territory. For instance, as Paddy Scannell (2002: 198) pointed out recently, the simple attempt to bridge film and television as similar media because they were both visual in effect rendered radio "the Cinderella" of media studies, even if radio and television news were deeply impacted by each other. Such demarcations had direct impact on the evolution of the historical study of journalism and the degree to which communication and media historians could regard journalism as an area independent of other kinds of mediated fare.

Thus, questions of whose journalism history was at focus remained open to interpretation. Interestingly, the tension over the placement of journalism history raised fundamental issues about how best to broaden a discipline and the degree to which scholars were able to look beyond their own neighborhood to legitimate their profession. Each lamentation about historical inquiry into journalism argued for a valorization of theory at some level, a contextualization of history within some kind of larger picture, and a linking of history with other disciplinary fields, moving away from traditional modes of history making. Significantly, the claim to broaden the field was made not only across the populations that "did journalism history" but also among those scholars interested in a more interdisciplinary blend of historical inquiry. The ability to maintain disciplinary integrity and its value when the standard of blended disciplines became, by definition, the norm thus drew attention to the conditions under which external legitimation became the preferred way of broadening a given area of inquiry; it also suggested that the repeated invocation of the social sciences as the scale and standard against which to judge and evaluate historical inquiry had its effect on the positioning of the historical study of journalism.

Classifying Historical Inquiry Into Journalism

An enormous body of literature has tackled journalism's past. Like other fields of study, historical inquiry promoted its own picture of what counted as journalism scholarship, and journalism's past was selectively told in its many geographic contexts. In the United States, most historical studies considered major urban newspapers primarily in large northeastern cities, to the general exclusion of semiurban, suburban, or rural news organizations and until very recently to the exclusion as well of the specialized and alternative press. In the United Kingdom, a bias privileged the long-standing mainstream journalistic settings of Fleet Street, while arenas like the provincial press or the Welsh press were not as readily examined. In the Middle East, more historical scholarship focused on the journalistic settings connected to Israel than those of the surrounding nation-states, and in Israel the emphasis was on journalism following the establishment of the nation-state. Australian scholarship focused more actively on the colonial period and on New South Wales than on the journalism of other periods and regions. And in Latin America, existing work focused most extensively on Mexico, Argentina, and Brazil, reflecting but a small portion of journalistic life in the region. In each case, the tabloid, oppositional, and localized journalistic settings received scant scholarly attention. As a perspective, then, existing studies painted portraits of journalism's past that were partial and largely singular in focus.

And yet, various classificatory schemes emerged in response to the ongoing debates about the appropriate shape of historical scholarship on journalism. In keeping with larger patterns of knowledge acquisition (Lakoff 1987), such classifications allowed journalism historians to draw consensus from some quarters of the academy if not all, engaging in what Nelson Goodman (1978: 21) described as "finding a fit."

But classifications, and the work of interpretation on which they were based, change. Historians—like other kinds of public scribes—were affected by the times in which they wrote, facing new material to be excavated and encountering new research tools for uncovering the past as time progressed. The interest in redoing "old" scholarship alongside the ascent of new computer technologies, data basing, and other means of declassifying formerly inaccessible files thereby made sense. Yet the variation across different interpretive schemes for thinking about the past depended on historically dependent positions. Questions of what might be appropriate for a given historical period—including how news was produced, who attended to it, and what it was composed of—depended on the habits, conventions, and technologies at play in a given historical period. This point undercut an unspoken assumption of universality about much inquiry into journalism, where it was often implied that news continued to be the same for all places and time periods.

All of this suggested that in any inquiry combining history and journalism, the following questions remained pertinent:

- The time of historical inquiry into journalism: From which time period is the analysis taken? When does it begin? When does it end? Historical visions of journalism that look back in time to examine journalism make a degree of evolutionary or chronological perspective as much a part of the constructed frame of inquiry as an attribute of the target of inquiry.

- The space of historical inquiry into journalism: From which geographic areas is history most able to generate broad statements about journalism's workings? The history of journalism in Europe is markedly different from that in the United States. How, then, is it possible to bring them together in a meaningful fashion?

- The focus of historical inquiry into journalism: Who and what is being studied? Is the focus on individual journalists, news organizations, or news institutions? Does the study use a broader scope in shaping its focus, such as the news coverage of a given event or adaptation to a new technology?

While these questions arise easily, we have clear-cut answers to none of them. About the subjects in many of the questions, we have no primary knowledge. To understand these claims, all we need consider is an example such as how the reporting of the U.S. civil rights movement looks if the black press is not included as part of the historical analysis. Just as there are many ways to draw the boundaries of the field of journalism scholarship, so are there many ways to legitimate an event's positioning in history. The predominance of white, privileged, and male perspectives defining so much of the field has created an aura by which its givens appear natural and commonsensical. Where are the voices of the women, the ethnic minorities, and the working class who have typically not been allowed to participate in the ongoing processes of collective definition? In that the field of journalism history is shaped differently depending on who engages in its definition, their absence deserves consideration.

Faced with the enormity of the material they must address, scholars interested in journalism's past have often found it more difficult to organize and hence legitimate their work than have other types of scholars. Due to the daunting nature of the task, very few followed Michael Bromley and Tom O'Malley's (1997: 1) lead in compiling what they called "a reader in the history of [British] journalism." Rather, regardless of whether or not they were associated with journalism history per se, communication and media history, or generalized history, scholars invested in journalism's past tended to slice the time of their scholarship by positioning it in a series of spatially nested frames. Differing in scale but not mutually exclusive, frames of the past ranged from the very specific, like the individual memoir, to the very broad, like the nation-state, as an organizing principle for analysis. In each case, different kinds of chronicles, including the anecdotal account and the case study, were used to address the past, whereby the familiarity of a certain frame offered a way to establish the continued legitimacy for telling the story in a certain way.

Journalism History Writ Small: Memoirs, Biographies, Organizational Histories

Framing journalism history as the past of individuals and individual organizations has been a valuable way of organizing material on the past. Most specific in nature of the alternatives discussed here, these works included memoirs, autobiographies, biographies, and insider accounts, as well as the histories of specific news organizations. Implicit in much of this work was the assumption that the detailed relay of an individual past bore or embodied more generalizable tenets for understanding the history of journalism in broader strokes.

The anecdotal chronicles that provided the backbone of most memoirs and autobiographies long remained a popular way of making sense of the past. Usually written by a former journalist acting as historian, who re-counted his or her experiences and celebrated or denigrated a given news organization or institution, these chronicles varied across news setting and nation-state. As Hanno Hardt (1995: 5) noted, their prevalence meant that many of "the first journalism historians had their roots in the profession. They were trained in neither history nor the social sciences; rather they had often left careers in journalism without ever telling their own stories."

In the United Kingdom, for example, memoirs written "by reporters and editors about their early lives, their entry into journalism . . . and the transition to work in Fleet Street" helped track how journalists faced the dilemmas and pressures of their work in different time periods (Bailey and

Williams 1997: 352). The central history of the press was the five-volume *The History of the Times* (Anonymous 1935–1958), largely written by people in the business rather than professional historians and concerned "with significant individuals . . . and the politics of their day" (Scannell 2002: 199). Memoirs and autobiographies appeared to have an unusual staying power as explanatory texts in the United Kingdom, with early memoirs and autobiographies (Payne 1932, 1947; Reith 1949; Jones 1951; Fienburgh 1955; Cameron 1967) continuing to grace contemporary lists of journalistic memoirs (e.g., Boyce, Curran, and Wingate 1978; Curran and Seaton 1985). At the same time, more contemporary memoirs—Harold Evans's *Good Times, Bad Times* (1994), which recounted his years at the *Sunday Times,* and John Pilger's (1986) story of his time at the *Daily Mirror*—provided reminiscences that drew equal popularity and acclaim.

In Australia, where journalism history was slower to arrive as an integral part of inquiry into journalism (Henningham 1988; Curthoys 1999), early reminiscences appeared and were reprinted (e.g., Gullett 1913, cited in Curthoys 1999), given a durability over time that supported a certain transparency with which 19th and early 20th century journalism was generally regarded (Curthoys 1999). As efforts were made from the 1960s onward to introduce a more critical voice in historical scholarship on journalism, memoirs by Lloyd Dumas and Cecil Edwards appeared (Henningham 1988), as did John Douglas Pringle's *Have Pen: Will Travel* (1973), detailing his career with the *Guardian* and *Times* and editorship of the *Sydney Morning Herald.* The memoirs of other Australian journalists—Ita Buttrose's *Early Edition: My First Forty Years* (1985) and Philip Knightley's *A Hack's Progress* (1998)—also appeared by the late 1980s.

Memoirs and autobiographies in the U.S. context tended to have more of a rotational quality that privileged the more recent books; books on contemporary figures tended to displace books on earlier figures such as Benjamin Franklin (Parton 1864), Lincoln Steffens (1931), Edward R. Murrow (1941), and Harrison Salisbury (1983), so as to highlight the memoirs of individuals such as Fred Friendly (1967), Linda Ellerbee (1986), Walter Cronkite (1997) and Tom Brokaw (1998), all of which detailed experiences at the TV networks. These memoirs conveyed an immediacy that was no doubt lost in the earlier chronicles, and as technological advancements raced forward, the newer memoirs were able to draw pictures of increasing relevance to contemporary understandings of the news. As the back cover blurb to Dan Rather's (1977) book proclaimed, "here are his first-hand reports from the front lines of our most shattering events—Dallas the day JFK was killed, Watergate, the Vietnam jungle, the death of Martin Luther King." Contemporary journalistic memoirs continued to draw popular acclaim as questions persisted about more recent permutations of journalistic authority. Bernard Goldberg's *Bias: A CBS Insider Exposes How the Media Distort the News* (2001), written by a former CBS reporter, received considerable publicity for tracking three decades of dealings with what he saw as television news' liberal bias, and Katharine Graham's (1998) autobiography, which detailed the ups and downs at the *Washington Post,* also topped the bestseller lists.

The memoirs and autobiographies of journalists in Latin America tracked the reminiscences largely of retired journalists (e.g., Dines 1986; Abramo 1989). Developing as a body of historical scholarship later than was the case in other regions, many of these books recounted tragedies and triumphs in lives that were often politically at odds with either the political climate or the institutions in which the journalists worked. Claudio Abramo (1989) detailed the unusual circumstance of editing a conservative paper through a leftist political perspective. Alberto Dines (1986) offered reminiscences of his stint as long-time managing editor of the *Jornal de Brasil,* while Bernardo Kucinski (1991) detailed his experiences in the *jornalismo de causa,* the overtly politicized Brazilian alternative press. By and large, however, memoirs in Latin America reflected a largely uncritical literature that, in one view, remained "without criteria, . . . consist[ing] purely of simple, uncontextualized monographs" (Marques de Melo 1988: 406).

In each case, the value of these memoirs and autobiographies was limited. They evoked a "journalism which was looked back upon with nostalgic affection, and seen as endangered by economic, political and technological change" (Curthoys 1999: 3). It was no surprise that even the trade literature played its part in publishing reminiscences to mark anniversaries or other special occasions, such as a special issue of *The Journalist* published in November of 1971 to mark the 60th anniversary of the Ausralian Journalists' Association (Curthoys 1999).

A related mode of historical recounting was the large number of biographies of key journalistic personalities, which provided an important dimension of historical scholarship but tended to be only slightly more critical than the autobiographies and memoirs. In one view, these books "constituted the most significant category of historical research in journalism at least until the early 1980s," when social history came on the scene (Hardt 1995: 7). The targets of inquiry were predictable: in the U.S. context, biographies appeared on Joseph Pulitzer and his son (Ireland 1969; Pfaff 1991), William Randolph Hearst (Nasaw 2000), Edward R. Murrow (Kendrick 1969; Sperber 1986; Persico 1988), I.F. Stone (Cottrell 1993), and Bob Woodward and Carl Bernstein (Havill 1993). Two biographical series were begun in the United States in the 1980s (Ashley 1983–1985; Riley 1988–89), which reflected an ongoing interest in building up a repertoire of biographical sketches that journalism could call its own. In the United Kingdom biographers wrote about Lord Northcliffe (Ryan 1953; Thompson 2000) and Evelyn Waugh (Sykes 1977), while in Australia books tracked Rupert Murdoch (Munster 1985), James Harrison, William Mellefont, and John Gale (Henningham 1988), as well as a "growing industry devoted to one of Australia's most influential and best-remembered journalists, C.E.W. Bean" (Curthoys 1999: 4). Some books combined numerous biographical sketches, such as Fred Inglis's tracking of "the giants of the genre" in *People's Witness: The Journalist in Modern Politics* (2002). That book, written by an otherwise critical analyst of the news media, combined historical and biographical writing but nonetheless bore remnants of a sometimes breathless celebration of the individuals it profiled.

Some work in this vein provided a critical understanding of the news organization, produced generally by academics using autobiographies or biographies to make broader points about journalism. Linda Steiner, for instance, analyzed the autobiographies of U.S. women journalists as the basis for her discussion of the gendered basis of their professional lives (Steiner 1996, 1997), while Michael Schudson (1988) contrasted the autobiographies of Lincoln Steffens and Harrison Salisbury as a means of discussing journalistic mind-sets of different eras.

Counting as historical record insofar as they recounted what happened at various points in time, these chronicles were valuable because they provided a first-person view of a complex organizational or institutional setting. At the same time, they were limited in usefulness from an evidentiary point of view, for their perspectives were largely subjective, singular, and highly personalized.

A third type of historical account that addressed the small scale of journalism's past was the case study of individual news organizations. Case studies, which tracked certain news organizations over time, also tended to vary by nation-state. Scholarship in the United Kingdom chronicled the establishment of the *Financial Times* (Kynaston 1988), *The Guardian* (Ayerst 1971), the *New Statesman* (Hyams 1963), the *Sun* (Chippendale and Horrie 1992), and the *Daily Telegraph* (Burnham 1955; Hart-Davis 1991). In the United States, scholars addressed the history of the *Washington Post* (Roberts 1977, 1989; Bray 1980), the *New York Times* (Davis 1921/1969; Berger 1951; Diamond 1995; Tifft and Jones 2000), and the *Baltimore Sun* (Williams 1987), among others. Gary Paul Gates's chronicle of CBS News, *Airtime: The Inside Story of CBS News* (1978), written after he left his job as a writer for CBS News, drew popular acclaim for its tracking of 15 years of experiences with the network. In each case, the news organization provided a finite and identifiable filter through which the evolution of news could be more broadly considered. Garnering acclaim were the works of two former *New York Times* reporters,

David Halberstam's *The Powers That Be* (1979) and Gay Talese's *The Kingdom and the Power* (1978), which offered in-depth comparative examinations of some of the key news empires, combining insiders' authoritative views with rich and often critical detail.

In all its cases—memoirs, autobiographies, biographies, and case histories of individual news organizations—this body of historical scholarship established a ground on which more theoretically-complicated and complexly formed histories could be crafted. Particularly attuned to long-standing premises for doing history, by which the individual circumstance, case study, or example stood in for the more general terrain of which it was representative, this scholarship was valuable for setting historical inquiry on the map of journalism's study. At the same time, its often uncritical celebration of journalism's high points left uncovered many of the contradictions and problems resonant in journalism's performance.

Journalism History Writ Midway: Periods, Themes, Events

A second mode of historical scholarship offered a larger scale of inquiry that contextualized the discrete target of scholarly attention against some broader impulse. Contextualizing the past as midway between the individual focal points of the works mentioned above and the large-scale contexts offered by others, scholars writing journalism history "midway" organized their approach to the past in a number of ways—by periods, by themes, and by events. The research produced here was particularly valuable to scholars conducting ahistorical inquiry on journalism, in that it hinted at broader explanatory mechanisms by which to understand the specific instance being examined. At the same time, this research remained affected by both the smaller scale scholarship and the nation-states that figured into the larger scale journalism histories. In other words, journalism history, writ midway, was shaped by both individual histories and the histories of nation-states.

Journalism by temporal period remained a frame of choice across the terrain of journalism scholars, but it seemed to draw particular attention among journalism educators, whose delivery of periodicized histories of journalism was consonant with the provision of a professionalized curriculum in journalism schools. Often categorizing journalism by temporal demarcations and positioning research within either named, familiar temporal periods, decades, or centuries, much of this scholarship (e.g., Smith 1977) imposed a temporal unity on different sets of practices. For example, references in the U.S. context to journalism of the colonial period were immediately thought to address the origins of the press during the 1600s and 1700s. Similarly, the penny press was repeatedly positioned between certain years, regardless of the fact that many of its practices extended beyond those years (Nerone 1987). Periodicized histories reflected broader, consensually-driven historical time-periods—such as the Revolutionary Press in the United States and the period of the American Revolution or the Victorian Press in the United Kingdom and Victorian England. The periods that tended to generate the most extensive scholarship were typically those that reflected some critical tension in the evolution of journalistic practice. In that regard, the penny press remained one of the most frequently addressed topics in U.S. period histories of journalism.

In framing their scholarship around a given time period, scholars also tended to adopt more specifically defined temporal demarcations, such as the journalism of a certain political administration. In the United States, for instance, journalism was said to be connected with the Eisenhower administration (Allen 1992) or the Kennedy years (Watson 1990). Sometimes scholars developed a roll call of personalities associated with a given time period, so that studies of colonial period journalism invariably paid attention to Benjamin Franklin. In fact, chronicling the activities of individual journalists was prominent in colonial period journalism because part of the reigning mythology about American journalism tracked the ascent of the individual journalist, as embodied by Franklin.

Framing by period facilitated the construction of thoughtful observations about pieces of journalism's past in ways that eased their comparison with the present. Charles E. Clark's (1994) discussion of the colonial press pointed out both the craft and business dimensions of newspaper publishing and showed how the press acted simultaneously as a force for both Anglicization and Americanization; in this regard, it established a precedent for community building that persisted long beyond the colonial period. Jeffrey Pasley's (2003) discussion of Thomas Jefferson's use of the press during the Jacksonian era overturned many conventional notions about the origin of newspaper-based politics, as did Michael McGerr's (2001) consideration of the decline in political voting, which he attributed to a change in political style during the post-Civil War years. Hazel Dicken-Garcia's *Journalistic Standards in Nineteenth Century America* (1989) diligently probed press standards, coverage, and criticism around the broad area defined as the Civil War period, and her analysis was helpful in thinking about standards in other wartime eras (Schwarzlose 1989, 1990). Joyce Hoffman (1995) analyzed the 25 years of Theodore White's journalism, arguing that his movement from journalist to political insider was reflective of larger changes in U.S. journalism of the time, and her analysis too set the stage for thinking about insider journalism of the contemporary era.

However, too often this kind of historical study invoked an arbitrary demarcation of temporal periods, with journalism divided so that it offered temporally bounded reflections of just about every era in history. For instance, in the U.S. context, one such attempt (Sloan 1991) included revolutionary journalism (1765–1783), the party or partisan press (1783–1833), the frontier press (1800–1900), the antebellum press (1827–1861), the industrial press (1865–1883), and new journalism (1883–1900). This latter category, offering a different name for yellow journalism, emphasized sensationalism and crusading for reform, as exemplified by Joseph Pulitzer's *World* and William Randolph Hearst's *New York Journal*. The inherent weakness of such demarcations seemed to be most vividly reflected when addressing the more recent past. Contemporary analysis somewhat arbitrarily divided modern journalism (1900–1945) from contemporary journalism (1945–present). The former included chronicles on muckraking (1901–1917), various new media (rise of radio), and media in wartime (both World War I and World War II), while the latter focused rather broadly on journalism's continued growth as a profession, its evolving economic structure, changing media technologies like the Internet, and the swing toward a more antagonistic government-media relationship. The overloading of such a wide range of topics on two temporal periods reflected not only the difficulty in separating periods from each other but also the broader inclination to reduce the pace of historical inquiry as it neared the present.

By definition, journalism by period differed according to the national settings in which journalism evolved. For instance, in France, Robert Darnton's (1985) discussion of the prerevolutionary French press offered an alternative glimpse of the function of the press in tweaking official sensibilities, while Jeremy Popkin (1980; also Popkin, Kaplan, and Baker 1990) elaborated on a repertoire of practices by which journalism connected with its public during that same time period. Extending his analysis to the French revolutionary press, Popkin (2001) established the ways in which the press then shaped new identities for members of marginalized groups, like workers, women, and members of the middle class. In the United Kingdom, temporal demarcations were established via historical periods related to British history: Lucy Brown's (1985) analysis was limited to the Victorian press, while Aled Jones (1996) focused on the British press of the 19th century. George Boyce, James Curran, and Pauline Wingate (1978) divided the bibliography attached to their survey of the British press into the following historical periods: before 1780, from 1780 to 1850, from 1850 to 1914, from 1914 to 1945, and post 1945. Again, the more recent period seemed to be the hardest on which to generate consensus. Other works, such as Joseph Frank's (1961) analysis of the beginnings of the British newspaper, limited the period of inquiry—in

Frank's case to a mere 40 years (1620–1660). And Matthew Engel's *Tickle the Public* (1996), a chronological tracking of the British tabloids, was subtitled "One Hundred Years of the Popular Press."

Even the availability of temporal markers like eras or centuries, however, did not ensure a unified view of the period in question. For instance, the nearly 30 years of the penny press era (1833–1861)—a period in which U.S. newspapers were assumed to have given way to the modern press and to a cheaper, more popular, and more sensationalistic newspaper—was variously analyzed by scholars arguing both for and against its regularly articulated features. While mainstream journalism historians saw the appearance of the penny press and the rise of the "common man" as closely integrated (e.g., Emery and Emery 1996: 121; also Mott 1941/1962), revisionist historians like Michael Schudson (1978) and Dan Schiller (1981) argued for a more nuanced and less celebratory interpretation of its virtues. Nearly a decade later, John Nerone (1987) offered a more critical view, which took most of the leading scholars of the penny press to task for what he saw as errors of judgment and interpretation that exaggerated what had in fact occurred during the era. In response, some of those same scholars publicly refuted Nerone's claims, accusing him of erroneously lumping together mainstream and revisionist historians, understating the unique features of the penny press, and not recognizing the critical edge of their own scholarship. And even today, much of the same interest reappears in adapted narratives (Mindich 1998). In addition, many of these works were reduced to simplified associations with identifiable periods: Schudson's *Discovering the News* (1978) was referenced repeatedly in conjunction with the penny press, despite the fact that the book addressed the 1920s in detail.

Framing journalism's past by theme offered a second way of writing journalism midway. Contextualizing the past through a predetermined thematic interest and borrowing from broad theoretical understandings about how journalism worked, these histories provided a useful explanatory mechanism for organizing the material about journalism's past. Various themes were invoked, such as the adaptation of journalistic practices to developing technologies or the evolution of certain journalistic practices in response to market pressures, as in William Solomon and Robert McChesney's (1993) discussion of the marginalization of journalistic forms over the years that had challenged a widespread acceptance about the interdependency of capitalism and democracy in journalistic settings. In that volume, for instance, Michael Warner (1993) used critical theory and deconstruction to explain the meaning of print in the colonial period, while Albert Kreiling (1993) examined the different journalistic modes necessarily activated by the African American press in response to commercialism. Tracked elsewhere were issues such as violence against the press (Nerone 1994), women's history and journalism (Steiner 1997; Beasley 2001), and the interplay of religion and journalism (Nord 2001, in press). Thomas Leonard (1995) rethought how people over time used the news. Despite a decline in the number of daily papers and the percentage of individuals who read them, a reduction in the number of newspaper owners, and a narrowing of the represented political views, the power of individuals to select the news they wanted grew over time, bringing different interpretive communities and settings surrounding the news back to life.

Some of these histories thematically tracked the evolution of certain kinds of journalistic practices (e.g., Schwarzlose 1989, 1990; Baldasty 1999), positioning them against a broader context that explained their development. Perhaps the most well-known work in this regard, written by an Australian but largely seen as an in-depth chronicle of journalism at large, was that of Philip Knightley (1975), a former war correspondent and investigative reporter with the *Sunday Times* who turned journalism historian (Hobson, Knightley, and Russell 1972; also Knightley 1998). His book, *The First Casualty* (Knightley 1975), remains among the most widely referenced histories of journalism in wartime. Another body of well-known work here was that addressing the history of the notion of objectivity. In *Discovering the News,* Michael Schudson (1978) offered a comprehensive and insightful analysis of the journalistic practices of news writing that evolved from the penny press onward. Providing a sociological lens on historical inquiry, he tackled the changes in communal standards by which U.S. journalism was prone to constitute itself. Locating those standards in the mind-sets of journalists rather than in external pressures to professionalize, Schudson drew a complicated map of the contradictory tensions in journalistic practice by which the penny press crafted its arrival. And in so doing, he set in place a history of the practices of objectivity that became a standard against which numerous other works were evaluated (Smith 1978; Schiller 1981; Nerone 1987; Hackett and Zhao 1998; Mindich 1998).

The evolution of other journalistic practices—like muckraking (Shapiro 1968), the alternative press (Kessler 1984), horse-race journalism (Littlewood 1998), or newspaper design (Barnhurst and Nerone 2001)—also drew scholarly attention. Certain backgrounds were offered schematically as a way of explaining the shaping of journalistic practices over time, as in the ascent of commercialism in the U.S. press of the 19th century (Baldasty 1992), the crafting of early forms of press freedom (Smith 1988, 1999), and the rise of business practices in news (Kielbowicz 1986). Here, the history of journalism in wartime produced a groundswell of scholarship that discussed how each wartime period developed its own journalistic register. In the

United Kingdom, journalistic practices during both the Crimean War and the Falklands War occupied a place in the register of scholars interested in establishing historical contexts (Knightley 1975; Harris 1983; Morrison and Tumber 1988; Lambert and Badsey 1997), while similar studies were written by scholars in the United States around Vietnam (Braestrup 1977; Hallin 1986; Arlen and Thompson 1997), the Pentagon Papers (Sheehan, Smith, Kenworthy, and Butterfield 1971; Rudenstine 1996), and the Gulf War (Gerbner, Mowlana, and Schiller 1992; Kellner 1992; Denton 1993; Moore 1993: Bennett and Paletz 1994; Taylor 1998). Journalism in World War II was examined either by discussing that war's widespread military fronts and press pools (e.g., Schwarzlose 1989, 1990) or by analyzing certain practices like photography (Moeller 1989; Zelizer 1998b) and the military press (Cornebise 1993). Some studies were narrowly focused, as in work on the history of photography and wartime (Lewinski 1978; Taylor 1991; Brothers 1997). Such research, which provided extensive analyses of journalism in war, was only rarely linked to the practices of nonwar journalism.

Against this background, a considerable amount of work addressed journalism's past through the theme of technological advancement. Here studies were published that tracked the broad contours of journalism's history, with an emphasis on its technologies and the so-called great men who used its devices. Following upon a large body of work in communication that drew technologically deterministic parameters for understanding practice (e.g., Innis 1951, 1972; McLuhan 1964), and adopting what is often known as a grand narrative, these chronicles delineated the ways in which new news media evolved from the days of cave painting onward (e.g., Streckfuss 1998). Foremost here was Mitchell Stephens's *A History of News* (1988), which bore the subtitle "From the Drum to the Satellite" and provided a wide-ranging journey through journalism history that laid emphasis on the ongoing impulses that moved journalism from early times to the news of today. Some of this work addressed technological advancement by telling the story of the history of media rather than journalism per se, offering discussions of certain large-scale technological settings and the ways in which they impacted journalism. Diamond (1975) and Smith (1998), for instance, helped lay a foundation for thinking critically about how the medium of television challenged, shaped, and altered more traditional forms of news. The history of press photography was tracked in Australia, the United Kingdom, and the United States (Carlebach 1992, Griffin 1994). Technological themes similarly shaped examinations of precursors to the press (Frank 1961; Schaaber 1967), the wire services (Boyd-Barrett 1980b; Blondheim 1994), and radio (Douglas

1987; Smulyan 1994), though work on the internet (e.g., Borden and Harvey 1998) has yet to produce its own historicization.

Finally, journalism's past was addressed by focusing on one event or series of events that reflected broader problems with journalistic practice. In this regard, filtering the past through an event served to refine broad-ranging discussions by limiting them to a focal point that was identifiable and somewhat finite. Often this work focused on a major watershed or public event of a given nation-state—such as wars, political changes, alterations of the socioeconomic order, and political scandals. Thus, U.S. journalism history was seen through McCarthyism (Bayley 1981), Watergate (Schudson 1992), or the JFK assassination (Zelizer 1992b). Sometimes events of one country were analyzed for their impact on another country, such as how the British press covered the American revolution (Lutnick 1967). Journalism was also at times seen through its coverage of a particular contested public issue, political campaign, war, or moral panic. For example, Leo Chavez (2001) offered a comprehensive examination of 35 years of immigration's coverage in the U.S. press.

This approach to classifying historical scholarship demarcated a certain temporal logic by which journalism was thought to operate in different periods. Its limitations, however, were obvious. It created an arbitrary demarcation that cut off the temporal development of journalism from developments in other eras. For example, in the case of colonial period journalism and its emphasis on the origins of the press, what some have argued were in fact the first media—pamphlets and broadsides—disappeared from analytical focus. Furthermore, this approach lent an analytical unity to each era that made the era overly autonomous from the longer cycling of history. Adopting an event, a period, or a theme as a framing device served a certain legitimating function when doing history, for it obviated the need to develop an analytical frame that required agreement by others. That said, the value of such devices was somewhat limited by the singularity of the analysis.

Crafting journalism midway drew interest as journalism historians turned their attention to the internal nuances by which journalism was set in place, and it was particularly prevalent in the social history of journalism. In the words of Boyce, Curran, and Wingate (1978: 13–14), "the way in which the role of the press is perceived, the expectations audiences have of audiences, the values and beliefs of newspapermen, the attitudes of elites to the press are all significant in helping us to understand the nature and development" of journalism. Focusing on an issue, a problem, or a concept through an evolutionary lens enabled scholars to craft broad arguments about journalism through discrete and understandable targets of analysis.

Journalism History Writ Large: The Nation-State

One of the long-standing motivations for doing journalism history was its relevance to the development of the nation-state. In this regard, there evolved a substantial amount of literature tracking the history of journalism as associated with the history of nations. Often written in journalism schools for pedagogical purposes, these works ranged from naturalist and often atheoretical recountings of the past to theorized critical reconsiderations of how journalism took shape in conjunction with the larger aims of nation building. Writ large, this scholarship embraced the broadest frame of inquiry of the alternatives discussed here, providing a large-scale address to the institutional nexus connecting journalism and the nation-state.

Histories of journalism and histories of nation-states were connected first by studies that saw journalism filling tasks related to nation building. In the United Kingdom, histories of newspapers dated to the mid-19th century, when Alexander Andrews (1859) published his two-volume *History of British Journalism,* which tracked the role of the press in building British society. Similar studies followed over time (e.g., Fox Bourne 1887, cited in Boyce, Curran, and Wingate 1978; Morison 1932, Stutterheim 1934; Williams 1958; Taylor 1961), drawing a detailed picture of the institutional setting in which the British press was established and then maintained in the postwar era (Seymour-Ure 1991). That setting was later used as the basis for discussing other journalistic institutions, such as broadcasting (e.g., Briggs 1961–1995). Differences between the two, however, remained stark, as James Curran (2000c) noted in contrasting the successful broadcasting reform in the United Kingdom with the failure of press reformism. The central Australian study of the press, Henry Mayer's *The Press in Australia* (1964), remained a landmark study for some time after its publication, due to the fact that, as he complained in the preface, there had been insufficient historical work on journalism to that date: "I have been compelled to do my own spade-work in a field in which I have no special competence" (quoted in Curthoys 1999: 4). Others, such as R.B. Walker (1980), Rod Kirkpatrick (1984), and John Henningham (1988), in later years provided some of the additional details Mayer felt hard-pressed to uncover during the 1960s. Raymond Kuhn's *The Media in France* (1995; also see Ferenczi 1993) provided a comprehensive tracking of the evolution of French media from 1945 onward, concentrating on the relationship between journalism and the state.

Relevant here was a mode of naturalist history that followed the tenets of the different schools of historical interpretation associated with stages of nation building. Yoking the telling of history to the reigning mythologies of the country in which it was told, six "schools" of historical interpretation—nationalist, romantic, developmental, progressive, consensus, and cultural—were identified in the U.S. context as relevant ways of telling the past (Startt and Sloan 1989; also Sloan 1991). Although they were never self-conscious forms of interpretation, these schools of interpretation together comprised a range of interpretive positions invoked to tell the stories of journalism's past as it impacted on the development of the U.S. nation-state. In each case, the interpretive schools changed with the altered trends of historical inquiry, reflecting, for example, more of an interest in social context when social history became more of a norm.[9]

Thus, for instance, works that tracked journalism's past as the evolution of professionalism topped the lists of large-scale journalism histories. Fredric Hudson's acclaimed *Journalism in the United States, From 1690 to 1872* (1873), published in response to the rise of the penny press in the early 1800s (particularly the rise of the *New York Sun* in 1833), introduced an altered set of expectations about journalism to U.S. journalism schools that were tied to notions of professionalism; however, Hudson himself was not a historian per se but a managing editor at the *New York Herald.* Two other similarly framed scholarly examples included James Melvin Lee's *History of American Journalism* (1917) and Willard Bleyer's *Main Currents in the History of American Journalism* (1927). The entry of women into the profession set the stage for the publishing of one landmark early text, Ishbel Ross's *Ladies of the Press* (1936), which traced the evolutionary goals that women hoped to achieve as journalists. But the classic text produced along these lines in the United States remained Frank Luther Mott's *American Journalism: A History of Newspapers in the United States Through 250 Years: 1690–1940.* Written originally in 1941 and reprinted numerous times (in 1947, 1950, 1953, 1962, and 2000), the book was organized around the concept of progress and tied journalism's development to larger advances in professionalism and their link to the nation-state and institutions of democracy. The themes resonant here found their way into the foundational tenets for organizations of journalism educators, including the American Society of Journalism School Administrators. As one journalism educator wrote in 1958,

In a half-century, journalism education in this country has grown from the fumblings of infancy and the uncertainties of childhood into an adolescence marked by a surprised recognition of increasing power. Now it is entering a period of maturity, a maturity notable, thus far, for introspective self-criticism and self-conscious striving toward improvement. (quoted in Sloan 1991: 219)

Against this background, works like those of Fred Friendly (1967), A.M. Sperber (1986), and Joseph Persico (1988) all established premises against which to evaluate particular individuals, organizations, and institutions under the guise of professionalism and its linkage with democratic freedom.

Another much-favored way of linking the history of journalism to the history of the nation-state was through progressivism, which developed the idea of journalists working within society to effect change central to democracy's betterment. The villains here were media owners, businessmen, industrialists, or anyone with money or power, and the development of the press was thereby seen as an instrument of reform. Oswald Garrison Villard's *Some Newspapers and Newspapermen* (1923) critiqued the materialism of American publishers, whose financial goals were thought to sacrifice quality in their news making. Similarly, Harold Ickes's *America's House of Lords* (1939) and George Seldes's *Freedom of the Press* (1935) argued against big business's control of the press and the potential destruction of press freedom. Much of the contemporary critical history of journalism drew upon many of the tenets of progressivism, in spirit if not in name. Writing from a liberal economic perspective, their goal, in William Sloan's (1991) view, was to critically assess the shortcomings of the press in conjunction with the larger economic motivations of media owners. For instance, Barbara Matusow's (1983) discussion of television anchorpersons saw television's weaknesses in its economic dependence on advertisers and profits. Similarly, George Boyce, James Curran, and Pauline Wingate's masterful examination of press history in the United Kingdom was directed at elucidating issues related to the "ownership of capital, system of production, division of labor, and the institutionalization of knowledge" (Boyce et al. 1978: 13).

Other more consensually driven interpretations of the link between journalism and nation included a body of work that tracked journalism's role in upholding unity. Examples here included Bernard Bailyn's *Pamphlets of the American Revolution, 1750–1776*. Written in 1965, Bailyn's book was reprinted as the Pulitzer Prize winning *The Ideological Origins of the American Revolution* 2 years later (Bailyn 1967). Revolution, in his view, was seen as an ideological rather than a class struggle, and pamphlets were seen as a forum for expressing public opinion. A more recent example was George H. Douglas's *The Golden Age of the Newspaper* (1999), which traced 130 years in which the press was used to form a collective of the public it served. Douglas surveyed journalism's giant figures—James Gordon Bennett, Charles Dana, Adolph Ochs—and concluded that the heyday of the press was already reached by the 1920s, when a personal bond created an intimacy between journalists and their public. More consensual histories of journalism tended to proliferate whenever the nation-state faced trouble.

For example, numerous studies emerged adhering to this perspective during wartime, when media owners were seen as individuals of high principle who contributed to society, and researchers tracked pressing issues like wartime performance and censorship (Larson 1940; Moffett 1986). Consensual interpretations also tended to emerge in nation-states undergoing periods of instability or degrees of destabilization, as seen in accounts of journalism in Israel and elsewhere in the Middle East, parts of Latin America, and regions in Africa.

Grand narratives were a favored way of retelling journalism's past when connecting it to the emergence and development of the nation-state. Typical here was *The Press and America* (Emery and Emery 1999), which in numerous reprintings told the story of the development of the U.S. press from its early days in the colonial period and American revolution through the changing journalism of the 19th and 20th centuries. In each edition, it ended with a slightly different discussion of the challenge of contemporary technology. Roger Streitmatter's *Mightier Than the Sword: How the News Media Have Shaped American History* (1997) delivered a tale of journalism's high and low moments, which swung up toward the triumphs of turning public opinion against slavery and attacking municipal corruption and down toward the embarrassments of offering radio forums for the spread of anti-Semitism and facilitating what later came to be called a "talk show election." Arguing that the pen was mightier than the sword (hence, the title), Streitmatter contended that the media did much of this on their own. In his words, "the news media have shaped history. Absolutely. Boldly. Proudly. Fervently. Profoundly" (Streitmatter 1997: 234). In Australia, Graeme Osborne and Glen Lewis (1995) tracked the media of the press, film, and broadcasting, showing how the broad functions of nation building, cultural impact, and social control developed differently.

As a mode of shaping inquiry of the past, however, the grand narrative drew criticism for its simplified retelling of complex and nuanced circumstances. As one British overview of press history argued, grand narratives appeared often at the expense of an elucidation of underlying structural features: "too much newspaper history has been written in terms of 'great personalities,' rather than the underlying social and economic forces that have shaped the press" (Boyce et al. 1978: 13). Or, as Peter Golding and Philip Elliott (1979: 7) put it, "there is an awful lot of history and not many great men."

It is no surprise, then, that more critical, less naturalistic historical scholarship evolved that addressed the linkage between the nation-state and journalism. Much of this work came from the cultural sphere, where sociologist Robert Park's classic articles "The Natural History of the Newspaper"

(1925) and "News as a Form of Knowledge" (1940) argued that journalism resulted from its interaction with the surrounding culture over time. In the U.S. context, this work was furthered by Sidney Kobre, who in a series of books argued that media history could not be understood without taking into account environmental influences. Over a quarter century, Kobre's five books—*Development of the Colonial Newspaper* (1944), *Foundations of American Journalism* (1958), *Modern American Journalism* (1959), *The Yellow Press and Guilded Age Journalism* (1964), and *The Development of American Journalism* (1969)—took account of the influence of factors like the growth of a city or the need of businesses for advertising media. In a similar fashion, in the United Kingdom Alan J. Lee's *The Origins of the Popular Press in England, 1855–1914* (1976) covered the environmental influences surrounding the popular press.

This scholarship ushered in a slew of differently framed critical historical studies addressing the nexus of journalism and the nation-state. It is no surprise that many of these large-scale histories were tightly structured around the linkage between journalism and the political sphere. For instance, Whiggish interpretations of history, seen as the reigning theme by which British press history came to be told, offered a patterned accounting that told the story of the emergence of a "free" political press that emerged victorious over government censorship and control (Curran and Seaton 1985: 5–113). Citing the widely read histories of Stephen Koss (1981, 1984) as a prime articulator of this view, James Curran and Jean Seaton claimed that the market was seen as having acted in a positive light because it guaranteed both civil liberties and press autonomy. By contrast, Curran and Seaton argued that the real "hero" of the period was the suppressed radical press of the early 19th century and that the villain was the market, which destroyed the viability of the political press (Curran and Seaton 1985; also Scannell 2002). Advertising helped rewrite the financial base of the press and in so doing helped bring about the decline of the radical press.

Often this work traced the evolution of one particular news medium in conjunction with a nation-state. For instance, in *Dangerous Estate*, Francis Williams (1958) traced 300 years of British press history. Broadcasting drew extensive attention around the globe—in the United Kingdom (Smith 1973, 1998; Scannell and Cardiff 1991), United States (e.g., Diamond 1975; Hilmes 1997), France (Meadel 1994), and Australia (Inglis 1983; Johnson 1988). Some of these works represented Herculean efforts to encompass all relevant details. A three-volume set by Eric Barnouw on the history of U.S. broadcasting was published (Barnouw 1966–1970), though its compressed version received more acclaim (Barnouw 1975). British historian Asa Briggs (1961–1995) produced the premier institutional history of British broadcasting, with five volumes published over 35 years and a sixth volume recently commissioned from Jean Seaton (Scannell 2002). As Paddy Scannell told it, the problems that Briggs faced were monumental:

> He wanted to write a "total history" that covered all aspects of the activities of the BBC. . . . There were real difficulties of narrative organization and coherence as his narrative moved forward slowly on all fronts: home broadcasting, overseas broadcasting, radio, and, later, television. There were difficulties of writing an institutional history, which might result in a "history from above." . . . There was the danger of not being able to see the wood for the trees. . . . There was, finally, the issue of perspective. (Scannell 2002: 200)

In that Briggs wanted his history to be definitive, he in effect provided "a historian's history," which allowed subsequent researchers to conduct scholarship "without having to reconstruct yet again the house that Briggs built" (Scannell 2002: 201). Even historians of other broadcasting systems in other countries voiced the debt owed Briggs (e.g., Dahl 1976; also Scannell 2002). At the same time, however, the relative lack of attention to either Welsh or Scottish media in Briggs's original work was compounded as it served an example for later scholarship.

The connection between journalism and the nation generated its own specific narratives about journalism's past. The drawn-out campaign in the United Kingdom against the "taxes on knowledge" generated discussion of the triumph of a free press and libertarian ideals (Curran and Seaton 1985), while the concept of the Fourth Estate was challenged with evidence from the Victorian period (Boyce 1978; Curran 1978). The evolution of new patterns of ownership and economic regulation was addressed as a common corporate challenge to journalism's autonomy in numerous societies of advanced capitalism, including France (Belanger, Godechot, Giral, and Terrou 1969–1974) and the United Kingdom (Hoyer, Hadenius, and Weibull 1975, Murdock and Golding 1978). Work on the Northcliffe "revolution" in the United Kingdom from the 1890s onward (Catterall, Seymour-Ure, and Smith 2000), on British popularization of the press more generally and its connection to the market economy and the public sphere (Williams 1978; Conboy 2002), and on the development of tabloidization during the late 20th century (Engel 1996) offered other examples by which the connection between journalism and nation was queried.

At the same time, scholars excavated an unspoken consensus about certain kinds of practices connecting journalism and the nation that were taken for granted in much existing historical scholarship. Jean Chalaby (1998), for instance, argued that journalism itself was an "Anglo-American invention," whereas the focus on information and facts so central in the United States and United Kingdom was simply not followed in France; he also raised the strong possibility that European journalists repaired to a literary ideal that occupied the "psychological space" taken up by a professional ideal among U.S. journalists (Chalaby 1996).

Debates About History and Journalism

Legitimating the inquiry of journalism's past by framing it as one of three nested frames—by which history was writ small as memoirs, autobiographies and organizational histories; writ midway as histories organized by period, theme, and event; and writ large as histories of the nation-state—made journalism history more accessible. Not only did it provide a relatively facile way of traversing enormous amounts of documentation, but the tight logic of historical evolution lent coherence to what might have otherwise remained a mess of contradictory data. In some cases, historical inquiry put human faces behind otherwise faceless social forces and structures. In others, it offered a main story by which to understand complex and often contradictory processes and events, though displaying the downside of simplifying complexities and muting contradictions for the sake of narrative cohesion. Thus, often histories of journalism strayed too much from the circumstances whose story they sought to tell and were at times ungeneralizable beyond the specific instance examined.

And yet, the point here is telling: It remained unclear who could lay claim to the past. Scholars were not agreed about who was qualified to discuss history, how to evaluate those who discussed history, which bodies of evidence could best be used and to what aim, and how to classify and distinguish historians from each other. In other words, as Robin Winks (1968) argued, scholars had no other way to establish evaluations than on the basis of evidence. Often, however, the value of that evidence was difficult to assess.

Against this background, fundamental points about the historical study of journalism remain. Historical inquiry is subject to both internal debates within communication and journalism scholarship and larger debates about the shape of historical inquiry. This double whammy positions journalism history in an odd place and introduces the disadvantage to its perspective of an uncertainty as to whether one can know for sure that what is being argued matters. And yet, the advantage of historical inquiry remains clear, particularly when it comes to journalism scholarship. Historical inquiry lends depth to a field sorely in need of it, and it enhances understanding by setting up patterns of practice over time. At heart here are fundamental assumptions about what historical inquiry lends other types of inquiry. Not only does it deepen the field, but, in Mary Mander's (1983: 11) view, "it provides context—a phenomenon closely related to meaning." Without the historical dimension and the social context it offers, she argued, the meaning of a communicative act cannot be fully understood and historical works "run the risk of becoming charming period pieces" (Mander 1983: 11).

In sum, then, as with other disciplinary perspectives, history is only as good and as bad as a limited perspective can be. It brings temporal advantages to journalism's study, calling for a recognized and established place in the larger world of journalism scholarship. At the same time, however, historical inquiry is always partial and thus dependent on the mechanisms for legitimation by which we, as scholars, agree to support or contest the interpretations of the past that it offers.

5

Language Studies and Journalism

The examination of the languages of journalism has been a relatively novel phenomenon in the world of inquiry into journalism. Although language is at the heart of journalism, only over the past 30 years or so have scholars shown a sustained interest in investigating its languages. The combination of formal features of language—such as grammar, syntax, and word choice—and less formal ones—such as storytelling frames, textual patterns, and formulaic narratives—creates a multilayered system of information relay, which has grown in complexity as journalism has embraced not only the printed press but also radio, television, cable, and new media. Today, sound, still photographs, moving visuals, and patterns of interactivity have become part of the languages by which journalists provide information. As journalism has progressed toward increasingly complex systems of information relay, the notion of what constitutes a journalistic language has grown as well.

Language studies are an outgrowth of the idea that the messages of journalism are not transparent or simplistic but encode larger messages about the shape of life beyond the sequencing of actions that comprise a news event. A simple reading of a text can be found nowhere obvious; instead, reading a text is always the product of a socially contingent and negotiated process of meaning construction. Reading necessarily involves a nuanced examination of a text's fit with a larger cognitive, social, cultural, political, and/or economic context. In moving away from a somewhat empiricist bias on the world—the stance of "what you see is what you get" that is readily touted by journalists as part of their self-presentation as arbiters of reality—language studies provide a wide-ranging rubric in which to examine language in different, often competing contexts. Key to this rubric, which connects the microanalytic and macroanalytic dimensions of news work, has been an a priori acceptance of the premise that journalism involves construction.

The Study of Language

Inquiry of the languages of journalism has taken shape alongside broader developments in the academy around the world, primarily after scholars in communication, sociology, anthropology, and linguistics independently began to broaden their level of analysis concerning language during the late 1960s and early 1970s. According to Teun van Dijk (1987), four major historical developments paved the way for more creative and integrated interdisciplinary investigations of language. In linguistics, the primary unit of grammatical analysis moved from the "sentence" to the "text" or "discourse." Anthropologists developed an interest in the ethnography of speaking, which promoted investigations of language use in its socio-cultural context (e.g., Hymes 1972). Sociologists became interested in microsociology, an interest that gravitated in two directions: (1) toward the tradition of political sociology, where primarily British sociologists began to examine issues of class and other power distributions through Marxist leanings that geared them toward language (e.g., Lukes 1975) and (2) toward the examination of the rules and methods of everyday interaction, commonly known in the United States as conversation analysis and ethnomethodology (e.g., Sacks 1972). Finally, developments in cognitive psychology brought scholars closer to social psychology: they moved from largely experimental studies of text comprehension focusing on the formal grammatical rules by which reading and learning took shape to studies that examined the strategies of context-dependent practices associated with information processing. In the United Kingdom, a parallel move was made via Freudian and Lacanian theorizations of the centrality of language to human subjectivity.

The theories and methods that found a home in language studies were widespread and strongly European in origin, though some efforts were displayed in the United States. Semiology, discourse analysis, critical linguistics, narrative analysis, rhetoric, and content analysis were but a few of the research perspectives employed by scholars seeking to examine language. At the heart of each perspective was a combination of one or more of three basic approaches to language—structuralism, culturalism, and functionalism.

Structuralism typically considered language as an autonomous abstract system that existed in an arbitrary relationship with reality. Language in this view was predicated on the universality of linguistic structure that followed its own set of rules independent of the context at hand. Culturalism, sometimes called the "anthropological perspective" on language, promoted the idea that cultures develop different languages for perceiving reality. An extension of the Sapir-Whorf hypothesis, this view popularized the twin assumptions of linguistic relativity and linguistic determinism in offering the perspective that languages changed according to the cultures using them. Functionalism, which both sociolinguists and ethnomethodologists employ, saw language use as determined by the function it fulfilled in those who used it. This view offered a correlation between certain linguistic features and aspects of social context.

The analysis of journalism's languages typically employed a combination of these different perspectives on language use. In that each approach presumed that language resulted from construction, rendering language the focal point of analysis, each went against the grain of journalists' self-presentation by undermining their insistence that they mirrored reality. The enthusiasm for studying the languages of news accompanied an ascending recognition of the construction work underlying journalistic practice. At the same time, this assumption allied language research strongly with critical and ideological studies and thus saw journalists as agents of the ideological order.

The emphasis on language played to both formalistic and less formalistic attributes that were repeatable and patterned, hence analytically accessible due to what appeared to be a static and seemingly stable nature. Differences that came to the fore when considering the use of passive or active voice or the differentiation across gender terms came to be seen as useful information in understanding the mind-set of journalists and journalism, and language gradually came to be regarded as a unique analytical setting for these reasons. For instance, it offset sociological inquiry's relative lack of interest in news texts. Conversely, sociological inquiry's greatest strength—the emphasis on interactions across groups of people—remained beyond the interest of most scholars engaged in language studies.

Against this background, inquiry into language and journalism developed in numerous parts of the globe, its establishment facilitated by the ascent of computers in conducting searches. Tools such as Lexis-Nexis, a search engine that looked for a single phrase or word across newspapers, and other software, which allowed scholars to search for the pairing of certain words, made it easier to trace language use in the news. Language studies primarily emerged from analyses of English-language news, though some scholars also analyzed the news in German (Burger 1984), Italian (Mancini 1988), French (Brunel 1970), Chinese (Scollon 1998), Dutch (van Dijk 1988), and Hebrew (Roeh 1982; Blum-Kulka 1983; Nir 1984). Certain scholars provided comparative analyses across nation-states and languages (e.g., van Dijk 1988). Leitner (1980), for instance, compared two cases of official radio-talk—BBC English and *Deutsche Rundfunksprache* (the designated language of German radio)—finding that the sociopolitical structure determined which sociolinguistic categories became designated news languages. In all cases, different invocations of part or all of three bodies of scholarship targeted the verbal and visual languages of journalism as follows:

- An orientation to the informal attributes of the languages in which journalistic texts were relayed: Such attributes ranged from the number of times a word or phrase was mentioned to the linkage across the connoted meanings of a news photograph or front-page headline. Typical approaches here included content analysis and semiology.

- An orientation to the formalistic aspects of a journalistic text: Included were its grammar, syntax, morphology, semantics, lexical meanings, and pragmatics. Typical approaches here included sociolinguistics, critical linguistics, discourse analysis, and formalistic studies of the visual attributes of news.

- An orientation to the pragmatic use of journalistic language: Examples of such scholarship included those focused on the act of telling a story and its narrative formula and storytelling conventions, on rhetoric, and on the use of news as a framing device. Typical approaches here included the various modes of narrative analysis, rhetorical analysis, and framing studies. In recent years, this category of scholarship drew particular interest from those interested in alternative types of journalistic storytelling, as evidenced by the tabloids, and in visual storytelling.

Journalism and the Informal Study of Language

Interest in the languages of journalism was slower in coming to inquiry into journalism than were the focal points of other disciplinary perspectives. It was primarily in the mid-1970s that journalism scholars began to respond to the fact that language had not been systematically studied as part of journalism. Some efforts had been made, but they were generally isolated and unrelated to each other. As the Glasgow University Media Group (1976: 21) noted, there was an "almost complete lack of convergence between the discipline of linguistics, the literary and stylistic criticism of texts and the rag-bag of sociological content analysis," all of which made the analysis of news language a highly unattractive proposition. And yet, the growing and often competing presence of content analysis and semiology, and eventually of framing, in inquiry into journalism began to force the question of language's relevance, offering divergent alternatives for thinking about how language might function as part of journalism. Although none of these approaches offered the type of formalistic analysis of language that would later come with the more linguistically driven analytical perspectives, content analysis in particular positioned language as a given that merited generalized scholarly attention. Over time these approaches facilitated the sustained recognition of language as a complex and patterned venue worthy of analytical attention.

Content Analysis

Although content analysis does not consider the formal attributes of news languages per se, its attention to news texts made the centrality of language an unavoidable aspect of journalism's study. In its purest form, content analysis was clarified most extensively by Klaus Krippendorff (1980/2004), who delineated precise formulations about inference making and a conceptual framework for how to move between a text and its context. Simply put, it involved counting the number of times a phenomenon—a word, a phrase, a story, or an image—appeared in a text, classifying each of them according to predefined categories, and offering latent and manifest explanations for their patterned appearance. Although Krippendorff's template was extensive and painstakingly laid out, few works that eventually labeled themselves "content analyses" actually developed along the lines he suggested (Krippendorff 1980/2004; Rosengren 1981). Over time, many procedures he suggested for connecting a phenomenon with the larger world it represented were simply cut out of analysis, and contemporary instances of content analysis often tended to do little more than count frequencies of appearance of a given phenomenon.

Early attempts at content analysis of the press were implemented earlier than other language approaches, already at the turn of the 20th century in both Europe and the United States: Kurt Lang, for instance, listed numerous efforts at that time, among them a U.S. study in 1900 of different kinds of news content, a French 1902 examination of Parisian and provincial dailies, and a German 1910 study of 30 Berlin and provincial newspapers (Lang 1996). Krippendorff (1980/2004) mentioned yet another study that, in setting up a bookkeeping system that monitored the number of column-inches of coverage on certain news topics, sought to reveal "the truth about newspapers" (Street 1909). Approximately 30 years later, as propaganda became an issue of concern in the years leading up to and following World War II, social science scholars began to apply their own analytical tools to the systematic study of content patterns of press coverage (Simpson 1934; Kingsbury 1937). Julian Woodward (1934), for instance, saw it as a technique of opinion research and a reflection of the uses to which social science methodology could be put. Topics ranged from the *New York Times'* disastrously optimistic reporting of the end of the Russian Revolution (Lippmann and Merz 1920) to Communist propaganda (Lasswell and Jones 1939) to general patterns of war coverage (Foster 1937). Harold Lasswell (1941) invoked certain tenets of the perspective while examining the circulation of political symbols in news editorials.

Over time efforts became more sophisticated. In that the perspective involved the counting and summation of phenomena, it was seen as an empirical method worthy of recognition by scholars in the social sciences and rapidly became a perspective of choice, offering them a way to account for a phenomenon's variance over time, geographic region, or issue. Scholars like Bernard Berelson (1952), Ithia de Sola Pool (1959), and Ole Holsti (1969) used content analysis to make broad statements about political life. In 1959, Wilbur Schramm's *One Day in the World's Press* used content analysis to show how the ideological prism of 14 major world newspapers affected the reporting of two international crises—the attack on Egypt by European and Israeli forces during the Suez Canal crisis and the entry of Soviet tanks into Budapest.

The method behind the early studies was simple, was easy to understand, and promoted an implicit emphasis on journalistic language. And yet it assumed implicitly that if journalists made a given statement or reference to a phenomenon in their news reports, that statement or reference was sufficient evidence that the phenomenon existed. Much work here did not consider the selection and construction work implicit in language's shaping, assuming instead that the articulation of a phenomenon was primarily what was relevant. Moreover, it did not consider numerous embedded dimensions of language use, such as its social situatedness, tone, style, and other affective qualities. Language, then, was seen as a neutral carrier, a conduit for events to be articulated in the public sphere.

The simplicity of that logic had an impact on broader understandings of how journalism worked. One issue frequently examined through content analysis was journalistic bias. Beginning with Richard Hofstetter's (1976) analysis of bias in the coverage of political campaigns—where it was largely reduced to the linguistic evidence of a deliberative choice for or against a candidate—content analysis became a means for implementing a slew of similar studies of news over the decades that followed (e.g., Robinson and Sheehan 1983, Moriarty and Popovich 1991, Kuklinski and Sigelman 1992, Kenney and Simpson 1993, Patterson 1993, Dickson 1994, Domke et al. 1997). Studies examined the bias of verbal reports and visual images across national and international contexts, each time relying at least partly on the number of times a certain phrase or theme was mentioned or a certain image appeared. Although the notion of bias has since been complicated as a given in journalistic practice and discourse (see, e.g., Hackett 1984; Zelizer, Park, and Gudelunas 2002), the repeated studies proclaiming degrees of its absence or presence in news on the basis of the number and frequency of certain linguistic or visual markers deserve pause. Their prevalence helped instantiate a widespread reliance on language without due consideration of the factors that influenced language's shaping. In other words, much early work in content analysis treated language like an empirical reality, rendering it a given for examining journalism's workings without considering the features that went into its making.

From the 1970s onward, certain work in content analysis helped establish the ideological leanings of the news. The Glasgow University Media Group (GUMG) saw content analysis as one of its central analytical methods. Using the most sophisticated technologies then available—the video cassette recorder and the software system SSPS—the group found itself recalculating the time and effort its content analysis would entail but used it to uphold findings about an antilabor bias in British TV news (GUMG 1976, 1980). Other work combined content analysis with interviews to examine the working patterns of editors of the book review sections of U.K. newspapers (Curran 2000b).

Though still in use for studies that primarily enumerate frequencies of a given phenomenon in the news, content analysis has been critiqued for its oversimplification of the complexities it addressed (e.g., Schroder 2002). In one contemporary media critic's words, most studies are "rarely 'scientific' in the generally understood connotation of the term. Many are merely pseudo-science, ideology masquerading as objectivity" (Alterman 2003: 15). Although content analysis did much to focus scholars' attention on the relevance of language to inquiry into journalism, and it increased in prominence with the more frequent use of computers, the ascendance of other language-based approaches to journalism created a more complicated stream of language studies on journalism.

Semiology

Semiology's arrival in inquiry into journalism forced a rethinking of the empiricist notion of "what you see is what you get" in language. Of all language approaches, semiology, also called semiotics, was perhaps most responsible for moving the study of journalism's languages toward a consideration of texts in context. Following the work of Ferdinand de Saussure (1916/1965), Claude Lévi-Strauss (1958/1968), Roland Barthes (1957/1972, 1967), Charles Peirce (1893–1913/1998), Umberto Eco (1976, 1984), and Thomas Sebeok (1964, 1979), semiologists, also called semioticians, promoted the notion that the form of a message was as important as its content. Drawing on the one hand from de Saussure's insistence on the arbitrary relationship between signs and the real world and Lévi-Strauss's concern with myth's capacity to dissolve distinctions between nature and culture, and on the other hand from an interest in the science of signs drawn from philosophy and logic, these scholars set about excavating the various sign systems at play in journalistic texts (Leach 1976). News texts provided a captive corpus, in which journalism scholars saw significant opportunity for furthering existing understandings of news.

The relevance of semiology to journalism was evident already from Barthes's provocative collection of essays *Mythologies* (1957/1972), in which he analyzed photographs of politicians, the language of the press during the Algerian war, and politicians' political speeches as a means of uncovering the semiological patterns in public discourse. Using what he later developed as an approach to narrative analysis (Barthes 1967), he examined how the French media strategically manipulated codes of signification while proclaiming that no such codes existed. But it was the application of his work to news photographs—in a seminal essay in cultural studies by Stuart Hall (1973a) of the Birmingham School—that directly piqued the interest of scholars wanting to account for the twofold ability of news language to both signify and impact larger power structures. By the time the Birmingham School published *Culture, Media, Language* in 1980 (Hall, Hobson, Lowe, and Willis 1980), language's study had begun to be seen as an important analytical entry for understanding the ideological positioning of the media.

Parallel efforts in earlier years by the U.S. philosopher Charles Peirce (1893–1913/1998) developed a second strand of semiological work, focused on a philosophy of signs derived from logic. Developing a distinction between a sign's representation, the object to which it referred, and the interpreted version of the sign, Peirce was interested in explaining how the cognitive activities involved in interpretation gave rise to an ongoing process called semiosis, by which the interpretation of signs continually generated other interpretations. Semiosis over time became invoked as a useful basis for extensive theories of the communication process, although Peirce's work was applied to journalism more slowly. Scholarship in Italy by Umberto Eco (1976) extended Peirce's work and further elaborated the importance of distinguishing between natural and cultural codes of meaning in the news. In the United States, Thomas Sebeok (1964, 1979) led the way in introducing semiotics to more traditional modes of language analysis.

By the late 1970s and early 1980s, semiology began to be adopted by British and Australian researchers, working independently to understand the languages of news. Focusing on the role of language in helping explain how meanings were socially produced rather than individually constructed, as well as subject to power relations, these scholars developed the idea that news consisted of both signs and codes—the former referring to any items that produced meaning, the latter to how they were organized in conjunction with the surrounding social and cultural order.

Within this paradigm, the two most well-known texts were John Fiske and John Hartley's *Reading Television* (1978) and John Hartley's *Understanding News* (1982). Both were responsible for introducing those studying journalism to a set of focal points and analytical terms that significantly changed understandings of the centrality of journalistic language. In *Reading Television* (1978), Fiske and Hartley reproduced an entire television news bulletin for analysis, offering a point-by-point examination of it in terms of line up, word choice, and verbal and visual sequencing. They argued that journalists primarily functioned as bards in providing and selectively constructing social knowledge for the public, supplanting individuals who in earlier times had fulfilled the same function—priests, patriarchs, intellectuals. Hartley's book, *Understanding News* (1982), called by one scholar "of great importance in restoring semiotic concepts to the theory of news representation" (Fowler 1991: 223), extended the work of *Reading Television* into a wide-ranging consideration of journalism's verbal and visual dimensions. Offering simple definitions for fundamental concepts from a semiological standpoint—signs and codes, denotation and connotation, paradigm and syntagma, myths and icons—the book applied the basic premises of semiology to journalism by elaborating the broad cultural codes in which journalism's languages took shape. Hartley argued that audiences learned not only to understand the information they received but also to interpret the world in terms of the codes they learned from the news.

Both Hartley and Fiske continued their semiological excavation of news in later work, extending it to a broader mode of cultural analysis that over time met criticism due to its wide-ranging applications and because it initially assumed that all readers decoded in basically the same way (e.g., McGuigan 1992). Fiske (1988, 1996) examined the ideological positioning of journalists and journalism in a wide span of news events, including the O.J. Simpson court trial and the Anita Hill-Clarence Thomas hearings. Hartley (1992, 1996) primarily considered the visual dimensions of journalism, where he used semiology to examine the function and role of photography in the news.

The Glasgow University Media Group also followed semiological perspectives in some of its later examinations of language (GUMG 1980) but more directly in its consideration of the visuals of news (GUMG 1976, 1980). Focusing on a combination of film logic and its adaptation to simultaneous audio commentary, the group showed how presentational cues in the news guided viewers in assessing the legitimacy of what they heard. Other work here was visual in focus, as in Zelizer's (1990b) analysis of how visual codes on broadcast news conveyed a false sense of proximity between anchorperson and event. Although later work by other scholars utilized many of the premises set in place by semiology, particularly its emphasis on cultural codes, much of this later work tended to be codified as cultural studies (e.g., Allan 1998), where issues like meaning and power became central imperatives for studying texts.

Other work of a semiological bent developed in France, where, following on the legacy of Barthes, scholars focused on language in the media, paying particular attention to political discourse (e.g., Dayan 1999, 2001). The establishment of the review *Mots,* dedicated to "the languages of politics," explored different dimensions of the language underlying the intersection of journalism and politics, including political speeches, political cartoons, journalistic reviews, and journalistic rhetoric. For example, socialist discourse of the mid-1980s began repeatedly to reference modernization in the news, revealing a change in the lexicon of terms related to French social democracy (Neveu 1998). In addition, scholars argued that journalistic representations of foreigners as "immigrant workers" linked them to law and order discourses or that the scene construction for a French political talk show was built to reflect a mock House of Commons, where political guests were divided spatially by political loyalties (Neveu 1998).

Over time many semiological studies of journalism ceased to be called such even though they continued to adopt certain tenets of semiology, particularly given the ascent of critical cultural scholarship that insisted on a wider range of responses to news than semiology initially allowed. Nonetheless, semiology's attentiveness to the form of a news text and to the nuanced intersection between journalism's textual and contextual features introduced vital focal points that were taken up in other language studies of journalism.

* * * * *

The informal study of journalism's languages was important in that it established a setting for thinking about language as a valuable analytical venue of inquiry into journalism. Although content analysis and semiology did not offer a close analysis of the detailed features of news language and each profited instead from thinking broadly about its positioning as evidence of either a concrete phenomenon, as in content analysis, or cultural meaning, as in semiology, their positioning in inquiry into journalism facilitated the development of other language-based approaches to journalism.

Journalism and the Formal Study of Language

The formal inquiry of the languages of journalism paralleled a broader interest in the academy. Developing primarily in Western Europe, Australia, and New Zealand, from the 1960s onward, an interest in syntax, morphology, phonology, and lexicology was used to engage larger units of meaning in language studies. In the view of one journalism scholar, "the most important development in linguistics for our work has been the emergence of sociolinguistics as a proper field of study . . . the study of language as a means of establishing, maintaining, and mediating social relationships" (Glasgow University Media Group 1980: 126). Alongside sociolinguistics, the analysis of critical linguistics, discourse analysis, and the visual attributes of news made for a wide-ranging analytical setting. Its topics, moreover, extended across the wide range of journalism's performances, as in the analysis of the language employed in sportscasting (Kuiper 1996), the study of DJ conversations on radio (Heritage 1985), analyses of the visual forms of news (Barnhurst 1994; Barnhurst and Nerone 2001), or even Erving Goffman's (1981) seminal discussion of radio talk.

Sociolinguistics

This primarily functionalist approach to language, which considered language use through the functions it filled in those who used it, typically examined correlations between linguistic features and aspects of social context. Following the work of U.S. scholar William Labov (1972), who argued that variants in pronunciation corresponded with the socioeconomic classes of speakers, this work examined journalistic language in its social context throughout the 1970s. It extended along two main analytical tracks: (1) conversational analysis and ethnomethodology (Garfinkel 1967; Sacks 1972) and (2) the ethnography of speaking (Hymes 1972; Bauman and Sherzer 1974).

For most sociolinguists interested in journalism, the work of the Glasgow University Media Group was seen as having most actively promoted the salience of news language. By showing that news was always reported from a particular angle, the group established that news "imposed a structure of values, social and economic in origin, on whatever is represented; and so inevitably news, like every discourse, constructively pattern[ed] that of which it speaks" (Fowler 1991: 4). The group succeeded in establishing a constructionist view of news work that was a necessary starting point for further linguistic inquiry into journalism.

The Glasgow University Media Group was explicit about its ties to sociolinguistics. Dedicating its first volume to the memory of conversational analyst Harvey Sacks, it concerned itself with how issues germane to conversational analysis—how successive utterances were organized, who controlled conversations, and how speaker turns were negotiated—could be applied to the mediated languages of news. Using Sacks's consistency rule, by which categories of speakers were characterized by the rules of their conversation, the group demonstrated that the aim of scripted news talk was "to create preferential hearings which invite the competent listener to hear the talk as neutral. . . . [closing] off any questions about evidence and the problematics of production and . . . [resting] upon unexamined causal inferences" (GUMG 1976: 25). Borrowing also from William Labov's ideas about speech variations across social classes (1972) and Basil Bernstein's distinction between restricted and elaborated codes—the former spoke to particular groups, whereas the latter offered more universal framings of events—to analyze British television news, the group argued that news language functioned as a restricted code (GUMG 1980). Characterized by a high degree of predictability, a simplified framing of public events, and a high level of redundancy, these attributes encouraged audiences to align themselves as part of a group rather than express individual differences. In other words, language itself underscored the maintenance of the status quo.

Other work followed the tenets of conversation analysis and ethnomethodology with similar vigor. Concerned with the micromechanics of verbal interaction, scholars looked primarily at broadcast journalism. Their studies ranged from examinations of accents and pronunciation patterns on the news, as in Martin Montgomery's (1986a) discussion of the tensions between BBC English and the wider range of accent types in U.K. broadcasting to the broad range of talk patterns displayed in interviews, talk shows, radio DJ talk, and sports broadcasting (Bell 1982; Crow 1986; Montgomery 1986b; Heritage 1985; Kuiper 1996). Sociolinguistic work on news grew particularly over the last decade. Paddy Scannell put together one of the first edited collections on broadcast talk (Scannell 1991). In 1998, Allan Bell and Peter Garrett tracked the key issues in the analysis of news language, with each chapter of their edited volume addressing a different aspect of the languages of journalism, including discourse structure, word choice in editorials, and layout design of front pages, to name a few. John

Heritage and David Greatbatch used conversational analysis separately and together to analyze British news interviews (Heritage 1985; Greatbatch 1988, 1997; Heritage and Greatbatch 1991). Philip Bell and Theo van Leeuven (1994) used a combination of different sociolinguistic methods to consider the news interview. Steven Clayman (1990) showed how the interactional style of the interview was transposed into the print media. Barbie Zelizer (1989) used Dell Hymes's (1972) framework of the ethnography of communication to examine journalistic quoting practices and notions of differential address in U.S. radio news.

Work on the sociolinguistics of journalism received particular acclaim in New Zealand, where journalist Allan Bell produced one of the most extensive examinations of the language of radio news. Following the work of William Labov (1972), Bell (1991, 1994) considered the level of comprehension evident in the various linguistic features of news registers. Maintaining the singularity of media discourse from a sociolinguistic perspective—in that it did not allow for a co-present listener able to affect conversational flow—Bell showed that the language of news displayed a set of characteristics both typical of and different from those of other conversational settings.

Critical Linguistics

Critical linguistics developed in the late 1970s, when interest in the properties of mediated language grew among British and Australian linguists at the University of East Anglia. The approach sought to establish links between the language of media texts and the production of ideology, reflecting in turn on the reproduction of a social order that perpetuated inequalities. Jointly developed by Roger Fowler, Bob Hodge, Gunther Kress, and Tony Trew as a systemic linguistic template by which to analyze news language, the group produced a series of books elaborating the importance of language's lexical and syntactic choices in demonstrating ideological meanings. Under titles like *Language and Control* (Fowler, Hodge, Kress, and Trew 1979) and *Language as Ideology* (Hodge and Kress 1979), this approach showed the widespread and patterned use of language in all institutional settings.

One work that effectively demonstrated the potential relevance of critical linguistics to journalism was a study of press coverage of racial tension in South Africa, which used language to level criticisms on the variations in media coverage by showing how linguistic variations shaped perceptions of social violence in the news (Trew 1979a). Arguing that linguistic variations encouraged certain public perceptions of the world over others, Trew's work underscored the degree to which journalists' invocations of preferred ways of describing social violence seemed commonsensical to those who encountered them. In *Language, Image, Media* (Davis and Walton 1983), scholars investigated the parallels across the institutional settings that were impacted by language, with Kress (1983) addressing the linguistic and ideological pairing that characterized the rewriting processes of news reporting. Other works by the same group (Kress and Trew 1978; Trew 1979b) further elaborated the discursive features of the press, while still others extended across numerous case studies (e.g., Hodge and Kress 1988).

Concerned with the "fixed, invisible ideology permeating language" (Fowler 1991: 67), these scholars moved from an a priori recognition of language's constructedness and ideological positioning to a delineation of the syntactic, lexical, semantic, pragmatic, and textual features that made it possible. Critical linguists believed that the style of language was critical because it encoded ideology. In that each choice concerning language use—whether it involved syntax, grammar, or word choice—reflected an invocation of some kind of broader ideological positioning, all aspects of linguistic structure were thought to carry ideological significance. Style constituted ideology's most obvious embodiment and offered a primary link between journalists and readers, who decoded and encoded through a shared familiarity with certain social and discursive practices.

For instance, Fowler (1991) examined how ideological significance was encoded in discourse about gender groups. He argued that the reliance on personalization—and its emphasis on individuals and individual details—hid a more basic thrust in news discourse toward categorization, which provided a discursive basis for discriminatory practices by grouping people, things, and activities into culturally organized sets of categories. Discourse allowed these categories to be traded freely, and discriminatory discourse reinforced stereotypes. This was important to examine because of its effect: Individuals who were placed into discriminatory categories enjoyed less power than did other people.

Critical linguistics was also applied to journalistic visuals. Although *Reading Images: The Grammar of Visual Design* did not center directly on journalism, newspaper photographs figured liberally in the book as examples of the larger visual grammar deployed (Kress and van Leeuwen 1996). Elsewhere, the same authors provided a provocative reading of newspaper front pages (Kress and van Leeuwen 1997). Theo van Leeuwen examined the proxemics, or spatial codes, of the TV news interview (van Leeuwen 1986).

In each case, critical linguistics provided a systematic and wide-ranging mode of engaging with journalistic languages. The perspective's insistence on ideological positioning and its embodiment in language made it attractive to journalism scholars interested in finding a vehicle to substantiate ideology's presence. At the same time, however, its attentiveness to small, discrete features of language limited its applicability for scholars interested in journalism's "big picture."

Discourse Analysis

Another approach to language and news was developed by numerous European researchers under the rubric of discourse analysis. Established along largely parallel trajectories, these attempts made significant headway in connecting language to its social situations.

Dutch text linguist Teun van Dijk (1983, 1987, 1988) led the way in this regard. He provided what has evolved into probably the most systematic exploration of the discursive features of mediated language, using tools culled from linguistics, literary studies, anthropology, semiotics, sociology, psychology, and speech communication. His approach, developed at the end of the 1960s and beginning of the 1970s in the Netherlands, provided a highly interdisciplinary theoretical and methodological approach to language and language use that was concerned primarily with group-based forms of inequality in the news. Teun van Dijk centered on the ways in which journalistic texts supported an unequal distribution of power in society and argued that it could be found in language along lines of class, gender, ethnicity, race, or other indices related to status, domination, and power.

Discourse, for van Dijk, referred to the language patterns that were associated with social action and the ways in which people interacted in real situations. In this attempt to merge the microanalysis and macroanalysis of social phenomena, discourse analysis aimed to show how social relationships and processes were accomplished at a micro level through routine practices. In a number of books, including *News as Discourse* (1987), *Communicating Racism* (1989), and *News Analysis* (1988), van Dijk combined text linguistics, narrative analysis, stylistics, and rhetorical analysis to help explain the fundamental legitimation of inequality in society. Discourse analysis, in his view, could not be separated from the larger world but was necessarily associated with what people in a given culture knew, believed, and valued as appropriate.

Another central figure in the development of the discourse analytic work on journalism was British scholar Norman Fairclough (1992, 1993, 1995). Offering a model of language use that conceptualized language as nested within what he saw as a combination of discursive and social practices, Fairclough examined certain types of journalistic relays—such as interviews or news reports—in terms of their dependence on texts from other contexts, like government reports or press releases. Fairclough argued that these different kinds of texts constituted a blended environment in which the spread of informal speech and colloquial expression helped legitimate certain ways of seeing the world (Fairclough 1996, 1998; Chouliaraki and Fairclough 2000). More so than other approaches, this work stressed the centrality of intertextuality as a way of acceding to certain worldviews and was therefore less impacted by theories of social cognition than by those of cultural impact.

Other scholars developed additional versions of discourse analysis and the news. Working from an analysis of the news in Chinese and English, Ron Scollon (1998) developed a conceptualization of journalistic discourse as a form of social interaction, arguing for more focus on the interactions that shaped journalistic language because they reflected the various discursive identities brought to bear on journalism. Certain scholars (Deacon, Pickering, Golding, and Murdock 1999) applied a combined approach of the work of van Dijk and Fairclough when analyzing the language of British newspapers. Some focused tightly on word choice, voice, or tense as a way of establishing broader meanings about the news, such as newspaper accounts of riots (Potter and Wetherell 1987; also Potter 1996), while others employed somewhat broader notions of discourse to examine the discursive features in talk that appeared both in journalism and elsewhere (e.g., Billig 1995).

In recent years, the invocation of "discourse theory" to describe the work of scholars as diverse as Jurgen Habermas, Ernesto Laclau, Chantal Mouffe, and Slavoj Zizek somewhat muddied the recognition of discourse analysis as a distinct set of methodological tools for analyzing language. None of the latter researchers engaged in the kind of focused analysis of language that the discourse analysts mentioned here were intent on implementing.

Visual Attributes of News

Related here was a growth of literature focusing on the visual aspects of journalism, which exhibited an approach to its formal attributes in ways that drew upon the positioning of visuals as a language. Scholars, though, remained divided about whether or not to call the visual domain a language per se.

The work in this area ranged broadly, including literature on the layout, design, and visual architecture of the news. Leading the scholarship on the visual attributes of print journalism was the work of Kevin Barnhurst (1994), and a later book on the evolution of newspaper design by Barnhurst and Nerone (2001). In both books, the careful and meticulous practices by which different newspapers displayed the news were chronicled; in the latter case, the connection between front-page design and the self-images of certain cities offered a striking way to consider the salience of visual languages in news. The work of other scholars focused on specific kinds of visuals in the news, such as maps (Monmonier 1989), photographs (Schwartz 1992; Griffin 1999; Newton 2001), and even the visual display of quantitative information (Tufte 2001). In each case, scholars comprehensively laid out the attributes by which journalism visually crafted its messages. Certain work focused on the visuals used in journalistic coverage of specific events, as in Theo Van Leeuwen and Adam Jaworski's (2003) analysis of the images of the Israeli-Palestinian conflict in the British and Polish press. Yet others addressed the broader function of visuals as an integral, though not always accepted, tool of information relay (e.g., Stephens 1998).

Of particular interest were the visual dimensions of online journalism. From issues as wide-ranging as web design to computer graphics, journalism's visual domain was seen as particularly relevant, with a large amount of literature tracking the issues of visual design and visual communication from a professional perspective (e.g., Lester 1995; Harris and Lester 2001; Holland 2001). In that regard, numerous websites, such as "News Page Designer" (www.newspagedesigner.com), and professional organizations—including the Society for News Design (with chapters in the United States, Latin America, and Scandinavia) and the Society of Publication Designers—were established as ways of sharing design tips in journalism. Under the heading "There are no facts, only interpretations," Visualjournalism.com was established as a European resource site to discuss visual aspects of the news. In the United Kingdom, the Royal Photographic Society set up a new group called Visual Journalism, under the caveat that it included, according to its website, "television news and film documentaries, in addition to newspapers, magazines, and books, and now, of course, the Internet."

Accompanying the focus on the visual attributes of news was the question of whether or not the visual domain could in effect function as a language. While certain researchers explicitly adopted the terms of linguistic relay (e.g., Kress and van Leeuwen 1996), the issue remained unclear for many scholars interested in visual journalism.

* * * * *

The formal study of journalism's languages was crucial for it drew a comprehensive and systematic portrait of the patterned reliance of journalists on certain kinds of verbal and visual tools in crafting the news. It demonstrated that regardless of context or issue or national boundary, the choices inherent in language's construction offered a highly strategic view of how the world worked. Perhaps more so than other types of inquiry, these studies strongly offset the popular notion that journalistic accounts reflect the world as it is. Though often difficult for nonlinguistic scholars to follow, due to its tight focus on linguistic and other language-related details, the formal study of news language nonetheless performed a critical service for the inquiry of journalism that established a thorough and multivariant picture of choices available to journalists in making news and the patterned ways in which decisions about a news text were typically made.

Journalism and the Pragmatic Study of Language

A third body of language-based research on journalism—the study of the pragmatic use of language invoked in telling a story, as rhetoric, or as framing—drew extensive attention over the years. This research examined how journalists structured accounts of reality through stories, narratives, rhetoric, and frames, using language to affect a cause or service a specific aim. Drawing on the constructivist impulse that characterized the other kinds of language-based scholarship, this body of research offered an extended applicability to journalism texts because it drew upon the broader uses of language in numerous settings. The familiarity of such uses of language—familiar from a wide range of contexts, including history, the family setting, even the Bible—made journalism appear more like other kinds of public expression and made journalists more like other groups of public speakers, such as members of the clergy or politicians. As the pragmatic approach to language gained in popularity as a viable way to think about journalism's study, it became more difficult for journalists to claim exclusive status, such as that surrounding objectivity or truth, for the stories, rhetoric, or frames they crafted.

Dating to the work of Aristotle, who emphasized the importance of both storytelling and rhetoric in his *Poetics,* language in this view offered a way to craft a coherent sequencing of events across time and space, and its relay referred to the processes involved in the act of putting that sequencing into play. This research borrowed from a widespread interest, particularly prevalent in the disciplines of folklore, literature, rhetoric, and anthropology in the United States and Europe, in the works of scholars in Russian formalism and its related scholarship (Propp 1930/1984; Hjelmslev 1943/1963; Jakobson 1962–1966; Todorov 1978), scholarship in the United States on dramatism (Burke 1945, 1950), the Anglo-American tradition of language use (Booth 1961; White 1987), and, particularly in France, European modes of literary criticism (Barthes 1977). In each case, scholars focused on how language was used to structure—through narratives, rhetoric, and frames—broader understandings of the world.

Narrative and Storytelling

Work on narrative and storytelling presumed that both offered a fundamental epistemological way of knowing the world. Theorists interested in
narrative helped bring certain notions about language to the fore, extrapo-
lating on the need to consider both form and content. From Tzvetan
Todorov's (1978) notions about narrative equilibrium to Vladimir Propp's
(1930/1984) ideas about narrative balance and function, narrative theorists
showed a concern for how representations of the social order imposed clo-
sure on understandings of the world. Roland Barthes (1977) discussed five
basic codes of signification or meaning in narrative—semic, referential,
symbolic, proiaretic, and hermeneutic—which together reflected the codes
in which the author and reader necessarily interacted. Seymour Chatman
(1978) argued for a distinction between the "what" of narrative (the story)
and the "way" of narrative (the discourse or the way in which the story is
transmitted), while elsewhere the distinction between form and content separated the "how" of narrative from the "what" of narrative (Kozloff 1992).
Narrative theorists raised scholarly sensitivities about a narrative's repeatable or formulaic dimensions, making distinctions between narrative similarity and narrative difference and arguing for degrees of narrative balance
and fidelity (Kozloff 1992). The notion of discourse emerged here too,
as a reference to the wider distribution of social and cultural power: for
instance, how a teen news magazine interwove discourse about delin-
quency, urban life, and college together to fashion meaningful stories for
its readers.

Central to thinking about narrative and storytelling in journalism was a
broader tension derived from how journalists themselves saw their work.
Particularly in the U.S. context, scholars tracked an evolution in storytelling
that separated those who saw journalism as "information" from those who
saw journalists as producing stories (e.g., Schudson 1978). As cultural critic
Walter Benjamin put it, the lingering emphasis on "information" rather than
"story" was a choice of form that was highly strategic for journalists: It laid
"claim to prompt verifiability" and was "shot through with explanation"
(Benjamin 1970: 89). Focusing on the informative rather than narrative
aspects of news emphasized "the causes of events rather than their meanings," removing "astonishment and thoughtfulness" from the relay and
replacing them with the "clarifications of a report" (Inglis 1990:11). Over
time, however, there grew a gradual recognition that not one but both
choices, information *and* stories, constituted equivalent alternatives of narrative style (Manoff and Schudson 1986). However, even then, the recognition of narrative's importance was fraught with ambivalence, making it no

surprise that, to quote Jack Lule (2001: 3), "we run the words 'news story' together so often that their meaning gets lost."

The interest in journalistic narrative in the United States grew substantially during the 1980s, when an interest in narrative made its way into communication. In 1985, the *Journal of Communication* published a special issue entitled "Homo Narrans," which underscored the centrality of the storytelling and narrative paradigm in communication. In that forum, scholars debated storytelling's relevance and efficacy as a potential explanatory metaphor for explaining communicative practice. John Lucaites and Celeste Condit (1985) in particular argued for narrative's functionality. Summarizing the forum, Walter Fisher (1985) argued that narrative was fundamental in establishing effective communication. Humans, in his view, were ultimately storytellers, and people chose sets of stories through which to elaborate their life experiences (see also Fisher 1987).

As narrative scholars turned toward journalism's study, the early targets of analysis were the more traditional forms of journalistic relay. Early work focused on those attributes of journalistic storytelling most closely aligned with journalism's sense of self. Hard news was established as the background setting for considering narrative parameters, and news content was seen to be timely, important, interesting, and novel. In the U.S. context, the form of most news stories was expected to take the shape of brief, thematized, concrete accounts of public events, and language was expected to include few adjectives or descriptive phrases, relying on an omniscient, authoritative third-person voice. Both Robert Darnton (1975) and Michael Schudson (1982) elaborated on the formulaic narrative attributes of U.S. news, showing how journalistic storytelling was patterned, predictable, and systemic. Mary Mander (1987) observed that journalistic storytelling was shaped so as to establish an all-knowing and prophetic moral order of events in the news, while Jack Lule (1995) and Ronald Jacobs (1996) focused on the ritual aspects of news narrative. W. Lance Bennett (1988) discussed how journalists personalized, dramatized, fragmented, and normalized the public events whose stories they told. Barbie Zelizer (1990a) argued that reporters used the narrative techniques of synecdoche, omission, and personalization to marshal both individual and collective professional authority. Both Theodore L. Glasser and James Ettema (1993) and Itzhak Roeh (1982, 1989) showed how irony permeated news narrative.

Scholarship on news narrative was set in place with a certain degree of opposition from journalism professionals and traditional journalism scholars, for the narrative qualities of news from the onset were seen as posing problems for journalists. Steve Barkin was first to point out that the act of telling a story was unevenly paired with the act of reporting (1984).

Although Helen Hughes's *News and the Human Interest Story* (1940) was among the first attempts to differentiate one type of storytelling from the setting of hard news, in fact there existed a split between research on the storytelling of hard news and that of the rest of journalism, because hard news was supposed to count as true, not stylized, accounts of the real world. To be a good storyteller meant that one was not a good journalist, and the more objective a story became, the more unreadable it also was thought to become. Narrative style was thus encoded as antithetical to the process of producing neutral news reports, and a good journalist became one whose presence as a storyteller was muted (Barkin 1984; Bird and Dardenne 1988).

At the same time, narrative analysis was well positioned to account for the varieties of journalistic practice. Although not part of journalists' self-presentation, much of journalists' authority rested not in what they did but in how they represented what they knew. Narrative, then, was a way of figuring out how journalists constructed their own authority (Zelizer 1990a, 1993b), and extensive research on journalistic storytelling set out to show how this was accomplished. In one valuable discussion, S. Elizabeth Bird and Robert Dardenne claimed that journalism of all kinds owed equal parts to real life happenings and to the codes and conventions of storytelling. Arguing to put aside the "interesting/important" dichotomy, they suggested that news stories needed to be considered as one whole with different parts, as a particular kind of mythological narrative "with its own symbolic codes that are recognized by its audience" (Bird and Dardenne 1988: 72–73). Similarly, James Carey (1986a) offered extended discussions of the way in which story forms privileged certain ways of knowing the world through news. He argued that such story forms underemphasized the "how" and "why" behind the news, inflating the focus on descriptive but not necessarily instrumental details. Beyond the United States, in which the idea of storytelling seemed to raise less strident a response from journalism professionals, scholars focused on alternative narrative modes that were regularly used to structure the news (e.g., Chalaby 1996, 1998; Benson 2002).

For those narrative analysts who pushed beyond the professional resistance to regard news as narrative, narrative analysis showed how all kinds of journalism were part of the same family and that differences between them were differences of degree rather than kind. Because it assumed that journalistic storytelling was a choice between alternatives for creative expression, narrative analysis necessarily regarded storytelling across the continuum of different kinds of journalism—hard and soft, elite and tabloid, mainstream and oppositional, television and press, broadcast and internet. While journalists themselves historically insisted on demarcations between the "high" and "low" lives of journalism—which over time switched from distinctions between tabloid and mainstream to distinctions between television and print, TV news magazines and regular television programming, tabloid TV and TV news magazines, cable TV and internet—their defense had a familiar quality, distinguishing repeatedly between information and entertainment, substance and style, public interest and commercialism, responsibility and sensationalism. In each case, they tended to exclude the lower end of the comparison from evaluation. Narrative analysis, however, forced the comparison on both ends.

Journalism scholars examined journalistic narratives in three main areas of research—in the mainstream press, on television news, and in the alternative journalistic forms of tabloids, reality television, and the internet. In each area, questions persisted regarding the privileged and less privileged forms of journalistic storytelling, and how each came to be thus positioned. Much of this research developed among U.S. scholars.

Storytelling in the Mainstream Press

There have been many narrative forms in the mainstream press. As G. Stuart Adam (1993) recounted, in the British context alone, journalism of the 17th and 18th centuries took the alternative forms of news briefs, literary essays, polemical writing, and legislative reports.

But the most regular invocation of storytelling technique, of how the news is told, was the oft-cited distinction between hard and soft news. As noted earlier, during the rise of the penny press, practices of storytelling were central to distinctions made between journalism that informed and journalism that told a gripping tale (Schudson 1978). For some time, the development of the less privileged form, at least in the United States, was more readily associated with storytelling, while hard news was thought, at least among journalism professionals, to involve no narrative technique whatsoever.

The so-called softer form focused on dramatic or heartrending stories, moral imperatives, and compelling plotlines. In part, this reflected the narrative features of the human-interest story, which Helen Hughes (1940), a student of Robert Park at the University of Chicago, was first to mark as a necessary and important deviation from the brief, dispassionate chronicles of the newspaper's front pages. A sidebar of the penny press in the 1830s, the human interest story was a form that addressed events in the lives of the individual and community in accessible and often emotional ways. Regarding the human interest story as part of a historical evolution that introduced the masses to reading, Hughes saw it as necessarily democratic and crucial for facilitating the transformation of the masses into a public. Storytelling was also associated with other alternative, often softer narrative forms in the mainstream press. Literary journalism, called also "new journalism," was articulated by its visionaries as a way to highlight the narrative style of journalism over the substance of the stories it told (e.g., Pauly 1990; Sims 1990; Sims and Kramer 1995).

But as narrative analysis grew in scope and interest, the hard news of mainstream journalism drew the interest of narrative analysts. The language considered here was what one observer called "the plain style" (Kenner 1990). In G. Stuart Adam's view, it invoked simplicity and explicitness, and its attributes were as follows:

> The storyteller in newspapers and newsmagazines is often disguised behind the device of an anonymous third person. That third person may be the publisher, the persona in the mind of the writer who writes authoritatively that the war has ended or has been declared, or that the election campaign has begun or the vote tallied. (Adam 1993: 33)

According to Adam, the plain style was uniform and consistent, delivered in a "stylized, published, and routinized voice" and often in an official tone. In every case, the journalist "is a presence who guides the reader through a story. He or she shows, tells, and explains." Finally, "the devices the narrator in journalism uses are those used by all storytellers: 'plot, characterization, action, dialogue, sequencing, dramatization, causation, myth, metaphor, and explanation'" (Adam 1993: 33–34; also Roeh 1982, 1989).

One of the first articles to explore mainstream journalistic storytelling directly was Robert Darnton's "Writing News and Telling Stories" (1975). Interested in the impact of the journalist's working milieu on news narrative, Darnton used his early experiences as a reporter at the *New York Times* to consider factors as varied as the spatial arrangement of the newsroom, the reporter's relation to primary and secondary reference groups, patterns of the reporter's occupational socialization, and storytelling techniques. Arguing that there were preestablished categories for both news form and content, Darnton (1975: 189) showed that "the story" ultimately involved the "manipulation of standardized images, cliches, angles, slants, and scenarios, which call forth a conventional response in the minds of editors and readers." For example, there existed a certain kind of "bereavement quotes" for bereavement stories. Journalists engaged in a sort of "search and find" process in writing news that upheld standardization and stereotypy.

Other scholars soon followed suit. British sociologist Philip Elliot (1980) advanced the notion that press rituals in the mainstream press functioned as folk literature. In "The Politics of Narrative Form," Michael Schudson (1982) examined the effect of narrative codes on the representation of reality. Although Schudson's interest in storytelling dated back to *Discovering the News* (1978), where he had pointed to two kinds of journalistic accounting, information and stories, here he focused exclusively on narrative form as a way of understanding U.S. journalistic practice. Journalism's ultimate power, he argued, rested in the forms by which declarations about reality could be made, and his tracking of reporting of the U.S. President's State of the Union Address over 200 years showed how reporting conventions like the summary lead and inverted pyramid, a focus on the U.S. President as the most important actor, a focus on a single rather than continuous event, highlighting political speeches, and contextualizing political acts moved journalists from reporting events to interpreting them. Emerging as expert analysts of the political world rather than partisans of political causes, journalists thus came to be seen as interpreters of political events rather than mere reporters, with the meaning of political events found not in the events themselves but in the political aims of the actors within them. The article's main point was central: Narrative form had a tremendous effect on news content, which in turn directly inflected the shape of what was regarded as news.

Elsewhere, much work on journalism and storytelling suggested that journalists fashioned stories according to definitive narrative patterns. Phyllis Frus (1994) elaborated on the historical differences between journalism and literature and concluded that current movements inside journalism were more open to embracing the narrative forms of storytelling. John Hartsock (2001) charted the evolution of literary journalism from the late 19th century onward, arguing that its particular form of storytelling developed its own resonance with the public over time, while Louise Woodstock (2002) reflected on the therapeutic elements of public journalism's narratives about itself. By the mid-1990s, even journalism professionals experienced a rebirth of interest in writing as part of mainstream journalism (e.g., Clark 1994).

Related here was a substantial amount of work on the visual languages of the mainstream press, and work on photography, video, and photojournalism drew substantial academic attention across the board of scholars interested in narrative. While work by Barthes (1967, 1977), Peirce (1893–1913/1998), and Hall (1973a) on the iconic, indexical, and symbolic dimensions of photographic authority had existed for years, it was only with the advent of narrative as a way of making sense of a text, combined with some of the alternative sites for analysis favored by cultural studies, that this work took hold. For instance, work here focused both on the general patterns of news photography (Schwartz 1992; Perlmutter 1998) and on the function of photography in response to certain types of circumstances (J. Taylor 1991, 1998; Brothers 1997; Moeller 1989; Zelizer 1998).

Also of relevance was extended work on the mythological parameters of journalistic narratives. John Pauly and Melissa Eckert (2002) addressed what they called the "myth of the local" in U.S. journalism, while Carolyn Kitsch (2000, 2002) looked at the various narrative elements that took on mythological proportion in U.S. newsmagazines. Jack Lule considered how myth played a part in journalism generally (2001) and in mainstream editorial pages following September 11 (2002). In his view, the daily news remained "the primary vehicle for myth in our time," and seven master myths—the victim, the scapegoat, the hero, the good mother, the trickster, the other world, and the flood—offered patterned ways for audiences to make sense of surrounding events (Lule 2001: 19).

Storytelling in Television News

Other scholars considered the stories of television news, with an emphasis on its narrative structures (e.g., Hartley 1982). James Lett (1987) delineated the narrative traits characteristic of TV news programming, such as pandering to the visual dimensions of a message or stressing the dichotomous aspects of the conflicts reported. Dan Nimmo and James Combs (1983, 1985) discussed the narrative style of crisis reporting across three U.S. television networks, finding that each network had its own style of telling the story of crisis: CBS was interpretive and official, ABC focused on the common people involved in the crisis, and NBC resigned to move on beyond the chaos that the crisis introduced. Certain scholars focused on televisual style more generally (e.g., Griffin 1992; Postman and Powers 1992; Griffin and Kagan 1996), with Justin Lewis (1994) arguing that television news in effect functioned in the absence of narrative codes, rendering it disjunctive and ineffectual. The narrative structure of TV news, he said, resembled more "a shopping list than a story" (Lewis 1991: 131). Narrative style was tracked across different kinds of journalistic coverage. Katherine Fry (2003) looked at television's representation of natural disasters, while Matthew Ehrlich (2002) examined the "On the Road" television reports of Charles Kuralt for CBS News. Barbie Zelizer (1992b) examined U.S. television's news relays of the John F. Kennedy assassination.

TV news magazines and current affairs programs drew particular attention from scholars interested in narrative (e.g., Nichols 1991). In *60 Minutes and the News* (1991), Richard Campbell argued that storytelling helped establish the authority of the TV news magazine, which evolved in the late 1960s as an application of the magazine—rather than the newspaper or film—to television. While narrative style was antithetical to the neutral reports favored by hard-core reporters, Campbell maintained that

"60 Minutes," as a news program, was more interested in narrative than were other news programs. The style of personal reporting and its drama were as much connected to the program's popularity as the facts it reported. Thus, the program strategically developed certain formulaic narrative conventions by which viewers could understand the world: Reporters were either characters or narrators, storylines were multiple, dramatic tension was mediated so as to build narrative conflict, and the camera frame was controlled in a way to give the reporter control over the story. Campbell identified four news frames through which the program framed the world—as mystery, therapy, adventure, and arbitration—and maintained that through them "60 Minutes" persisted as a support for middle-American morality. Elsewhere (Fiske 1988; Postman and Powers 1992), scholars focused on the ways in which TV news magazines either enhanced or detracted from the attributes of basic TV news programming.

Storytelling in Alternative Journalistic Forms

A substantial amount of work focused of late on the narrative parameters of still-evolving, less obvious modes of journalistic relay. In particular, as work in cultural studies forced open some of the boundaries by which journalism constituted itself (e.g., Dahlgren and Sparks 1992), the relevance of narrative and storytelling in delineating the formulaic features of a broadened repertoire of journalistic forms became evident. In less celebratory terms, these genres showed that, as had been predicted with the advent of television, "organized journalism is dead" (Altheide and Snow 1991: 51). Such alternative forms included tabloid journalism, reality television, sports and weather journalism, and online journalism.

Tabloid forms of storytelling had long been part of journalism across the world. The readiness with which certain journalistic practices were lumped together as "tabloid" varied across contexts and historical periods. For instance, Colin Sparks argued for five kinds of journalism in regard to tabloidization—the serious press, semi-serious press, serious-popular press, newsstand tabloid press, and supermarket tabloid press—each of which offered variant versions of the traits thought to characterize all tabloid forms (Sparks 2000). At the same time, the existence of tabloid journalism was widespread.

In the U.S. context, tabloid versions of the news bubbled up with the penny press of the 1830s, the rise of the sensationalist Pulitzer and Hearst newspaper empire of the 1890s, the jazz journalism of the 1920s, and the supermarket tabloids and tabloid television of today (Bird 1992), though it was argued that the U.S. fascination with crime, gossip, and sex had been ongoing at least since the 16th century (Stephens 1988). In the United Kingdom, tabloids had a more even and continuous history, dating to the introduction of compulsory education in the mid 1800s (Engel 1996). Elsewhere, they were connected with localized modes of popularization in the broader culture, as seen in Australia (Lumby 1999), Hungary (Gulyas 2000), and Germany (Klein 2000). Certain differences prevailed, as in Mexico, where the tabloid remained primarily a television phenomenon (Hallin 2000). And yet, in each case of their analysis, the narratives of the tabloids were fairly uniform: more sensationalistic, accessible, provocative, and popular in tone, more textually fragmented and concerned with spectacle and messages of exclusion. Their function was to provide partisan sources of collective knowledge, teaching readers how to disbelieve what they read or saw while learning to exploit the contradictions in news storytelling (Fiske 1992b).

Perhaps the most articulate discussion of tabloid journalism as storytelling was that offered by S. Elizabeth Bird. In a range of works, Bird (1990, 2000) discussed tabloid forms by exploring the common storytelling traits that were shared by the mainstream and tabloid press. In *For Enquiring Minds* (1992), she showed how the narrative traits of the tabloids—timelessness, high moralism, political conservatism, predictability, and individualism—aligned with the trajectory of oral tradition. Packed with news about natural disasters, unusual births, omens and murders, tabloids typically focused on stories of human gore, celebrity gossip, and human interest. Bird also showed how a number of journalistic values—such as objectivity and credibility—were realized through parallel practices among tabloid and mainstream journalists.

Other scholars investigated additional variants on the split between mainstream and tabloid news. Matthew Ehrlich (1997) found that tabloids differed almost inconsequentially from their mainstream cohorts, with storytelling conventions ultimately reflecting the various modes of cultural production from which they borrowed. Kevin Glynn (2000) examined the tabloid's generic and historic functions, arguing that the particular generic form of tabloid television became the central impulse of the media environment of the 1980s and 1990s. Narrative was key here. As John Langer (1998: 6) phrased it, tabloid journalism needed to be examined precisely because of, and not despite, its peculiar narrative qualities: "its commitment to storytelling, its formulaic qualities as well as its search for visual impact." In contrast to those types of journalism that "could be described as the 'purer' forms of political culture," tabloid forms profited mostly from attempts "to track down and account for the 'trivialities'" (Langer 1998: 7). They remained the "other news . . . the remaindered news, recognized in passing, but left aside in order to focus full attention on what was perceived as more serious and more pressing news matters" (Langer 1998: 8–9).

In addition, journalistic talk shows, sometimes called "assertion journalism," where journalists provoked conflict instead of presenting so-called reasoned analysis, or vox pop shows, where audiences took the place of journalistic experts, constituted further elaborations on the tabloid themes of popularization and individualization. Related here was what broadcasters—and certain scholars—preferred to call reality programming. Indicating a slew of programming types that stretched from cop shows to tabloid talk shows, these forms of journalism were seen to inhabit the borders of recognized journalistic practice (e.g., Fishman 1999; Friedman 2002). And yet, the similarities were tangible. In the United States, shows like "A Current Affair," "Hard Copy," "America's Most Wanted," and "Inside Edition" offered stories of moral disorder and deviance that were personalized through subjective treatments, the use of music videos, and the recreation of actuality—all of which had long been considered inappropriate for mainstream television news, yet all of which offered representations of the so-called real world for their audiences. These hybrids of the narrative forms of newscast, telethon, documentary, cop show, and family drama (Glynn 2000), which were further developed by shows like "Big Brother," "Survivor," and "A Makeover Story," offered a new version of what journalism could be. Similarly, work on sports journalism and weather journalism offered an ongoing complication to traditional notions of what journalism was for (e.g., Hargreaves 1986; Rowe 1999; Miller 2002).

Narrative work on the internet also began to draw interest as online journalism became a more integral aspect of journalistic work. Allan (2002) delineated some of the ongoing problems that the internet posed to traditional notions of journalistic narrative: the lack of editing and related instantaneous replay, the diminished authority of the journalist, the personalized fashioning of news preferences, and the interactivity. Elsewhere (Hauben and Hauben 1997; Borden and Harvey 1998), scholars extrapolated on the narrative potentials that could develop as online journalism continued its expansion. Seen informally as a kind of collaborative journalism, the narratives of online news were thought to provide an alternative twist to the ways in which the news had been traditionally presented, and thus the storytelling attributes that they adopted were seen of particular value.

Rhetoric

Rhetorical scholars offered a separate set of analytical tools through which to consider the authority and power of journalism. By far the earliest set of ideas available for analyzing texts, rhetorical study drew in broad strikes from the writings of Aristotle and Plato. Concerned with the study of persuasion, it shaped its analyses by considering texts in conjunction with the five stages of preparing a speech as identified in the rhetorical tradition—*inventio* (collecting and conceptualizing subject matter), *disposito* (structuring a speech), *elocutio* (giving a speech linguistic articulation), *memoria* (memorizing the speech), and *actio* (performing the speech). This scholarship also drew from the more contemporary work of Kenneth Burke (1945, 1950, 1978), whose notion of language as action provided a fruitful starting point for the analysis of news texts. Concerned with the attribution of motive, Burke developed the notion of the "dramatistic pentad," by which act, scene, agent, agency, and purpose were thought to come together in explaining human action, and that of the "terministic screen," by which certain aspects of action were presumed to come to the forefront of attention while others dropped to its backstage. Both notions, together with the broad range of Burke's work, facilitated an address to language use in conjunction with pragmatic aims.

The rhetorical analysis of journalism's languages developed primarily in the United States and largely at the margins of rhetoric or English departments. As notions of power and authority came to be attributed to journalism, rhetoric came to be seen as particularly relevant to news and of particular interest to scholars interested in political communication. In this regard, rhetorical scholars elaborated the ways in which journalism could be thought of as an act of rhetoric. Interviewers or anchorpersons were seen as conveying journalistic authority by constructing arguments in certain ways and not others. Which figures of speech figured into which kinds of talk were seen as strategic and patterned choices that in turn supported the positioning of journalists in the public sphere.

A wide range of scholars applied Burke's premises to understanding the work of the media in shaping language and vice versa (e.g., Edelman 1964, 1985; Duncan 1968; Combs and Mansfield 1976). Burke's (1978) notion of the terministic screen, for instance, was seen as relevant to a wide range of discussions about the filters journalists used in coverage. Celeste Condit and J. Ann Seltzer (1985) addressed the rhetorical attributes of the press coverage of a murder trial. Bruce Gronbeck (1997) used Burke's notions to examine local newscasts, whereas Barry Brummett (1989, 1991) examined the popularization of journalism in conjunction with Burke's understanding of public action. Burke was invoked in Carol Wilkie's (1981) discussion of pretrial publicity in the scapegoating of Bruno Richard Hauptmann and in John Marlier's (1989) analysis of coverage of Oliver North's testimony. Few of these studies, however, linked the discussions of coverage with an understanding of journalistic routine. In addition, many of the events they examined were contested events whose deliberation took shape in an institutional setting, such as a courtroom.

In that rhetoric was particularly concerned with persuasion, much work focused on acts of political communication as situated against the broader journalistic frame. Thus, work by Kathleen Hall Jamieson (1984, 1988) and Roderick Hart (1987) focused on the ways in which coverage of campaigns established a certain rhetorical authority for political candidates. Other scholarship focused on the visual dimensions of the journalistic text, as in the work by Robert Hariman and John Lucaites (2002, 2003, in press) on iconic photographs.

Certain scholarship here employed a looser definition of rhetoric, focusing on the rhetorical dimensions of news in ways that did not necessarily date back to the early origins of the field but clarified rhetorical authority nonetheless. Burke was loosely invoked in Jack Lule's analyses of coverage of both the Challenger disaster (Lule 1989a) and the downing of KAL Flight 007 (Lule 1989b). Itzhak Roeh (1989) discussed the rhetorical modes of address employed in the news in a variety of contexts, including coverage of the war in Lebanon (Roeh and Ashley 1986), late-night TV news broadcasts (Roeh, Katz, Cohen, and Zelizer 1980), and newspaper headlines (Roeh and Feldman 1984). In *The Rhetoric of News* (1982), Roeh elaborated how irony was brought to bear in the news and argued that news language functioned as what he called a "rhetoric of objectivity," whereby journalists used objective modes of address in a rhetorical fashion.

Framing

One of the more recent approaches to journalism that drew upon a grounding in language was scholarship on framing. Borrowed from early work by Erving Goffman (1974) and Gregory Bateson (1972) in which all public life was seen as organized by frames through which individuals perceived surrounding action, framing offered a way to understand the systematic and often predetermined organization of news stories into types facilitated by patterned selection, emphasis, and presentation (Gitlin 1980; also Gamson 1989).

Called by Todd Gitlin (1980: 7) a way to "organize the world both for journalists who report it and, in some important degree, for us who rely on their reports," framing studies offered journalism scholars a means of examining the filters that made the news sensical to both journalists and the public. Favored largely by U.S. scholars in political science and political communication, framing research constituted a way to account for the lack of neutrality in news and provided "a standard set of themes and values common to much of the information American news audiences receive" (Price and Tewksbury 1997: 174). Often invoked in conjunction with scholarship on agenda setting and priming, framing research focused on story presentation as a way of explaining the news (Iyengar and Kinder 1987; Iyengar 1991); in Robert Entman's (1993a: 52) view, "to frame is to select some aspects of a perceived reality and make them more salient." At the same time, framing was thought to occur in conjunction with the public at which it was directed. In this regard, it differed from the other approaches to language use.

Over time defined as a "central organizing idea or story line that provides meaning" (Gamson and Modigliani 1987: 143) and as "mentally storied clusters of ideas that guide individuals' processing of information" (Entman 1993a: 53), framing among journalists came to be seen as working both culturally and cognitively (Reese 2001). Frames drew upon numerous tools of language, including metaphors, exemplars (or historical lessons), catchphrases, depictions and visual images such as icons (Gamson and Modigiliani 1989: 3). In this way, framing was thought to reflect both journalistic interpretations of events and the contexts by which they were made sensical, with journalists setting the frames of reference by which audiences interpreted the news (Gamson 1992; Neuman, Just, and Crigler 1992). Much of the research on framing focused on ascertaining the systematic effect of the frames through which the news was relayed or, in Vincent Price and David Tewksbury's (1997: 175) words, on clarifying "issue-framing effects—the ability of media reports to alter the kinds of considerations people use in forming their opinions."

Much of the more recent literature on framing focused on the patterns of news coverage in types of discourse, as in Shanto Iyengar's (1991) discussion of political coverage on television or the coverage of particular issues or events. On the latter count, literature ranged across discussions of risk (Hornig 1992), the Intifada (Cohen and Wolfsfeld (1993), the antinuclear movement (Entman and Rojecki 1993b), the Gulf War (Iyengar and Simon 1993), the crash of TWA flight 800 (Durham 1998), and European reception of the Euro (de Vreese 2001). Others used framing to draw comparisons across different kinds of news events (e.g., Gerstle 1992).

At the same time, scholars invoked framing in a wide variety of ways, prompting Robert Entman (1993a) to call it a "fractured paradigm." Zhongdang Pan and Gerald Kosicki (1993) argued that other structures, such as themes, schema, and scripts, filled many of the same functions as frames. Maxwell McCombs, Donald Shaw, and David Weaver (1997) maintained that framing performed a second-level agenda setting in linking salient characteristics of journalistic stories with the audiences' interpretations of them. Others pondered whether or not framing constituted a method, a theory, or neither. A collection of essays edited by Stephen Reese, Oscar Gandy, and August Grant (2001), for instance, surveyed the range of theoretical and methodological issues that arose in framing research, including its relation to agenda setting, public deliberation, and postmodernism. In certain views, the fractured nature of the literature did not improve over time (e.g., Scheufele 1999).

Nonetheless, framing provided an important pathway for thinking about language use in conjunction with the intersection between journalists and their public. In this regard, and more broadly than many other arenas examining the languages of journalism, it highlighted the centrality of language for disciplines in which language was not necessarily an obvious target of analysis. In so doing, framing thereby critically extended the domain of language studies and journalism.

* * * * *

Work on the pragmatic uses of language in journalism was noteworthy in that it not only allowed scholars to consider journalism through one of its most obvious, proven, and patterned manifestations—language—but it also helped make journalistic work comprehensible by connecting it to the broader uses of language. The scholarship on journalistic narrative, rhetoric, and framing also played an important role in helping scholars focus beyond the discontinuous episodes and events that constituted the news. Offering an accessible and patterned template of sorts to which journalists repaired while crafting news of most sorts, work on news narrative, rhetoric, and framing helped force recognition of the systematically constructed nature of journalistic work, even if journalists were reluctant to admit as much in their own discussions of journalism.

The Centrality of Language Studies and Journalism

What did the study of news languages more generally offer the inquiry into journalism? To begin with, its emphasis on journalistic texts displayed the strengths and weaknesses associated with language study. While this scholarship offered a prolonged and detailed view of what a journalistic text looked like, it also stressed the text over the larger environment and the processes by which journalism was made. In this regard, language studies offset the relative disinterest in news texts that characterized many of the other disciplinary perspectives.

At the same time, language studies did not offer equal scholarly attention to all aspects of news making. Absent from this approach was a consideration of production, the audience, the historical context and diachronic dimension of journalism, and journalists per se. In fact, this scholarly view, like certain other disciplinary work, remained largely unpeopled, with texts shaped and analyzed in a somewhat disembodied fashion. The study of the languages of journalism, then, overstated journalistic language by considering it in isolation from the larger surround in which journalism took shape.

In addition, the language-driven study of journalism focused only on certain kinds of texts in generalizing about how language worked in this setting. In that the perspective offered highly focused glimpses of different news texts, it did not go beyond the boundaries of those texts as much as it might have. Such extensions could profitably include examinations of different kinds of news segments, different kinds of news texts (such as the trade literature), and the various patterns of intertextuality within and beyond news organizations. For instance, much of the mainstream narrative work took shape within the United States and thus established a familiarity with mainstream U.S. news that was not matched by an attention to other narrative forms in other regions. By contrast, work on the narratives of tabloid journalism seemed to reach far more stridently across the journalisms of different nation-states.

Like other microanalytical work, these language-based approaches to journalism tended to be extensive, systemic, and comprehensive. However, also like much microanalytical work, the detailed material that emerged from this type of inquiry did not generate many attempts at replication because its detail was highly particularistic, minutely focused, and difficult to connect with the broader aspects of the analysis of journalism. For example, invoking the tenses of broadcast news commentary as an illustration of a journalist's proximity to a news event required an a priori sensitivity to the importance of language, which was not characteristic of most journalism scholars. Indeed, the opposite has appeared to be the case, where scholars who were not invested in the language-based inquiry into journalism paid the findings related to language an uneven degree of attention.

And yet, language study moved journalistic inquiry in definitive ways. Each of the discussed studies on journalistic language proceeded from a belief that examining the constructed nature of texts could help establish the elaborated dimensions by which journalism worked. Focusing on the text itself, as a starting point for understanding journalism more broadly, was a useful alternative to the heavy emphasis on people established by other modes of inquiry. Questions did remain concerning the degree to which journalism's various "textual" attributes needed to be delineated and examined before moving on to more general issues related to the craft and processes of journalism. Similarly, reaching clarification and consensus on how to best locate evidence of the ideological positioning implicit in journalism's languages remained at issue. And yet, the fact that all three approaches to language—informal, formalistic, and pragmatic—started with the premise that language was ideological offered a critical counterassumption not only to the more mainstream scholarship on journalism but also to claims of journalism professionals that journalism was a reflection of the real. Other domains of inquiry would take these notions beyond language and apply them to a broader repertoire of additional aspects of the journalistic world.

6

Political Science and Journalism

When compared with other scholarly views on journalism and journalistic practice, the perspective offered by most scholars in political science has been decidedly normative. Falling under the rubric of "interested research," this scholarship typically examines journalism through a vested interest in the political world. In large part concerned with the optimum functioning of the political system that rests alongside journalism, its considerations derive from long-standing expectations about the news media acting in democracies as government's fourth estate. Questions about "mediated democracy" (Orren 1986; McNair 2000a), "mediacracy" (Taylor 1990), "mediated political realities" (Nimmo and Combs 1983), "media politics" (Arterton 1984; Bennett 1988), and "whether the media govern" (Iyengar and Reeves 1997) are key here, derived from an assumption of interdependency of the political and journalistic worlds in certain kinds of political systems. In this regard, those engaged with the political research on journalism often take the position of advocates for the public who are invested in figuring out how journalism can better serve the public, primarily according to premises operating in democratic and generally capitalist societies.

The underlying normative concern of much of this research—which largely focused on the United States, though a parallel concern was raised in the United Kingdom in departments of government and politics—was how the news media could be expected to operate by serving its citizenry in the surrounding political environment. Dating back to the early work of Walter Lippmann (1914, 1922/1960, 1925), the concern with journalism's political role was uppermost. Arguing that the crisis of modern democracy was a crisis of journalism, he called on journalists to act as experts in mediating the information that the wider public received. As Denis McQuail (1987: 4) observed, normative theory queried how an institution "ought to operate if certain social values are to be observed or obtained," a concern that in turn has influenced what the public can and should expect from the news media or what Fred Inglis (1990: 110) called "the study of how the world is and how it ought to be." Driven primarily by large-scale observation, scholarship here often concluded with a suggestion of practices for journalistic reform, by which the efficacy of a given media system could be expected to improve. It examined how the world of journalism ought to operate in conjunction with certain political systems, with an emphasis on whether, to what extent, and how journalism influenced electoral and decision-making processes and policies. In this sense, simply by relegating its focus to the intersection of journalism and politics rather than inside journalism alone, political science research of journalism offset what Philip Schlesinger (1990) called "the media-centric bias" of much journalism research undertaken in accordance with other disciplinary frames.

Evolution of Political Science Research Into Journalism

Expectations of political behavior go back to the days of Plato and Aristotle, though the academic discipline of political science primarily emerged half a century ago in the United States. Defined as the study of government and other political institutions and processes, political science has had both social scientific and humanistic sides—the former produced large-scale surveys of political orientations, values, and behavior, the latter probed the aspirations of moral and ethical conduct in the political world. Dubbed informally as the study of "who gets what, when and how," political science has long been concerned with what the political scientist Hans J. Morgenthau (1948/1985) defined as the "nature, accumulation, distribution, exercise, and control of power on all levels of social interaction, with special emphasis on the power of the state." In that regard, the targets of political science inquiry were those institutions, features, and issues that impacted upon the conduct of politics in the interaction of nation-states.

Collective expectations that journalism has a political role to play in the world are not new: Alexis de Tocqueville was among the first to outline the effect of the press on public opinion in both France and America (1900), though the work of Gabriel Tarde (1898, 1901/1969), Ferdinand Tonnies (1923/1971), John Dewey (1927/1954), and Walter Lippmann (1922/1960) independently targeted the intersection of the press, public, and polity. Noting the influence of the press on public opinion, Tarde saw journalism as fueling the conversation that made democratic action possible, though he did not address the problematic link between journalists and politicians (Blumler and Gurevitch 1995). Tonnies regarded the press as an instrument used by government to shape public opinion, while Dewey and other pragmatists looked to journalism as a means to ensure the autonomy and vitality of public community and sentiment. In a more contemporary formulation, expectations about journalism's political role were driven by the notion that journalism constituted a fourth estate of government, a notion introduced during the late 18th century with the evolution of modern forms of democracy, when the press was thought to exist as a guardian of democracy and defender of the public interest (Carlyle 1905). More modern commentators interpreted the fourth estate as a check and balance on the other three forms of power—executive, judicial, and legislative (Cater 1959). Bedfellows to the notion of the fourth estate included the notion of "public opinion" and an emphasis on the centrality of public debate in political decision making (Boyce 1978; McNair 1998; Splichal 1999), each of which accompanied journalism's evolving linkage with the political world. From outright ownership by political parties in the early days of the Republic through the incessant presence of press officers and on to the intricate bonding of journalists and politicians in what is commonly called the "sound-bite age," politics and journalism displayed an ongoing orientation to each other. It is no surprise, then, that the evolving and changing notions about democracies promoted similarly evolving expectations of journalism, particularly the kind of journalism seen as capable of protecting the public in what appeared to be an increasingly sophisticated environment of political interest. While certain scholars went so far as to query why we don't "call journalists political actors" (Cook 1998:1), the interweaving of journalistic and political missions, as brought to bear on journalistic practice, was long-standing. And in the United States, political scientists were enthusiastic about analyzing its workings in that vein.

In other parts of the world, however, the examination of the synergistic relationship between the political and journalistic domains was not necessarily examined through the disciplinary frame of political science, at least not in its U.S. form. Other disciplines—sociology, communication, philosophy, semiology and literary studies, international relations—played an important role in shaping how scholars thought about journalism and political life. For instance, in the United Kingdom, despite a considerable degree of interest in issues of political power, such issues were often framed under a sociological rubric, where even scholars trained in political science rejected claims that British society was pluralistic and adopted instead sociological premises of inquiry that facilitated a critical unpacking of journalism's political dimensions (e.g., Morrison and Tumber 1988). In Germany, where the term "Publizistik"—a traditional term for "political journalism"—was at first appended to nearly all the professorships and research institutes created in the immediate post-World War II decades, political or public communication remained the self-evident core of German communication curricula (Schulz 1997). French research on journalism and politics evolved equally under the rubrics of semiology and literary studies, on the one hand, and political science, on the other (Neveu 1998). Philosophy played a part in tracking journalism's political dimensions in both France and the United Kingdom (Ellul 1965; Keane 1991; Sfez 1993). Certain work on globalization and journalism, particularly in the Middle East, was framed as international communication, borrowing in part from the field of international relations (e.g., Mowlana 1996). Moreover, certain political scientists leveled substantial critiques at the way in which the preferred disciplinary conversation in political science shunted aside competing premises, interests, and geographic locations (e.g., Downing 1996).

And yet, in the United States, as journalism was co-opted by the social sciences as part of their core interest, political science was at the top of the list of relevant disciplines. Dating back both to Walter Lippmann's work on public opinion (1922/1960, 1925) and Harold Lasswell's (1927/1971, 1941, 1948) exploration of propaganda after World War I and of post-World War II media "herding behavior," political science from the 20th century onward conceived of journalists as potentially powerful, influential actors in the political world. A concern with studying the impact of propaganda particularly during the post-World War II period brought journalists to the forefront of analysis. Although political scientists did not always agree on the extent of journalism's political role—as recently as the mid-1990s, for instance, Stephen Hess (1981, 1996) characterized journalism as merely "another public policy institution," while Thomas Patterson (1993) argued that the news media were remarkably powerful brokers of American politics—a connection between journalism and politics was presumed rather than debated and challenged. This connection and the various assumptions about it not only offered an early understanding of the linkage between government and journalism but set the pitch for much political science scholarship that followed.

Developments in both journalism and politics enhanced journalism's political role. In many views, the U.S. political process in effect grew through an intricate dependence on the press (e.g., Davis 1992). With both political actors and the public relying on journalism to disseminate and provide information about the political world, the political system was thought to use journalism's speedy and far-reaching address to the public to make comprehensible the weakening and decentralization of its major political parties, the enhanced significance of national government, and the rise of the so-called modern presidency. In this regard, much political science inquiry into journalism was negative in tone, displaying what Brian McNair (2000b) called a "pervasive pessimism" about the relationship between journalism and politics in advanced capitalist, liberal democracies. Invested with considerable power in theory, journalists and their institutional settings were critiqued for what they failed to provide. To borrow a phrase from Jay Blumler and Michael Gurevitch (1995), the ongoing "crisis of public communication" in advanced capitalism was seen as a threat to democracy itself.

Political science's inquiry into journalism developed in three main directions, each of which scoped out a largely normative and abstract view of different levels of journalistic practice. At the heart of each route of inquiry was a concern for how journalism was versus how it ought to be. As Timothy Cook (1998: 173) aptly phrased it, "most critiques of journalism, whether outside or inside the enterprise, operate from a tacit assumption that if we could only get journalists to change how they go about doing their job, the news would be much improved." Driven by a concern for the ideal and the optimum, political science developed a wide-ranging litany of tools by which to transform journalism's actual state into a more perfect enterprise.

These three directions of research differed in analytical scope and scale. Key was first a systematic concern with the "smallest picture" of the journalistic world—that embodied by the interaction between journalist and source. Although the literature on sourcing practices developed in line with sociological inquiry (e.g., Gans 1979, Fishman 1980, Ericson, Baranek, and Chan 1989), it also reflected a concern in political science over the intersection of journalism and partisan politics, found here in the interactions linking reporter and source. For that reason it is discussed here under the rubric of political science scholarship. Within this small-scale perspective was also scholarship on journalistic models and roles, abstractions by which the optimum practices of journalism could be set in place.

A second direction of political science's inquiry into journalism was a mid-scale consideration of the functioning of journalism's intersection with the political world, considered across the broad environment by which journalists connected to both political actors and audiences. Within this rubric was included work on journalists, political actors, and audiences during political campaigns and more recently scholarship on public journalism.

Most well known within political science's study of journalism was the establishment of large-scale typologies of interaction, which attempted to describe possible operating traits for journalism under different political orders. Such typologies, revised over the years, established and sustained an abstract standard for evaluating the efficacy of journalistic systems in alternative political environments around the world. At the same time, political science was the site for developing linkages with other domains of scholarly inquiry on journalism. Central here was scholarship on political language and its impact on the intersection linking journalism and politics.

Political Science and Small-Scale Journalistic Practices

Although the interest of political science researchers in small-scale journalistic practices might not seem to parallel their interest in large-scale media systems and their connection with the political world, a substantial amount of research was devoted to identifying the specific practices that individual journalists used to connect with the political apparatus. For instance, scholarship in the U.S. context provided research on journalistic work in the Washington press corps or on the campaign trail (Rosten 1937; Crouse 1973), on the relationship between journalists and key political figures such as U.S. presidents (Pollard 1947; Watson 1990; Allen 1993; Liebovich 2001), and on the workings of explicitly political beats such as the White House (Grossman and Kumar 1981; Hertsgaard 1988), Congress (Blanchard 1974), and the House of Representatives (Cook 1990). A smaller number of works focused on the press and city hall (Gieber and Johnson 1961; Kaniss 1995). At the heart of much of this scholarship was a concern with the shape of the small-scale journalistic-political intersection, which translated broad concerns with journalism's political dimensions into a finite, identifiable setting or set of interactions.

Sourcing Practices

From the beginning of political science's interest in journalism, numerous scholars, following upon the heels of sociology and the early newsroom studies, began to focus on the smallest interactional setting of journalism—the source-journalist relationship. Just as Warren Breed had narrowed a large-scale concern with journalism to a focused examination of the physical locale of the newsroom, others—Leon Sigal (1973), Stephen Hess (1981, 1984), and Herbert Strentz (1989) in the United States, Jeremy Tunstall (1970) and Colin Seymour-Ure (1974) in the United Kingdom, and Rod Tiffen (1990) in Australia—similarly focused on the link between journalists and sources as a way to consider broad questions about journalistic power and autonomy. The identification of each person or set of persons as an embodiment of a respective institutional setting helped concretize the abstract nature of the linkage between politics and journalism. Some scholars thought that sourcing practices reflected the whims and desires of officials and politicians (Cohen 1963), while others claimed that the reporter was better off or in greater control (Hess 1984; Press and Verburg 1988).

Over time, however, the scholarship on sourcing established with a wide degree of consensus that sourcing practices derived from a symbiotic and consensual process in which both parties had much to gain in making news (Sigal 1973; Gans 1979; Fishman 1980). Sourcing practices reflected a mutually dependent and advantageous set of interactions (Blumler and Gurevitch 1981; Ericson, Baranek, and Chan 1989; Schlesinger 1990). The source-reporter link was seen as a series of bargaining or exchange interchanges, most of which involved political reporters and governmental or administrative personnel. The material to be exchanged remained steadfast—media exposure for information.

Certain patterns were found repeatedly in scholarship that exposed the tenor of that exchange. Leon Sigal (1973) argued that just about half of the sources cited in the front-page stories of the *New York Times* and the *Washington Post* were U.S. government officials, underscoring a fundamental imbalance toward elites. Herbert Gans (1979) showed that sources divided unevenly into knowns and unknowns and demonstrated that the source-reporter relationship depended on a manageable and mutually advantageous exchange of positive exposure for beneficial or important information. Barbara Pfetsch (1998) focused on the patterns of news management among government officials. These studies were generally conducted in the United States and focused almost exclusively on national reporters and official bureaucracies in Washington, D.C. or New York City.

A similar patterning of source-reporter interactions was displayed elsewhere, typically in conjunction with the existing mainstream and elite bureaucratic news settings of different democratic and capitalist systems. For instance, in the United Kingdom, works targeted the Westminster-Whitehall lobby system (e.g., Tunstall 1970). Thomas Patterson (1998) showed how different kinds of journalists across national boundaries allowed varying degrees of independence from sources in their interactions: British journalists were both passive and neutral in their sourcing practices, U.S. reporters remained neutral but actively tried to shape the information that they received, Italian journalists were passive but acted as advocates in their sourcing practices, German journalists functioned as social and political analysts, and Swedish reporters remained active but neutral in their exchanges—all of which suggested that Western journalists played different roles in their relationships with sources. Other differences emerged elsewhere in the world.

In Latin America, for instance, sources tended to use journalists to tweak their own political rivalries more aggressively than in other regions (Waisbord 2000). In Mexico, governmental sources often paid reporters to publish their sides of stories (Benavides 2000), while in Israel, such sources displayed an often protracted source-reporter relationship due to the basic fact that many sources and reporters knew each other socially (Goren 1979; Roeh et al. 1980; Liebes 1997; Wolfsfeld 1997; Caspi and Limor 1999). In Japan, formal associations of journalists, called Kisha Clubs, determined which sources a reporter could access (Feldman 1993), and in the Netherlands, journalists operated from within a far more individualized and often atomized environment, activating source relationships unevenly (Cohen 1995).

Work on sourcing practices began to diversify as scholars looked more intensely at the different kinds of settings in which sources could be activated. Scholars who examined crime coverage (Hall, Critcher, Jefferson, Clarke, and Roberts 1978) noted a "primary definition" effect that occurred in news making, whereby a structured relationship between journalists and their powerful sources allowed sources to become the primary definers of topics covered by the media. But that notion was challenged by Philip Schlesinger (1990), and following with their own examination of crime coverage, Schlesinger and Howard Tumber (1995) argued that the negotiations between journalists and sources were more ongoing and less predetermined. Local journalistic settings similarly complicated notions about sourcing, as scholars in the United States and United Kingdom demonstrated a hierarchy effect that changed with circumstance (Cox and Morgan 1973; Berkowitz 1990; Kaniss 1991, 1995; Franklin and Murphy 1997), as did the study of oppositional news (Eliasoph 1988). A growing interest in the new specialisms of journalism, such as cultural, sports, and weather news (e.g., Allan 1999; Rowe 1999; Miller 2002), broadened the search for sources beyond the political setting.

Scholars also examined specific sourcing practices. Some of them— punditry (Hirsch 1991; Nimmo and Combs 1992), spin (Heffer 1995; Jones 1995; Kurtz 1998; Schlesinger, Miller, and Dinan 2001), and political consultants (Sabato 1981)—appeared in popular discourse, reflecting the growing familiarity with which the public began to regard a number of key sourcing practices. Research on television news provided an emphasis on talking heads, photo ops, and sound bites as a concrete consequence of the source-reporter relationship (Adatto 1994; Hallin 1994, 1997; Rosenbaum 1997). Raymond Kuhn and Erik Neveu (2002) tracked these practices beyond the Anglo-American sphere, including Italy and Thailand. Gianpetro Mazzoleni, Julianne Stewart, and Bruce Horsfield (2003) considered the new forms of source-journalist relations that emerged in eight geographic locations once extreme right-wing neo-populist political parties became active political players. With the increasing centrality of the internet, discussions about sourcing practices changed further in demeanor, as scholars noted the more democratic and equalizing impulses involved in journalistic work on the Web (Borden and Harvey 1998; Davis 1999; Pavlik 2001; Anderson and Cornfield 2002). Michael Cornfield (2002), for instance, looked at the dynamic websites of political candidates as a mark of politicians' recognition that an ongoing address to the public was necessary for them to win their campaigns. By extension, this changed journalism's role in the process considerably.

At the same time, public discussions of sourcing practices became markedly more critical. Terms like "feeding frenzy," "attack journalism," and "the boys in the bush" filled public conversations about the linkages between the journalistic and political worlds, as scholars sought to explain why journalists covered events "intensely, often excessively, and sometimes uncontrollably" (Sabato 1991: 6). In fact, Larry Sabato listed a string of adjectives that were typically appended to journalism in public discussions of how well it fulfilled its public mission. The adjectives were graphic: bloodsport, cheap-shot, gotcha, hit-and-run, keyhole, paparazzi, jugular, trash, voyeur (Sabato 1991: 2). The fact that none were complimentary suggested that at some level assumptions about the demeanor of the reporter-source connection—that is, *how* journalists secured their information—fueled the more intense reactions that members of the public tended to have about journalism's broader public role.

Scholarship on journalists' sourcing practices offset the naïve notion that the power of journalists was limitless. It positioned them within an identifiable set of interactions with people in other worlds, and it positioned journalism in the context of other institutions. While certain scholarship focused on one kind of source—the government press officer (Hess 1984) or the Congressional reporter (Blanchard 1974)—other work focused on the patterning implicit in the balancing act between source and reporter. This link between reporter and official drew academic attention because it appeared to embody many larger concerns about how journalism in a democracy worked, rendering both journalistic and political bureaucracies personal, concrete, and understandable. Because the exchange of information implicit in sourcing was also dependent on a given exchange relationship, the work here was comprehensible while suggesting a broader need for the contextualization by which sourcing occurred. Excluded from analysis, however, were the informal locales for sourcing (such as informal networking or clubs), as well as the simultaneous pack practices that produced other relevant interactions, such as those between reporters and editors.

Journalistic Models and Roles

In light of the normative setting in which much of political science inquiry into journalism took shape, it is not surprising that a substantial proportion of scholarship developed prototypes of the link between journalistic and political worlds. In some cases, these took the form of models, or abstractions of how the intersection of journalism and politics might look in a controlled environment. In other cases, scholars focused on roles, or prescriptive abstractions of particular kinds of journalistic behavior.

Modeled here was the tenor of the intersection expected when journalists encountered the political world in different kinds of political systems. Schudson (1999), borrowing from U.S. history, discussed three models of journalism in democratic systems—the market model (in which journalists gave the public what it wanted), the advocacy model (in which journalists transmitted political party perspectives), and the trustee model (in which journalists provided the news citizens needed to be informed participants in democracy). Elsewhere, a model of dissociation between the press and politicians was suggested (McQuail, Graber, and Norris 1998), while scholars argued for recognition of the "journalism of opinion" prevalent in France, Italy, the United Kingdom, and Latin America (Mancini 1992; Chalaby 1998; Waisbord 2000). Competing impulses within one kind of political system were often tracked, as in the parallel development of two democratic news models—politicized and objective: the former, common in Northern European nations, saw news as "politicized on behalf of competing parties" and dependent on an engaged and ideologically committed public; the latter, common in the United States, depended on audience interest and attention to survive (McQuail et al. 1998: 252). Journalism students were found to aspire to three models of journalism—journalism to enlighten, to wield power, and to entertain (Splichal and Sparks 1994). Developmental journalism, a model of practices set in place to address the needs surrounding the media in developing nation-states, critiqued the values and standards of traditional journalism. By focusing directly on community and the journalist's role in activating a sense of collectivity, proponents of developmental journalism saw themselves promoting a type of journalism that was fundamentally different from Western models of news making (Gunaratne 1998). "Asian values," an authoritarian and paternalistic approach to journalism across Asia and Southeast Asia, gained currency over the last decade or so to describe a set of journalistic practices, now prevalent primarily in Singapore and Malaysia, that in earlier years characterized much journalism in the region (Gunaratne 2000). Culled from a debate over Asian values that set out to explain the circumstances of Asian economic success, journalism adhering to Asian values was seen among its promoters as upholding a deference to order and authority, the twinning of press freedom and responsibility, and the privileging of national interests over individual ones, in which journalism was harnessed to aims of national betterment (Xu 1998). Critics argued that the fundamentally authoritarian nature of such news work precluded the practice of effective journalism (Masterton 1996; Lee 2001).

Scholars sought to describe models of journalistic practice that reflected particular local circumstances, such as "the jihad model of journalism," a name coined over journalists' response to Islam (Karim 2000: 158). In Latin America, despite a historical absence of muckraking, journalists developed their own version of watchdog journalism, which forced a new moral and political role on Latin American journalists (Waisbord 2000). Journalists seeking to authoritatively cover Latin America were advised to come to grips with local realities, like the *gacetilla* (roughly, "reading notice," the Mexican version of political advertisements) (Benavides 2000) or the concept of *mestizaje* (roughly, "hybridity") as a way of claiming identity across the region (Martin-Barbero 1993). In Africa, journalists were counseled to consider *ubuntu* (roughly, "humanness" or "collective responsibility") in covering African society and culture (Blankenberg 1999; also Scannell 2002). Journalists in Asia operated in an environment guided by wide-ranging Orientalist behaviors, including Confucianism, Buddhism, fortune telling, and face-saving practices (Ramanathan and Servaes 1997; Servaes 2000; Sim 2000). Zhao (1998) discussed the particularities of party journalism in China, arguing that journalists experienced more autonomy in practice than theoretical discussions of the media's role in Communism suggested.

Related work focused on the establishment of journalistic roles. Following the groundbreaking study by Bernard Cohen (1963), one of the first scholars to establish a typology that separated the "neutral" role from the "participant" role, and early work in sociology (e.g., Janowitz 1975), the notion of roles offered a valuable way to think about the journalist's positioning in the broader political environment. In that regard, political science inquiry into journalism often offered abstract prescriptions by which a journalist could be both a reporter and a citizen, and how to best accommodate the political tensions, interests, and agendas encountered while doing work as a journalist was constructed here as an ongoing problem.

Following that line of reasoning, a number of ongoing surveys and overviews of journalists, particularly in the United States, applied revised versions of Cohen's early distinctions between types of journalists to new periods and contexts (e.g., Johnstone et al. 1976; Weaver and Wilhoit 1986, 1996). Renata Kocher (1986) contrasted the roles exemplified by journalistic work in the United Kingdom and in Germany. Thomas Patterson (1998;

also Patterson and Donsbach 1996), working with European scholars Wolfgang Donsbach, Paolo Mancini, Jay Blumler, and Kent Asp, elaborated the conceptionalization of roles by examining how the degree of attachment to ideological or partisan interests differed across journalists in five nation-states. Querying the degree of partisanship, objectivity, and critical perspective among journalists, their survey of 1,300 journalists found that those in Western societies generally showed a tendency toward a more active journalistic political role, though differences remained regarding the journalist's positioning as a political actor. However, the selection of countries in the survey—all advanced industrialized democracies—left unexamined the ways in which the journalistic-political relationship differed in emerging democracies and in nondemocratic regimes.

By contrast, other research extensively examined journalistic roles across Eastern Europe, particularly in the post-Soviet era. A Glasnost Defense Foundation survey of 1,200 journalists in Russia's regional newspapers and television found complex relations in the intersection of the journalistic and political worlds, with news often paid for by political organizations (Glasnost Defense Foundation 1995). Ellen Mickiewicz (1997, 1998) showed how the post-Soviet transitions to the new political systems of Eastern Europe forced a rethinking of old journalistic practices and norms. In her words,

> for countries shedding an authoritarian past, in contrast to longtime democracies, objectivity in news reporting may be understood differently. Subjectively reported news was for many the first bold step toward accurate coverage and an alternate meaning to the state-dominated message. (Mickiewicz 1998: 52)

Other work focused on the nuances and problematics of being political or not among journalists in East Germany (Boyle 1992), Russia (McNair 1991; Mickiewicz 1997), Poland (Curry 1990), the Czech and Slovak republics (Wilson 1994), and across the entire Central and Eastern European landscape (Splichal 1994; Paletz, Jakubowicz, and Novosel 1995; Downing 1996). Karol Jakubowicz (1995) found that journalists in Poland were as driven by private publishers in the post-Communist era as they had been by party commissars while under Soviet domination.

Still other research focused on Latin America (Fox 1988; Skidmore 1993). Michael Salwen and Bruce Garrison (1991) examined how the routine work of journalists was impacted by unstable economic and political conditions, on the one hand, and by quasi-governmental organizations such as hit squads and terrorist organizations, on the other. Juan Corradi, Patricia Fagen, and Manuel Garreton (1992) addressed the problem of living under authoritarian rule and the way in which fear infiltrated all public dealings.

Silvio Waisbord (2000) traced how watchdog journalism had evolved as a response to the peculiarities of the Latin American political world.

* * * * *

In much of this work, an emphasis on how journalists both did accommodate the broader political environment and could accommodate it better was uppermost. Alongside substantial considerations of the small-scale practices by which journalists negotiated their ways in and out of the political world was a persistent trajectory that propelled many of these discussions toward a more optimum operation of journalism. In that regard, those aspects of the journalistic-political intersection which obstructed that functioning were often codified here as problematic.

Political Science and Mid-Scale Journalistic Practices

Other work on the political dimensions of journalism was represented by an array of mid-scale journalistic practices, seen here through their impact on the polity and the political process. Work in this vein again remained primarily normative, though a critical subset offered alternative glimpses of the intersection of journalism and politics. Both normative approaches to journalism and their normative-critical subset of research stayed close to the abstract elucidation of problems that obstructed the political effectiveness of news.

Relevant here was a large area of scholarship dealing with freedom of expression. In the United States, this work was associated with First Amendment issues and effectively used many premises of political science inquiry on journalism to address norms of free expression and the press (Mill 1859; Lippmann 1925; Chafee 1941; Allen and Jensen 1995; Hensley 2001; Baker 2002, Magee 2002). Elsewhere, the issue of freedom of expression was woven into broader discussions of democracy, and freedom of the press was seen as a main safeguard of the civil liberties associated with freedom of expression. Often associated with the free flow of information in developing nation-states, the role of journalism in these circumstances was seen as integral to the effective functioning of democracy. As such, much of the nurturing and maintenance of freedom of expression issues was addressed by journalists and journalist-supported organizations, which through their institutional presence attempted to redress violations of freedom of expression issues around the world.

Unarticulated but central here was the notion that the press could exist as a vehicle not intended for party advantage and political propaganda.

This primarily U.S. version of the press-politics linkage was not supported in much of Western, Central, or Eastern Europe, in Latin America, or in other locations in which political parties received public funding. However, it persisted as the default setting against which to think about mid-scale journalistic practice from a political science perspective.

Normative Scholarship on Mid-Scale Practices

A number of premises underpinned the normative discussion of mid-scale journalistic practices, which applied a concern with the journalist's optimum functioning in the political environment to discussions of the environment itself. The triumvirate of press, public, and polity was uppermost here, as discussions broadened from the concrete behavior of journalists to the broader impact and influence of that behavior. Most of these discussions took place under the rubric of democratic systems of government, either established or emerging. As articulated by Doris Graber, Denis McQuail, and Pippa Norris (1998: 1), this was worth thinking about because "the public policy agenda—what happens in political life—is influenced by the news media." Journalists were thus expected to adhere to certain rules of behavior, be free from political coercion, and have credible evidence to support their stories. The choice of acting as an impartial observer of the political world, as an advocate of certain interests, or as a watchdog requiring performance evaluation was central here, with the implications of each alternative seen as centrally impacting the tenor of the surrounding democratic world.

In much the same way that the work on small-scale journalistic practices targeted the link between sources and journalists, here too much scholarship focused on the evolving ties of democratic and journalistic systems. Although the possibility of an inefficient linkage had been in early years associated with totalitarian regimes (e.g., Ellul 1965), by the early 1980s many scholars assumed that the growth of government and the media would alter the political process, arguing that a "media democracy" would alter the tenor of both settings. Journalism would take over the "vital functions of political parties and [move] into the center of the political system; and institutions and practices of politics and government [would adapt to] the central role of mass media, particularly television" (Pfetsch 1998: 70). In this scenario, media democracy was to be held accountable for both the deficits and disadvantages associated with mass politics and the consequent institutional, stylistic, and strategic changes they would bring. Different negative effects were thought to have resulted from the ascent of the so-called media democracy, including a decline in social trust (Putnam 2001), the undermining of effective politics

(Sabato 1991), and the strategized shaping of the information provided as news (Jamieson and Waldman 2002).

Much work in this vein sought to establish journalism's failure to ensure a viable democratic public life (Graber, 1984). In *News: The Politics of Illusion,* Lance Bennett (1988) argued that the news media failed to create the conditions necessary for people to participate in public life. Because three groups of actors—politicians, journalists, and the public—systematically created and used political information that was comprehensible and believable but not particularly useful for democracy and citizenship, the public remained a prisoner of the news cycle created by the other groups. In its best case scenario, then, journalism provided news that was fragmented, dramatic, personalized, and normalized, often in ways that chipped away at the full information thought necessary for citizens in a democracy.

A similar impulse was demonstrated in Robert Entman's *Democracy Without Citizens* (1989). Entman extended Bennett's criticism of journalism's failure to stimulate public life into an attack on its dependence on a market economy. He argued that U.S. market competition prevented journalists from supplying the kind of news that would nurture sophisticated citizenship, rendering the marketplace of ideas an unachievable goal. With journalists and self-interested elites competing for control of the news, U.S. elites exchanged minimal information for the maximum amount of positive coverage, and journalists extracted information for stories that generated acclaim from their superiors. This had woeful implications for U.S. democracy, where "people who participate regularly and knowledgeably form a distinct minority" (Entman 1989: 28). The most important product of news was not ideas, but news, and the expectation that journalists could both be part of market driven, profit-oriented organizations and act as autonomous scribes of public life was unattainable, rendering untenable the notion of a marketplace of ideas nourished by economic competition.

Other scholars located additional nuances in the public's responses to the journalism-polity intersection. Samuel Popkin (1991), for instance, argued that the public was not as disadvantaged by journalism's offerings about the political world as other scholars had claimed. Russell Neuman, Marion Just, and Ann Crigler (1992) offered evidence to suggest that the public played a far more active role in interpreting the news than was typically assumed. They found that feelings of powerlessness often exacerbated public disinterest in national and international affairs and rendered public interest uneven in those same affairs.

How journalism affected democratic process also drew attention here, and scholars considered journalism's impact on agenda setting (Iyengar and Kinder 1987; Iyengar 1991; Brosius and Kepplinger 1992), on the shaping of the work and beliefs of elites (Lichter et al. 1986), and on the polity as a whole (Paletz and Entman 1982). Thomas Patterson (1993) argued that the contemporary press in effect hijacked campaigns from both the politicians and the public. In tracking public cynicism and apathy toward U.S. politics, Kathleen Hall Jamieson and Joseph Cappella (1997) held journalism responsible and suggested a revamping of journalistic routines of coverage so as to energize public attitudes toward the polity. Doris Graber, Denis McQuail, and Pippa Norris (1998) considered the shaping of news as an intermediary between politicians and the public, while Michael Janeway (2001) surveyed the long-standing complaint that the news media contributed to a loss of public faith in American political institutions. Timothy Cook (1998) claimed that the news media had in effect become a bona fide political institution, integral to government's daily political functioning. In *The Press Effect* (2002), Kathleen Hall Jamieson and Paul Waldman argued that the U.S. press failed the public during the 2000 to 2002 time period. Claiming that journalists adopted frames to fill roles they felt the public wanted, Jamieson and Waldman saw less than exemplary coverage—of the 2000 election, of the Supreme Court follow-up to that election, and of the governmental response to September 11, 2001—as a reflection of journalism's limitations. In surveying journalism's role in peace negotiations in the Middle East and Northern Ireland, Gadi Wolfsfeld (2003) found that the news values of journalists and the nature of peace negotiations worked oppositionally, making it difficult for journalists to play an effective role in the peace process.

Of central importance here were numerous, large-scale analyses of election campaigns. Loosely grouped as the "election studies," these works were critical in establishing valuable data about the public's electoral preferences, behavior, and attitudes, and studies of the electoral process were elaborated by the establishment of institutional settings whose intent was to track elections over the years. In the United States, the NES (National Election Studies) time series involved 23 sites conducting surveys of presidential and midterm election years. Begun at the University of Michigan in the 1950s and supported by the National Science Foundation from the 1970s onward, the NES compiled wide-ranging data on issues such as expectations of the electoral process, interest in campaigns, and assessment of political values. The BGES (British General Election Study) tracked how and why people voted from 1964 onward (e.g., Butler and Stokes 1969; Evans and Norris 1999). In Europe, under the initial aegis of scholars like Jay Blumler, Jean-Jacques Rabier, Karlheinz Reif, and Hermann Schmitt, EES (European Election Studies) took the form of surveys, campaign analyses, and analyses of the role of the media (Reiff and Shmitt 1980; Blumler 1983; Reiff 1985). Over the next 30 years, the group broadened, including numerous scholars from Baltic and Central Europe, who analyzed the broad picture of public electoral involvement (e.g., Schmitt and Thomassen 1999, 2000; Perrinau, Grunberg, and Ysmal 2002), and other independent efforts were taken by members of the group, such as the influential study conducted by Jay Blumler, Roland Cayrol, and Michel Thoveron (1978) in France. Other groups also evolved; under the title "Democracy in the Western Hemisphere—Election Studies," other scholars affiliated with the privately funded Center for Strategic and International Studies to track electoral preferences and behaviors in Latin America (e.g., Grayson 1994). Centered in Germany during the early 1990s, the Fritz Thyssen Foundation tracked electoral processes in 13 emerging democracies across Eastern Europe. By 2000, scholars engaged in studying elections began to query whether or not the studies had reached the limit of the useful questions they could ask (Franklin and Wlezien 2002).

Although there was little work offering a comparative view of how normative practices might differ according to the broader political environment, certain scholars made headway in that direction. Akiba Cohen and his colleagues (Cohen 1987; Cohen, Levy, Roeh, and Gurevitch 1996) and Thomas Patterson (1998) tracked the implications of broad-ranging global news practices on local populations in different nation-states. In Israel, Gadi Wolfsfeld (1997) offered a comparative view of the Israeli news media across different kinds of political events—demonstrations, protests, war, and acts of terror—while Cohen and Wolfsfeld (1993) tracked the media involved in covering the Palestinian Intifada.

Normative-Critical Scholarship on Mid-Scale Practices

Yet other political science researchers were less wedded to the normative implications of their research, though they were still driven by a broad, primarily abstract interest in journalism's effective functioning. These researchers focused critically on the gaps between the state of journalism as it tried to be and the state of things as they were, and in so doing they provided an inventory of those aspects of journalism that did not measure up to the standard they anticipated.

Key here was the work of Jurgen Habermas (1989), whose notion of the public sphere complicated long-standing notions about how journalism served its public. Seeing news and conversation as elements necessary for democracy, Habermas reacted against technocratic rationality in arguing to reposition the public within the framework of a community (Dahlgren and Sparks 1991: 16). Describing 18th-century England, in which the public sphere mediated between society and the state, and the public, with the help of journalists, organized itself as an arbiter of public opinion, Habermas lamented that such was no longer the case. Instead, journalism could not effectively generate rational public opinion because its intertwining with advertising, entertainment, and public relations mixed those realms into public opinion's development. Other circumstances then present—such as the infrastructure for social communication evidenced by libraries, the press, and publishing houses, as well as by places for social engagement (e.g., coffeehouses, the theater, and libraries)—could no longer be counted on to help develop the opportunity for reasoned public discussion. And without reasoned public discussion, people could no longer impact government by articulating their views (Habermas 1989).

Other scholars interested in journalism's role enthusiastically took up the mantle suggested by Habermas. The spirit of discussion and dissent that he raised were seen as crucial to democracy (Poster 1995), and scholars began to rethink journalism's role in light of Habermas's public sphere, with his views becoming the anchor of critical debates about journalistic performance (Garnham 1986; Tiffen 1990; Keane 1991; Glasser and Salmon 1995). For while he idealized the purist form of the public sphere in earlier days, he also argued that it was downgraded during the 19th century when the press reflected the economic interests of the state rather than the informational needs of the public. Habermas's views took on increased relevance with the ascent of online journalism and the space for public discussion provided by blogs, listservs, and other internet forms of journalistic relay. In France, for instance, the work of Dominique Wolton and Jean-Louis Missika (1983) was instrumental in creating a regard for television as a setting that created the conditions for Habermas's notion of a public sphere, thereby offsetting long-standing lamentations about its eradication. In Erik Neveu's view (1998), the birth of the French media journal *Hermes* was largely related to the stream of research that developed along these lines. Over time, however, the abstract nature of Habermas's views made them difficult to apply to journalism in concrete ways, and certain scholars revised their evaluations, calling his notion of the public sphere "little more than an idealized reminder that we have an unsolved problem on our hands" (Katz 1996: 3).

While the triumvirate of press, public, and polity central to normative research here too provided an analytical cornerstone, each of these terms was complicated by the scholars invoking it. For instance, in his discussion of journalism in Russia, Poland, and Hungary, John Downing (1996) elaborated on how the lexical and semantic imprecision underpinning the central terms of "civil society" and "the public sphere" rendered the application of political science concepts in these nation-states difficult. More broadly, one needed to think only of how often over time terms like "the public" and "the polity" were placed between quotation marks to arrive at a similar conclusion. The borders across these terms were also seen as permeable and ever changing. To quote James Carey (1999: 53), the "press, public and politics mutually constitute one another; they create spaces and roles in relation to one another, and, when any of the parties opts out of the symbiosis, it necessarily breaks up."

And yet, this normative-critical research was opportunely positioned to level a sustained critique of the environment of influence created by the politics-journalism linkage. Daniel Hallin (1986, 1994) produced wide-ranging research that, in borrowing from both political science inquiry and the sociological study of journalism, injected critical nuances into existing understandings of how journalism and politics were entwined. In *The Uncensored War: The Media and Vietnam* (1986), he rejected the claims that the living room war constituted a graphic daily portrayal of violence and that television was consistently negative toward U.S policy, thereby offsetting the common understanding of TV's so-called negative role in covering Vietnam. Studying journalistic coverage over nearly a 10-year period during the war, he showed a significant degree of interdependence between journalism and the political system, and he argued that television was initially patriotic in its war coverage and only shifted as the political climate shifted. Using earlier work on sourcing practices and the sociology of news production, Hallin's study was important in that it used internally studied premises about journalism to examine popular understandings of an event that went beyond journalism's own parameters.

Hallin forged similar pathways in later scholarship. In *We Keep America On Top of the World* (1994), he invoked the broader notion that modern societies—particularly liberal capitalist ones—distorted political dialogue, and he showed how journalism took technical knowledge as its model for reporting news in a way that muted public participation in the news. The professionalization of news narrowed the nature of political discourse, undermining the long-held expectation that journalism would act as a mid-wife to the birth of a new political order. With Paolo Mancini, Hallin tracked the ways in which U.S. and Italian reporters portrayed presidential elections on television differently (Hallin and Mancini 1984), and elsewhere (Hallin 1992) he lamented the passing of the high modernism of American journalism, during which journalists were able to smooth over the contradictory dimensions of their profession. No longer simultaneously powerful and prosperous, independent and public spirited, contemporary journalists lacked both political consensus and economic security, and they were increasingly called on to fill a vacuum left open by other key institutions of debate and interpretation, such as the presidency or the political parties. In later years, Hallin and Mancini (in press) compared the strain toward homogenization across global media in different nation-states, arguing that the public sphere simultaneously became more open due to the eradication of political limitations in certain regions and less open due to the constraints imposed by the ascent of commercial imperatives.

Other normative-critical work on the mid-scale practices of journalists exhibited a similarly broad evaluative tone. In *Journalism and Democracy* (McNair 2000a) and in a subsequent summary article on the state of journalism and democracy (McNair 2000b), Brian McNair took a more positive tack in suggesting that ongoing changes in both the journalistic and political worlds necessitated a more optimistic appraisal of their relationship. Arguing against what he saw as overextended expectations of contemporary journalism, he contended that journalism had improved its linkage with the public over the generations of contact. He suggested that by broadening one's field of vision—to the different kinds of journalisms, to the counterspin developed in response to spin doctors, to the difficulties of maintaining impartiality in a commentary-driven culture—one could see that journalism's role in connecting with the public was less dire than was usually assumed.

As globalization made its way into the everyday realities of journalism, a substantial amount of critical work focusing on the political-journalistic intersection turned discussions toward the jockeying of nation-states for power and journalism's role in that jockeying. Focusing on Russia, Poland, and Hungary, John Downing (1996) argued that complex issues like secrecy and surveillance complicated the functioning of the news media in unanticipated ways in the post-Soviet era. Monroe Price (1995, 2002) provided a detailed analysis of journalistic autonomy in the United States and Eastern and Western Europe—both alongside television's regulation and with regard to the more far-reaching policy imperatives that accompanied globalization. Others (e.g., Mohammadi 1997; Sreberny-Mohammadi, Winseck, McKenna, and Boyd-Barrett 1997) offered detailed views of how globalization affected journalism and politics in a variety of regions, including Asia, Europe, the Middle East, and Latin America.

Scholarship on Public Journalism

Many criticisms leveled at journalism by scholars investigating mid-scale journalistic practices over the past decade were channeled in the United States into a redefinition of journalism and journalistic practice on behalf of the public. Commonly called public or civic journalism, this branch of scholarship evolved from a sense of public despair with the news media following the U.S. political campaigns of the mid-1980s. Providing a way to argue for an alternative mode of journalistic practice, public journalism was seen as attending to the public as much as to the journalists who practiced it. Called alternately an argument, an experiment, a movement, a debate, and an adventure, public journalism, argued lead scholar Jay Rosen (1994, 1999), offered a way to reinvigorate a tired set of journalistic practices and at the same time provided the public with a way to become involved in news making. Although the public journalism movement in the United States had parallels with the Third Way in the United Kingdom, the development of the former rendered it singularly different from the latter and reflective of what Michael Schudson (1999) called a conservative reform movement, shaped in the tradition of social reforms in the United States during the Progressive Era.

The movement to reinvigorate U.S. journalism's linkage to its public evolved from a general sense, to paraphrase James Carey, that "the public" was the god-term, or legitimating notion, of journalism (Carey 1995). If journalism were grounded in anything, it was in the public, yet there existed ambivalence over who, what, and where the public was. Moreover, there was need for a new form of public community life, by which journalists and the public would come together in a newly spirited communal belonging.

Seen as a variant on the model of trustee journalism (Rosen 1996; Schudson 1999), public journalism, with its emergent characteristics, was outlined in numerous treatises (Charity 1995; Rosen 1996, 1999). Even work not written explicitly in the name of public journalism but following its tenets (Fallows 1996) helped set in place a number of premises for thinking differently about how journalism might better serve the public. Such premises included a journalistic willingness to break with old routines, a desire to "reconnect" with citizens, an emphasis on serious discussions as the foundation of politics, and a focus on citizens as actors rather than spectators (Rosen 1996; Merritt 1995). Public journalism was defined as journalism for the public, with Arthur Charity (1995: 2) calling it a journalism that would "make it as easy as possible for citizens to make intelligent decisions about public affairs."

In that it explicitly articulated many normative premises upon which political science's inquiry into journalism had been initiated, public journalism drew the attention of those scholars interested in journalism's political role. Called "a clear step in the right direction" (Cook 1998: 176), it was largely seen as a "well-intentioned attempt to reduce the sensationalism and blatant political manipulation of mainstream journalism" (McChesney 1999: 300). Furthermore, its ideals struck a chord elsewhere in the world. Likening it to the developmental journalism common in developing nations,

Shelton Gunaratne (1998) argued that both kinds of journalism drew from and toward the community in facilitating the adoption by journalists of more active roles to support social change. As recently as 1999, the proposed New World Information and Communication Order (NWICO) was seen as stressing the kinds of models of coordinated civic action for development journalists, which led scholars to characterize it as dependent on "a network of networks based in civil society" (Vincent, Nordenstreng, and Traber 1999: x; also Pauly 1999a).

But public journalism also met with criticism. Theodore L. Glasser and Stephanie Craft (1998) argued for a modification of some of public journalism's key tenets. In the edited collection *The Idea of Public Journalism* (Glasser 1999), a number of scholars decried what they saw as an insufficient degree of attention being paid to the realization of public journalism. John Peters (1999) and Michael Schudson (1999) both contended that the notions of "democracy" and "public" as supported by public journalism were difficult to achieve. John Pauly (1999b) pondered the (im)possibilities of journalism becoming a democractic institution, while Barbie Zelizer (1999) argued that public journalists neglected a slew of "neighbors"—journalism history, other kinds of journalism, the public, and the politicians—in crafting their movement into action. Tanni Haas and Linda Steiner (2001) contended that in the rush to popularize the movement, public journalism was never sufficiently theorized, consequently stymieing attempts to practice, defend, and evaluate its practices.

Nonetheless, the attention that public journalism drew suggested that it struck a chord, that it focused attention on what was in need of resolution about contemporary journalistic practices. It may be that the normative impulse embodied by political science remained securely at the core of much thinking about journalistic practice, and in this regard, public journalism attended to as many unresolved issues about inquiry into journalism as about journalistic practice.

Much of the mid-scale research on journalism was driven by the concern, characteristic of political science inquiry into journalism, to set things right—in the polity, among and for the public, and with journalism. The issue that remained at the end of the day, however, was an old one, which was articulated early in the last century by Walter Lippmann: "The problem of the press is confused because the critics and the apologists expect the press to . . . make up for all that was not foreseen in the theory of democracy" (Lippman 1922/1960: 31–32). Whose welfare was being addressed by focusing on the triumvirate of the press, public, and the polity remained, despite much well-intentioned scholarship, as unclear as in the early days of political science's inquiry into journalism.

Political Science and Large-Scale Journalistic Systems

Journalism's large-scale relationship with the surrounding political system became a part of journalism's study in the immediate aftermath of World War II, when questions arose in the United States concerning how journalism could best attend to the vagaries and power of fascist governments. With the proximate impact of the war, scholars became invested in figuring out what would be the optimum shape of the relationship between government and journalism in democratic environments.

Typologies of Interaction

One of the most prevalent types of large-scale studies of politics and journalism involved crafting so-called typologies of the linkage between the two domains. In many cases, these efforts were seen as a way to delineate the ideal linkage in keeping with larger normative impulses.

The first attempt to delineate the optimum functioning of the news media was a much-heralded attempt of three individuals who had themselves been central in developing journalism as an academic field—Frank Siebert, Theodore Peterson, and Wilbur Schramm. Their book, *Four Theories of the Press* (1956), met with enthusiastic acclaim from the moment of its initial publication. The book, one of the classics in journalism research that was set in place in Peterson's words "by accident" (quoted in Merrill and Nerone 2002: 134), argued that the media took on the form of the surrounding social and political structures within which they operated. In reflecting the larger system of social control, media systems were thereby explained ultimately through the basic beliefs of the surrounding political environment, and understanding the distinction between media systems ultimately became an issue of philosophical and political difference.

Siebert, Peterson, and Schramm classified news media systems in accordance with the dominant political governance. On this basis, they argued for four basic theories of the press: an authoritarian approach, in which absolute power of the monarch restricted media use by royal patent; a libertarian approach, in which a general philosophy of rationalism and natural rights (developed from the writings of Locke, Milton, and Mill) expected the news media to uphold a self-righting process of truth and a free marketplace of ideas; a Soviet-totalitarian theory, in which journalism was controlled through surveillance implemented in accordance with Marxist thought; and a social responsibility theory, which evaluated journalism in conjunction with professional ethics, community opinion, and the ability to air conflict.

The news media's functioning changed in accordance with the variable features of the political system alongside it.

Four Theories of the Press constituted a landmark study whose primary value was delineating the features thought to connect journalism with its political environment. These included patterns of regulation, ownership, censorship, and licensing. In so doing, it laid out certain relevant features to consider when theoretically situating journalism in the larger world. At the same time, the models it offered assumed more of a distinction between worldviews than was actually the case. As Denis McQuail (1987: 110) saw it, most media systems were in fact applications "of different (even inconsistent) elements from different theories." Even in democratic systems, the appearance of press controls, licensing of printers, and discouragement of press opposition aligned themselves with the authoritarian model. In addition, the approach's dependence on a stable and static notion of what a political system could be necessitated its continued updating. John Merrill and John Nerone (2002: 135) argued that although the book was readable and dared to "talk confidently about big issues," it was profoundly ideological rather than scientific, optimistic rather than realistic, and affected unilaterally by World War II and its aftermath. The book's strong appeal, then, was also its shortcoming, in that its confidence and unidimensional approach to large issues somewhat shortcircuited its applicability to even slightly divergent circumstances.

Not surprisingly, the book ushered in a long string of applied studies, which took its basic ideas and applied them to an increasing number and range of political systems. The journalism of developing nations posed a particular challenge to the theories of the press, in that none of the theories adequately addressed the role of journalism in shaping and facilitating development. Called a "triangular interaction of news, communication and community" (Gunaratne 1998: 301), development journalism followed the work of Daniel Lerner (1958) and Lucian Pye (1963) in examining those situations in which journalism operated outside of government-press relations as envisioned in democratic, capitalist, industrial societies. On the premise that the four theories were limited in their applicability to developing nations, a developmental theory of journalism was established following premises set forth in UNESCO's MacBride Report (International Commission for the Study of Communication Problems 1980). The application of the model, however, required substantial elaboration in developing countries. Not only did it uncritically call for the media's active role in national development through grass-roots involvement, but, in McQuail's (1987: 110) view, it did so without the conditions necessary for a developed mass communication system—such as professional skills or a communicative infrastructure—and where instead there existed a dependence on the developed world for missing technology or skills. Additional applications tried to more effectively address the needs of developing nations: Herbert Altschull (1984) argued for three forms of the press—First World, or the "market" journalism of liberal-capitalist nations; Second World, or the "Marxist" journalism of Soviet-socialist nations; and Third World, or the "advancing" journalism of developing nations. These different combinations referred loosely to a mixture of libertarian and social responsibility in the first instance, to the totalitarian model in the second, and to development theory in the third. However, as East-West conflicts gave way to North-South tensions, the relevance of a model for developing nations became problematic because it assumed different premises about the power linkage across different regions and political systems than those adopted by the more long-standing models of journalistic practice.

Other applications of *Four Theories of the Press* involved recombining attributes of the different theories into other contemporary applications. One such attempt included relabeling the libertarian approach "free press theory" (Rivers, Schramm, and Christians 1980; Curran and Seaton 1985), which basically argued that the freedom to publish was an extension of other fundamental rights—of assembly, opinion, and expression. Another attempt involved combining elements of libertarianism and socialism to create the democratic participant media theory, also called the democratic socialist theory (McQuail 1987). This application addressed the value of horizontal communication and an active receiver in an open political society, and positioned itself against commercialization and the mono-polization of privately owned media, centralism, and bureaucratization of public broadcasting institutions, arguing for the right to use interactive media and access relevant information (McQuail 1987). Yet another approach was the "revolutionary model of the press" (Hachten 1981), in which the press was seen as overthrowing the system in power. James Curran (1991) argued for distinguishing among liberal, Marxist, and Communist radical democratic theories of the press.

It is not surprising that these theories of the press, in all of their evolving formulations, generated a steady stream of discourse, both for and against their applicability. Karol Jakubowicz (1998/99) accused the theories of impos-ing a "straight-jacket on the world's media." Kaarle Nordenstreng (1997) called for a distinction between normative theories and those that described the actual practices of media systems. In one of the most prevailing critiques, Denis McQuail (1987) contended that the evaluation criteria applied to the theories were both general and positioned differently across the different mod-els: The criteria involved issues of freedom and equality (usually measured by the degree of control exercised by owners and managers over high-level com-municators, such as editors, and by them over subordinates), issues of order and solidarity (the integration of society and its component groups, as forged from below by individuals), issues of diversity and access (seen as a goal of journalism and often measured by the number of separate independent media), and issues of objectivity and information quality (as correlates of journalistic independence). These issues became points of argument in each typology's discussion of press and media ownership, diversity of opinion and access to information, and transnational operations and political sovereignty.

One more recent discussion of the *Four Theories of the Press—Last Rights: Revisiting the Four Theories of the Press* (1995), edited by John Nerone and written by present and former academics from the University of Illinois, where the first book originated—provided a tracking of the long trajectory of the work and addressed its centrality to much contemporary thought on large-scale journalistic practices. The authors praised the volume for both its curricular centrality and its effectiveness in helping scholars address the contradictions of classical liberalism. At the same time, they argued that the original volume spoke to a world beset by a no longer existent cold war and noted that its invocation of liberal premises had caused it to ask the wrong constitutive questions from the onset: "It seemed to succeed in mapping *all* the normative theories because it mapped them from just one" (Nerone 1995: 184).

Following the lead established by *Four Theories of the Press*, each of the typologies discussed above bore the strengths and weaknesses of typologies in general. At best partial in their examination of the phenomenon at hand and directly dependent on the assumption of an identifiable inter-action between the journalistic and political worlds, these typologies were valuable in that they charted comparisons among different members of a given category, in this case the press in differing political systems. By the same token, however, the comparative dimension so prevalent here simpli-fied the nuances and complexities evident within each member of the cate-gory being examined. Journalism was envisioned solely as an intersection with the political system, and the roles promoted here were not as much testable theories as descriptions of how press-government relations might be structured. In assuming identifiable interactions between the press and government, evidence was often reduced to only that which upheld expected interactions. In other words, typologies were better at offering comparisons than they were at examining each phenomenon being compared.

Politics, Journalism, and Language

The political science inquiry into journalism also promoted an additional area of study that by definition blended into other disciplinary fields, due to its interest in the language of politics and journalism. Specifically, this work emphasized journalism and its impact on political rhetoric and political language.

One arena of this scholarship originally came from a sustained interest in presidential speech making (e.g., Campbell and Jamieson 1990). Represented largely by rhetoric scholars like Kathleen Hall Jamieson and Roderick Hart, the emphasis was on wedding rhetorical criticism with political science. In that vein, in *Packaging the Presidency* (1984) Jamieson examined the history of the linkage of political advertising and news, arguing that political candidates needed advertising to convince the public of the value of their candidacies. In *The Sound of Leadership*, Hart (1987) traced the role of journalists in encouraging what he called the "soundbite culture" of American political leaders. In *Eloquence in an Electronic Age* (1988), Jamieson examined changes in the art of political speech making with the advent of radio and television, such as the shrinking of hour-long oratory to sound bites and television's ability to seduce audiences through visual eloquence.

Work on political narrative and storytelling also made inroads in political science's inquiry into journalism. In W. Lance Bennett and Murray Edelman's "Toward a New Political Narrative" (1985), the narrative paradigm was used as a way of understanding the nature of political news. Concerned with the kinds of narrative cycles that bred short-term optimism and long-term policy failures, they tracked the ideological implications of news reported as truth by arguing that narrative facilitated presenting ideological understandings as natural. Political narrative displayed an either-or character that posited producers and readers of news on one side of an ideological divide (rich vs. poor, south vs. north), and the complexities of political debate were simplified and cast in "mutually exclusive terms" (Bennett and Edelman 1985: 158). In this way, the continuity of the political system depended on the efficacy of persuasiveness of its journalistic narratives. Similarly, Edelman (1964, 1988) demonstrated that politics was a basically ambiguous text, inherently symbolic in nature, and that the news produced by journalists was constructed in line with particular beliefs about the political world. Bennett (1988) tracked the language biases of the news and the way in which strategic communication forced a certain kind of news relay. In *The Politics of Misinformation*, Edelman, Bennett, and Robert Entman (2001) considered how the deployment of power in society helped produce mediated language that was image based, simplistic, vague, emotional, and misleading, reneging on journalism's mission to the public to provide clear information about the polity.

Each of these studies examined journalism's mission with regard to the public, as expressed through journalism's production of language in the news, a mission stressed in political science inquiry into journalism (see Neveu 1999). Language here was seen as an embodiment of larger inequities in journalism's realization of its connection to the political world, and these researchers looked to the analysis of language as a way of highlighting those inequities.

* * * * *

What did political science establish about journalism that was different from what was offered by other disciplinary approaches? In its more traditional clothes, political science remained enchanted by journalism's big picture, though without the deterministic view that was common in some historical scholarship. In most cases, this big picture highlighted notions of distance and impartiality—the notion that journalists could be and should be impartial or at the least working for the good of the public—over attachment and opinion, and it presumed an ongoing, somewhat isolated, and largely symbiotic linkage between journalism and the political world. That linkage helped explain how journalism reported the world. In this regard, journalism was seen as a tool used to serve larger political ends; it was an indicator not only of itself but of the larger system that it either upheld or undermined.

The flip side of this point revealed a restriction of journalism to its intersection with politics. It is not surprising, then, that absent from the picture provided by political science were numerous dimensions of journalism that went beyond the connection between journalists, the public, and the polity. Largely missing were the texts per se of journalism and its history, the notion that journalists could be working for themselves, and the fact that journalists had their own communal ways of knowing.

It is important to note that the definitions on which political science depended in order to engage its own questions for scholarly inquiry were different in significant ways from those being advanced elsewhere in the academy. Attempts elsewhere to reconceptualize journalism and journalistic practice (e.g., Manoff and Schudson 1986; Carey 1997) challenged this body of inquiry on a number of foundational fronts, raising questions about the basis of political science's inquiry into the news. For instance, definitions of what counted as "political" in much of this research were narrow and usually restricted to hard news, despite the fact that a substantial literature outside of political science had established that other kinds of journalism— tabloid (Bird 1992), human interest (Hughes 1940), television magazine (Campbell 1991), online (Davis 1999)—helped orient the public to the world of politics. Definitions of what counted as "journalism" were also narrow, adopting journalism's professional sense of self as the lynchpin for many of the arguments developed. This meant that deriding journalism for a lack of impartiality or for a failure to serve the public were positions that drew from journalists' professional expectations of themselves more actively than they reflected the broad picture of how journalists operated.

The Future of Political Science Inquiry Into Journalism

The political science inquiry of journalism grows and recedes as a prospect with tangible implications for the world of news. Although the symbiotic link between journalism and politics can be seen to benefit the workings of certain kinds of political systems, the strains arising from changes in the contemporary links between the political and journalistic worlds suggest a possibly necessary reworking of certain tenets detailed here.

To extend upon the views of Denis McQuail, Doris Graber, and Pippa Norris, when considered from a political science perspective, journalism simply does not deliver what it promises. This has both positive and negative ramifications; in their words, "Whatever the aims or expectations of the news media, they never seem to inform adequately, at least not well enough to meet formal criteria of adequacy." Moreover, "what passes for news of politics is often an inextricable mixture of messages from. . . . advertising, public relations, reports of opinion polls, and propaganda." However journalists try to side step the negative effects of these other domains, "the news is inevitably tarred to some degree with the brush of manipulation" (McQuail, Graber, and Norris 1998: 253–254).

What this means is that existing ways of explaining how the political and journalistic worlds intersect may not have captured the entire picture of what journalism does, even if they have done a stellar job of portraying what it ought to be. Both modernist assumptions about how the media work and normative impulses about how they should work belie the basic notion that politics "more than ever appears to be a minority sport, not a uniquely compelling subject of interest for all"(McQuail, Graber, and Norris 1998: 255). At the very least, this calls for a closer examination of the relevance of the triumvirate terms of analysis in political science inquiry into journalism.

As with all disciplinary views, much of this research introduced its own biases into the descriptions of journalism it produced. It remained largely unpeopled. To borrow from John Downing, political science inquiry "is in serious danger of treating political actors as mute, albeit astute, pieces on a chessboard, and thus of producing a very curious abstraction from societal reality" (Downing 1996: 17). The focus here on the high echelons of power paid insufficient attention to oppositional and emergent political impulses. And despite forays into various parts of the world, this inquiry still remained primarily a U.S. affair, with the examination of other kinds of intersections of politics and journalism filtered largely through the U.S. experience.

7

Cultural Analysis
and Journalism

One of the most fertile arenas of journalistic inquiry has evolved in conjunction with the cultural analysis of journalism. Given a wide range of titles—including the collective knowledge journalists need to function as journalists (Park 1940), the "culturological" dimensions of the news (Schudson 1991), and the examination of "journalism as popular culture" (Dahlgren 1992)—this type of inquiry has produced a fruitful line of scholarship that links the untidy and textured *materiel* of journalism—its symbols, rituals, conventions, and stories—with the larger world in which journalism takes shape. The world of news, approached here as more than just reporters' professional codes of action or the social arrangements of reporters and editors, is viewed in the cultural analysis of journalism as a complex and multidimensional lattice of meanings for all those involved in journalism, "a tool kit of symbols, stories, rituals and world views, which people use in varying configurations to solve different kinds of problems" (Swidler 1986: 274).

Pronouncedly interdisciplinary and self-reflexive, the cultural inquiry of journalism employs diverse research perspectives and scholarly tools that are used to variously consider journalism broadly as a culture. "Culture" itself has many invocations, not all of them mutually exclusive. On the one

Author's Note: Parts of this chapter appear in the article "When Facts, Truth, and Reality Are God-Terms: On Journalism's Uneasy Place in Cultural Studies" in *Communication and Critical/Cultural Studies,* 1(1), March 2004, 100–119.

hand, it refers to a phenomenon of concerted action that uses conventional understandings to guide members of collectives in doing things in consensual ways. In this regard, culture is one of the resources journalists draw upon to coordinate their activities as reporters and editors. On the other hand, news itself is seen as cultural, ultimately relative to the givens of the groups and individuals engaged in its production.

Cultural inquiry addresses journalism by traversing an analytical track with two somewhat incompatible edges. It both sees journalism through journalists' own eyes, tracking how being part of the community comes to have meaning for them, and queries the self-presentations that journalists provide. Emphasizing "the constraining force of broad cultural symbol systems regardless of the details of organizational and occupational routines" (Schudson 1991: 143), the cultural analysis of journalism moves decidedly in tandem with but oppositionally to the pronounced and conventional understandings of how journalism works. Undercutting the pronounced sense of self that journalism professionals have long set forth regarding their practices and their position in the world, cultural inquiry assumes that journalists employ collective, often tacit knowledge to become members of the group and maintain their membership over time (see, e.g., Goodenough 1981), yet presumes that what is explicit and articulated as that knowledge may not reflect the whole picture of what journalism is and tries to be. Cultural inquiry thus travels the uneven road of reading journalism against its own grain while giving that grain extended attention.

Analysis here considers the meanings, symbols and symbolic systems, rituals, and conventions by which journalists maintain their cultural authority as spokespeople for events in the public domain. Work elsewhere in the academy—in philosophy, sociology, anthropology, and linguistics—helped legitimate an interest in culture as a lens through which to consider journalism. This was accompanied by the two strains of cultural studies—British and U.S.—which also helped create cultural focal points in journalism's study. In the United Kingdom, the blend of neo-Marxism, psychoanalysis, feminist studies, critical theory, literary theory, semiotics, and ethnography that constituted early British cultural studies complemented the interest in pragmatism, symbolic interactionism, cultural anthropology, and cultural sociology in the United States. While the broad analytical template these fields provided for studying journalism's cultural dimensions was certainly targeted in part by other disciplinary approaches to journalism, specific issues about journalism become critical from the perspective of cultural studies—its subjectivity of expression, the constructed nature of its meanings for events, the politics of its identity building, and the grounding of each of these premises in practice.

These tenets offer a wide-ranging analytical perspective that presumes journalism works differently from how it is understood to work in many of its more traditional academic approaches. First, cultural givens are thought to unite journalists in patterned ways with people who are not journalists yet are similarly involved in diverse modes of cultural argumentation, expression, representation, and production, suggesting as a starting-point commonalities rather than differences between journalists and others like filmmakers, poets, and politicians. Second, variables used elsewhere in the academy to keep the centers of journalism distinct from its margins— rendering, for instance, journalism distinct from fiction, mainstream journalism distinct from tabloid journalism, journalists' verbal reports distinct from the visual images they use—are here repositioned as bridges connecting differences, consequently presenting journalism as a whole of disparate, often self-contradictory impulses. The different tools of journalism, different kinds of journalism, and similarities between journalism and the world outside are brought together to illuminate the nuanced and textured character of journalism in all of its possibilities. And third, the cultural analysis of journalism views journalists not only as conveyors of information but also as producers of culture, who impart preference statements about what is good and bad, moral and amoral, and appropriate and inappropriate in the world. Their positioning as the creators and conveyors of views about how the world works is linked with the positionings of their audiences, who make sense of the news in ways that reflect their own identity politics.

It is no surprise, then, that this orientation facilitates the examination of facets of journalism that typically have not been examined in other scholarly perspectives. These include a worldview that underpins making sense of the world in certain ways, the inherent connections between form and content, the often strategic but always changing relation between "facts" and symbols, the ways in which journalists work themselves into the news they provide, and the uneven and often unpredictable function of images, collective memories, and journalistic stereotypes. Even journalists' vague renderings of how they know news when they see it take on a decidedly nuanced flavor when seen as part of the larger constraints of meanings and symbols available in the world. At the same time, those larger constraints do not figure into journalists' own presentations of self as much as do many of the categories of analysis employed by other disciplinary perspectives. This is because the insistence here on meaning making as a primary activity explicitly challenges two aspects of journalism's inquiry: the normative biases of much of existing journalism research and the professional notions of journalists themselves. By definition, a cultural consideration of journalism negates the worldview that underpins much of traditional journalism research, journalists' professional ideology, and the claim to exclusive status on which both are based.

The cultural inquiry into journalism creates and proceeds from its own strategic dissonance. Conventional givens about journalism are intentionally suspended, so as to address the practices, values, and attitudes that go beyond those deemed relevant by either existing journalism research or professional reporters. Cultural inquiry forces an examination of the tension between how journalism likes to see itself and how it looks in the eyes of others, while adopting a view of journalistic conventions, routines, and practices as dynamic and contingent on situational and historical circumstance.

All of this suggests that the cultural study of journalism strategically and pronouncedly interrogates the articulated foundations for journalism and journalistic practice that may be taken for granted elsewhere in the academy, offsetting the nearsightedness of journalism's inquiry. In Stuart Allan's words, cultural analysis moves beyond the presumption that journalism plays a "role everyone knows" of "afflicting the powerful . . . while comforting the afflicted" because it "severely limits . . . what sorts of questions can be asked about the news media in our society" (Allan 1999: 2–3). Dissipating the information bias that has taken entertainment and pleasure as information's opposite and broadening journalism beyond the particular loci in which it has traditionally been examined, in much of this research scholars work against the narrow, "metonymic" conception of journalism discussed by Peter Dahlgren (1992). In this regard, the cultural inquiry on journalism did much to keep journalism's study in step with some of the more contemporary developments in the news, which expanded without regard for the slower pace of change in journalism's study. Thus, seeing news and journalism through the lens of culture was valuable because it displayed a pronounced interest in the more recent transmutations by which people acted as journalists, including the internet, blogs, cybersalons, newsgroups, talk shows, and newzines.

Evolution of Cultural Inquiry Into News

An interest in the cultural dimensions of journalism was part of journalistic inquiry since its inception. Research on the sociology of culture in sociology, an interest in constructivism in philosophy, a turn in anthropology and folklore toward the analysis of symbols and symbolic forms, a move toward ethnography in linguistics, and growing scholarship in cultural history and cultural criticism all heightened interest in thinking about culture as an analytical locus. By extension, this broadened the template by which the cultural dimensions of journalism could be examined.

Interest in journalism's cultural sides was thus drawn from scholarship across the disciplines. In the United States, early work on American pragmatism (Dewey 1927/1954) and the symbolic side of collective life (Durkheim 1915/1965) helped create a focus on journalism's cultural dimensions by insisting on the collective codes of knowledge and the belief systems by which people made sense of the world. Among the most valuable scholarship for thinking about culture and journalism was the work of Robert Park (1925, 1940), who argued in the early days of the Chicago school of sociology for an examination of the collective codes of knowledge by which journalists typically structured their world. A former journalist, Park, whose interest in processes of social and cultural change came from his training at the University of Chicago, was instrumental in forwarding what he regarded as the journalistic knowledge necessary to developing a way of thinking about journalistic practice (Park 1940). Furthermore, believing that the journalistic techniques of observation and recording could be used as the foundation of academic inquiry, he helped set the ground for much of the qualitative inquiry that would later be used to address the mind-set of U.S. journalism. Developments in areas as diverse as humanistic sociology (Berger 1963; Wuthnow and Witten 1988), symbolic interactionism (Blumer 1969; Goffman 1974; Becker and McCall 1990), and cultural anthropology (Geertz 1973; Rabinow and Sullivan 1979) in different ways facilitated the recognition of culture as a way of understanding journalism. For instance, Clifford Geertz's regard for culture both as a frame of mind and as patterned conduct allowed for a simultaneous consideration of journalists' worldview and standards of action. Similarly, work in the sociology of culture moved scholars toward thinking about different kinds of cultural processes and cultural products (e.g., Becker 1984). Michael Schudson (1989), for instance, noted that the potency of a cultural product was determined by its rhetorical force, retrievability, resonance, institutional retention, and resolution, all of which came to play in the examination of journalism.

Elsewhere, particularly in the United Kingdom but also in Australia, Latin America, and other regions of the world, work in anthropology and sociology led the way to thinking about journalism as culture (e.g., Bocock 1974; Lukes 1975; Leach 1976; da Matta 1991). In addition, work on Marxism lent a pragmatic edge to journalism's study that, when paired with structuralism, forced a simultaneous consideration of its internal and external trappings. At the same time, work in cultural criticism (Williams 1978; Eagleton 1995) created a place in the academy for thinking critically about journalism's cultural dimensions.

Central to each of these efforts was a connection forged between the internal mind-sets about how the world worked and the external arrangements by which social life was set in place. Such a connection proved to have a demonstrative impact on contemporary thinking about journalism, in that it moved many scholars from supporting a long-held anthropological sense of culture as preceding people toward seeing it as a phenomenon also produced by people (Becker 1984). The application of this analytical lens by definition broadened journalism's study, in that it targeted journalism's cultural dimensions by accommodating its internal tensions. No longer was it necessary to maintain consonance with the actual and normative sides of what journalism was and what others wanted it to be.

This wide-ranging interest in journalism as culture and the recognition of the internal tensions involved in that perspective was in consonance with the work of Raymond Williams (1982). Williams argued for a tripartite view of culture, maintaining that it needed to be analyzed not only through its idealist side and its recorded or documentary side—or, put more simply, its aspired-to standards and the work that resulted from an application of those standards—but also through the social arrangements and circumstances by which the cultural settings were set in place. By definition, this turned inquiry simultaneously in the direction of journalistic texts, journalistic practices, and journalists themselves, seen here within their respective positioning as members of collectives.

Cultural Studies and Journalism

Perhaps nowhere in the academy was as much cultural interest paid journalism as by the two main strains of cultural studies scholarship, loosely connected to the U.S. and British experiences.[10]

On the U.S. side, journalism remained a fairly consistent area of inquiry. The invocation of early visionaries—John Dewey, Robert Park, and Thorsten Veblen, among others—led the way to the development of a strand of cultural studies concerned with problems of meaning, group identity, and social change (see Jensen and Pauly 1997). Largely fashioned as what came to be called the "Illinois strand of cultural studies," and led by James Carey at the University of Illinois, this school saw a resident evil in social science's positioning as the preferred mode of knowledge in the American academy, and it identified the critique of positivism as the charge for American cultural studies. Eschewing Marxism as the central problematic through which society was to be examined, the scholarship that developed here positioned the news media as conveyors of experience and shapers of broadly defined cultural systems. Within this arena of cultural studies, journalism emerged as a key strain of resonance for thinking about how culture worked.

Carey's work was central in that it wove discussions of journalism into the larger social and cultural fabric, including concerns about politics, technology, and the public. His argument for the recovery of journalism as a cultural form rather than as a profession was mounted in numerous contexts (1969, 1986, 2000), each of which demonstrated the complex nature of journalism's cultural world. In Carey's view, there was a dialogic and normative side to journalism's cultural life that

> required a mode of understanding actions and motives, not in terms of psychological dispositions or sociological conditions but as a manifestation of a basic cultural disposition to cast up experience in symbolic forms that are at once immediately pleasing and conceptually plausible, thus supplying the basis for felt identities and meaningfully apprehended realities. (Carey 1997a: 11)

Others at the University of Illinois followed in Carey's path. Albert Kreiling (1993), who had produced an important doctoral dissertation in the early 1970s, used the African-American press to address the shaping of middle class identities. Following the lead of Carey and Kreiling, a second generation of scholars, largely comprised of Carey's students—Joli Jensen (1990), Mary Mander (1983, 1987, 1998), Carolyn Marvin (1983, 1988, 1999), John Pauly (1988), Norman Sims (1990; Sims and Kramer 1995), and Linda Steiner (1992, 1998), among others—produced a substantial body of material emphasizing journalism's meaning-making capacities. That strain of cultural studies persists today, its tenets embodied particularly but not exclusively in the work of David Eason (1984, 1986), Richard Campbell (1991), S. Elizabeth Bird (1992), Thomas Connery (1992), and G. Stuart Adam (1993). At the same time, Michael Schudson (1978, 1995, 2002), coming from the sociology of culture, developed a parallel interest in the cultural domain of journalism, which was furthered by his students (e.g., Boyle 1992; Waisbord 2000).

On the British side, the interest in journalism was more problematic. The long revolution by which cultural studies turned from an idiosyncratic, uneven study of culture in various academic disciplines into a recognizable and identifiable program with its own journals, departments, and key figures has long been heralded as the birth narrative of cultural studies in both the United States and the United Kingdom. Though not always articulated as such, within that birth narrative British cultural studies took over the helm of much of what came to be recognized as the default setting for cultural studies as it spread more globally (see, e.g., Hartley 2003; Johnson 1986/ 1987). Within the drive to legitimate cultural studies across time and space, stress points emerged and took hold, while emphases that were initially secondary or adjunct by nature blossomed gradually into semi-autonomous subfields. Almost overnight, complaints about the absence of recognition became more of a concern than were complaints about recognition being shared with others (Nelson and Gaonkar 1996). And alongside its formidable growth, lingering points of neglect, misunderstanding, and omission became embedded within the newly broadened default setting.

In the early days of British cultural studies, journalism and the workings of news were a key focus of the Centre for Contemporary Cultural Studies (CCCS) in Birmingham, and much of its groundbreaking work then, in the early 1970s, explicitly involved journalism, usually in its hard news form. As British cultural studies emerged as a response to the formalism of Marxism and its resonance in literary theory, British scholars took as their mandate the elucidation of the conditions of the British working class.

Within this rubric, many of the early classic British texts on cultural studies based their groundwork on the news. CCCS director Stuart Hall himself was an early editor of the *New Left Review* and a frequent contributor to both *Marxism Today* and *New Times,* making it no surprise that his seminal essay "Encoding/Decoding" (1973b) dealt with news as a stand-in for other modes of cultural production. Heralded as "a turning point in British cultural studies" (Fiske 1992a: 292), the essay came to be regarded as the classic cultural studies formulation of the production-audience intersection, and its offering of audience decoding positions established different audiences for different contents and came to embody the active audience paradigm (Deacon, Fenton, and Bryman 1999). A similar generalizability greeted Hall's "The Determination of News Photographs" (1973a), which was his celebrated extension of Roland Barthes's 1967 work on the photographic image. Both works, firmly situated in the analysis of journalism, inspired analyses of a whole range of nonnews texts; for example, Charlotte Brunsdon and David Morley's (1978) study of *Nationwide* news audiences extended Hall's scholarship to become the primary text for thinking about a range of audience responses to different kinds of mediated messages (see also Morley 1980).

Other early work followed in this vein (e.g., Hall 1972; Hall, Connell, and Curti 1976). Stanley Cohen and Jock Young's *The Manufacture of News* (1973), labeled the "earliest 'standard' critical work on the media's construction of reality" (Turner 1990: 88), drew attention to symbolic construction by considering the patterns underlying journalism's treatment of crime and deviance and developing an understanding of the media's role in moral panics. *Policing the Crisis* (Hall et al. 1978) and Dick Hebdige's work on subcultural style, *Subculture: The Meaning of Style* (1979) and *Hiding in the Light* (1988), used the news as a background for thinking about more generalized modes of cultural production and the distribution of social and cultural power. No surprise, then, that one text on the evolution of British cultural studies, Graeme Turner's *British Cultural Studies: An Introduction* (1990), used press photographs of Oliver North and Ferdinand Marcos to illustrate culture's broad workings. In one view, much of this scholarship was in effect "a defense of the importance of journalism" because, for one of the first times in British academe, it took the news media seriously (Hartley 1999: 23).

A default regard for journalism was further echoed as British cultural studies extended to institutions beyond Birmingham. The foundation of the Center for Journalism Studies at Cardiff University, though slated as a center "offering training to a limited number of carefully selected students . . . destined for careers on *The Times* and in the BBC," attached to journalism a "veneer of learning in the humanities and [implicated] it in 'scientifically-direct' research" (Hopkinson 1982; Bromley in press). Under the auspices of its first head—former journalist Tom Hopkinson, who was also former editor of the *Picture Post* and the first journalism professor in the United Kingdom—the school was connected until 1996 with an academic group that specialized in English literature and language, cultural criticism, philosophy, and critical and cultural theory and produced celebrated cultural work on journalism by the mid-1970s. In 1996, it became part of a new alliance that was tellingly titled the school of Journalism, Media and Cultural Studies (Bromley in press). Nearby, at the Polytechnic of Wales, John Fiske and John Hartley were particularly renowned for advancing semiology as a way to read television and the news (1978), invoking journalism as the default case for understanding cultural power, cultural production, and the impact of culture and the media on audiences. Similarly, the Centre for Mass Communication Research at the University of Leicester, established in 1966, also drew attention to journalism's cultural dimensions, producing a groundbreaking study of the media's coverage of political demonstrations (Halloran et al. 1970) that set the analytical parameters for thinking about journalism's role in shaping public events. The Unit for Journalism Research, led by James Curran at Goldsmiths' College University of London, had a similar impact. In one view, alliances of this sort constituted a "migration away from the imaginative system of modernity (literature) towards its realist textual system (journalism)" (Hartley 2003: 49; also see Hartley 1996), establishing what seemed to some as an obvious natural connection between cultural studies and journalism.

The recognition of journalism as a way of thinking about culture continued along a trajectory of culturally oriented scholarship. The early interest in journalism's cultural nuances, displayed in the work of Fiske and Hartley, later became for both scholars an ongoing address to the more populist dimensions of the news (Hartley 1982, 1992, 1996; Fiske 1992b, 1996). Peter Dahlgren (1992, 1995) launched his own investigation of the cultural dimensions of the news and citizenship. The Glasgow University Media Group (1976, 1980, 1982) tackled news head-on in a way that simultaneously accommodated image and text. Simon Cottle (2000a, 2003) yoked the givens of journalistic practice and its study into one area of inquiry, while Michael Bromley (1997), Philip Schlesinger and Howard Tumber (1995), and Cynthia Carter, Gill Branston, and Stuart Allan (1998) investigated the intersection of journalism and so-called external inequities regarding class, gender, and other indices of cultural identity. Others (e.g., Sparks 1994) concentrated on how popular forms of journalism filled functions left unaddressed by the mainstream or traditional domain of journalistic practice. In each case, journalism was offered as a default case for understanding cultural power, cultural production, and the impact on audiences. Seen as "definite, if unlikely, bedfellows," journalism and culture remained inextricably aligned (Wark 1997: 111, 179–185; also Hartley 1999: 24)

This early linkage between journalism and cultural studies made sense. It evolved from a certain shared commitment to the real world. While cultural studies tended to be fueled by political commitment, journalism's commitment tried to account for real-life events in a way that enhanced public understanding of the key institutional processes at work in everyday life—government, economics, education. Born of a lingering dissatisfaction with existing explanations for culture as it impacted on the real world, cultural studies tried to mark life in and beyond the academy simultaneously, and journalism offered valuable terrain on which to gauge the shape of such life. The emphasis on power and discourse made journalism a natural setting for probing many of the issues relevant to cultural studies. In John Hartley's view, the disciplinary gaze of journalism and cultural studies was similar, licensing both to

> explore the full range of the social, describe other people's lives, generalize specialist knowledge for general readers, interrogate decisions and actions on behalf of "governmental" discourses of appropriate behavior (legal and ethical) and manageability (decision-making, policy), textualize the world in order to know it, and communicate by appropriate idiom to target demographics. (Hartley 2003: 137–138)

Furthermore, interest in citizenship and the rights and responsibilities of an informed citizenry rested at the foundation of both fields. As Graeme Turner

(2000: 362) argued, journalism and cultural studies pursued "a common ethical project aimed at reinforcing the principles of citizenship and the development of the skills of critical literacy which underpin the ideals of a democratic press and a democratic readership." Hartley (2003: 138) pushed the point even further, arguing that the fields "were in fact competitors in the social production of knowledge about everyday life," sharing an attraction to "the negatives of human life, the human cost of progress."

Yet as British cultural studies moved beyond the United Kingdom, first to the United States and then more globally, and as it grew to embrace broader and more varied forms of cultural production in and out of the UK, journalism's attractiveness as an analytical venue of choice waned. In fact, journalism all but disappeared from much of the work in British cultural studies published from the 1980s onward. A brief overview of some of the key lexicons and central texts published during this period bears this out.

While a number of lexicons denoting the "key words" of cultural analysis were published from the eighties onward, the terms of "journalism" and "news" rarely appeared in their indices (e.g., O'Sullivan et al. 1983; Brooker 1999, Edgar and Sedgwick 1999). Some of the fattest cultural studies anthologies (Nelson and Grossberg 1988; During 1993; Baker, Diawara, and Lindeborg 1996; Shiach 1999) did not mention news or journalism prominently. One anthology thoughtfully tracked the disciplinary intersections relevant to cultural studies, but its long list of connections with what it called "an array of knowledges"—including sociology, anthropology, law, philosophy, and archaeology—neglected to include journalism as a site of relevance (Miller 2001:12). A reader put forth by Lawrence Grossberg, Cary Nelson, and Paula Treichler (1992) offered 16 thematic headings for the study of culture, none of which mentioned journalism, while Marjorie Ferguson and Peter Golding's *Cultural Studies in Question* (1997), heralded as the "most aggressive attack" on the field (Erni 2001: 194), also excluded journalism from its discussion. Even introductory texts attempting to lay the groundwork for entry to the field discussed journalism nowhere at length (Brantlinger 1990; McGuigan 1992; Storey 1993; Davies 1995; Tudor 1999; Giles and Middleton 1999). In one case, a book whose index stretched to 10 pages, appended by a 14-page glossary of key terms in cultural studies, barely made reference to journalism (Barker 2000).

The uneven attention paid journalism had its effect on journalism's cultural inquiry. On the one hand, scholarship migrated to those dimensions of journalism that were most distant from its pronounced sense of self—the tabloid, the alternative newspaper, the online relay. While scholars produced a wealth of scholarship on these aspects of the news (see, e.g., Langer 1998; Lumby 1999; Sparks and Tulloch 2000), they nonetheless provided a vision of journalism that was differently narrowed, drawn on alternative lines that tended to eschew the mainstream dimensions of news most closely aligned with journalism's sense of self. In other words, while offering a valuable addition to journalism scholarship, this research furthered the separation between mainstream news and news of a different order—alternative, tabloid, oppositional. Lost were the nuances that legitimated both as part of one world.

On the other hand, articles on generalized or mainstream news, when they did appear, were couched as if journalism were but one choice of many background settings. Discussions of "the media" included the "news media," and yet, as Carey asserted (1997b: 332), "to confuse journalism with media or communications is to confuse the fish story with the fish." Thus positioned, journalism lost its singular features, hidden as the uneven and often unarticulated target of discussions of gender representation, government censorship, or democracy and the public sphere. Accordingly, this view of journalism rendered it more similar to than different from other cultural settings. While this premise initially motivated the cultural inquiry into journalism, it may have been too much of a good thing. For left relatively unexamined were the peculiarities connected to cultural authority that pertained exclusively or primarily to journalism, particularly its reverence for facts, truth, and reality. Moreover, as other kinds of cultural texts—like soap operas and James Bond films—became available for analysis on what were hitherto regarded as the margins of cultural production, journalistic settings began to look less interesting.

All of this is not to say that journalism professionals themselves welcomed the attention of cultural studies, as uneven as it was. Problems between the two fields persevered. When cultural studies targeted journalism as a viable analytical venue, it did so with the express aim of contextualizing its power, recognizing that journalism played an instrumental role in circulating powerful ideas about how the world worked. Thus, the scholarship that developed here often had much to say about culture and cultural power, in general, rather than valuable insights by which journalists could continue to work as journalists. Particularly in areas where the inquiry of cultural studies into journalism promoted turf wars over insufficient resources, the antipathy between the two camps was strident, as witnessed by the very public dispute in Australia between journalism educators and cultural studies scholars (Windshuttle 1998; Hartley 1999; Turner 2000). Keith Windshuttle's basic argument—that journalism education was being undone by cultural studies—brought to the surface many of the residual tensions over who had the right to study journalism. The disaffection between the two areas became pronounced, with Keyan Tomaselli (2000) saying in a critical paraphrasing of Windshuttle that cultural studies constituted "the central disorganizing principle in journalism education."

Why was there such an uneven interest in journalism among cultural studies scholars? Much of the dissonance derived from one of the foundations of journalism's own self-presentation, which rendered journalism fundamentally different from other sites of cultural analysis—its regard for facts, truth, and reality as god-terms.

Journalism's presumed legitimacy depended on its declared ability to provide an indexical and referential presentation of the world at hand. Insisting on the centrality of reality and on facts as its carrier, journalism maintained a clear distinction between itself and other domains of public discourse. Journalists claimed that their work had a capacity to narrativize the events of the real world in a way different from other cultural voices, because it retained an attentiveness to how things "really" happened. Moreover, against this template rested a preoccupation with something called "truth." Although the journalist's recognition of his or her capacity to reproduce a semblance of truth diminished in the contemporary era, the predilection for making truth claims certainly persevered. All of this meant that journalism's practices, conventions, breaches, and standards—indeed, the very gauges by which its growth and stultification were measured—rested on the originary status of facts, truth, and reality. And yet, this reliance created problems for the cultural analysis of journalism, which by definition subjected these very phenomena—facts, truth, and reality—to the measurements of relativity and subjectivity.

The complications surrounding journalism's reverence for facts, truth, and reality extended to additional aspects of its internal mind-set. Journalists' professional ideology was offset by an insistence, common in cultural analysis, that the production of knowledge is always accomplished in the interests either of those who hold power or of those who contest that hold. The growing trend to look toward audiences to locate journalism's workable dimensions, now prevalent in cultural studies, conflicted with a firm assumption among journalists that journalism takes shape in the newsroom, not amongst the public. Furthermore, in that much of cultural analysis privileged what came before or rests outside a phenomenon as the explanatory impulse for examining the phenomenon itself, the indifference to contextual factors shown by most journalists and many journalism scholars undermined much of the cultural study of journalism. As one scholar stated it, "nothing disables journalism more than thinking that current practice is somehow in the nature of things" (Carey 1997: 331), and there remained a reluctance about drawing on contexts—historical, economic, political—to explain journalism's internal trappings. As Theodore Glasser and James Ettema contended long ago, "among journalists . . . news is not a theoretical construct but a practical accomplishment" (Glasser and Ettema 1989a: 20–21). Or, as James Carey put it more recently,

> journalists do not live in a world of disembodied ideals; they live in a world of practices. These practices not only make the world, they make the journalist. Journalists are constituted in practice. So, the appropriate question is not only what kind of world journalists make but also what kinds of journalists are made in the process. (Carey 1997b: 331)

All of this suggested that journalism posed a special challenge for cultural analysis. Unlike the modes of cultural argumentation favored by poets and clergy, unlike the patterns of cultural production displayed on reality television and action films, and unlike the cultural similarities that brought together so-called chick flicks and romance novels, journalism remained constrained by its somewhat reified but nonetheless instrumental respect for facts, truth, and reality. Criticized for remaining a bastion of positivism when relativity and subjectivity have become in many quarters the more endearing tropes for understanding public expression, journalism's adherence to the facts, both real and strategic, and related reverence for the truth and some version of reality rendered it sorely outdated and out of step with academic inquiry of a cultural bent. And yet were it to loosen its adherence to these foundational tenets, journalism would have lost its distinctiveness from the other modes of cultural expression, argumentation, representation, and production that frequently comprised the targets of cultural analysis.

The basic dissonance this created impacted upon various sides of the connection between cultural studies and journalistic inquiry. It was in part connected with cultural studies' own critique of Enlightenment thinking and the lack of confidence in the emancipatory power of reason that increasingly underpinned much of its mandate for looking at the real world. Journalism's persistent loyalty to modernism and to what Toby Miller called "technologies of truth" (1998) kept it at odds with cultural studies' worldview, with cultural studies scholars increasingly regarding journalism as unthinkingly supporting the underside and problematic dimensions of facts, truth, and reality. In other words, journalism's god-terms were themselves seen by cultural studies scholars as troubling evidence of a somewhat blind devotion to a deity gone rotten.

Cultural studies' uneven interest in journalism also derived from journalism's powerful institutional status, which encouraged the examination of certain aspects important for critique—its establishment bias, its collusion with political and economic powers, its failure to provide ongoing independent investigation. Once these aspects were attended to and seemingly depleted, however, journalism as a whole tended to be abandoned by much of cultural studies as no longer a worthwhile target of analysis. The less obvious—and less fruitful—routes for studying journalism's power and authority, such as the profoundly conflicted performances that emerge when power and authority begin to break down while a belief in facts and truth perseveres, drew less energized interest from many cultural scholars. Their reluctance to break apart the institutional presence of journalism persisted both because the power associated with that presence offered a rich target of analysis and because the picture that emerged when institutional presence dissipated was not as compelling for cultural studies. While some notable exceptions (see, e.g., Eliasoph 1988; Reese 1990) offered a picture of journalism that was both internally and externally divisive and contradictory, they were not frequent enough to constitute a substantial body of scholarship.

Finally, cultural studies' uneven interest in journalism also reflected fundamental differences over what counted as evidence. Journalism's positivism and concomitant attention to notions of facts, truth, and reality all seemed to be at odds with cultural studies' examination of culture via its contingencies—historical, social, political, and economic. Cultural studies' insistence on constructivism, subjectivity, and relativity was ill-matched to journalists' proclaimed invocations of accuracy, balance, and objectivity. Some of this may have derived from the problems associated with applying British cultural studies to the U.S. context. As Hanno Hardt warned in 1986, British cultural studies' appropriation and professionalization in the U.S. scene facilitated the loss of its original political commitments. Perhaps nowhere was this seen more clearly than in journalism's subsequent reduction to a world of marginal practices, popular auras, and generalized otherness.

When combined, all of this made journalism, particularly its mainstream dimensions, uninteresting for much of British cultural studies in its global spread. And yet, there is need to ask whether cultural studies took its subject of inquiry too much at face value. In defining journalism and its study on its own terms—that is, in adopting journalism's self-presentation as indicative of what journalism is or could be—cultural studies left the nuances of journalism's workings out of its analysis. Rather than tackle the unpronounced, illogical, and dissonant sides of journalism—the contingencies and contradictions involved in the constant, often tiresome, and frequently fruitless negotiations to yoke popular and official, private and public, lay and professional, dishonest and truthful, biased and balanced impulses—cultural studies closed its eyes. It catered to official journalism's pronounced sense of itself, which articulated an adherence to each of the latter choices and a disavowal of each of the former, largely dismissing the study of journalism as a whole. The uneven response in cultural studies to journalism played to the modernist bias for its official self-presentation, a presentation that promoted the informative, civic, and rational sides of its practices over their pleasure-inducing, entertaining, or simply affective ones. Playing to this side of journalism, however, recognized only part of what it was.

For much of cultural studies, then, mainstream journalism was examined through the nearsighted eyes used by much of the academy. In many of its forms, journalism became codified as an extension of the sciences and the scientific model of knowledge production, oppositionally positioned to cultural studies' dominant scholarly stance of criticism and sometimes parody. Cultural studies reduced the impact of positivistic knowledge about journalism to a whisper and missed the nuances of the journalistic world, failing to realize that in so doing it neglected to examine much of what contradicted journalists' own parameters of professional practice. Yet these nuances were worth addressing precisely because they rested underneath the articulated core of how much of journalism saw itself.

It is not surprising that this tendency generated divergent interpretations, which echoed the differences between British and U.S. cultural studies: In fact, the lack of recognition of U.S. cultural studies as an occupant of the same field of study persisted. Although the adoption of British cultural studies elsewhere was uneven (see, e.g., Stratton and Ang 1996; Mariscal 2001; Yudice 2001), its potential recognition as a global field of inquiry was far more assured than that of its U.S. counterpart, which at times was shunted from the conversation altogether. To wit, one recent discussion characterized U.S. cultural scholars James W. Carey, Elihu Katz, and Carolyn Marvin as distanced from the field, noting that "few would have identified themselves as practitioners of cultural studies" (Hartley 2003: 102). Similarly, a recent mapping of the various geographic trajectories of cultural studies scholarship by Richard Maxwell mentioned Carey and some of his likeminded colleagues but not his progeny (cited in Miller 2001: 4). The lack of recognition, despite the consistently vocal role that Carey and others took to identify cultural studies as a field at least partially consonant with their own interests (see, e.g., Carey 1989b; Munson and Warren 1997), marked a dissonance between the two strains of cultural studies. Its persistence, discussed independently by Hanno Hardt (1986), Lawrence Grossberg (1997), and John Erni (2001), exacerbated journalism's precarious positioning in the larger domain of cultural study.

Thus, the divergent interpretations of journalism's absence in much of this scholarship reflected broader differences in the U.S. and British schools of cultural studies. Some saw cultural studies as representative of a mode of knowledge that sought "nothing less than to rethink received truths and remake inherited frameworks of explanation," becoming a "symptom of widespread doubt and disillusion about the contriving ability of inherited truths to command assent" (Hartley 2003: 2). Others saw it as buying into "a moral and political vocabulary that [was], if not anti-democratic, at least insufficiently sensitive to the ways in which valued political practices intertwine with certain intellectual habits" (Carey 1989b).

All of this suggested that the originary premises of journalism and much of cultural studies positioned them at odds with each other. The former believed in truth, reality, and facts, the latter in construction, subjectivity and relativity. A fundamental difference about what counted in the compilation and interpretation of evidence, even if both arenas provided strategies for shaping that compilation, concretized a broader dissonance in journalism's cultural study that underscored the difficulty, if not impossibility, of figuring out *how* to study the cultural dimensions of a phenomenon that made claim to an indexical and referential presentation of the world at hand. The effect of such a difference de facto encouraged journalism's gradual transformation into material that looked more like the stuff of contemporary journalism education and journalistic professionalism, resembling less a set of practices of symbolic expression in the public domain than a narrowly conceived intersection of the political and the economic. As the insects of positivism—reality, truth, facts—were exterminated from analysis with a self-righteous zeal, for a time and in considerable scholarship journalism retreated to the territory from which it had originally come, the atheoretical world of journalism education, training, and professionalization and the valorization of its capacity to account for the real, the true, and the factual. The centrality of "facts" and a migration toward positivistic knowledge as a way of tamping a fundamental self-doubt about the profession became obstructions to cultural studies' interest in the journalistic world, and journalism's claims to the real—invoking objectivity, balance, accuracy—muted the capacity of many cultural scholars to consider the nuances of journalistic practice. Largely unrecognized as a cultural form in itself, it became positioned as "the other," codified by much of British cultural studies as uninteresting territory and resembling in growing degree what had been claimed originally of it by journalism educators. This meant that despite auspicious beginnings, scholarship on journalism in much of cultural studies came to look less like other kinds of cultural phenomena and more like the material in which cultural analysis had no interest. In other words, many cultural studies scholars led the way of those who took journalism professionals and educators too much at their word, reducing the cultural inquiry of journalism to a marginal interest, a sideshow.

It is important to note, though, that this trend may be dissipating in certain quarters. John Hartley's latest key concept reader, *Communication, Cultural and Media Studies* (2002), included terms relevant to news such as "bias," "news values," "objectivity," and "gatekeeper," as did the updated version of another reader (O'Sullivan, Hartley, Saunders, Montgomery, and Fiske 1994). Nick Lacey (1998) used a text from the British television program "News At Ten" to illustrate what he meant by "institutional analysis" in his key concept reader on media studies and visual culture. Roberta Pearson and John Hartley offset journalism's neglect by opening their volume, *American Cultural Studies: A Reader* (2000), with a section of reprints of politically progressive journalistic articles, as well by including an academic article in a section titled "Media" that specifically addressed journalism. Jeff Lewis (2002) not only wove a discussion of journalism and news throughout his examination of cultural studies, but he even tackled certain journalism forms, like paparazzi. John Storey devoted a chapter to the press and magazines in his overview of the field, *Cultural Studies and the Study of Popular Culture* (1996b), and in *Inventing Popular Culture* (2003) he began his discussion of globalization with a consideration of television news. Meenakshi Durham and Douglas Kellner (2001) addressed the status of newspapers in different cultural contexts in their cultural studies reader, and Kees Brants, Joke Hermes, and Lisbet Van Zoonen (1998) dedicated an entire section to "the ethics of popular journalism." John Hartley's recent *A Short History of Cultural Studies* (2003) tracked a consistent regard for journalism alongside an interest in larger questions of cultural power.

Questions remain over how to engage the epistemological uneasiness at the core of journalism and cultural studies' coexistence in a way that maintains the integrity of both journalism and cultural studies. There have been numerous calls of late to reinvigorate the charter of cultural studies, particularly in its British form (e.g., Frow 1995; Bennett 1998; Couldry 2000a, 2000b). There have also been calls to better address the merger of cultural studies and journalism (Hartley 1999; Tomaselli 2002; Turner 2000). The trajectory traced here suggests that journalism offers a litmus test of sorts regarding the future of cultural studies. Repositioning journalism at the forefront of cultural studies inquiry could help cultural studies on its own road to academic maturation, by which cultural studies might become a fuller fledged discipline of knowledge rather than one positioned in opposition to the surrounding fields of study. Cultural studies' capacity to instantiate itself as a field of knowledge secure in its own claims and in what counts as evidence is key here. Its maturation into a field with enough self-knowledge to grow depends on its capacity to expand and include a phenomenon like journalism rather than shrink to keep it outside. There is enough evidence to suggest that it can do so even if journalism partly challenges some of cultural studies' own claims. While it is possible that cultural studies has neglected incorporating journalism at its core because doing so would necessitate a close look at the limitations of cultural inquiry, it may now be time for cultural studies to confront the problems embodied by journalism and the limitations such problems suggest for the study of any long-standing inquiry into the real. Recognizing that there is a reality out there and that in certain quarters truth and facts have currency does not mean letting go of relativity, subjectivity, and construction. It merely suggests yoking a regard for them with some cognizance of the outside world.

Trends in the Cultural Analysis of Journalism

All of this is not to say that cultural analysis, in all of its forms, did not produce a substantial body of journalism research. Journalism expanded, even if its study was slower to do so, and sites as diverse as tabloid journalism, the alternative press, the internet, and other more populist forms of news making forced such inquiry to open its eyes. The analytical offset introduced by the cultural study of journalism left it well positioned to lead a hitherto nearsighted field of scholarship into different targets of analysis. Much of this work employed tenets of both cultural studies and other modes of cultural analysis; some of it operated independently of the twinned existence of the two fields (e.g., Hardt 1992).

In that cultural analysis worked against the grain of the conventional understandings of how journalism worked, it was particularly valuable in tracking across the fault lines left relatively untouched by other modes of inquiry. Six strands of research helped set this in motion—analysis of the worldviews of journalism, the practices of journalism, the forms of journalism, the breaches of journalism, the representations of journalism, and the audiences of journalism. In each case, cultural inquiry stretched across the broad terrain of what was recognized as journalistic scholarship and in doing so it offset the often unarticulated default by which numerous kinds of journalism had been unilaterally thought to work. This included addressing journalism in numerous geographic regions rather than just in its Anglo American applications, addressing newer forms of news gathering—such as tabloids, the internet, cybersalons—rather than just the triumvirate of radio, television, and the press, and addressing localized modes of journalistic address rather than the unilateral and often irrelevant dispensation of information. In all six strains of research, scholars used available self-generated data—such as news texts, media columns, autobiographies, proceedings of professional forums and conventions, and the trade press—to track how journalists felt about themselves as journalists, how they communicated to the public notions about the ways in which the world worked, and how their representations of the world were engaged by audiences.

Cultural Analysis and the Worldviews of Journalism

The collective mind-set of journalists—the establishment and maintenance of certain ways of knowing, or how journalists came to think both of themselves as journalists and of the world around them—offered a fertile entry point for much of the cultural inquiry of journalism. One early attempt to adopt a wide-ranging notion of journalism as culture, though it did not make the claim explicitly, was Robert Karl Manoff and Michael Schudson's edited volume, *Reading the News* (1986). Marketed as a "Pantheon Guide to Popular Culture," the volume made clear that the professional prism of most journalists required tweaking, and it organized its discussion of culture's intrusion into news by adapting the fundaments of "doing a news story"—the "who, what, when, where, why, and how" of public events—into categories for analyzing journalism's performance.

Numerous other scholars took close looks at how journalism came to mean. Key here were the ways in which journalists created the collective knowledge they needed to maintain group membership, and scholars examined primary journalistic texts—handbooks, career manuals, autobiographies, conference proceedings, media criticism columns—so as to ascertain how journalism was presumed to work. For instance, in the United States, John Pauly (1988) and Linda Steiner (1992) showed how phenomena as varied as journalistic handbooks and discourse about key journalistic personalities served as boundary markers for the group. Michael Schudson used journalistic autobiographies to expose professional mind-sets from different temporal eras (1988). Barbie Zelizer (1993b) used journalistic responses to McCarthyism and Watergate to illustrate how journalists fashioned themselves into interpretive communities. In Canada, G. Stuart Adam (1989, 1993) unveiled the contradictions in journalism education and their impact on journalistic inquiry.

Related here were the numerous works that connected journalistic views on the world with the world itself, particularly with "external" indices of identity—gender, ethnicity, race, sexual orientation. Here a variegated amount of scholarship emerged, an unsurprising development given the articulated interest in issues of identity from much of cultural scholarship and most of cultural studies inquiry. Although much of this work gravitated to address the characteristics of news and its decoding by audiences, some of it also targeted the demographics of journalistic settings. Work on journalism and gender underscored the masculine bias of journalistic worldviews (e.g., Steiner 1997; Carter et al. 1998), work on journalism and race showed the whiteness of the news (e.g., Ainley 1998), work on journalism and ethnicity displayed the limited ethnic representation of journalistic settings (e.g., Gabriel 1998; Cottle 2000c), work on journalism and class both linked more populist journalistic forms of journalism with class identity and showed the prevalence of class-based judgments in the news (e.g., Bird 1992; Fiske 1992b; Hartley 1992; Meinhof and Richardson 1994; Reeves and Campbell 1994), and work on journalism and sexual orientation challenged the default setting of straightness in journalism (e.g., Moritz 1992; Alwood 1996; Gross 2002). Stuart Allan (1999) focused on the functions of news discourses, which he argued were used to depoliticize the dominant meanings derived from reported events.

In each case, work ranged from discussions of how journalistic settings worked to how journalistic representations provided a way of thinking about the world. Scholars concentrated on the contingencies involved in news making and on the fact that news was relative to the givens of those who engaged in its production.

Cultural Analysis and the Practices of Journalism

Much cultural work also targeted certain journalistic practices, bringing together action and symbolic form in a way that reflected the often conflicting tensions at the core of journalistic practice. Key here was the work of Theodore Glasser and James Ettema, which unpacked the background assumptions for the set of sovereign journalistic practices known as investigative reporting. Their studies (Glasser and Ettema 1989b, 1998) showed how investigative journalism could coexist in numerous but patterned ways with the dominant moral order.

Others took a similar direction of inquiry. For instance, Caryl Rivers (1996) tackled some of the enduring notions about journalistic work—professional detachment, pack journalism, and the notion of the newspaper as a historical record—by working backward to highlight their status as discursive constructions contingent on certain points in the evolution of the profession. David Eason (1984) discussed the ways in which different modes of experience—specifically, ethnographic realism and cultural phenomenology—constructed journalists' very approaches to their subject matter and the stories they needed to produce. Jimmie Reeves and Richard Campbell (1994) focused on journalistic work and drug campaigns, Claire Wardle

(2003) worked on coverage of U.S. and U.K. murder trials, and Keith Tester (1994) examined the ways in which morality shaped news culture. In Latin America and Mexico, Armand Mattelart (1980), Jesus Martin-Barbero (1993), and Elizabeth Fox and Silvio Waisbord (2002) led the conversation on thinking about journalistic practices, with Silvio Waisbord (2000) showing how the Anglo American tradition of investigative journalism was differently codified as watchdog journalism in four South American countries. Bonnie Brennen and Hanno Hardt followed historical trajectories for thinking about the practices of photojournalism (Brennen and Hardt 1999) and the rank and file of journalism (Hardt and Brennen 1995), while William Solomon and Robert McChesney (1993) tracked the marginalizing impulses that had shaped media history. Both John Huxford (2000, 2001) and Oren Meyers (2002) detailed the vagaries that went into photographic representation in the news.

The list of journalistic practices considered relevant for inquiry grew as journalism itself expanded. Karin Wahl-Jorgensen (2001, 2003), for instance, joined the list of scholars keeping an eye turned to journalism's cultural dimensions when she analyzed journalistic responses to letters to the editor. Others moved inquiry in the direction of even newer journalistic practices, such as reality television (Friedman 2002), television talk shows (Shattuc 1997), and the internet (Allan 2002). In particular, the increasing popularity of weblogs and other journalistic practices connected with the Web rendered editing irrelevant and brought to the surface long-standing questions about the definitions of journalism and journalists, as well as about the recognition of practices as journalistic or not.

Cultural Analysis and the Breaches of Journalism

A third body of cultural work was instrumental in questioning the givens by which journalism worked while retaining a fundamental respect for the integrity of journalism, as an ideal if not as a practice. This work elucidated how journalism worked by examining its breaches—breaches of codes of so-called appropriate behavior, ethical violations of collective knowledge, and ruptures of consensual though often unarticulated conventions. These included the ruptures by which journalists' collective mind-set was violated or breached and then reinstated.

Leading this line of cultural inquiry was David Eason, who elaborated the ways in which journalists shaped public events by focusing on the internal breaches within the journalistic community. His landmark study of the Janet Cooke affair, the story of a young black *Washington Post* reporter who received a 1981 Pulitzer Prize for a fabricated story about an 8-year-old heroin user, showed how the scandal provided a chance for journalists to "reflect publicly on the social and cultural processes whereby their accounts gain[ed] authority in society" (Eason 1986: 430). By using the scandal to discuss issues of concern to them as professionals—the increased presence of African American journalists, changes in journalistic conventions, and changes in reporting routines—journalists lent the scandal the status of an originary tale about journalistic authority that articulated what Eason (1986: 430) called "the boundaries of the permissable in journalism." Revealing a journalistic community sliced apart by issues of race, age, gender, and assumptions about reporting, the "facts" and "fictions" of journalism were seen to be no longer given but "the product of interpretive communities whose work is the making of the two categories and explaining how they interrelate." Journalism's evolution, then, was "in part, that of establishing, repairing and transforming the authoritative base for accounts of 'the way it is'" (Eason 1986: 430–431).

Other work followed Eason's example. The notion of examining practice through its violations was connected with a significant body of cultural work on the critical incidents of journalism, ranging across revelations about political ideology, wars, plagiarism, terrorism, political assassinations, and other kinds of media spectacles (Pauly 1988; Reese 1990; Zelizer 1992a, 1992b, 1998b; Garber, Matlock, and Walkowitz 1992; Zelizer and Allan 2002), In many of these works, the focus on journalism's critical incidents helped shed light on how journalists rose to the challenging circumstances occasioned by their work.

Other scholarship on journalistic breaches also tracked work that was less disruptive but different in shape and function. Daniel Dayan and Elihu Katz's (1992) notion of media events established a way of thinking differently about the high moments of live news coverage.

Cultural Analysis and the Forms of Journalism

Another way of thinking about journalism from a cultural perspective involved tracking the forms by which journalism presented and circulated its information and views of the world to audiences.

In *The Form of News* (2001), Kevin Barnhurst and John Nerone tracked the ways in which journalistic presentational form changed over time. Martin Shingler and Cindy Wieringa (1998) traced the journalistic forms that persisted in the so-called blind medium of radio. Scholars focused on the emancipatory power that surrounded radio news, particularly in marginalized settings (Daley and James 1998; Land 1999). Other scholars traced the particular forms of photojournalism (Hall 1972; Taylor 1991,

1998; Zelizer 1998b), cartoons (Hess and Northrup 1996; Rall 2002), and televisual forms (Miller 2002). Public television and public service broadcasting drew extensive scholarly attention (Scannell 1989; Linder 1999; Ouellette 2002), with research often primarily drawn around issues of public interest and an informed citizenry that they did or did not activate.

Particularly valuable here was an array of work detailing alternative or expanded forms of journalism. Forms as varied as television newsmagazines (Campbell 1991), sports journalism (Hargreaves 1986; Rowe 1999), reality television (Friedman 2002), and video activism and guerrilla television (Boyle 1992; Aufderheide 1993) showed the parameters of the ever-changing journalistic landscape. Scholarship on debate program and call-in talk shows were analyzed by cultural scholars interested in the participatory potential such forms made possible (e.g., Franklin 1997; Gibian 1997). The internet and the new forms of journalism that it facilitated—unedited journalism, personalized downloads of information, listservs, weblogs—drew the interest of cultural scholars, who saw an altered future for journalism (Carey 1998; Allan 2002).

Here, much crucial work was conducted on tabloid journalistic forms, much of it addressing how journalism's popular forms filled functions left unaddressed by the mainstream of journalistic practice. Many scholars elaborated the closing of the distance between tabloid and mainstream forms of news (Bird 1992; Hartley 1992, 1996; Ehrlich 1997; Langer 1998; Lumby 1999; Glynn 2000; Sparks and Tulloch 2000). In "Popularity and the Politics of Information," John Fiske (1992b: 49) argued that "the people" and "the power-bloc" each needed to be defined as sifting allegiances of interests rather than classes or social categories, rendering journalistic information "not simply a set of objective facts to be packaged and delivered around the nation" but a choice about addressing the interests of certain audiences. Similarly, Colin Sparks and John Tulloch (2000) argued that popular journalism's appeal to personal experience lent its coverage of news events an immediacy and totality absent in traditional journalism's fragmented picture of the world.

Cultural Analysis and the Representations of Journalism

Other cultural work addressed the representation of journalists in various domains of cultural production, including books, television, and film (Barris 1976; Good 1989, 2000; Ehrlich 1996; Brennen 2003).

This work had a long history, which predated the interest of scholars in the cultural analysis of journalism per se. From classic pieces like Evelyn Waugh's *Scoop* (1938) to Arnold Wesker's *Journey Into Journalism* (1977) and *Journalists* (1980), writers, playwrights, and filmmakers have long used journalism as a source of inspiration in their work. The interest of journalism scholars in analyzing these representations was slower in coming.

Like the gangster or detective film, the journalist genre was seen as the representation of the "cultural middle man" excavating the trappings of urban life (Saltzman 2002). Gerald Stone and John Lee (1990) found that journalists were highly visible on prime time television but given less than favorable depictions.

Although the portrayals of journalists and their work settings became increasingly realistic over time, many representations of journalism provided a romanticized view of how journalism operated. As Peter Dahlgren (1992: 1) noted, much of this literature offered a consistent, somewhat mythic portrayal of journalists: "The heroic image of the journalist defending the truth against the many dragons of darkness in the modern world." In fact, journalists long displayed a bias toward glorifying their own existence in the world's eyes (Schudson 2002). What tended not to be included were the more mechanistic, less dramatic sides of journalistic life—the endless door stepping and phone calls, minute excavation of bureaucratic documents, persistent nudging of sources who revealed less than they could. In other words, these representations played to the aspects of journalism that could be dramatically and vividly portrayed in fiction and on film and television.

At the same time, some of this literature used representations of journalism to query the problems of professionalism in everyday life. For instance, in *The Drunken Journalist* (2000), Howard Good addressed the stereotype of the hard-drinking journalist as a way of thinking about the role of alcohol in shaping our images of certain professional and often marginalized groups. Elsewhere, in *Girl Reporter* (1998), Good examined Hollywood's infatuation with the image of the female journalist, and in *Outcasts* (1989) the drudgeries of working class journalism, all as represented in cinema. Matthew Ehrlich (1991, 1997) addressed the cinematic portrayals of journalism and the function that they played in journalistic education.

Interestingly, some of this literature made its way into the professional trade journals (e.g., Gersh 1991; Rowe 1992; Sessions Stepp 2000), suggesting that the representations of journalism had an impact on how journalists maintained their enthusiasm about the field.

Cultural Analysis and the Audiences of Journalism

Yet an additional arena for thinking about journalism as culture was through its audiences. Emanating primarily from a variety of complications on Stuart Hall's encoding/decoding model and linked to the work of David Morley and Charlotte Brunsdon (Brunsdon and Morley 1978; Morley 1980), cultural scholars tracked the question of how different audiences made sense of the news.

Relevant here was a widespread recognition of the notion that journalism worked differently in conjunction with the identity positioning of its audiences, and following the early work primarily in British cultural studies in this regard, scholarship made substantial headway in establishing the notion that different audiences engaged with the news in different ways.

Much work here targeted the ways in which audiences—seen primarily as consumers or citizens—made sense of the news. In Germany, for instance, Hans Bausinger (1984) demonstrated how newspaper reading became a collective process shared among family, friends, and colleagues. Klaus Bruhn Jensen (1986, 1990) provided an ethnographic basis for thinking critically about different news audiences. Journalism's role in forming communities drew a substantial amount of attention, particularly among alternative communities (Atton 2002) and the communities surrounding the radical press (Downing 1996).

Not only did this work address mainstream audiences, but it variegated such collectives by gender, age, ethnicity, and other indices of identity. Work on tabloid journalism, particularly by S. Elizabeth Bird (1992) and Colin Sparks (1994), stressed the ways in which tabloid news depended on a certain sensibility of how the world worked, that was in turn shaped by class, gender, age, and the like. Ann Gray (1992) focused on the audiences of video and the particular practices it facilitated. Thomas Leonard (1995) focused on the readers of the press by showing the durability of readers' sentiments despite the growing and receding destinies of media organizations. David Mindich (in press) tackled the probing question of how young people attended to journalistic representations of the world. Numerous scholars (e.g., Jankowski, Prehn, and Stappers 1992; King and Mele 1999) addressed the phenomenon of localized audiences for news and community video. Marie Gillespie (1995) addressed the role of television news in diasporic communities in London.

A somewhat related area of inquiry here was the study of journalistic inquiry itself, that is, looking at scholars as audiences. Although the work here was less extensive than it was in the other areas of interest, nonetheless headway was made in tweaking the ways in which journalism scholars conceive of journalistic practices and worldviews. For instance, an examination of news ethnographies offered a critical view of the outdatedness of much of traditional news scholarship (Cottle 2000a). Similarly, queries were made of the positioning and relative status of humanistic lenses for thinking about journalism (Zelizer 1993a) and the uneven positioning of journalism's scholarship in the academy (Zelizer 1998a).

* * * * *

What, then, has the cultural inquiry of journalism given us? The real value of such study has been that it tried to offset much of the disciplinary nearsightedness of traditional journalism scholarship. Taking interdisciplinarity as its key and constituting feature, it provided a variegated voice for addressing head-on what had long stymied the development of journalism scholarship, particularly as it connected with new forms of journalism, new technologies, and altered expectations of what journalism ought to be doing when journalists acted as journalists. Not all cultural work on journalism was of equal value, however. Much of it provided an analysis of individual cases under such close focus that it was difficult to extrapolate findings across different kinds of circumstances. Moreover, still unclear were the answers to numerous questions about the recognition of journalism as a legitimate domain of cultural inquiry. How to more effectively yoke the fertile move toward the cultural study of journalism with a pronounced and explicit insistence on facts, truth, and reality as part of journalism's own raison d'etre remained largely unresolved in the cultural analysis of journalism, and journalism's persistence in what seemed to many an antiquated position of how to think about the world lingered uneasily. Whether or not such a notion reflected the limitations of cultural inquiry itself or the limitations of journalism underscored an ambivalence within cultural analysis about more fully accommodating journalism's study, in all of its dimensions, including its mainstream ones.

8

Taking Journalism Seriously

A s we begin the 21st century, journalism strikes an unsteady chord in the public imagination. Recently, over the last few months of 2003, it showed up in odd places and did not appear in expected ones. Arnold Schwartzenegger announced his candidacy for California governor on the Jay Leno Show, to the horror and amazement of mainstream political reporters. A poll reported that U.S. children and teenagers spent more time on the internet than reading or watching television, practices presumed to have direct impact on their ability to act as news audiences. Individuals involved with an FBI probe of the Philadelphia mayor's office were accused of contacting journalists with information about the probe before the targeted individuals were given the same information. And that is only in the United States. Across the world, the conditions under which journalism shows its faces are shifting, to the extent that it pops up when least expected and hibernates when its presence is deemed most crucial.

Surprise, however, tends to visit those who lack a way to make sense of what they observe, and *Taking Journalism Seriously* has suggested taking a direction in which journalism can be understood more broadly. Contending that the shaping of scholarly inquiry on journalism is at least partly responsible for the incomplete and often strategic picture that is painted of journalism, this book has offered one way to circumvent the isolated pockets of inquiry that generate conversation internally far more actively than they encourage dialogue with each other. It offers the beginnings of a more programmatic way of taking journalism seriously and moves us toward a place where conversations across disciplinary pockets might continue. Suggesting that the numerous disciplinary perspectives through which journalism has been studied offer more than one angle by which to understand journalism's workings, *Taking Journalism Seriously* has argued that across those angles we are best able to recognize that journalism matters—not in one prescribed way but in many ways and across many circumstances. And recognizing that journalism matters is the first step to taking journalism seriously.

That journalism matters was addressed differently in the various chapters discussed here. Taken together, these discrete views establish the various circumstances that ought to go into thinking about journalism, because doing so enriches the ground against which journalism makes its name as a field, a profession, a practice, and a cultural phenomenon.

Numerous developments in the academy point already in the direction of taking journalism seriously. As outlined in this book, scholars engaging with journalism in interdisciplinary ways are appearing more regularly across the curriculum than they used to. Scholarship that long inhabited the margins of journalism research—on tabloids, for instance—now finds itself referenced increasingly in mainstream discussions about journalism. And academic curricula are beginning to recognize that some attention is worth paying journalism, even in disciplinary fields that bear no obvious linkage with the news.

And yet an existential angst continues to permeate conversations about journalism's viability. During the past decade, no fewer than four articles by major scholars on journalism were titled or subtitled "The End of Journalism" (Katz 1992; Manoff 1995; Hardt 1996; Bromley 1997). On any given day, close to 300 titles of newsletters, columns, and professional roundtables and symposia pondering the same issue clutter the internet. Just over the last decade or so, the phrase was used to describe a long list of potential ills, earmarking journalism's status as a conveyor of misfortune. The list is so broad it seems almost shapeless: the rise of CNN, market-driven newspapers, the end of objectivity, the fate of the independent media in Serbia, online journalism and blogging, the threat to *Nightline* by David Letterman's *Late Show*, journalists' failure to protect their sources, infotainment and "soft" journalism, press releases posing as mainstream journalism, and the Jayson Blair incident. Regardless of its target or source, then, a pervasive sense of concern permeates ongoing conversations about journalism and raises fundamental questions regarding its future. Perhaps this should not be surprising. For as Michael Bromley and Tom O'Malley eloquently stated, journalists

> emerge as a group of people uncertain about how useful their work is or how acceptable they are as a group. . . . The journalist's very tendency to write in a swift, unreflective form produces impressionist accounts of the practice and

purpose. The prevalence of this form of writing suggests that journalism has existed, in some senses, on the margins of social acceptability. Unlike other activities, there is something about journalism which is permanently troubled and contradictory. (Bromley and O'Malley 1997: 8)

Existential angst rears its head in concrete phenomena. Dips in newspaper circulation, the avid tracking of television ratings, and symposia lamenting the rising popularity of reality television have all left their imprint on the degree of resilience with which journalists contemplate their future. As longtime British editor Harold Evans was said to have noted, "the problem that many media organizations face is not to stay in business, but to stay in journalism" (quoted in Gardner, Csikszentmihalyi, and Damon 2001: 131).

While this book can offer little to stabilize the future of journalism, it has much to say about the future of journalism's scholarship. As it has tried to show, the anxiety over journalism may derive in part from the very limitations of scholarly inquiry. As scholars invested in clarifying the phenomenon that we call journalism, we may have missed the mark. For in fine-tuning our analytical endeavors to the contours offered by a given disciplinary lens, we may have produced scholarship that obscures more than it clarifies and that by definition keeps its sights more on the premises of a given discipline than on the impulses underlying journalism, as contradictory and unclear as they might be. In other words, this book suggests that we have replaced old biases against journalism—against which it struggled to establish for itself a place on the curriculum—with a new situation of disciplinary nearsightedness. While this is an obvious consequence of disciplinary scholarship, it begs the question of how true to journalism—in all of its forms and variations—journalism's study can be.

On the Relevance of Disciplinary Lenses in Journalism's Study

This book has examined five academic lenses through which journalism has been perceived: sociology, history, language studies, political science, and cultural analysis. Though not the only lenses for considering journalism, they offer a wide range of issues through which to think differentially about journalism's operation. While their development has no doubt enriched the field, they reside in places that are distinct and separate from each other, unintegrated parts of one whole. The question remains, then, as to whether a lack of active cross-referencing across the often contradictory scholarship advanced by various types of inquiry has inadvertently stunted the development of journalism's study, causing scholars to miss the full range of activities, beliefs, and practices that give it its name.

To recap, each lens offered its own picture of journalism's study, magnifying different answers to the question of why journalism matters. Sociology focused on *how journalism matters,* examining the people, practices and behavior, structures, and institutions that went into the making of news. History targeted *how journalism used to matter.* Establishing its longevity, it considered the long-standing authority of journalism both over time and at different times. Language studies concentrated on *the verbal and visual tools by which journalism matters.* In focusing on its languages, it offered formal and informal templates for considering how the messages of news were structured. Political science developed a focus on *how journalism ought to matter.* It considered journalism's larger political role in making news, accounting for numerous dimensions of the intersection between journalism and politics. And cultural analysis described *how journalism matters differently,* seeing it as relative to the givens of those engaged in its production, presentation, and reception while dissipating the consensus that grounded more traditional inquiry.

The differences between the various lens loom large. So too do the possibilities suggested by their potential integration. For our present state of disciplinary nearsightedness comes as a warning sign to those interested in the viability of journalism's study, necessitating more interdisciplinary sensitivity if the inquiry on journalism is to reflect journalism with greater resonance than has been the case till now.

How Journalism Differs Across Disciplinary Lenses

A number of key differences between the disciplinary lenses that are largely akin to the commandment questions of journalism—who, what, where, when, why, and how—are worth considering in detail. Roughly put, they address first the who, what, where, and when of journalism's study, each of which appears to a different degree across the disciplinary frames. Second, they come together in various combinations to build an elaborated ground on which to respond to the how and why of journalism's study, ultimately establishing why journalism matters.

Who Was the Target of Inquiry?

Who was targeted as the focus of academic inquiry has been key to shaping the various areas of journalism's study. The question of whether a scholarly work was shaped around questions about journalism that examined journalistic elites, mid-ranked journalists, low-ranked journalists, or the public clearly motivated studies that differed substantially from each other. For instance, an examination of the impact of electoral campaigns on the public (Entman 1989) differed from a study of campaign political rhetoric (Jamieson 1988) and from a study of newsroom practices during political campaigns (Kaniss 1995). While each of the three studies focused on journalism and electoral campaigns, the material seen as relevant in one study did not parallel that put forward by the others: one focused on the public, one on campaigning officials, one on journalists. Yet each had much to say about journalism and campaigns that complemented the findings offered by the other studies.

All five lenses focused on the people of journalism, but not always and not to equal degree. Scholars in language studies, for instance, depended on an implication or abstraction of people behind the tools of verbal and visual relay that they examined, but as a field of inquiry they rarely examined individual persons per se, leaving their analyses largely unpeopled. Researchers in political science tended to examine different kinds of people in their studies, grouping them either by rank or by their relation to the political process. Thus, analysts of sourcing practices tended to consider the practices or beliefs of elite journalists, mid-ranked journalists, and the officials with whom they made contact (e.g., Schlesinger and Tumber 1995), while scholars conducting election studies defined their populations as those individuals casting votes in an election (e.g., Blumler 1983). The majority of political science scholars, however, shaped the "who" of their inquiry as a construct, whereby an abstract notion of "the public" took the place of real people (e.g., Patterson 1993). In this regard, political science scholarship too remained generally unpeopled.

Other frames were more actively motivated by the "who" of inquiry. For instance, people remained at the core of both sociological analysis and cultural analysis. Scholars associated with sociology tended to shape inquiry through an emphasis on people, grouping them by rank and examining elite, mid-ranked, and lower ranked journalists with a fair degree of equivalence across the groupings. While ethnographers tended to examine the lower and middle ranked participants in journalistic settings (e.g., Tuchman 1978a; Fishman 1980), scholars conducting more ideologically driven studies generally focused on those individuals holding power in a news setting (e.g., Gitlin 1980). Researchers engaged in occupational analyses and demographic studies of the journalistic population examined people across the board (e.g., Splichal and Sparks 1994; Weaver and Wilhoit 1996). Furthermore, in that scholars following the lines of sociological inquiry frequently examined dominant rather than deviant practices and settings, most people examined were mainstream. By contrast, much work in cultural analysis tended to bypass the mainstream and orient itself toward groups of people who were not regularly examined elsewhere— people of color, marginalized individuals, oppositional groups, journalists with alternative political mind-sets (Meyers 1994; Carter et al. 1998; Gabriel 1998). In both sociological and cultural work, the "who" of inquiry tended to be groups, not individuals, and the analytical focus generally underscored their relations with each other.

The people targeted in historical studies tended to be of two types— primarily elites and then mid-ranked individuals. Scholars who examined the histories of news organizations or institutions tended to consider both those holding power and those helping to exercise that power (e.g., Tifft and Jones 2000), but not from the lower-ranked echelons of the journalistic setting. Biographers and autobiographers tended to be more uniformly focused on elites and were usually interested in people of high rank, such as top editors or publishers like William Randolph Hearst and Rupert Murdoch (Munster 1985; Nasaw 2000). These efforts actively drew many of the individual portraits associated with journalism.

The "who" of journalism's study, then, differed substantially across the frames of inquiry. Scholars associated with sociology and cultural analysis scoped the individuals of their analyses most broadly when shaping inquiry, though those in political science led the way in terms of thinking abstractly about the public and its relationship with journalism and those in history almost single-handedly established the existing picture of individual journalists. Researchers in language studies paid less attention to the people of journalism than did scholars associated with other disciplinary frames.

What Was the Target of Inquiry?

The question of what constituted the target of inquiry has varied by disciplinary frame, in that each frame's focus differed as to which kinds of practice mattered. Generally speaking, targets of inquiry were differentiated by the point in the news-making process at which analysis was conducted. Thus, different studies focused a priori on the production of news, on its presentation, or on its reception among publics, and that difference was crucial in shaping the studies that ensued.

Cultural scholars tended to stretch broadly across the entire news-making process when developing sites of study. Although they focused most directly on presentation and reception (e.g., Fiske and Hartley 1978; Morley 1980), in keeping with the long-standing traditions set in place with Stuart Hall's two emblematic studies of news—"Encoding/Decoding" (1973a) and "The Determinations of News Photographs" (1973b)—cultural scholars examined the production of news too, particularly as it was differentiated across alternative sites of production, such as oppositional news, reality television, and online journalism (e.g., Boyle 1992; Friedman 2002).

Scholars in history and sociology focused on both production and reception, though unequally, as both tended to favor the former. Most historical scholars studying production tracked journalism's development over time by chronicling the evolution of certain journalistic practices, as in Michael Schudson's (1978) tracking of objectivity or Joyce Hoffman's (1995) study of insider journalism, although some researchers, particularly of late, looked at the evolution of practices by which audiences made sense of the news (e.g., Leonard 1995). Sociological scholars also tended to focus more on production than reception (e.g., Tuchman 1978a), though certain analysts (e.g., Gitlin 1980; Schudson 2002) linked reception and production in sophisticated overviews of how news making existed symbiotically with the public it targeted. Scholars studying the effects of journalism maintained a focus on reception (e.g., Lang and Lang 1953, 1983; Bogart 1956, 1981). Across these cases, sociologically minded scholars elaborated a wide range of practices and activities associated with production and reception. Neither historical nor sociological scholars tended to emphasize presentation, though there were exceptions, as in Thomas Leonard's (1986) discussion of political cartoons during the 1800s or Kevin Barnhurst and John Nerone's (2001) examination of the evolution of U.S. newspaper design. By contrast, scholars associated with language studies emphasized both production and presentation, though favoring the latter over the former in the formal, informal, and pragmatic study of language use (e.g., van Dijk 1987; Schudson 1992; Pan and Kosicki 1993; Fairclough 1995). Their studies of journalism's languages extensively elaborated the presentational tools by which journalism structured its messages, developing a ground to which other scholars, not studying presentation per se, could refer.

Political science scholars produced studies primarily concerned with questions of reception. In that scholars associated with this frame saw journalism in conjunction with its effect on the public, their emphasis on reception was consonant with larger notions about political science inquiry. However, scholars conducting smaller scale research on sourcing (e.g., Sigal 1973; Tiffen 1990) at times tracked the issues surrounding the production of news too.

On this matter, cultural scholars were the most wide-ranging in conducting inquiry across all points of the news-making process. Researchers associated with language studies were instrumental in leading scholars to focus on presentation, while those in political science kept scholarly attention attuned to the problems of reception. Scholars in history and sociology led the way in thinking about production, then and now.

Where Was the Target of Inquiry?

Where the analytical focus was located—in individual, organizational, or institutional settings—has been an important distinction between the different types of inquiry. Scholars associated with all five lenses produced studies shaped through considerations of individuals, organizations, and institutions, but to unequal degree: No one lens produced equivalent amounts of research across all three analytical settings.

Scholars concerned with broad questions of power—political, cultural, economic, or social—were interested in journalism's institutional settings, and in that regard those associated with sociology, language studies, political science, and cultural analysis all gravitated in such a direction. Their studies, which focused on journalism's broadest parameters, tended to bypass the individual dimension of journalism and linked an interest in institutional settings with a lack of real people in inquiry. In that institutions provided the broadest evidence for tracking the questions of power and authority that underlined much cultural inquiry (e.g., Sparks and Tulloch 2000; Waisbord 2000), cultural analysts were strong in institutional inquiry, though certain cultural scholars also examined individual journalists (Pauly 1988) and news organizations (Ehrlich 2002). Scholars in language studies concentrated on the patterned languages that characterized journalism's institutional settings, as in the work of Roger Fowler (1991) and S. Elizabeth Bird (1992), while political science researchers concerned themselves with the institutional impact of journalism on the public (e.g., Cook 1998). Some of this work paired an interest in institutions with a focus on organizations. Scholars associated with language studies emphasized the verbal and visual tools used to relay the news in certain organizational settings, as in the Glasgow University Media Group's discussion of news language in the BBC (GUMG 1976, 1980) or of journalistic storytelling on CBS's "60 Minutes" (Campbell 1991), while certain political science scholars focused on sourcing practices in identifiable news organizations (e.g., Eliasoph 1988; Kaniss 1991), though institutional settings remained more at the core of the interests of political science scholars. Sociological scholars seemed to focus equally on organizational (Epstein 1973; Golding and Elliott 1979; Volkmer 1999; Curran 2000a) and institutional (Herman and Chomsky 1988; Curran and Gurevitch 1991;

Bagdikian 1997) settings, largely because it was in such settings that the issues relevant to sociological inquiry—people and the interactions across them, as well as the interplay between organizations, institutions, and structures—could be easily examined. Sociological studies rarely, if ever, analyzed the individuals of journalism. There were, however, exceptions, as in James Ettema and D. Charles Whitney's (1982) edited volume *Individuals in Mass Media Organizations.*

Historical researchers unevenly addressed all three analytical settings—individual, organizational, and institutional—though not at one period in time. Much of the distinction among the three had to do with the type of historical research being conducted. Thus, many of the anecdotal chronicles that were typical of memoirs, autobiographies, and biographies helped develop in the early years of historical inquiry a ground for understanding the individuals connected with journalism (e.g., Steffens 1931; Reith 1949; Hopkinson 1982), while the large-scale histories of specific news organizations (e.g., Hart-Davis 1991; Kynaston 1988) and of journalistic institutions like broadcasting (Scannell and Cardiff 1991; Hilmes 1997; Smith 1998) and the press (Curran and Seaton 1985; Emery and Emery 1996) played a similar role in later years in developing organizational and institutional settings.

On the question of where analysis was located, then, historical scholars offered the most broadly scoped research, followed by sociological analysts. At the same time, institutional analyses seemed to draw the most attention across the disciplinary frames, addressed across the range of alternative lenses, suggesting that much of journalism scholarship was shaped by a bias toward the examination of institutional settings.

When Was the Target of Inquiry?

The issue of temporality has been central in distinguishing modes of inquiry. When journalism was studied became key, and the importance of time in shaping the inquiry at hand facilitated the development of different kinds of studies. To no surprise, historical scholars led the way in thinking about inquiry through some notion of temporality, using the lessons, triumphs, and tragedies of the past as an impulse for understanding journalism. But even among historical scholars, temporality was shaped in various ways: at times, it was invoked as a general background for exploring thematized issues (Solomon and McChesney 1993; Nerone 1994). At other times, it was employed as a variable that shaped the target of inquiry, as in, for example, discussions of journalistic practices during certain time periods (Dicken-Garcia 1989; Hartsock 2001). Given that temporality was historical inquiry's defining attribute, this made sense.

Cultural scholars, like historical researchers, displayed an interest in questions of time, though to a lesser degree. Particularly since the early days of cultural studies, when notions of historical time were woven into inquiry—as in the work of Stuart Hall, Dorothy Hobson, Andrew Lowe, and Paul Willis (1980), for example, in which historical scholarship was segmented as nearly a third of their book on culture and the media—time was frequently used as a background variable for shaping the cultural inquiry of journalism. Thus, numerous scholars (e.g., Reeves and Campbell 1994; Bromley and O'Malley 1997) tracked the cultural parameters of journalism over time or in a given time period.

By contrast, scholars conducting research along the lines of sociology, language studies, and political science were less invested in shaping inquiry around issues of temporality, although in each field scholars framed their studies in given time periods that were generally stipulated but not developed. There were exceptions, however, as in Colin Sparks's (2000) classification of tabloid forms of storytelling over time and in Timothy Cook's (1998) discussion of the evolution of the news media as a political institution.

To no surprise, then, historical scholars were the most focused on the question of "when" in shaping their inquiry. With help from researchers in cultural analysis, they elaborated this question as a ground on which other kinds of inquiry could be situated without needing to develop it anew.

Why Journalism Matters:
The How and Why of Journalism's Inquiry

Journalism, like most phenomena, is easier to look at from afar than from up close, where its many contradictory impulses come to light. Writing in the period of World War II, George Orwell complained about his freelance journalism, calling it drudgery and "made-to-order stuff" (quoted in Bromley 2003: 123), while at the same time he admitted that he found it difficult to write books because journalism kept him motivated and at the center of things. His journalistic work was prolific during those years—during which he wrote for over a dozen different journals, including *Tribune, New Leader, New Statesman and Nation, The Observer,* and *Partisan Review*— yet some scholars disparaged the very energy that kept him enmeshed in its daily grind (Bromley 2003). Raymond Williams (1972: 65), for instance, claimed that Orwell's journalism was "lively, but not his best work." Orwell's first book was denigrated by a critic who, on seeing that he had added newspaper quotations, accused him of turning "what might have been a good book into journalism" (Orwell 1946, cited in Bromley 2003), and his collected works were compiled decades later under the unambivalent title

Smothered Under Journalism, 1946 (Orwell 1999). Yet it was Orwell's early journalistic work that formed the basis for the celebrated novels yet to come.

Stories such as this one repeat over and over, and their persistence—in accounts of Charles Dickens, Arthur Ransome, Samuel Johnson, John Dos Passos, Andre Malraux, Dylan Thomas, Norman Mailer, John Hersey, and others—underscores the fact that the boundaries of what is and is not journalism remain necessarily unclear. Other writers—like Martha Gellhorn, Ernest Hemingway, and Joan Didion—drew high regard for their journalism but remained troubled by their movement between journalistic and non-journalistic worlds. All of this suggests that the contradictory impulses surrounding journalism are not going away. If we are to take journalism seriously, then, we need to develop scholarly frameworks that can accommodate its vagaries, downsides, and inconsistencies as easily as they address the more coherent dimensions of the journalistic world. All of this supports a way of thinking about journalism and its study through a necessarily interdisciplinary lens.

Five lenses have been offered in these pages as separate refractions of journalism's world. None of the lenses was shaped by all of the issues delineated above, and yet all were shaped by each of them partly. In other words, no one disciplinary lens held all of the angles relevant to generating authoritative statements about how journalism works, while each lens offered distinctive stress points as to which kinds of evidence mattered in conducting research on journalism. Across the various angles offered by our inquiry, then, we may have a better way of tracking journalism's multiple sides.

Perhaps nowhere is this as evident as when thinking about the various purposes for which scholars study journalism. Certain researchers have looked for the internal patterning within certain kinds of journalistic practices, circumstances, or settings, creating subsets of circumstances that were internally cohesive to the discipline being invoked. Thus, historical scholars focused on finding internal patterns within a given time period (Schwarzlose 1989, 1990) or around certain events (e.g., Schudson 1992), while cultural analysts focused on delineating the internal characteristics of journalism that were associated with indices of identity—race (e.g., Ainley 1998), ethnicity (e.g., Gabriel 1998; Cottle 2000c), class (e.g., Bird 1992; Hartley 1992), or sexual orientation (e.g., Alwood 1996; Gross 2002). Although many of the studies produced here were motivated by an interest in the more general patterning that went beyond the circumscribed parameters in which they were set up, the scholarly goal in many studies of journalism tended to remain more firmly within those parameters than beyond them. In other words, there was little articulation of a concern with establishing any kind of broader generalizability to the findings presented in many existing studies.

But the studies produced here had immeasurable impact in drawing a clear picture of journalism in certain circumstances.

Other scholars have been explicitly invested in establishing a fuller external generalizability across different kinds of journalistic settings. In these cases, scholars, often working from within political science and sociology, extrapolated from the internal patterning to suggest a broader generalizability about journalism and a representativeness to the cases being examined. For instance, Doris Graber, Denis McQuail, and Pippa Norris used examinations of a specific set of circumstances to generate broader statements about how journalism worked, as they noted in their conclusion to *The Politics of News/The News of Politics:* While the material mainly "relates to the United States," they said, "many of the same features have been observed in other Western democracies or are anticipated in varying degrees before too long" (Graber et al. 1998: 251). Similarly, Jay Blumler and Michael Gurevitch (1995: 221) argued that the crisis of public communication, which they examined in a series of separate essays, could be more broadly found because it "inheres in the massification of Western societies." Such a focus offered grounds for evaluating journalism more commonly in the social sciences than in the humanities, and it therefore tended to appear more often in studies associated with both political science and sociology than in those associated with culture, history, or language. The value of the aforementioned studies was clear, in that they helped establish the broader environment in which certain circumstances could be established.

The two purposes at hand in studying journalism thus offer complementary ways of drawing journalism's academic boundaries, boundaries that together impact more fully on our understanding of why journalism matters. In Tom Hopkinson's autobiography, he wrote that by the time *Picture Post*—the journal he edited for decades—closed, it had become "not one, but many different magazines" (Hopkinson 1982: 297). Journalism too comprises not one, but many different journalisms, and more interdisciplinary sensitivity in its scholarship is needed if as scholars we are to continue drawing and redrawing its boundaries. This calls for both a more vigorous integration of the various frames traditionally used to consider journalism and the use of such frames as active variables in shaping contemporary inquiry. Were we to enhance our examinations of news by vigorously engaging alternative perspectives as a more integral part of our thinking, we might better appreciate each type of inquiry for what it offers and offset the long-held assumption that one type of inquiry can tell us all that we seek to know. In other words, journalism's study might come to reflect more of journalism than of the academic world that observes it. And that is the best hope we have for ensuring that both journalism and its study continue to matter.

This is not the first call to reorient the study of journalism. Such calls have been made across the world (Phillips and Gaber 1996; Bierhoff, Deuze, and de Vreese 2000; Cottle 2000a, 2000b). Scholars have pondered the split between the social sciences and the humanities, wondering from where journalism could most effectively blossom (Katz 1992; Carey 2000; Schudson 2002). They have called to realign journalism education within institutional settings that address the professional arts and creative industries and wondered over the digital divide and its impact on notions of "optimum" journalism (Downing 1996; Bromley in press). And they have come together in one concern: Will journalism survive? This book suggests another, related thread to that concern: Will journalism's academic inquiry survive? And if so, should and can they survive alongside each other or in separate domains? *Taking Journalism Seriously*, it is hoped, kicks off a conversation about those issues, mapping out ways in which we might take journalism seriously by seeing its shadows as well as its lights—broadly, creatively, and without prejudice.

Notes

1. The response to Hemingway's work as a journalist has been widespread. See, for instance, John Atkins's *The Art of Ernest Hemingway* (1964), Earl Rovit's *Ernest Hemingway* (1961), and J.F. Kobler's *Ernest Hemingway: Journalist and Artist* (1985). Interestingly, Hemingway disparaged his time as a journalist himself, worrying incessantly that it had destroyed his creativity and furious when others mentioned his news reports in the same breath as his short stories and novels (see *Ernest Hemingway: Selected Letters,* 1981, edited by Carlos Baker).

2. James W. Carey acted as a respondent to a conference panel on humanistic inquiry and journalism, in which he praised the papers for the simple reason that they tried to "take journalism seriously." The panel, which included S. Elizabeth Bird, Robert Dardenne, Barry Dornfeld, and myself, was convened at the 1993 meetings of the International Communication Association in Washington, D.C.

3. These included frequency (the time span of an event), threshold (the size or magnitude of an event), unambiguity (the clarity of an event), meaningfulness (both the cultural proximity and relevance of an event), consonance (the predictability of an event), unexpectedness (the unpredictability of an event within the meaningful and the consonant), continuity (the running story), composition (the balance in lineup or on the front page), reference to elite persons and nations (primarily involving North America, Japan, Europe, and Russia), personalization (with events codified as the actions of individuals), and negativity (with bad news seen as good news).

4. Tuchman spent a day a week at a television station from 1966 to 1969, an additional 6 months at a newspaper from 1967 to 1968, a period of interviewing reporters in New York City in 1975, and an additional 3 months of observation of reporters assigned to the New York City Hall pressroom from 1975 to 1976.

5. Gans's ethnography was based on several months that he spent at each of the four news organizations between 1965 and 1969, an additional month of observation in each place in 1975, and a spate of interviews conducted in 1978. He also did numerous content analyses, completed over a year. The news values he identified included ethnocentrism, altruistic democracy, responsible capitalism, small-town pastoralism, individualism, and moderatism.

6. The filters included an organizational size and concentrated elite ownership that made a profit orientation the preferred managerial mode of news organizations,

a dependence on advertising as the primary source of income, a dependence on government and business as sources of information, the employment of flak— negative responses such as letters, petitions and law suits—to keep news organizations in line, and the invocation of anti-Communism as a way of mobilizing the population against "the enemy."

7. Carey's call drew both supporters (e.g., Marzolf 1975; Ward 1978) and detractors (e.g., Nord 1988), who lamented that Carey's suggestions could not be operationalized and that his proposed changes had already been in existence for some time. Yet Carey's statement lingered as one of the most provocative summations of the state of affairs in journalism history. And indeed, as a template for engaging in the historical inquiry of journalism, it was reproduced in other works on journalism over time (Carey 1978, 1985, 1989).

8. In many ways, Nerone's lament described the similarities between historians and journalists, whose development into a professional community during the 19th century followed a line similar to that of historians. Particularly in the United States, journalists, like historians, depended on a common method for doing their work, developed into professionals with an explicit embrace of the doctrine of objectivity, sought to tell the world of yesterday or today as it was, and were dependent on narrative and narrativity, which, while not coded explicitly into practice, nonetheless helped develop news-making codes (see Novick 1988 for a discussion of historians).

9. According to Sloan (1991), these schools differed as follows: Nationalist interpretations, developed in the early 19th century, saw the news media as instruments contributing to the progress of the nation-state. They focused on ideas such as freedom of the press or journalists' positioning as nationalist patriots in the U.S. context (Thomas 1810) and on Whiggish interpretations of journalism history in Britain (Sloan 1991: 3; also Curran and Seaton 1985). Nationalist interpretations tended to emerge when nation-states needed support from the environment, such as during times of national instability or insecurity. Romantic interpretations, developed in the late 18th century, offered a personalized, nostalgic view of the progress of mankind. Tending to blend autobiography, memoir, and narrative biography, they saw history as a literary art generally crafted by persons of leisure—printers or publishers—who were familiar with the people about whom they wrote (e.g., Parton 1864). This school reemerged in the post-Watergate era (e.g., Halberstam 1979), when "authors had the enticing events of that decade and the 1960s to consider" (Sloan 1991: 336). As Sloan (1991: 335) told it, "many authors wrote of television in passionate, adventurous and idealistic terms . . . in bigger-than-life terms." The developmental school of interpretation emerged in the United States from the early 1900s onward as professionalism became a way of thinking about journalism; journalism's history was seen as the evolution of journalistic practices, rules, and standards; and the press itself was seen as a setting through which the journalistic professional could continually evolve. These chronicles emphasized how the press became a tool for journalists to advance their own professional identity (e.g., Hudson 1873; Lee 1917; Bleyer 1927; Mott 1941/1962, 2000). Renewed during the post-Watergate years, when history was viewed as a clash between the media and other established institutions, such as

religion, government, and big business (Startt and Sloan 1989), the developmental school reemerged in discussions of press freedom in wartime and media autonomy in times of increased national security, all codified as professional issues relevant to democratic existence (e.g., Braestrup 1977). Progressive interpretations remained one of the most discussed interpretive schema, primarily because much of U.S. journalism as we know it today found its beginnings in this era, making it the obvious candidate for telling the story of journalism's past. Emerging in the United States around 1910, they offered reform-oriented historians who had been influenced by general historians like Frederick Jackson Turner or Charles Beard the opportunity to pit journalists against the upper class, while invoking freedom, democracy, equality, and civil reform. Ideological conflict was seen here as central and was more often than not seen in economic terms. The chroniclers in this school, not always professional journalists but rather historians graduated from departments of journalism, began to see historical inquiry more as a science than an art, due partly to changes by which historians themselves became professionals (Villard 1923; Seldes 1935; Ickes 1939). The consensus school of interpretation developed during the first half of the 1900s in response to the Depression and the First World War, when certain scholars of historical inquiry sought to effect consensus rather than conflict through their chronicles. Emphasizing agreement and unity, journalistic performance in general was seen as a tool to achieving national unity and helping the government. Consensus historians praised media owners as entrepreneurs who had performed admirably for the war effort (Bailyn 1965; Douglas 1999). The last school of interpretation was the cultural school, developed around the premise that the media operated in close links with their environment. Media were seen here as a part of society, influenced by factors outside the media themselves, and cultural historians were largely interested in the impact of society on media, rather than the other way around. This school promoted the disappearance of the "great men" chronicles and supported seeing individuals not as powerful or important but instead as agents of the larger cultural frameworks in which they worked (Kobre 1944, 1958, 1959, 1964, 1969; Carey 1974; Lee 1976; Schudson 1978). The limitations of the schools of interpretation approach are implied by its title: In adopting a given "school of interpretation," scholars imposed an a priori analytical unity on the events being described. While this no doubt produced a highly coherent and cohesive account of events in history, it also tended to generate a unitary aura to the explanations it provided.

10. Although there has been extensive work challenging the so-called unitary character of British cultural studies (see, in particular, Stratton and Ang 1996 and Miller 2001), I maintain it here as a heuristic device to differentiate the treatment accorded journalism by both the U.S. and British schools.

Bibliography

General Sources

Allen, Robert (ed.). *Channels of Discourse, Reassembled* (2nd ed.). Chapel Hill: University of North Carolina Press, 1992.

Baker, Houston A., Jr., Manthia Diawara, and Ruth H. Lindeborg (eds.). *Black British Cultural Studies: A Reader.* Chicago: University of Chicago Press, 1996.

Barker, Chris. *Cultural Studies: Theory and Practice.* Thousand Oaks, CA: Sage, 2000.

Barthes, Roland. *Elements of Semiology.* London: Jonathan Cape, 1967.

Barthes, Roland. *Mythologies.* London: Jonathan Cape, 1972 (1957).

Barthes, Roland. "Introduction to the Structural Analysis of Narratives," in *Image/Music/Text.* New York: Hill and Wang, 1977, 79–124.

Bateson, Gregory. *Steps to an Ecology of Mind.* New York: Ballantine, 1972.

Bauman, Richard, and Joel Sherzer (eds.). *Explorations in the Ethnography of Speaking.* Cambridge, UK: Cambridge University Press, 1974.

Becker, Carl L. "Everyman His Own Historian," *American Historical Review* 37 (January 1932), 221–236; reprinted in Robin Winks (ed.), *The Historian as Detective.* New York: Harper Torchbooks, 1965, 3–25.

Becker, Howard. *Art Worlds.* Berkeley: University of California Press, 1984.

Becker, Howard. "Culture: A Sociological View," in *Doing Things Together.* Evanston, IL: Northwestern University Press, 1986, 11–24.

Becker, Howard, and Michal McCall (eds.). *Symbolic Interaction and Cultural Studies.* Chicago: University of Chicago Press, 1990.

Bell, Allan, and Peter Garrett (eds.). *Approaches to Media Discourse.* Oxford, UK: Blackwell, 1998.

Benjamin, Walter. "The Storyteller," in Hannah Arendt (ed.), *Illuminations.* London: Jonathan Cape, 1970, 83–109.

Bennett, Tony. *Culture: A Reformer's Science.* London: Sage, 1998.

Berger, Peter. *Invitation to Sociology: A Humanistic Perspective.* Garden City, NY: Doubleday, 1963.

Black, Max. *Models and Metaphors.* Ithaca, NY: Cornell University Press, 1962.

Blumer, Herbert. *Symbolic Interactionism: Perspective and Method.* Englewood Cliffs, NJ: Prentice Hall, 1969.

Bocock, Robert. *Ritual in Industrial Society*. London: Allen and Unwin, 1974.

Booth, Wayne. *The Rhetoric of Fiction*. Chicago: University of Chicago Press, 1961.

Bourdieu, Pierre. *Homo Academicus*. Cambridge, UK: Polity, 1988.

Brantlinger, Patrick. *Crusoe's Footprints: Cultural Studies in Britain and America*. New York: Routledge, 1990.

Brants, Kees, Joke Hermes, and Liesbet van Zoonen (eds.). *The Media in Question: Popular Cultures and Public Interests*. London: Sage, 1998.

Brooker, Peter. *A Concise Glossary of Cultural Theory*. London: Edward Arnold, 1999.

Brummett, Barry. *Rhetorical Dimensions of Popular Culture*. Tuscaloosa: University of Alabama Press, 1991.

Burke, Kenneth. *A Grammar of Motives*. New York: Prentice Hall, 1945.

Burke, Kenneth. *A Rhetoric of Motives*. New York: Prentice Hall, 1950.

Burke, Kenneth. *Language as Symbolic Action*. Berkeley: University of California Press, 1978.

Carey, James W. *Communication as Culture*. London: Unwin Hyman, 1989a.

Carey, James W. "Overcoming Resistance to Cultural Studies," in *Communication as Culture*. London: Unwin Hyman, 1989b, 89–112.

Carey, James W. "Afterword: The Culture in Question," in Eve Stryker Munson and Catherine A. Warren (eds.), *James Carey: A Critical Reader*. Minneapolis: University of Minnesota Press, 1997a, 308–340.

Carey, James W. "Reflections on the Project of (American) Cultural Studies," in Marjorie Ferguson and Peter Golding (eds.), *Cultural Studies in Question*. London: Sage, 1997b, 1–24.

Carlyle, Thomas. *The French Revolution*. New York: AMS Press, 1974 (1905).

Chatman, Seymour. *Story and Discourse*. Ithaca, NY: Cornell University Press, 1978.

Chatman, Seymour, *Coming to Terms*. Ithaca, NY: Cornell University Press, 1990.

Chouliaraki, Lilie, and Norman Fairclough. *Discourses in Late Modernity*. Edinburgh: Edinburgh University Press, 2000.

Clifford, James. "Introduction: Partial Truths," in James Clifford and George Marcus (eds.), *Writing Culture: The Poetics and Politics of Ethnography*. Berkeley: University of California Press, 1986, 1–26.

Couldry, Nick. *Inside Culture: Re-Imagining the Method of Cultural Studies*. London: Sage, 2000a.

Couldry, Nick. *The Place of Media Power: Pilgrims and Witnesses in the Media Age*. London: Routledge, 2000b.

Davies, Ioan. *Cultural Studies and Beyond*. London: Routledge, 1995.

Douglas, Mary. *How Institutions Think*. Syracuse, NY: Syracuse University Press, 1986.

Duncan, Hugh. *Symbols in Society*. New York: Oxford University Press, 1968.

Durham, Meenakshi Gigi, and Douglas M. Kellner (eds.). *Media and Cultural Studies: Keyworks*. Malden, MA: Blackwell, 2001.

During, Simon (ed.). *The Cultural Studies Reader*. London: Routledge, 1993.

Emile. *The Elementary Forms of the Religious Life*. New York: Free Press 1965 (1915).

Eagleton, Terry. *The Crisis of Contemporary Culture*. Oxford, UK: Oxford University Press, 1995.

Eco, Umberto. *Theory of Semiotics*. Bloomington: Indiana University Press, 1976.

Eco, Umberto. *The Role of the Reader: Explorations in the Semiotics of Texts*. Bloomington: Indiana University Press, 1984.

Edgar, Andrew, and Peter Sedgwick. *Key Concepts in Cultural Theory*. London: Routledge, 1999.

Erni, John Nguyet. "Media Studies and Cultural Studies," in Toby Miller (ed.), *A Companion to Cultural Studies*. Malden, MA: Blackwell: 2001, 187–213.

Evans, Jessica, and Stuart Hall (eds.). *Visual Culture: The Reader*. London: Sage, 1999.

Fairclough, Norman. *Discourse and Social Change*. Cambridge, UK: Polity, 1993.

Fairclough, Norman. *Media Discourse*. London: Edward Arnold, 1995.

Fairclough, Norman. *Language and Power*. London: Addison-Wesley, 1996.

Ferguson, Marjorie, and Peter Golding (eds.). *Cultural Studies in Question*. London: Sage, 1997.

Fish, Stanley. *Is There a Text in This Class?* Cambridge, MA: Harvard University Press, 1980.

Fisher, Walter. "The Narrative Paradigm: In the Beginning," in "Homo Narrans: Storytelling in Mass Culture and Everyday Life," *Journal of Communication* 35, 1985, 74–89.

Fisher, Walter. *Human Communication as Narration: Toward a Philosophy of Reason, Value, and Action*. Columbia: University of South Carolina Press, 1987.

Foucault, Michel. *The Archaeology of Knowledge*. London: Tavistock, 1972.

Foucault, Michel. *Power/Knowledge*. New York: Pantheon, 1980.

Fowler, Roger, Bob Hodge, Gunther Kress, and Tony Trew (eds.). *Language and Control*. London: Routledge and Kegan Paul, 1979.

Friedson, Elliot. *Professional Powers*. Chicago: University of Chicago Press, 1986.

Frow, John. *Cultural Studies and Cultural Value*. Oxford, UK: Oxford University Press, 1995.

Gardner, Howard, Mihaly Csikszentmihalyi, and William Damon. *Good Work: When Excellence and Ethics Meet*. New York: Basic Books, 2001.

Garfinkel, Harold. *Studies in Ethnomethodology*. Englewood Cliffs, NJ: Prentice Hall, 1967.

Geertz, Clifford. *The Interpretation of Cultures*. New York: Basic Books, 1973.

Gibian, Peter (ed.). *Mass Culture and Everyday Life*. London: Routledge, 1997.

Giddens, Anthony. "What Do Sociologists Do?" in *Social Theory and Modern Sociology*. Stanford, CA: Stanford University Press, 1987, 1–21.

Giles, Judy, and Tim Middleton. *Studying Culture: A Practical Introduction*. Malden, MA: Blackwell, 1999.

Goffman, Erving. *Frame Analysis*. Boston: Northeastern University Press, 1974.

Goodenough, Ward. *Culture, Language, and Society.* Reading, MA: Addison-Wesley, 1981.

Goodman, Nelson. *Ways of Worldmaking.* Indianapolis, IN: Hackett, 1978.

Gramsci, Antonio. *Selections from the Prison Notebooks.* New York: International Publishers, 1971.

Grossberg, Lawrence, Cary Nelson, and Paula Treichler (eds.). *Cultural Studies.* New York: Routledge, 1992.

Grossberg, Lawrence. *Bringing It All Back Home: Essays On Cultural Studies.* Durham, NC: Duke University Press, 1997.

Hall, Stuart, Dorothy Hobson, Andrew Lowe, and Paul Willis (eds.). *Culture, Media, Language,* London: Hutchinson and Co., 1980.

Hardt, Hanno. "British Cultural Studies and the Return of the 'Critical' in American Mass Communications Research," *Journal of Communication Inquiry* 10(2), Summer 1986, 117–124.

Hardt, Hanno. *Critical Communication Studies: Communication, History and Theory in America.* New York: Routledge, 1992.

Hartley, John. *Communication, Cultural and Media Studies: The Key Concepts.* London: Routledge, 2002.

Hartley, John. A Short History of Cultural Studies. London: Sage, 2003.

Hebdige, Dick. *Subculture: The Meaning of Style.* London: Methuen, 1979.

Hebdige, Dick. *Hiding in the Light.* London: Comedia, 1988.

Hjelmslev, L. *Prolegomena to a Theory of Language.* Madison: University of Wisconsin, 1963 (1943).

"Homo Narrans: Story-telling in Mass Culture and Everyday Life," *Journal of Communication* (Special issue) 35(4), Fall 1985.

Hughes, Everett C. *Men and Their Work.* Glencoe, IL: Free Press, 1958.

Hymes, Dell. "On Communicative Competence," in J.B. Pride and Janet Holmes, *Sociolinguistics: Selected Readings.* London: Penguin, 1972, 269–293.

Jakobson, Roman. *Selected Writings* (Vols. 1–4). The Hague, The Netherlands: Mouton, 1962–1966.

Jensen, Joli, and John J. Pauly, "Imagining the Audience: Losses and Gains in Cultural Studies," in Marjorie Ferguson and Peter Golding (eds.), *Cultural Studies in Question.* London: Sage, 1997, 155–167.

Johnson, Richard. "What Is Cultural Studies, Anyway?" *Social Text* 6(1), 1986/1987, 38–80.

Kirk, Jerome, and Marc L. Miller. *Reliability and Validity in Qualitative Research.* Beverly Hills, CA: Sage, 1986.

Kozloff, Sarah. "Narrative Theory and Television," in Robert Allen (ed.), *Channels of Discourse, Reassembled* (2nd ed.). Chapel Hill: University of North Carolina Press, 1992, 67–100.

Krippendorff, Klaus. *Content Analysis.* Beverly Hills, CA: Sage, 1980.

Krippendorff, Klaus. *Content Analysis* (2nd ed.). Thousand Oaks, CA: Sage, 2004.

Kuhn, Thomas. *The Structure of Scientific Revolutions.* Chicago: University of Chicago Press, 1964.

Labov, William. "The Study of Language in its Social Context," in J.B. Pride and Janet Holmes, *Sociolinguistics: Selected Readings*. London: Penguin, 1972, 180–202.

La Capra, Dominick. *History and Criticism*. Ithaca, NY: Cornell University Press, 1985.

Lacey, Nick. *Image and Representation: Key Concepts in Media Studies*. London: St. Martin's, 1998.

Lakoff, George. *Women, Fire, and Dangerous Things: What Categories Reveal About the Mind*. Chicago: University of Chicago Press, 1987.

Lakoff, George, and Mark Johnson. *Metaphors We Live By*. Chicago: University of Chicago Press, 1980.

Larson, Magali Sarfatti. *The Rise of Professionalism*. Berkeley: University of California Press, 1977.

Leach, Edmund. *Culture and Communication*. Cambridge, UK: Cambridge University Press, 1976.

Lévi-Strauss, Claude. *Structural Anthropology*. London: Allen Lane 1958.

Lusted, David, and Philip Drummond. *TV and Schooling*. London: British Film Institute, 1985.

Mariscal, Jorge. "Can Cultural Studies Speak Spanish?" in Toby Miller (ed.), *A Companion to Cultural Studies*. Oxford, UK: Blackwell, 2001, 232–245.

Matta, Roberto da. *Carnivals, Rogues, and Heroes: An Interpretation of the Brazilian Dilemma*. Notre Dame, IN: University of Notre Dame Press, 1991.

Mattelart, Armand. *The Invention of Communication*. Minneapolis: University of Minnesota Press, 1996.

Mattelart, Armand, and Michele Mattelart. *Rethinking Media Theory*. Minneapolis: University of Minnesota Press, 1992.

McGuigan, Jim. *Cultural Populism*. London: Routledge, 1992.

Miller, Toby (ed.). *A Companion to Cultural Studies*. Oxford, UK: Blackwell, 2001.

Moore, Wilbert Ellis. *The Professions: Roles and Rules*. London: Russell Sage, 1970.

Morgenthau, Hans J. *Politics Among Nations: the Struggle for Power and Peace*. New York: Alfred A. Knopf, 1985 (1948).

Munson, Eve Stryker, and Catherine A. Warren (eds.). *James Carey: A Critical Reader*. Minneapolis: University of Minnesota Press, 1997.

Nelson, Cary, and Dilip Parameshwar Gaonkar (eds.). *Disciplinarity and Dissent in Cultural Studies*. New York: Routledge, 1996.

Nelson, Cary, and Lawrence Grossberg (eds.). *Marxism and the Interpretation of Culture*. Urbana: University of Illinois Press, 1988.

Novick, Peter. *That Noble Dream*. Cambridge, UK: Cambridge University Press, 1988.

O'Sullivan, Tim, John Hartley, Danny Saunders, and John Fiske. *Key Concepts in Communication*. London: Methuen, 1983.

O'Sullivan, Tim, John Hartley, Danny Saunders, Martin Montgomery, and John Fiske. *Key Concepts in Communication and Cultural Studies*. London: Routledge, 1994.

Peirce, Charles. *The Essential Peirce: Selected Philosophical Writings, 1893–1913*. Bloomington: Indiana University Press, 1998.

Poster, Mark. *The Second Media Age*. Cambridge, UK: Polity, 1995.

Propp, Vladimir. *The Morphology of the Folktale*. Minneapolis: University of Minnesota Press, 1984 (1930).

Purcell, Edward A., Jr. *The Crisis of Democratic Theory: Scientific Naturalism and the Problem of Value*. Lexington: University of Kentucky Press, 1979.

Rabinow, Paul, and William M. Sullivan. *Interpretive Social Science: A Reader*. Berkeley: University of California Press, 1979.

Sacks, Harvey. "An Initial Investigation of the Usability of Conversational Data for Doing Sociology," in David Sudnow (ed.), *Studies in Interaction*. New York: Free Press, 1972, 31–74.

Saussure, Ferdinand de. *Course on General Linguistics*. New York: McGraw-Hill, 1965 (1916).

Schudson, Michael. "How Culture Works," *Theory and Society* 18(2), March 1989, 153–180.

Schutz, Alfred. *Life Forms and Meaning Structure*. Boston: Routledge and Kegan Paul, 1982.

Sebeok, Thomas. *Style in Language*. Cambridge: MIT Press, 1964.

Sebeok, Thomas. *The Sign and Its Masters*. Lanham, MD: University Press of America, 1979.

Shiach, Morag (ed.). *Feminism and Cultural Studies*. London: Oxford, 1999.

Stone, Lawrence. *The Past and the Present Revisited*. New York: Routledge and Kegan Paul, 1987.

Storey, John. *An Introductory Guide to Cultural Theory and Popular Culture*. Athens: University of Georgia Press, 1993.

Storey, John. *Cultural Studies and the Study of Popular Culture: Theories and Methods*. Athens: University of Georgia Press, 1996b.

Storey, John. *Inventing Popular Culture*. Oxford, UK: Blackwell, 2003.

Stratton, Jon, and Ien Ang. "On the Impossibility of A Global Cultural Studies: 'British' Cultural Studies in an 'International' Frame," in David Morley and Kuan-Hsing Chen (eds.), *Stuart Hall: Critical Dialogues in Cultural Studies*. London: Routledge, 1996.

Swidler, Ann. "Culture in Action: Symbols and Strategies," in *American Sociological Review* 51, April 1986, 273–286.

Thompson, John B. *Ideology and Modern Culture*. Stanford, CA: Stanford University Press, 1990.

Thompson, John B. *The Media and Modernity*. Cambridge, UK: Polity, 1995.

Todorov, Tzvetan. *The Poetics of Prose*. Ithaca, NY: Cornell University Press, 1978.

Tudor, Andrew. *Decoding Culture: Theory and Method in Cultural Studies*. London: Sage, 1999.

Turner, Graeme. *British Cultural Studies: An Introduction*. London: Routledge, 1990.

Van Maanen, John. *Tales of the Field: On Writing Ethnography*. Chicago: University of Chicago Press, 1988.

Wark, McKenzie. *The Virtual Republic: Australia's Culture Wars of the 1990s*. Sydney: Allen and Unwin, 1997.

Watson, James, and Anne Hill. *A Dictionary of Communication and Media Studies* (3rd ed.). London: Edward Arnold, 1994.

White, Hayden. *The Content of the Form: Narrative Discourse and Historical Representation*. Baltimore: Johns Hopkins University Press, 1987.

Williams, Raymond. *George Orwell*. New York: Viking, 1972.

Williams, Raymond. *The Sociology of Culture*. New York: Schocken, 1982.

Williams, Raymond. *Writing in Society*. London: Verso, 1983a.

Williams, Raymond. *Keywords*. New York: Oxford University Press, 1983b.

Winks, Robin. *The Historian as Detective*. New York: Harper and Row, 1968.

Wuthnow, Robert, and Marsha Witten. "New Directions in the Study of Culture," in *Annual Review of Sociology*, 1988, 49–67.

Yudice, George. "Comparative Cultural Studies Traditions: Latin America and the U.S.," in Toby Miller (ed.), *A Companion to Cultural Studies*. Oxford, UK: Blackwell, 2001, 217–231.

Sources on Journalism

Aarons, Leroy, and Sheila Murphy. *Lesbians and Gays in the Newsroom: 10 Years Later*. Report prepared by Annenberg School for Communication, USC, in collaboration with the National Lesbian and Gay Journalists Association, 2000 (http://www.nlgja.org/pdf/survey2k.pdf.).

Abramo, Claudio. *A regra do jogo: O jornalismo e a etica do marceneiro*. Sao Paulo: Companhia das Letras, 1989; cited in Waasbord 2000.

Adam, G. Stuart. "Journalism Knowledge and Journalism Practice: The Problems of Curriculum and Research in University Schools of Journalism," *Canadian Journal of Communication* 14, 1989, 70–80.

Adam, G. Stuart. *Notes Toward a Definition of Journalism*. St. Petersburg, FL: Poynter Institute, 1993.

Adatto, Kiku. *Picture Perfect*. New York: Basic Books, 1994.

Ainley, Beulah. *Black Journalists, White Media*. Stoke on Trent, UK: Trentham, 1998.

Allan, Stuart. "News and the Public Sphere: Towards a History of Objectivity and Impartiality," in Michael Bromley and Tom O'Malley (eds.), *A Journalism Reader*. London: Routledge, 1997, 296–329.

Allan, Stuart. "News From NowHere: Televisual News Discourse and the Construction of Hegemony," in Allan Bell and Peter Garrett (eds.), *Approaches to Media Discourse*. Oxford, UK: Blackwell, 1998, 105–141.

Allan, Stuart. *News Culture*. Buckingham, UK: Open University Press, 1999.

Allan, Stuart. "Reweaving the Internet: Online News of September 11," in Barbie Zelizer and Stuart Allan (eds), *Journalism After September 11*. London: Routledge, 2002, 119–140.

Allan, Stuart, and Barbie Zelizer (eds.). *Reporting War: Journalism in Wartime.* London: Routledge, in press.

Allen, Craig. *Eisenhower and the Mass Media: Peace, Prosperity, and Prime-Time TV.* Chapel Hill: University of North Carolina Press, 1993.

Allen, David S., and Robert Jensen (eds.). *Freeing the First Amendment: Critical Perspectives on Freedom of Expression.* New York: New York University Press, 1995.

Alterman, Eric. *What Liberal Media? The Truth About Bias and the News.* New York: Basic Books, 2003.

Altheide, David, and Robert Snow. *Media Worlds in the Postjournalism Era.* New York: Aldine de Grutyer, 1991.

Altschull, Herbert. *Agents of Power: The Role of the News Media in Human Affairs.* New York: Longman, 1984.

Alwood, Edward. *Straight News: Gays, Lesbians, and the News Media.* New York: Columbia University Press, 1996.

Anderson, David, and Michael Cornfield. *The Civic Web: Online Politics and Democratic Values.* Lanham, MD: Rowman and Littlefield, 2002.

Andrews, Alexander. *History of British Journalism* (Vols. 1 and 2). London: Richard Bentley. 1859; cited in Boyce, Curran, and Wingate 1878.

Anonymous. *The History of the Times* (Vols. 1–5). New York: Macmillan, 1935–1958.

Arlen, Michael J., and Robert J. Thompson. *Living Room War.* Syracuse, NY: Syracuse University Press, 1997.

Arterton, F. Christopher. *Media Politics: The New Strategies of Presidential Campaigns.* Lexington, MA: Lexington, 1984.

Ashley, Perry J. (ed.). *American Newspaper Journalists, 1690–1950* (Vols. 1–4). Detroit, MI: Gale Research, 1983–1985.

ASNE. *What Is News? Who Decides? And How?* American Society of Newspaper Editors as part of the Newspaper Reader Project, by Judee Burgoon, Michael Burgoon, and Charles K. Atkin of Michigan State University, May 1982.

Atkins, Joan. *The Art of Ernest Hemingway.* London: Spring Books, 1964.

Atton, Chris. *Alternative Media.* London: Sage, 2002.

Aufderheide, Patricia. "Latin American Grassroots Video: Beyond Television," *Public Culture 5,* 1993, 579–592.

Ayerst, David. *The Manchester Guardian—Biography of a Newspaper.* London: Collins, 1971.

Bagdikian, Ben. *The Media Monopoly* (5th ed.). Boston: Beacon, 1997.

Bailey, Sally, and Granville Williams. "Memoirs Are Made of This: Journalists' Memoirs in the United Kingdom, 1945–95," in Michael Bromley and Tom O'Malley (eds.), *A Journalism Reader.* London: Routledge, 1997, 351–377.

Bailyn, Bernard. *The Ideological Origins of the American Revolution.* Cambridge, MA: Belknap Press of Harvard University Press, 1967.

Baker, C. Edwin. *Media, Markets, and Democracy.* New York: Cambridge University Press, 2002.

Baker, Carlos (ed.). *Ernest Hemingway: Selected Letters.* New York: Scribner, 1981.

Baldasty, Gerald L. *The Commercialization of News in the Nineteenth Century.* Madison: University of Wisconsin Press, 1992.

Baldasty, Gerald L. *E.W. Scripps and the Business of Newspapers.* Urbana: University of Illinois Press, 1999.

Bantz, Charles. "News Organizations: Conflict as a Crafted Cultural Norm," *Communications* 8, 1985, 225–244.

Barkin, Steve. "The Journalist as Storyteller," *American Journalism* 1(2), Winter 1984, 27–33.

Barnhurst, Kevin G. *Seeing the Newspaper.* New York: St. Martin's, 1994.

Barnhurst, Kevin G., and John Nerone. *The Form of News.* New York: Guilford, 2001.

Barnouw, Eric. *A History of Broadcasting in the United States* (Vols. 1–3). New York: Oxford University Press, 1966–1970.

Barnouw, Eric. *Tube of Plenty: The Evolution of American Television.* New York: Oxford University Press, 1975.

Barris, Alex. *Stop the Presses! The Newspaperman in American Film.* South Brunswick, NJ: Barnes, 1976.

Batscha, Robert M. *Foreign Affairs News and the Broadcast Journalist.* New York: Praeger, 1975.

Bausinger, Hans. "Media, Technology and Daily Life," in *Media, Culture and Society* 6(4), 1984, 343–351.

Bayley, Edwin R. *Joe McCarthy and the Press.* Madison: University of Wisconsin Press, 1981.

Beasley, Maurine. "The Women's National Press Club: A Case Study of Professional Aspirations," *Journalism Quarterly* 15(4), Winter 1988, 112–121.

Beasley, Maurine. "Recent Directions for the Study of Women's History in American Journalism," *Journalism Studies* 2(2), May 2001, 207–220.

Becker, Howard S. *Art Worlds.* Berkeley: University of California Press, 1984.

Becker, Lee B., Jeffrey W. Fruit, and Susan L. Caudill. *The Training and Hiring of Journalists.* Norwood, NJ: Ablex, 1987.

Belanger, Claude, Jacques Godechot, Pierre Giral, and Fernand Terrou. *Histoire generale de la presse francaise* (Vols. 1–5). Paris: Presses Universitaires di France, 1969–1974.

Bell, Allan. "Radio: The Style of News Language," *Journal of Communication* 32(1), 1982, 150–164.

Bell, Allan. *The Language of News Media.* Oxford, UK: Blackwell, 1991.

Bell, Allan. "Climate of Opinion: Public and Media Discourse on the Global Environment," *Discourse and Society* 5(1), January 1994, 33–64.

Bell, Philip, and Theo van Leeuven, *The Media Interview: Confession, Contest, Conversation.* Kensington, NSW, Australia: New South Wales University Press, 1994.

Belsey, Andrew, and Ruth Chadwick (eds.). *Ethical Issues in Journalism and the Media.* London: Routledge, 1992.

Benavides, Jose Luis. "*Gacetilla*: A Keyword for a Revisionist Approach to the Political Economy of Mexico's Print News Media," *Media, Culture and Society* 22(1), 2000, 85–104.

Bennett, W. Lance. *News: The Politics of Illusion* (2nd ed.). New York: Longman, 1988.

Bennett, W. Lance, and Murray Edelman. "Toward A New Political Narrative," *Journal of Communication* 35(4), Autumn 1985, 156–171.

Bennett, W. Lance, and David Paletz (eds.). *Taken By Storm: The Media, Public Opinion and U.S. Foreign Policy in the Gulf War.* Chicago: University of Chicago Press, 1994.

Benson, Rodney. "The Political/Literary Model of French Journalism: Change and Continuity in Immigration News Coverage, 1973–1991," *Journal of European Area Studies* 10(1), 2002, 49–70.

Benson, Rodney, and Erik Neveu (eds.). *Bourdieu and the Sociology of Journalism: A Field Theory Approach.* Cambridge, UK: Polity, in press.

Berelson, Bernard. "What Missing the Newspaper Means," in Paul Lazarsfeld and Frank Stanton (eds.), *Communications Research, 1948–1949.* New York: Harper, 1949, 111–129.

Berelson, Bernard. *Content Analysis in Communication Research.* Glencoe, IL: Free Press, 1952.

Berger, Meyer. *The Story of the New York Times, 1851–1951.* New York: Simon and Schuster, 1951.

Berkowitz, Dan. "Refining the Gatekeeping Metaphor for Local Television News, *Journal of Broadcasting and Electronic Media* 34(1), 1990, 55–68.

Berkowitz, Dan. "Non-Routine News and Newswork: Exploring a What-a-Story," *Journal of Communication* 42(1), 1992, 82–94.

Bierhoff, Jan, Mark Deuze, and Claes de Vreese. "Media Innovation, Professional Debate and Media Training: A European Analysis," *European Journalism Centre Report.* Maastricht: EJC, 2000 (http://www.ejc.nl/hp/mi/contents.html).

Billig, Michael. *Banal Nationalism.* London: Sage, 1995.

Bird, S. Elizabeth. "Storytelling on the Far Side: Journalism and the Weekly Tabloid," *Critical Studies in Mass Communication* 7(4), 1990, 377–389.

Bird, S. Elizabeth. *For Enquiring Minds.* Knoxville: University of Tennessee Press, 1992.

Bird, S. Elizabeth. "Audience Demands a Murderous Market: Tabloidization in U.S. Television News," in Colin Sparks and John Tulloch (eds.), *Tabloid Tales.* Lanham, MD: Rowman and Littlefield, 2000, 213–228.

Bird, S. Elizabeth, and Robert W. Dardenne. "Myth, Chronicle and Story: Exploring the Narrative Qualities of News," in James W. Carey (ed.), *Media, Myths and Narrative.* Newbury Park, CA: Sage, 1988, 67–86.

Blanchard, Margaret A. "The Ossification of Journalism History," *Journalism History,* 25(3), Autumn 1999, 107–112.

Blanchard, Robert. *Congress and the News Media.* New York: Hastings House, 1974.

Blankenberg, Ngaire. "In Search of a Real Freedom: *Ubuntu* and the Media," *Critical Arts* 13(2), 1999, 42–65.

Bleske, Glen L. "Ms. Gates Takes Over: An Updated Version of a 1949 Case Study," *Newspaper Research Journal* 12, 1991, 88–97.

Bleyer, Willard. *Main Currents in the History of American Journalism*. Boston: Houghton Mifflin, 1927.

Blondheim, Menahem. *News Over the Wires: The Telegraph and the Flow of Public Information in America, 1842–1897*. Cambridge, MA: Harvard University Press, 1994.

BlueEar.com. *9/11: Documenting America's Greatest Tragedy*. BookSurge.com, 2001.

Blum-Kulka, Shoshana. "The Dynamics of Political Interviews," *Text* 3(2), 1983: 131–153.

Blumler, Jay G. *Communicating to Voters: Television in the First European Parliament Elections*. London: Sage, 1983.

Blumler, Jay, Roland Cayrol, and Michel Thoveron. *La television fait-elle l'election?* Paris: Presses de Science Po, 1978.

Blumler, Jay G., and Michael Gurevitch. "Politicians and the Press: An Essay on Role Relationships," in Dan Nimmo and Keith R. Sanders (eds.), *Handbook of Political Communication*. London: Sage, 1981.

Blumler, Jay G., and Michael Gurevitch. *The Crisis of Public Communication*. London: Routledge, 1995.

Blumler Jay G., and Elihu Katz. *The Uses of Mass Communications: Current Perspectives on Gratifications Research*. Beverly Hills, CA: Sage, 1974.

Blumler, Jay G., and Denis McQuail. *Television in Politics: Its Uses and Influence*. London: Faber, 1968.

Bogart, Leo. *The Age of Television: A Study of Viewing Habits and the Impact of Television on American Life*. New York: F. Ungar, 1956.

Bogart, Leo. *Press and Public: Who Reads What, When, Where, and Why in American Newspapers*. Hillsdale, NJ: Lawrence Erlbaum, 1981.

Borden, Diane L., and Harvey Kerric (eds.). *The Electronic Grapevine*. Mahwah, NJ: Lawrence Erlbaum, 1998.

Bourdieu, Pierre. *On Television and Journalism*. London: Pluto, 1998.

Boyce, George. "The Fourth Estate: Reappraisal of a Concept," in George Boyce, James Curran, and Pauline Wingate (eds.), *Newspaper History from the Seventeenth Century to the Present Day*. Beverly Hills, CA: Sage, 1978, 19–40.

Boyce, George, James Curran, and Pauline Wingate (eds.), *Newspaper History From the Seventeenth Century to the Present Day*. Beverly Hills, CA: Sage, 1978.

Boyd-Barrett, Oliver. "The Politics of Socialization: Recruitment and Training for Journalism," in Harry Christian (ed.), *The Sociology of Journalism and the Press* (Sociological Review Monograph 29). Keele, UK: University of Keele, 1980a, 307–340.

Boyd-Barrett, Oliver. *The International News Agencies*. London: Constable, 1980b.

Boyd-Barrett, Oliver, and Terhi Rantanen (eds.). *The Globalization of News*. London: Sage, 1998.

Boyd Barrett, Oliver, Colin Seymour-Ure, and Jeremy Tunstall. "Studies on the Press," *Working Paper–Royal Commission on the Press*. London: HMSO, 1977.

Boyle, Dierdre. "From Port-pak to Camcorder: A Brief History of Guerrilla Television," *Journal of Film and Video* 44(1/2), 1992, 67–79.

Boyle, Maryellen. "The Revolt of the Communist Journalist: East Germany," *Media, Culture, and Society* 14(1), January 1992, 133–139.

Braestrup, Peter. *Big Story: How the American Press and Television Reported and Interpreted the Tet Offensive in Vietnam and Washington.* New Haven, CT: Yale University Press, 1977.

Bray, Howard. *The Pillars of the Post: the Making of a News Empire in Washington.* New York: Norton, 1980.

Breed, Warren. "Social Control in the Newsroom: A Functional Analysis." *Social Forces* 33, 1955, 326–335.

Brennen, Bonnie, and Hanno Hardt (eds.). *Picturing the Past: Media, History, and Photography.* Urbana: University of Illinois Press, 1999.

Brennen, Bonnie. "What the Hacks Say: The Ideological Prism of U.S. Journalism Texts," *Journalism: Theory, Practice and Criticism* 1(1), 2000, 106–113.

Brennen, Bonnie. "Sweat Not Melodrama. Reading the Structure of Feeling in *All the President's Men*," *Journalism: Theory, Practice, and Criticism* 4(1), 2003, 115–133.

Briggs, Asa. *The History of Broadcasting in the United Kingdom* (Vols. 1–5). Oxford, UK: Oxford University Press, 1961–1995.

Brokaw, Tom. *A Long Way From Home: Growing Up in the American Heartland.* New York: Random House, 2002.

Bromley, Michael. *Media Studies: An Introduction to Journalism.* London: Hodder and Stoughton, 1995.

Bromley, Michael. "The End of Journalism? Changes in Workplace Practices in the Press and Broadcasting in the 1990s," in Michael Bromley and Tom O'Malley (eds.), *A Journalism Reader.* London: Routledge, 1997, 330–350.

Bromley, Michael. "Objectivity and the Other Orwell: The Tabloidism of the *Daily Mirror* and Journalistic Authenticity," *Media History* 9(2), 2003, 123–135.

Bromley, Michael. "One Journalism or Many? Confronting the Contradictions in the Education and Training of Journalists in the United Kingdom," in K.W.Y. Leung, J. Kenny, and P.S.N. Lee (eds.), *Global Trends in Communication Research and Education.* Cresskill, NJ: Hampton, in press.

Bromley, Michael, and Tom O'Malley (eds.). *A Journalism Reader.* London: Routledge, 1997.

Bromley, Michael, and Hugh Stephenson (eds.). *Sex, Lies and Democracy: The Press and the Public.* London: Addison-Wesley, 1998.

Bronstein, Carolyn, and Stephen Vaughn. "Willard G. Bleyer and the Relevance of Journalism Education," *Journalism and Mass Communication Monographs,* June 1998, 1–36.

Brosius, Hans-Bernd, and Han Mathias Kepplinger. "Beyond Agenda-Setting: The Influence of Partisanship and Television Reporting on the Electorate's Voting Intentions," *Journalism Quarterly* 69, 1992, 893–901.

Brothers, Caroline. *War and Photography.* London: Routledge, 1997.

Brown, Lucy M. *Victorian News and Newspapers*. Oxford, UK: Clarendon, 1985.

Brummett, Barry. "Perfection and the Bomb: Nuclear Weapons, Teleology, and Motives," *Journal of Communication* 39(1), 1989, 85–95.

Brunel, Gilles. *Le francais radiophonique à Montreal*. Unpublished master's thesis. Montreal: University of Montreal; cited in Bell 1991.

Brunsdon, Charlotte, and David Morley. *Everyday Television*. London: BFI, 1978.

Bundock, Clement J. *The National Union of Journalists: A Jubilee History*. Oxford, UK: NUJ, 1957.

Burger, Harald. *Sprache der Massenmedien*. Berlin: Walter de Gruyter, 1984; cited in Bell 1991.

Burnham, Lord. *Peterborough Court: The Story of the Daily Telegraph*. London: Cassell, 1955.

Burns, Thomas. "Public Service and Private World," in Peter Halmos (ed.), *The Sociology of Mass Media Communicators*. Keele, UK: University of Keele, 1969, 53–73.

Burns, Thomas. *The BBC: Public Institution and Private World*. London: Macmillan, 1977.

Butler, David, and Donald E. Stokes. *Political Change in Britain*. New York: St Martin's, 1969.

Buttrose, Ita. *Early Edition: My First Forty Years*. London: Macmillan, 1985.

Cameron, James. "Journalism: A Trade," in *Point of Departure*. London: Arthur Barker, 1967, reprinted in Michael Bromley and Tom O'Malley (eds.), *A Journalism Reader*. London: Routledge, 1997, 170–173.

Campbell, Karlyn Kohrs, and Kathleen Hall Jamieson. *Deeds Done in Words: Presidential Rhetoric and the Genres of Governance*. Chicago: University of Chicago Press, 1990.

Campbell, Richard. *60 Minutes and the News*. Urbana: University of Illinois Press, 1991.

Carey, James W. "The Communications Revolution and the Professional Communicator," *Sociological Review Monographs* 13, 1969, 23–38.

Carey, James W. "The Problem of Journalism History," *Journalism History* 1(1), Spring 1974, 3–5, 27.

Carey, James W. "A Plea for the University Tradition," *Journalism Quarterly* 55(4), Winter 1978, 846–855.

Carey, James W. "Putting the World at Peril: A Conversation With James W. Carey," *Journalism History* 12(2), Summer 1985, 38–53.

Carey, James W. "The Dark Continent of American Journalism," in Robert K. Manoff and Michael Schudson (eds.), *Reading the News*. New York: Pantheon, 1986a, 146–196.

Carey, James W. "Journalists Just Leave: The Ethics of an Anomalous Profession," in M.G. Sagan (ed.), *Ethics and the Media*. Iowa City: Iowa Humanities Board, 1986b, 5–19.

Carey, James W. "The Press and Public Discourse," *Center Magazine* 20(2), 1989c, 4–32.

Carey, James W. "The Press, Public Opinion and Public Discourse," in Theodore L. Glasser and Charles L. Salmon (eds.), *Public Opinion and the Communication of Consent.* New York: Guilford, 1995, 373–402.

Carey, James W. "The Internet and the End of the National Communication System," *Journalism and Mass Communication Quarterly* 75(1), 1998, 28–34.

Carey, James W. "In Defense of Public Journalism," in Theodore Glasser (ed.), *The Idea of Public Journalism.* New York: Guilford, 1999, 49–66.

Carey, James W. "Some Personal Notes on Journalism Education," *Journalism: Theory, Practice, and Criticism* 1(1), 2000, 12–23.

Carlebach, Michael L. *The Origins of Photojournalism in America.* Washington, DC: Smithsonian Press, 1992.

Carter, Cynthia, Gill Branston, and Stuart Allan (eds.). *News, Gender and Power.* London: Routledge, 1998.

Caspi, Dan, and Yehiel Limor. *The In/Outsiders: The Media in Israel.* Cresskill, NJ: Hampton, 1999.

Cater, Douglass. *The Fourth Branch of Government.* Boston: Houghton Mifflin, 1959.

Catterall, Peter, Colin Seymour-Ure, and Adrian Smith (eds.). *Northcliffe's Legacy: Aspects of the British Popular Press, 1896–1996.* New York: St. Martin's in association with Institute of Contemporary British History, 2000.

Chafee, Zechariah. *Free Speech in the United States.* Cambridge, MA: Harvard University Press, 1941.

Chaffee, Steven H., Carlos Gomez-Palacio, and Everett M. Rogers. "Mass Communication Research in Latin America: Views From Here and There," *Journalism Quarterly* 64(4), 1990, 1015–1024.

Chalaby, Jean K. "Journalism as an Anglo-American Invention," *European Journal of Communication* 11(3), 1996, 303–326.

Chalaby, Jean K. *The Invention of Journalism.* London: Macmillan, 1998.

Chaney, David. *Processes of Mass Communication.* London: Macmillan, 1972.

Charity, Arthur. *Doing Public Journalism.* New York: Kettering Foundation, 1995.

Chavez, Leo. *Covering Immigration: Popular Images and the Politics of the Nation.* Berkeley: University of California Press, 2001.

Chibnall, Steve. *Law and Order News: An Analysis of Crime Reporting in the British Press.* London: Tavistock, 1977.

Chippendale, Peter, and Chris Horrie. *Stick It Up Your Punter: The Rise and Fall of The Sun.* London: Mandarin, 1992.

Christians, Clifford. "An Intellectual History of Media Ethics," in Bart Pattyn (ed.), *Media Ethics: Opening Social Dialogue.* Leuven, Belgium: Peeters, 2000, 15–46.

Christians, Clifford C., Mark Fackler, Kim B. Rotzoll, and Kathy B. McKee (eds.). *Media Ethics: Cases and Moral Reasoning.* New York: Longman, 1983.

Christians, Clifford C., and Michael Traber (eds.). *Communication Ethics and Universal Values.* Thousand Oaks, CA: Sage, 1997.

Clark, Charles E. *Public Prints: The Newspaper in Anglo-American Culture, 1665–1740.* New York: Oxford University Press, 1994.

Clark, Roy Peter. "Return of the Narrative: The Rebirth of Writing in America's Newsrooms," *The Quill* 82(4), May 1994, 27.

Clayman, Steven E. "From Talk to Text: Newspaper Accounts of Reporter-Source Interactions," *Media, Culture and Society* 12(1), 1990, 79–103.

Cohen, Akiba A. *Dimensions of the Journalistic Interview*. Newbury Park, CA: Sage, 1987.

Cohen, Akiba A., Mark Levy, Itzhak Roeh, and Michael Gurevitch. *Global Newsrooms, Local Audiences: A Study of the Eurovision News Exchange*. London: John Libbey, 1996.

Cohen, Akiba A., and Gadi Wolfsfeld. *Framing the Intifada*. Norwood, NJ: Ablex, 1993.

Cohen, Bernard. *The Press and Foreign Policy*. Princeton, NJ: Princeton University Press, 1963.

Cohen, Bernard. *Democracies and Foreign Policy: Public Participation in the United States and the Netherlands*. Madison: University of Wisconsin Press, 1995.

Cohen, Stanley. *Folk Devils and Moral Panics*. London: McGibbon and Kee, 1972.

Cohen, Stanley and Jock Young (eds.). *The Manufacture of News*. Beverly Hills, CA: Sage, 1973.

Combs, James G., and Michael W. Mansfield. *Drama in Life: The Uses of Communication in Society*. New York: Hastings, 1976.

Conboy, Martin. *The Press and Popular Culture*. London: Sage, 2002.

Condit, Celeste, and J. Ann Selzer. "The Rhetoric of Objectivity in the Newspaper Coverage of a Murder Trial," *Critical Studies in Mass Communication* 2, 1985, 197–216.

Connery, Thomas (ed.). *A Sourcebook of American Literary Journalism*. Westport, CT: Greenwood, 1992.

Cook, Timothy E. *Making Laws and Making News: Media Strategies in the U.S. House of Representatives*. Washington, DC: Brookings Institution, 1990.

Cook, Timothy E., *Governing With the News: The News Media as a Political Institution*. Chicago: University of Chicago Press, 1998.

Cornebise, Alfred Emile. *Ranks and Columns: Armed Forces Newspapers in American Wars*. Westport, CT: Greenwood, 1993.

Cornfield, Michael. *Democracy Moves Online: American Politics Enters the Digital Age*. New York: Norton, 2002.

Corradi, Juan E., Patricia Weiss Fagen, and Manuel Antonio Garreton (eds.). *Fear at the Edge: State Terror and Resistance in Latin America*. Berkeley: University of California Press, 1992.

Cottle, Simon. "New(s) Times: Towards a 'Second Wave' of News Ethnography," *Communications* 25(1), 2000a, 19–41.

Cottle, Simon. "Rethinking News Access," *Journalism Studies* 1(3), 2000b, 427–448.

Cottle, Simon (ed.). *Ethnic Minorities and the Media: Changing Cultural Boundaries*. London: Open University Press, 2000c.

Cottle, Simon (ed.). *News, Public Relations and Power*. London: Sage, 2003.

Cottrell, Robert C. *Izzy: A Biography of I.F. Stone*. New Brunswick, NJ: Rutgers University Press, 1993.

Cox, Harvey, and David Morgan. *City Politics and the Press*. Cambridge, UK: Cambridge University Press, 1973.

Crawford, Nelson A. *The Ethics of Journalism*. New York: Alfred A. Knopf, 1924.

Cronkite, Walter. *A Reporter's Life*. New York: Ballantine, 1997.

Crouse, Timothy. *The Boys on the Bus*. New York: Random House, 1973.

Crow, Bryan K. "Conversational Pragmatics in Television Talk: The Discourse of 'Good Sex,'" *Media, Culture and Society* 8, 1986, 457–484.

Curran, James. "The Press as an Agency of Social Control: An Historical Perspective," in George Boyce, James Curran, and Pauline Wingate (eds.), *Newspaper History from the Seventeenth Century to the Present Day*. Beverly Hills, CA: Sage, 1978, 51–78.

Curran, James. "Rethinking the Media as a Public Sphere," in Peter Dahlgren and Colin Sparks (eds.), *Communication and Citizenship: Journalism and the Public Sphere in the New Media Age*. London: Routledge, 1991.

Curran, James. *Media Organizations in Society*. London: Edward Arnold, 2000a.

Curran, James. "Literary Editors, Social Networks and Cultural Tradition," in *Media Organizations in Society*. London: Edward Arnold, 2000b, 215–239.

Curran, James. "Press Reformism, 1918–1998: A Study of Failure," in Howard Tumber (ed.), *Media Power, Professionals and Policies*. London: Routledge, 2000c, 35–55.

Curran, James, Angus Douglas, and Garry Whannel. "The Political Economy of the Human Interest Story," in Anthony Smith (ed.), *Newspapers and Democracy*. Cambridge: MIT Press, 1980, 288–342.

Curran, James, and Michael Gurevitch (eds.). *Mass Media and Society*. London: Edward Arnold, 1991.

Curran, James, Michael Gurevitch, and Janet Woollacott (eds.). *Mass Communication and Society*. London: Edward Arnold, 1977.

Curran, James, and Jean Seaton. *Power Without Responsibility*. London: Fontana, 1985.

Curry, Jane Leftwich. *Poland's Journalists: Professionalism and Politics*. New York: Cambridge University Press, 1990.

Curthoys, Ann. "Histories of Journalism," in Ann Curthoys and Julianne Schultz (eds.), *Journalism: Print, Politics and Popular Culture*. St. Lucia: University of Queensland Press, 1999, 1–9.

Curthoys, Ann, and Julianne Schultz (eds.). *Journalism: Print, Politics and Popular Culture*. St. Lucia: University of Queensland Press, 1999.

Czitrom, Daniel. *Media and the American Mind: From Morse to McLuhan*. Chapel Hill: University of North Carolina Press, 1982.

Dahl, Hans Fredrik. "The Art of Writing Broadcasting History," *Gazette* 3, 1976, 130–137.

Dahlgren, Peter. "Introduction," in Peter Dahlgren and Colin Sparks (eds.), *Journalism and Popular Culture*. London: Sage, 1992, 1–23.

Dahlgren, Peter. *Television and the Public Sphere: Citizenship, Democracy and the Media*. London: Sage, 1995.

Dahlgren, Peter, and Colin Sparks (eds.). *Communication and Citizenship*. London: Routledge, 1991.

Dahlgren, Peter, and Colin Sparks (eds.). *Journalism and Popular Culture*. London: Sage, 1992.

Daley, Patrick, and Beverly James. "Warming the Arctic Air: Cultural Politics and Alaska Native Radio," *Javnost/The Public* 2(2), 1998, 49–60.

Darnton, Robert. "Writing News and Telling Stories," *Daedalus* 104(2), Spring 1975, 175–194.

Darnton, Robert. *The Great Cat Massacre and Other Episodes in French Cultural History*. New York: Random House, 1985.

Davis, Elmer Holmes. *History of the New York Times, 1851–1921*. New York: Greenwood, 1969 (1921).

Davis, Richard. *The Press and American Politics*. New York: Longman, 1992.

Davis, Richard. *The Web of Politics*. New York: Oxford University Press, 1999.

Dayan, Daniel. "Madame se meurt: Le jeu des medias et du public aux funerailles de lady Diana." *Quaderni* 38 (spring), 1999, 49–68.

Dayan, Daniel. "The Peculiar Public of Television." *Media, Culture, and Society* 23(6), 2001, 743–766.

Dayan, Daniel, and Elihu Katz. *Media Events*. Oxford, UK: Oxford University Press, 1992.

Deacon, David, Natalie Fenton, and Alan Bryman. "From Inception to Reception: The Natural History of a News Item," *Media, Culture, and Society* 21(1), 1999, 5–31.

Deacon, David, Michael Pickering, Peter Golding, and Graham Murdock. *Researching Communications: A Practical Guide to Methods in Media and Cultural Analysis*. London: Edward Arnold, 1999.

Delano, Anthony, and John Henningham. *The News Breed: British Journalists in the 1990s*. London: London College of Printing and Distributive Trades, 1995.

Dennis, Everette E. *Planning For Curricular Change: A Report on the Future of Journalism and Mass Communication Education*. Eugene: School of Journalism, University of Oregon, 1984.

Dennis, Everette E., and Edward C. Pease (eds.). *The Media in Black and White*. New Brunswick, NJ: Transaction, 1997.

Dennis, Everette E., and Ellen Wartella (eds.). *American Communication Research: The Remembered History*. Mahwah, NJ: Lawrence Erlbaum, 1996.

Denton, Robert B. *The Media and the Persian Gulf War*. Westport, CT: Praeger, 1993.

Denzin, Norman K., and Yvonna S. Lincoln (eds.). *9/11 In American Culture*. Walnut Creek, CA: AltaMira, 2003.

Dewey, John. *The Public and Its Problems*. Columbus: Ohio State University Press, 1954 (1927).

Diamond, Edwin. *The Tin Kazoo: Television, Politics, and the News*. Cambridge: MIT Press, 1975.

Diamond, Edwin. *Behind the Times: Inside the New New York Times*. Chicago: University of Chicago Press, 1995.

Dicken-Garcia, Hazel. *Journalistic Standards in Nineteenth-Century America*. Madison: University of Wisconsin Press, 1989.

Dickson, Sandra H. "Understanding Media Bias: The Press and the U.S. Invasion of Panama," *Journalism Quarterly* 71(4), 1994, 809–819.

Dijk, Teun van. "Discourse Analysis: Its Development and Application to the Structure of News," *Journal of Communication* 33(1), 1983, 22–43.

Dijk, Teun van. *News as Discourse.* Hillsdale, NJ: Lawrence Erlbaum, 1987.

Dijk, Teun van. *News Analysis.* Hillsdale, NJ: Lawrence Erlbaum, 1988.

Dijk, Teun van. *Communicating Racism: Ethnic Prejudice in Thought and Talk.* Beverly Hills, CA: Sage, 1989.

Dines, Alberto. *O papel do jornal.* Sao Paulo: Summus, 1986; cited in Waisbord 2000.

Domke, David, David P. Fan, Michael Fibison, Dhavan V. Shah, Steven S. Smith, and Mark D. Watts. "News Media, Candidates and Issues, and Public Opinion in the 1996 Presidential Campaign," *Journalism and Mass Communication Quarterly* 74(4), 1997, 718–737.

Donsbach, Wolfgang. "Journalists' Conception of Their Role," *Gazette* 32(1), 1983, 19–36.

Douglas, George H. *The Golden Age of the Newspaper.* Westport, CT: Greenwood Press, 1999.

Douglas, Susan J. *Inventing American Broadcasting: 1899–1922.* Baltimore: Johns Hopkins University Press, 1987.

Downing, John. *Internationalizing Media Theory: Transition, Power, Culture.* Thousand Oaks, CA: Sage, 1996.

Drudge, Matt. *Drudge Manifesto: The Internet's Star Reporter vs. Politics, Big Business, and the Future of Journalism.* New York: New American Library, 2001.

Durham, Frank D. "News Frames as Social Narratives: TWA Flight 800," *Journal of Communication* 48(4), 1998, 100–117.

Dyer, Richard. "Taking Popular Television Seriously," in David Lusted and Phillip Drummond (eds.), *TV and Schooling.* London: British Film Institute with the Institute of Education, University of London, 1985, 41–46.

Eason, David L. "The New Journalism and the Image-World: Two Modes of Organizing Experience," *Critical Studies in Mass Communication* 1(1), 1984, 51–65.

Eason, David. "On Journalistic Authority: The Janet Cooke Scandal," *Critical Studies in Mass Communication* 3, 1986, 429–447.

Edelman, Murray. *The Symbolic Uses of Politics.* Urbana: University of Illinois Press, 1964.

Edelman, Murray. *From Art to Politics.* Chicago: University of Chicago Press, 1985.

Edelman, Murray. *Constructing the Political Spectacle.* Chicago: University of Chicago Press, 1988.

Edelman, Murray, W. Lance Bennett, and Robert M. Entman. *The Politics of Misinformation.* New York: Cambridge University Press, 2001.

Ehrlich, Matthew. "The Romance of Hildy Johnson: The Journalist as Mythic Hero in American Cinema," *Studies in Symbolic Interaction* 12, 1991, 89–104.

Ehrlich, Matthew. "Thinking Critically About Journalism Through Popular Culture," *Journalism and Mass Communication Educator* 50(4), Winter 1996a, 35–41.

Ehrlich, Matthew. "The Journalism of Outrageousness: Tabloid Television News Versus Investigative News," *Journalism and Mass Communication Monographs* 155, 1997a, 3–27.

Ehrlich, Matthew. "Journalism in the Movies," *Critical Studies in Mass Communication* 14, 1997b, 267–281.

Ehrlich, Matthew. "Myth in Charles Kuralt's 'On the Road,'" *Journalism and Mass Communication Quarterly* 79 (2), Summer 2002, 327–338.

Eldridge, John (ed.). *Getting the Message: News, Truth and Power*. London, Routledge, 1993.

Eldridge, John. "The Contribution of the Glasgow Media Group to the Study of Television and Print Journalism," *Journalism Studies* 1(1), 2000, 113–127.

Eliasoph, Nina. "Routines and the Making of Oppositional News," *Critical Studies in Mass Communication* 5, 1988, 313–334.

Ellerbee, Linda. *"And So It Goes": Adventures in Television*. New York: Berkley, 1986.

Elliott, Deni (ed.). *Responsible Journalism*. Beverly Hills, CA: Sage, 1986.

Elliott, Philip. *The Sociology of the Professions*. London: Macmillan, 1972.

Elliott, Philip. "Press Performance as Political Ritual," in Harry Christian (ed.), *The Sociology of Journalism and the Press* (Sociological Review Monograph 29). Keele, UK: University of Keele, 1980, 141–177.

Elliott, Philip. *The Making of a Television Series: A Case Study in the Sociology of Culture*. London: Constable, 1992.

Ellul, Jacques. *Propaganda*. New York: Alfred A. Knopf, 1965.

Emery, Michael. *On the Front Lines: Following America's Top Foreign Correspondents Across the Twentieth Century*. Lanham, MD: Rowman and Littlefield, 1995.

Emery, Michael, and Edwin Emery. *The Press and America: An Interpretive History of the Mass Media* (9th ed.). Needham Heights, MA: Pearson, Allyn and Bacon, 1999.

Engel, Matthew. *Tickle the Public: One Hundred Years of the Popular Press*. London: Victor Gollancz, 1996.

Entman, Robert. *Democracy Without Citizens*. New York: Oxford University Press, 1989.

Entman, Robert. "Framing: Towards Clarification of a Fractured Paradigm," *Journal of Communication* 43(4), 1993a, 51–58.

Entman, Robert, and Andrew Rojecki. "Freezing Out the Public: Elite and Media Framing of the U.S. Anti-Nuclear Movement," *Political Communication* 10, 1993b, 155–173.

Epstein, Edward J. *News From Nowhere*. New York: Random House, 1973.

Epstein, Edward J. *Between Fact and Fiction*. New York: Random House, 1975.

Ericson, Richard V., Patricia M. Baranek, and Janet B.L. Chan. *Visualizing Deviance: A Study of News Organization*. Toronto: University of Toronto Press, 1987.

Ericson, Richard V., Patricia M. Baranek, and Janet B.L. Chan. *Negotiating Control: A Study of News Sources*. Toronto: University of Toronto Press, 1989.

Ericson, Richard V., Patricia M. Baranek, and Janet B.L. Chan. *Representing Order: Crime, Law and Justice in the News Media*. Toronto: Open University Press, 1990.

Ettema, James. "Press Rites and Race Relations: A Study of Mass-Mediated Ritual," *Critical Studies in Mass Communication* 7(4), 1990, 309–331.

Ettema, James, and D. Charles Whitney (eds.). *Individuals in Mass Media Organizations*. Beverly Hills, CA: Sage, 1982.

Ettema, James, and D. Charles Whitney. "Professional Mass Communicators," in Charles H. Berger and Steven H. Chaffee (eds.), *Handbook of Communication Science*. Newbury Park, CA: Sage, 1987, 747–780.

Evans, Geoffrey, and Pippa Norris. *Critical Elections: British Parties and Voters in Long-Term Perspective*. London: Sage, 1999.

Evans, Harold. *Good Times, Bad Times*. London: Orion, 1994.

Evans, Harold. "What a Century!" *Columbia Journalism Review*, January/February 1999, 27–37.

Fallows, James. *Breaking the News: How the Media Undermine American Democracy*. New York: Pantheon, 1996.

Feldman, Ofer. *Politics and the News Media in Japan*. Ann Arbor: University of Michigan Press, 1993.

Ferenczi, Thomas. *L'invention du journalisme en France*. Paris: Plon, 1993.

Fienburgh, Wilfred. *Twenty Five Momentous Years: A 25th Anniversary in the History of the Daily Herald*. London: Odhams, 1955.

Fishman, Jessica. "The Populace and the Police: Models of Social Control in Reality-Based Crime Television," *Critical Studies in Mass Communication* 16, 1999, 268–288.

Fishman, Mark. *Manufacturing the News*. Austin: University of Texas Press, 1980.

Fiske, John. *Television Culture*. London: Methuen, 1988.

Fiske, John. "British Cultural Studies and Television," in Robert C. Allen (ed.), *Channels of Discourse, Reassembled*. Chapel Hill: University of Carolina Press, 1992a, 284–326.

Fiske, John. "Popularity and the Politics of Information," in Peter Dahlgren and Colin Sparks (eds.), *Journalism and Popular Culture*. London: Sage, 1992b, 45–62.

Fiske, John. *Media Matters*. Minneapolis: University of Minnesota Press, 1996.

Fiske, John, and John Hartley. *Reading Television*. London: Methuen, 1978.

Foster, Harry S. "Charting America's News of the World War," *Foreign Affairs* 15, January 1937, 311–319.

Fowler, Roger. *Language in the News*. London: Routledge, 1991.

Fox, Elizabeth (ed.). *Media and Politics in Latin America: The Struggle for Democracy*. Newbury Park, CA: Sage, 1988.

Fox, Elizabeth, and Silvio Waisbord (eds.). *Latin Politics, Global Media*. Austin: University of Texas Press, 2002.

Fox Bourne, H.R. *English Newspapers*. London: Chatto and Windus, 1887; cited in Boyce, Curran, and Wingate 1978.

Frank, Joseph. *The Beginnings of the English Newspaper, 1620–1660*. Cambridge, MA: Harvard University Press, 1961.

Franklin, Bob. *Newszak and the News Media*. London: Edward Arnold, 1997.

Franklin, Bob, and David Murphy (eds.). *Making the Local News*. London: Routledge, 1997.

Franklin, Mark L., and Christopher Wlezien (eds.). *The Future of Election Studies*. New York: Pergamon, 2002.

Friedman, James (ed.). *Reality Squared. Televisual Discourse on the Real*. New Brunswick, NJ: Rutgers University Press, 2002.

Friendly, Fred W. *Due to Circumstances Beyond Our Control. . . .* New York: Random House, 1967.

Frus, Phyllis. *The Politics and Poetics of Journalism Narrative*. New York: Cambridge University Press, 1994.

Fry, Katherine. *Constructing the Heartland: Television News and Natural Disaster*. Cresskill, NJ: Hampton, 2003.

Gaber, Ivor, and Angela Phillips. "Practicing What We Preach: The Role of Practice in Media Degrees—and Journalism in Particular," *Journal of Media Practice* 1(1), 2000, 49–54.

Gabriel, John. *Whitewash: Racialized Politics and the Media*. London: Routledge, 1998.

Galtung, Johanne, and Marie Ruge. "The Structure of Foreign News: The Presentation of the Congo, Cuba, and Cyprus Crises in Four Foreign Newspapers," in *Journal of Peace Research* 2, 1965, 64–90.

Gamson, Joshua. *Freaks Talk Back: Tabloid Talk Shows and Sexual Non-Conformity*. Chicago: University of Chicago Press, 1998.

Gamson, William. "Political Discourse and Collective Action," in Bert Klandermans, Hanspeter Kriesi, and Sidney Tarrow (eds.), *From Structure to Action: Comparing Social Movements Across Cultures*. Greenwich, CT: JAI, 1988, 219–244.

Gamson, William. "News as Framing," *American Behavioral Scientist* 33(2), 1989, 157–161.

Gamson, William. *Talking Politics*. New York: Cambridge University Press, 1992.

Gamson, William, and Andre Modigliani. "The Changing Culture of Affirmative Action," in Richard G. Braungart and Philo Wasburn (eds.), *Research in Political Sociology*. Greenwich, CT: JAI, 1987, 137–177.

Gamson, William, and Andre Modigliani. "Media Discourse and Public Opinion on Nuclear Power: A Constructionist Approach," *American Journal of Sociology* 95(1), 1989, 1–37.

Gandy, Oscar. *Beyond Agenda Setting: Information Subsidies and Public Policy*. Norwood, NJ: Ablex, 1982.

Gandy, Oscar. *Communication and Race: A Structural Perspective*. London: Edward Arnold, 1998.

Gans, Herbert. "The Famine in American Mass-Communications Research: Comments on Hirsch, Tuchman, and Gecas," *American Journal of Sociology* 77(4), January 1972, 697–705.

Gans, Herbert. *Deciding What's News*. New York: Pantheon, 1979.

Gans, Herbert. *Democracy and the News*. New York: Oxford University Press, 2003.

Garber, Marjorie, Jann Matlock, and Rebecca L. Walkowitz (eds.). *Media Spectacles*. New York: Routledge, 1992.

Garnham, Nicholas. "Contribution to a Political Economy of Mass Communication," *Media, Culture and Society* 1(2), 1979, 123–146.

Garnham, Nicholas. "The Media and the Public Sphere," in Peter Golding, Graham Murdock, and Peter Schlesinger (eds.), *Communicating Politics: Mass Communications and the Political Process*. New York: Holmes & Meier, 1986, 37–53.

Gates, Gary Paul. *Airtime: The Inside Story of CBS News*. New York: Harper and Row, 1978.

Gerald, J. Edward. *The Social Responsibility of the Press*. Minneapolis: University of Minnesota Press, 1963.

Gerbner, George. "Ideological Perspectives and Political Tendencies in News Reporting," *Journalism Quarterly* 41, 1964, 495–506.

Gerbner, George. "Institutional Pressures on Mass Communicators," in Peter Halmos (ed.), *The Sociology of Mass Media Communicators*. Keele, UK: University of Keele, 1969, 205–248.

Gerbner, George, and Larry P. Gross. "Living With Television: The Violence Profile," *Journal of Communication* 27(1), 1976, 173–199.

Gerbner, George, Hamid Mowlana, and Herbert I. Schiller (eds.), *Trimuph of the Image: The Media's War in the Persian Gulf—A Global Perspective*. Boulder, CO: Westview, 1992.

Gersh, David. "Stereotyping Journalists," *Editor and Publisher*, 5 October 1991, 18–19, 37.

Gerstle, Jacques. *La communication politique*. Paris: P.U.F., 1992.

Gieber, Walter. "Across the Desk: A Study of 16 Telegraph Editors," *Journalism Quarterly* 33(4), Fall 1956, 423–432.

Gieber, Walter. "News Is What Newspapermen Make It," in Lewis Anthony Dexter and David Manning White (eds.), *People, Society and Mass Communications*. New York: Free Press, 1964, 172–182.

Gieber, Walter, and Walter Johnson. "The City Hall Beat: A Study of Reporter and Source Roles," *Journalism Quarterly* 38(3), Summer 1961, 289–297.

Gillespie, Marie. *Television, Ethnicity, and Cultural Change*. London: Routledge, 1995.

Gitlin, Todd. "Media Sociology: The Dominant Paradigm," *Theory and Society* 6, 1978, 205–253.

Gitlin, Todd. *The Whole World Is Watching*. Berkeley: University of California Press, 1980.

Gitlin, Todd. *Media Unlimited: How the Torrent of Images and Sounds Overwhelms Our Lives*. New York: Metropolitan, 2002.

Glasgow University Media Group (GUMG). *Bad News*. London: Routledge and Kegan Paul, 1976.

Glasgow University Media Group (GUMG). *More Bad News*. London: Routledge and Kegan Paul, 1980.

Glasgow University Media Group (GUMG). *Really Bad News.* London: Routledge and Kegan Paul, 1982.

Glasgow University Media Group (GUMG). *War and Peace News.* Milton Keynes, UK: Open University Press, 1986.

Glasnost Defense Foundation. *Journalists and Journalism of Russian Province.* Moscow: Nachala, 1995.

Glasser, Theodore L. (ed.). *The Idea of Public Journalism.* New York: Guilford, 1999.

Glasser, Theodore L., and Stephanie Craft. "Public Journalism and the Search for Democratic Ideals," in Tamar Liebes and James Curran (eds.), *Media, Ritual and Identity.* London: Routledge, 1998.

Glasser, Theodore L., and James S. Ettema, "Common Sense and the Education of Young Journalists," *Journalism Educator* 44 (Summer), 1989a, 18–25, 75.

Glasser, Theodore L., and James S. Ettema. "Investigative Journalism and the Moral Order," *Critical Studies in Mass Communication* 6, 1989b, 1–20.

Glasser, Theodore L., and James S. Ettema. "When the Facts Don't Speak for Themselves: A Study of the Use of Irony in Daily Journalism," *Critical Studies in Mass Communication* 10(4), December 1993, 322–338.

Glasser, Theodore L, and James S. Ettema. *Custodians of Conscience.* New York: Columbia University Press, 1998.

Glasser, Theodore L., and Charles T. Salmon. *Public Opinion and the Communication of Consent.* New York: Guilford, 1995.

Glynn, Kevin. *Tabloid Culture: Trash Taste, Popular Power, and the Transformation of American Television.* Durham, NC: Duke University Press, 2000.

Goffman, Erving. *Forms of Talk.* Philadelphia: University of Pennsylvania Press, 1981.

Goldberg, Bernard. *Bias: A CBS Insider Exposes How the Media Distort the News.* Washington, DC: Regnery, 2001.

Golding, Peter, and Philip Elliott. *Making the News.* London: Longman, 1979.

Golding, Peter, and Sue Middleton. *Images of Welfare: Press and Public Attitudes to Poverty.* Oxford, UK: Blackwell, 1982.

Golding, Peter, and Graham Murdock, "Culture, Communications, and Political Economy," in James Curran and Michael Gurevitch (eds.), *Mass Media and Society.* London: Edward Arnold, 1991, 70–92.

Goldstein, Tom. *The News at Any Cost: How Journalists Compromise Their Ethics to Shape the News.* New York: Simon and Schuster, 1985.

Good, Howard. *Outcasts.* Metuchen, NJ: Scarecrow, 1989.

Good, Howard. *Girl Reporter.* Lanham, MD: Scarecrow, 1998.

Good, Howard. *The Drunken Journalist.* Lanham, MD: Scarecrow, 2000.

Goodman, Geoffrey. "No Short Cuts, Lady O'Neill" (Editorial), *British Journalism Review* 13(2), 2002, 3–6.

Gordon, Paul, and David Rosenberg, *Daily Racism: The Press and Black People in Britain.* London: Runnymede, 1989.

Goren, Dina. *Secrecy and the Right to Know.* Tel Aviv, Israel: Turtledove, 1979.

Graber, Doris. *Processing the News: How People Tame the Information Tide.* New York: Longman, 1984.

Graber, Doris, Denis McQuail, and Pippa Norris (eds.). *The Politics of News: the News of Politics.* Washington, DC: CQ Press, 1998.

Graham, Katharine. *Personal History.* New York: Random House, 1998.

Gray, Ann. *Video Playtime: The Gendering of a Leisure Technology.* London: Routledge, 1992.

Grayson, George. *A Guide to the 1994 Mexican Presidential Election.* Washington, DC: Center for Strategic and International Studies, 1994.

Greatbatch, David. "A Turn-Taking System for British News Interviews," *Language in Society* 17(3), 1988, 401–430.

Greatbatch, David. "Conversation Analysis: Neutralism in British News Interviews," in Allan Bell and Peter Garrett (eds.), *Approaches to Media Discourse.* Oxford, UK: Blackwell, 1997, 163–185.

Greenberg, Bradley. "Person to Person Communication in the Diffusion of a News Event," *Journalism Quarterly* 41(4), Autumn 1964, 489–494.

Greenfield, Jeff. *The Real Campaign.* New York: Simon and Schuster, 1982.

Griffin, Grahame. "An Historical Survey of Australian Press Photography," *Australian Journal of Communication* 21(1), 1994, 46–63.

Griffin, Michael. "Looking at TV-News—Strategies for Research," *Communication* 13(2), 1992, 121–142.

Griffin, Michael. "The Great War Photographs: Constructing Myths of History and Photojournalism," in Bonnie Brennen and Hanno Hardt (eds.), *Picturing the Past: Media, History and Photography.* Champaign: University of Illinois Press, 1999, 122–157.

Griffin, Michael, and Simon Kagan. "Picturing Culture in Political Spots: 1992 Campaigns in Israel and the United States," *Political Communication* 13(1), Jan-Mar 1996, 43–62.

Gronbeck, Bruce E. "Tradition and Technology in Local Newscasts: The Social Psychology of Form," *The Sociological Quarterly* 38(2), Spring 1997, 361–374.

Gross, Larry. *Up From Invisibility.* New York: Columbia University Press, 2002.

Grossman, Michael, and Martha Kumar. *Portraying the President: The White House and the News Media.* Baltimore: Johns Hopkins University Press, 1981.

Gullett, Henry. "Journalism as a Calling: A Half-Century's Impressions," *The Australasian Journalist,* 25 April 1913, 1–2; cited in Curthoys 1999.

Gulyas, Agnes. "The Development of the Tabloid Press in Hungary," in Colin Sparks and John Tulloch (eds.), *Tabloid Tales: Global Debates Over Media Standards.* Oxford: Rowman and Littlefield, 2000, 111–128.

Gunaratne, Shelton. "Old Wine in a New Bottle: Public Journalism, Developmental Journalism, and Social Responsibility," in Michael E. Roloff (ed.), *Communication Yearbook* 21. Thousand Oaks, CA: Sage, 1998, 276–321.

Gunaratne, Shelton (ed.). *Handbook of Media in Asia.* London: Sage, 2000.

Gurevitch, Michael. "The Globalization of Electronic Journalism," in James Curran and Michael Gurevitch (eds.), *Mass Media and Society*. London: Edward Arnold, 1991, 178–193.

Haas, Tanni, and Linda Steiner. "Public Journalism as a Journalism of Publics: Implications of the Habermas-Fraser Debate for Public Journalism," *Journalism: Theory, Practice, and Criticism*, August 2001.

Habermas, Jurgen. *The Structural Transformation of the Public Sphere* (Trans. Thomas Burger). Cambridge: MIT Press, 1989.

Hachten, William A. *The World News Prism*. Ames: Iowa State University Press, 1981.

Hackett, Robert A. "Decline of a Paradigm? Bias and Objectivity in News Media Studies," *Critical Studies in Mass Communication* 1(3), 229–259, 1984.

Hackett, Robert A. *News and Dissent: The Press and the Politics of Peace in Canada*. Norwood, NJ: Ablex, 1991.

Hackett, Robert A., and Yuezhi Zhao. *Sustaining Democracy? Journalism and the Politics of Objectivity*. Toronto: Garamond, 1998.

Hagerty, Bill. "How Do We Balance Privacy With Freedom?" *British Journalism Review* 14(1), 2003, 3–6.

Halberstam, David. *The Powers That Be*. New York: Laurel Books, 1979.

Halimi, Serge. *Les nouveaux chiens de garde*. Paris: Liber-Raisons d'agir, 1997.

Hall, Stuart. "The Social Eye of *Picture Post*," *Working Papers in Cultural Studies* 2. Birmingham, UK: Centre for Contemporary Cultural Studies, University of Birmingham, 1972, 71–120.

Hall, Stuart. "The Determinations of News Photographs," in Stanley Cohen and Jock Young (eds.), *The Manufacture of News*. London: Sage, 1973a.

Hall, Stuart. "Encoding and Decoding in the Television Discourse" (also called "Encoding/Decoding"), *CCCS Position Paper*. Birmingham, UK: Centre for Contemporary Cultural Studies, University of Birmingham, 1973b.

Hall, Stuart. "The Rediscovery of Ideology: Return of the Repressed in Media Studies," in Michael Gurevitch, Tony Bennett, James Curran, and Janet Woolllacott (eds.), *Culture, Society, and the Media*. London: Methuen, 1982, 56–90.

Hall, Stuart, Ian Connell, and Lidia Curti. "The 'Unity' of Current Affairs Television," *Working Papers in Cultural Studies* 9. Birmingham, UK: Centre for Contemporary Cultural Studies, University of Birmingham, 1976, 70–120.

Hall, Stuart, Charles Critcher, Tony Jefferson, John Clarke, and Brian Roberts. *Policing the Crisis*. London: Macmillan, 1978.

Hallin, Daniel C. *The Uncensored War: The Media and Vietnam*. New York: Oxford University Press, 1986.

Hallin, Daniel C. "The Passing of High Modernism of American Journalism," *Journal of Communication* 42(3), Summer 1992, 14–25.

Hallin, Daniel C. *We Keep America on Top of the World*. London: Routledge, 1994.

Hallin, Daniel C. "Sound Bite News: Television Coverage of Elections," in Shanto Iyengar and Richard Reeves (eds.), *Do the Media Govern?* Thousand Oaks, CA: Sage, 1997, 57–65.

Hallin, Daniel C. "*La Nota Roja:* Popular Journalism and the Transition to Democracy in Mexico," in Colin Sparks and John Tulloch (eds.), *Tabloid Tales: Global Debates Over Media Standards.* Oxford: Rowman and Littlefield, 2000, 267–284.

Hallin, Daniel C., and Paolo Mancini. "Political Structure and Representational Form in U.S. and Italian TV News," *Theory and Society* 13(40), 1984, 829–850.

Hallin, Daniel C., and Paolo Mancini. "Americanization, Globalization and Secularization: Understanding the Convergence of Media Systems and Political Communication in the U.S. and Western Europe," in Frank Esser and Barbara Pfetsch (eds.), *Comparing Political Communication: Theories, Cases, and Challenges.* New York: Cambridge University Press, in press.

Halloran, James, Philip Elliot, and Graham Murdock. *Demonstrations and Communication.* London: Penguin, 1970.

Hannerz, Ulf. *Foreign News: Exploring the World of Foreign Correspondents.* Chicago: University of Chicago Press, 2004.

Harcup, Tony, and Deidre O'Neill. "What Is News? Galtung and Ruge Revisited," *Journalism Studies* 2(2), May 2001, 261–280.

Hardt, Hanno. *Social Theories of the Press: Early German and American Perspectives.* Beverly Hills, CA: Sage, 1975.

Hardt, Hanno. "Without the Rank and File: Journalism History, Media Workers, and Problems of Representation," in Hanno Hardt and Bonnie Brennen (eds.), *Newsworkers: Toward a History of the Rank and File.* Minneapolis: University of Minnesota Press, 1995, 1–29.

Hardt, Hanno. "The End of Journalism: Media and Newswork in the United States," in *Javnost/The Public* 3(3), 1996: 21–41.

Hardt, Hanno, and Bonnie Brennen. "Communication and the Question of History," *Communication Theory* 3(2), 1993, 130–136.

Hardt, Hanno, and Bonnie Brennen (eds.). *Newsworkers: Toward a History of the Rank and File.* Minneapolis: University of Minnesota Press, 1995.

Hargreaves, John. *Sport, Power and Culture.* Cambridge, UK: Polity, 1986.

Hariman, Robert, and John L. Lucaites, "Performing Civic Identity: The Iconic Photograph of the Flag Raising on Iwo Jima," *Quarterly Journal of Speech* 88, 2002, 363–392.

Hariman, Robert, and John L. Lucaites, "Morality and Memory in U.S. Iconic Photography: The Image of 'Accidental Napalm,'" *Critical Studies in Mass Communication* 20, March 2003, 33–65.

Hariman, Robert, and John L. Lucaites, "Liberal Representation and Global Order: The Iconic Photograph from Tiananmen Square," in Lawrence Prelli (ed.), *Rhetoric and Display,* University of South Carolina Press, in press.

Harris, Christopher R., and Paul Martin Lester. *Visual Journalism: A Guide for New Media Professionals.* Boston: Allyn and Bacon, 2001.

Harris, Robert. *Gotcha: The Media, the Government and the Falklands Crisis.* London: Faber and Faber, 1983.

Hart, Roderick. *The Sound of Leadership*. Chicago: University of Chicago Press, 1987.

Hart-Davis, Duff. *The House the Berrys Built: Inside 'The Telegraph,' 1928–1986*. London: Hodder and Stoughton, 1991.

Hartley, John. *Understanding News*. London: Methuen, 1982.

Hartley, John. *The Politics of Pictures: the Creation of the Public in the Age of Popular Media*. London: Routledge, 1992.

Hartley, John. *Popular Reality: Journalism, Modernity, Popular Culture*. New York and London: Edward Arnold, 1996.

Hartley, John. "What Is Journalism? The View From Under a Stubbie Cap," in *Media International Australia Incorporating Culture and Policy*, 90, February 1999, 15–34.

Hartsock, John C. *A History of American Literary Journalism: The Emergence of a Modern Narrative Form*. Amherst: University of Massachussetts Press, 2001.

Hauben, Michael, and Ronda Hauben. *Netizens: On the History and Impact of Usenet and the Internet*. Los Alamitos, CA: IEEE Computer Society Press, 1997.

Hauke, Kathleen. *Ted Poston: Pioneer American Journalist*. Athens: University of Georgia Press, 1999.

Havill, Adrian. *Deep Truth: The Lives of Bob Woodward and Carl Bernstein*. New York: Birch Lane Press, 1993.

Heffer, Simon. "Spinning for a Living," *British Journalism Review* 6(4), 1995, 6–10.

Henningham, John. "Journalism as a Profession: A Reexamination," *Australian Journal of Communication* 8, 1985, 1–17.

Henningham, John. "Two Hundred Years of Australian Journalism," *Australian Cultural History* 7, 1988, 49–63.

Henningham, John (ed.). *Issues in Australian Journalism*. Melbourne: Longman Cheshire, 1990.

Henningham, John. "Multicultural Journalism: A Profile of Hawaii's Newspeople," *Journalism Quarterly* 70, 1993, 550–557.

Hensley, Thomas R. (ed.). *The Boundaries of Freedom of Expression and Order in American Democracy*. Kent, OH: Kent State University Press, 2001.

Heritage, John. "Analyzing News Interviews: Aspects of the Production of Talk for an Overhearing Audience," in Teun van Dijk (ed.), *Handbook of Discourse Analysis: Discourse and Dialogue*. London: Academic Press, 1985, 95–119.

Heritage, John, and David Greatbatch. "On the Institutional Character of Institutional Talk: The Case of News Interviews," in Deirdre Zimmerman and Don H. Boden (eds.), *Talk and Social Structure: Studies in Ethnomethodology and Conversation Analysis*. Oxford, UK: Polity, 1991, 93–137.

Herman, Edward, and Noam Chomsky. *Manufacturing Consent*. New York: Pantheon, 1988.

Hertsgaard, Mark. *On Bended Knee: The Press and the Reagan Presidency*. New York: Farrar, Straus and Giroux, 1988.

Hess, Stephen. *The Washington Reporters*. Washington, DC: Brookings Institution, 1981.

Hess, Stephen. *The Government-Press Connection: Press Officers and Their Offices.* Washington, DC: Brookings Institution, 1984.

Hess, Stephen. *International News and Foreign Correspondents.* Washington, DC: Brookings Institution, 1996.

Hess, Stephen, and Sandy Northrup. *Drawn and Quartered: The History of American Political Cartoons.* Montgomery, AL: Elliott and Clark, 1996.

Hilmes, Michele. *Radio Voices: American Broadcasting, 1922–1952.* Minneapolis: University of Minnesota Press, 1997.

Hirsch, Alan. *Talking Heads: Television's Political Talk Shows and Pundits.* New York: St. Martin's, 1991.

Hjarvard, Sig. "TV News Exchange," in Oliver Boyd-Barrett and Terhi Rantanen (eds.), *The Globalization of News.* London: Sage, 1999, 202–226.

Hjarvard, Sig. "The Study of International News," in Klaus Bruhn Jensen (ed.), *A Handbook of Media and Communication Research.* London: Routledge, 2002.

Hobson, Harold, Philip Knightley, and Leonard Russell. *The Pearl of Days: An Intimate Memoir of the Sunday Times, 1822–1972.* London: Hamish Hamilton, 1972.

Hodge, Robert, and Gunther Kress. *Language as Ideology.* London: Routledge and Kegan Paul, 1979.

Hodge, Robert, and Gunther Kress. *Social Semiotics.* Cambridge, UK: Polity, 1988.

Hoffman, Joyce. *Theodore H. White and Journalism as Illusion.* Columbia: University of Missouri Press, 1995.

Hofstetter, C. Richard. *Bias in the News.* Columbus: Ohio State University Press, 1976.

Holland, D.K. *Design Issues: How Graphic Design Informs Society.* New York: Allworth Press, 2001.

Holsti, Ole R. *Content Analysis for the Social Sciences and Humanities.* Reading, MA: Addison-Wesley, 1969.

Hopkinson, Tom. *Of This Our Time: A Journalist's Story, 1905–1950.* New York: Arrow, 1982.

Hornig, Susanna. "Framing Risk: Audience and Reader Factors," *Journalism Quarterly* 69(2), 1992, 670–690.

Hoyer, Svennik, S. Hadenius, and L. Weibull. *The Politics and Economics of the Press: A Developmental Perspective.* Beverly Hills, CA: Sage, 1975.

Hudson, Frederic. *Journalism in the United States, From 1690 to 1872.* New York: Harper, 1873.

Hughes, Helen McGill. *News and the Human Interest Story.* Chicago: University of Chicago Press, 1940.

Hurst, John, and Sally A. White. *Ethics and the Australian News Media.* Melbourne: Macmillan, 1994.

Huxford, John: "Framing the Future: Science Fiction Frames and the Press Coverage of Cloning," *Continuum: Journal of Media and Cultural Studies,* 14(2), 2000, 187–199.

Huxford, John. "Beyond the Referential: Uses of Visual Symbolism in the Press," *Journalism: Theory, Practice and Criticism* 2(1), April 2001, 45–72.

Hyams, Edward. *New Statesmanship: An Anthology.* London: Longmans, 1963.

Ickes, Harold. *America's House of Lords.* New York: Harcourt, Brace, 1939.

Inglis, Fred. *Media Theory.* Oxford, UK: Blackwell, 1990.

Inglis, Fred. *People's Witness: The Journalist in Modern Politics.* New Haven, CT: Yale University Press, 2002.

Inglis, Kenneth Stanley. *This Is the ABC.* Melbourne: Melbourne University Press, 1983.

Innis, Harold A. *The Bias of Communication.* Toronto: University of Toronto Press, 1951.

Innis, Harold A. *Empire and Communications.* Toronto: University of Toronto, 1972.

International Commission for the Study of Communication Problems. *Many Voices, One World* (The MacBride Report). Paris: UNESCO, 1980.

Ireland, Alleyne. *Adventures with a Genius: Recollections of Joseph Pulitzer.* New York: E.P. Dutton, 1969 (1920).

Iyengar, Shanto. *Is Anyone Responsible: How Television Frames Political Issues.* Chicago: University of Chicago Press, 1991.

Iyengar, Shanto, and Donald Kinder. *News That Matters.* Chicago: University of Chicago Press, 1987.

Iyengar, Shanto, and Richard Reeves (eds.). *Do the Media Govern?* Thousand Oaks, CA: Sage, 1997.

Iyengar, Shanto, and Adam Simon. "News Coverage of the Gulf Crisis and Public Opinion: A Study of Agenda-Setting, Priming and Framing," *Communication Research* 20(3), 1993, 365–383.

Jacobs, Ronald. "Producing the News, Producing the Crisis: Narrativity, Television and News Work," *Media, Culture and Society* 18(3), 1996, 373–397.

Jacobs, Ronald. *Race, Media, and the Crisis of Civil Society: From the Watts Riots to Rodney King.* Cambridge, UK: Cambridge University Press, 2000.

Jakubowicz, Karol. "Media as Agents of Change," in David Paletz, Karol Jakubowicz, and Pavao Novosel (eds.), *Glasnost and After.* Cresskill, NJ: Hampton, 1995, 19–47.

Jakubowicz, Karol. "Normative Models of Media and Journalism and Broadcasting Regulation in Central and Eastern Europe," *International Journal of Communications Law and Policy* 2, Winter, 1998/99 (http://www.digital-law. net/IJCLP).

Jamieson, Kathleen Hall. *Packaging the Presidency.* New York: Oxford University Press, 1984.

Jamieson, Kathleen Hall. *Eloquence in an Electronic Age.* New York: Oxford University Press, 1988.

Jamieson, Kathleen Hall, and Joseph N. Cappella. *Spiral of Cynicism: The Press and the Public Good.* New York: Oxford University Press, 1997.

Jamieson, Kathleen Hall, and Paul Waldman. *The Press Effect: Politicians, Journalists, and the Stories That Shape the Political World.* New York: Oxford University Press, 2002.

Janeway, Michael. *The Republic of Denial: Press, Politics, and Public Life.* New Haven, CT: Yale University Press, 2001.

Jankowsky, Nick, Ole Prehn, and James Stappers (eds.). *The People's Voice: Local Radio and Television in Europe.* London: John Libbey, 1992.

Janowitz, Morris. "Professional Models in Journalism: The Gatekeeper and the Advocate," *Journalism Quarterly* 52(4), 1975, 618–626, 662.

Jensen, Joli. *Redeeming Modernity: Contradictions in Media Criticism.* Beverly Hills, CA: Sage, 1990.

Jensen, Klaus Bruhn. *Making Sense of the News.* Aarhus, Denmark: Aarhus University Press, 1986.

Jensen, Klaus Bruhn. "The Politics of Polysemy: Television News, Everyday Consciousness, and Political Action," *Media, Culture and Society* 12(1), 1990, 55–77.

Johnson, Gerald. *What is News: A Tentative Outline.* New York: Alfred A. Knopf, 1926.

Johnson, Lesley. *The Unseen Voice: A Cultural History of Early Australian Radio.* London: Routledge, 1988.

Johnson, Stanley, and Julian Harris. *The Complete Reporter.* New York: Macmillan, 1942.

Johnstone, John W.L., Edward J. Slawski, and William W. Bowman. "The Professional Values of American Newsmen," *Public Opinion Quarterly* 36(4), 1972, 522–540.

Johnstone, John W.L., Edward J. Slawski, and William W. Bowman. *The News People.* Urbana: University of Illinois Press, 1976.

Jones, Aled. *Powers of the Press: Newspapers, Power and Public in Nineteenth-Century England.* Aldershot, UK: Scolar, 1996.

Jones, Nicholas. *Soundbites and Spin Doctors.* London: Cassell, 1995.

Jones, Roderick. *A Life in Reuters.* London: Hodder and Stoughton, 1951.

Jowett, Garth. "Toward a History of Communication," *Journalism History* 2, 1975, 34–37.

Kaniss, Phyllis. *Making Local News.* Chicago: University of Chicago Press, 1991.

Kaniss, Phyllis. *The Media and the Mayor's Race: The Failure of Urban Political Reporting.* Bloomington: Indiana University Press, 1995.

Karim, Karim H. *Islamic Peril: Media and Global Violence.* Montreal: Black Rose, 2000.

Katz, Elihu. "Journalists as Scientists," *American Behavioral Scientist,* 33(2), 1989, 238–246.

Katz, Elihu. "The End of Journalism," *Journal of Communication* 42(3), 1992, 5–13.

Katz, Elihu. *Mass Media and Participatory Democracy.* Paper presented to Middle Tennessee State University, November 7–8, 1996.

Katz, Elihu, and Paul Lazarsfeld. *Personal Influence: The Part Played by People in the Flow of Mass Communications.* New York: Free Press, 1960 (1955).

Keane, John. *The Media and Democracy.* Cambridge, UK: Polity, 1991.

Kellner, Douglas. *The Persian Gulf TV War.* Boulder, CO: Westview, 1992.

Kellner, Douglas. *From 9/11 to Terror War*. Lanham, MD: Rowman and Littlefield, 2003.

Kendrick, Alexander. *Prime Time: The Life of Edward R. Murrow*. Boston: Little, Brown, 1969.

Kenner, Hugh. "The Politics of the Plain Style," in Norman Sims (ed.), *Literary Journalism in the Twentieth Century*. New York: Oxford University Press, 1990, 183–190.

Kenney, Keith, and Chris Simpson. "Was Coverage of the 1988 Presidential Race By Washington's Two Major Dailies Biased?" *Journalism Quarterly* 70(2), 1993, 345–255.

Kessler, Lauren. *The Dissident Press: An Alternative Journalism in American History*. Beverly Hills, CA: Sage, 1984.

Kielbowicz, Richard. *News in the Mail: The Press, Post Office and Public Information, 1700-1860s*. Westport, CT: Greenwood, 1986.

Kielbowicz, Richard, and Clifford Sherer. "The Role of the Press in the Dynamics of Social Movements," in Louis Kriesberg (ed.), *Research in Social Movements, Conflict and Change*, 9. Greenwich, CT: JAI, 1986, 71–96.

King, Donna L., and Christopher Mele. "Making Public Access Television: Community Participation, Media Literacy and the Public Sphere," *Journal of Broadcasting and Electronic Media*, 43(4), 1999, 603–623.

Kingsbury, Susan Myra. *Newspapers and the News: An Objective Measurement of Ethical and Unethical Behavior By Representative Newspapers*. New York: G.P. Putnam, 1937.

Kirkpatrick, Rod. *Sworn To No Master: A History of the Provincial Press in Queensland to 1930*. Toowoomba, Australia: Darling Downs Institute Press, 1984.

Kitch, Carolyn. "A News of Feeling as Well as Fact: Mourning and Memorial in American Newsmagazines," *Journalism: Theory, Practice and Criticism* 1(2), 2000, 169–193.

Kitch, Carolyn. "'A Death in the American Family': Myth, Memory, and National Values in the Media Mourning of John F. Kennedy, Jr.," *Journalism and Mass Communication Quarterly* 79(2), Summer 2002, 294–309.

Klaidman, Stephen, and Tom L. Beauchamp. *The Virtuous Journalist*. New York: Oxford University Press, 1987.

Klapper, Joseph T. *The Effects of Mass Communication*. New York: Bureau of Applied Social Research, 1949; expanded in *The Effects of Mass Communication*. New York: The Free Press, 1960.

Klein, Ulrike. "Tabloidized Political Coverage in the German Bild-Zeitung," in Colin Sparks and John Tulloch (eds.), *Tabloid Tales: Global Debates Over Media Standards*. Oxford: Rowman and Littlefield, 2000, 177–194.

Klinenberg, Eric. *Heat Wave: A Social Autopsy of Disaster in Chicago*. Chicago: University of Chicago Press, 2003.

Knightley, Philip. *The First Casualty: The War Correspondent as Hero, Propagandist and Myth-Maker from the Crimea to Vietnam*. London: Andre Deutsch, 1975.

Knightley, Philip. *A Hack's Progress.* Toronto: Random House of Canada, 1998.

Kobler, J.F. *Ernest Hemingway: Journalist and Artist.* Ann Arbor: University of Michigan Press.

Kobre, Sidney. *The Development of the Colonial Newspaper.* Pittsburgh, PA: Colonial Press, 1944.

Kobre, Sidney. *Foundations of American Journalism.* Tallahassee: Florida State University, 1958.

Kobre, Sidney. *Modern American Journalism.* Tallahassee: Florida State University, 1959.

Kobre, Sidney. *The Yellow Press and Guilded Age Journalism.* Tallahassee: Florida State University, 1964.

Kobre, Sidney. *Development of American Journalism.* Dubuque, IA: William C Brown, 1969.

Kocher, Renata. "Bloodhounds or Missionaries? Role Definitions of British and German Journalists," *European Journal of Communication* 1(1), 1986, 43–64.

Koss, Stephen. *The Rise and Fall of the Political Press in Britain* (Vols. 1 and 2). London: Hamish Hamilton, 1981, 1984.

Kreiling, Albert. "The Commercialization of the Black Press and the Rise of Race News in Chicago," in William S. Solomon and Robert W. Mcchesney (eds.), *Ruthless Criticism: New Perspectives in U.S. Communication History.* Minneapolis: University of Minnesota Press, 1993, 176–203.

Kress, Gunther. "Linguistic and Ideological Transformations in News Reporting," in Paul Walton and Howard Davis (eds.), *Language, Image, Media,* Oxford, UK: Blackwell, 1983, 120–139.

Kress, Gunther, and Tony Trew. "Ideological Transformations of Discourse: Or, How the Sunday Times Got Its Message Across," *Sociological Review* 26(4), November 1978, 755–776.

Kress, Gunther, and Theo van Leeuwen. *Reading Images: The Grammar of Visual Design.* London: Routledge, 1996.

Kress, Gunther, and Theo van Leeuwen, "Front Page: (The Critical) Analysis of Newspaper Layout," in Allan Bell and Peter Garrett (eds.), *Approaches to Media Discourse.* Oxford, UK: Blackwell, 1997, 186–219.

Kucinski, Bernardo. *Jornalistas e revolucionarios: Nos tempos da imprensa alternative.* Sao Paulo: Scritta Editorial, 1991; cited in Waisbord 2000.

Kuhn, Raymond. *The Media in France.* London: Routledge, 1995.

Kuhn, Raymond, and Erick Neveu (eds.). *Political Journalism: New Challenges, New Practices.* London: Routledge, 2002.

Kuiper, Koenraad. *Smooth Talkers: The Linguistic Performance of Auctioneers and Sportscasters.* Mahwah, NJ: Lawrence Erlbaum, 1996.

Kuklinski, James H., and Lee Sigelman. "When Objectivity is Not Objective: Network Television News Coverage of U.S. Senators and the 'Paradox of Objectivity.'" *The Journal of Politics* 54(3), 1992, 810–833.

Kumar, Krishan. "Holding the Middle Ground: The BBC, the Public and the Professional Broadcaster," in James Curran, Michael Gurevitch, and Janet

Woollacott (eds.), *Mass Communication and Society*. London: Edward Arnold, 1977, 231–248.

Kurtz, Howard. *Spin Cycle: Inside the Clinton Propaganda Machine*. New York: Free Press, 1998.

Kynaston, David. *The Financial Times: A Centenary History*. London: Viking, 1988.

Lafky, Sue A. "The Progress of Women and People of Color in the U.S. Journalistic Workforce," in Pam Creedon (ed.), *Women in Mass Communication*. Newbury Park, CA: Sage 1993, 87–103.

Lambert, Andrew, and Stephen Badsey. *The Crimean War (The War Correspondents)*. Dover, NH: Sutton, 1997.

Land, Jeff. *Active Radio: Pacifica's Brash Experiment*. Minneapolis: University of Minnesota Press, 1999.

Lang, Kurt. "The European Roots," in Everette E. Dennis and Ellen Wartella (eds.), *American Communication Research: the Remembered History*. Mahwah, NJ: Lawrence Erlbaum, 1996, 1–20.

Lang, Kurt, and Gladys Lang. "The Unique Perspective of Television and Its Effect," *American Sociological Review* 18(1), 1953, 103–112.

Lang, Kurt, and Gladys Lang. *The Battle for Public Opinion*. New York: Columbia University Press, 1983.

Langer, John. *Tabloid Television: Popular Journalism and the "Other News."* London: Routledge, 1998.

Larson, Cedric. "Censorship of Army News During the World War, 1917–1918," *Journalism Quarterly* 17(4), 1940, 313–323.

Lasswell, Harold. "A Provisional Classification of Symbol Data," *Psychiatry* (1), May 1938, 197–204.

Lasswell, Harold. "The World Attention Survey: An Exploration of the Possibilities of Studying Attention Being Given to the United States by Newspapers Abroad," *Public Opinion Quarterly* 5(3), 1941, 456–462.

Lasswell, Harold. "The Structure and Function of Communication in Society," in Lyman Bryson (ed.), *The Communication of Ideas*. New York: Harper, 1948, 37–51.

Lasswell, Harold. *Propaganda Technique in the World War*. Cambridge: MIT Press, 1971 (1927).

Lasswell, Harold, and Dorothy Jones. "Communist Propaganda in Chicago," *Public Opinion Quarterly* 3(1), January 1939, 63–78.

Lazarsfeld, Paul. "Remarks on Administrative and Critical Communications Research," *Studies in Philosophy and Social Science* 9(1), 1941, 2–16.

Lazarsfeld, Paul. "The Sociology of Empirical Social Research," *American Sociological Review* 27(6), 1962, 757–767.

Lazarsfeld, Paul, Bernard Berelson, and Hazel Gaudet. *The People's Choice*. New York: Duell, Sloan and Pearce, 1944.

Lazarsfeld, Paul, and Elihu Katz. *Personal Influence*. New York: Free Press, 1960.

Lazarsfeld, Paul, and Robert Merton. "Mass Communication, Popular Taste, and Organized Social Action," in Lyman Bryson (ed.), *The Communication of Ideas*. New York: The Institute for Religious and Social Studies, 1948, 95–118.

Lazarsfeld, Paul, William Sewell, and Harold Wilensky (eds.). *The Uses of Sociology*. New York: Basic Books, 1967.

Lee, Alan J. *The Origins of the Popular Press in England, 1855–1914*. London: Croom Helms, 1976.

Lee, Chin-Chuan. "Beyond Orientalist Discourses: Media and Democracy in Asia," *Javnost—The Public* 8(2), 2001, 7–19.

Lee, James Melvin. *History of American Journalism*. Boston and New York: Houghton Mifflin, 1917.

Leitner, Gerhard. "BBC English and *Deutsche Rundfunksprache*: A Comparative and Historical Analysis of the Language on the Radio," *International Journal of the Sociology of Language* 26, 1980, 75–100.

Leo, John. "Bloopers of the Century." *Columbia Journalism Review*, January/ February 1999, 38–40.

Leonard, Thomas. *The Power of the Press*. New York: Oxford University Press, 1986.

Leonard, Thomas. *News For All: America's Coming of Age With the Press*. New York: Oxford University Press, 1995.

Lerner, Daniel. *The Passing of Traditional Society*. New York: Free Press, 1958.

Lester, Paul Martin. *Visual Communication: Images With Messages*. New York: Wadsworth, 1995.

Lett, James. "An Anthropological View of Television Journalism," *Human Organization* 46(4), 1987, 356–359.

Levy, Mark. "Disdaining the News," *Journal of Communication* 31(3), 1981, 24–41.

Lewin, Kurt. "Channels of Group Life," *Human Relations* 1, 1947, 143–153.

Lewinski, Jorge. *The Camera at War: A History of War Photography From 1848 to the Present Day*. London: W.H. Allen, 1978.

Lewis, Jeff. *Cultural Studies: The Basics*. London: Sage, 2002.

Lewis, Justin. *The Ideological Octopus: An Exploration of Television and Its Audience*. London: Routledge, 1991.

Lewis, Justin. "The Absence of Narrative: Boredom and the Residual Power of Television News," *Journal of Narrative and Life History* 41(1–2), 1994, 25–40.

Lichter, Robert, Stanley Rothman, and Linda S. Lichter. *The Media Elite*. Bethesda, MD: Adler and Adler, 1986.

Liebes, Tamar. *Reporting the Arab-Israeli Conflict: How Hegemony Works*. London: Routledge, 1997.

Liebovich, Louis W. *The Press and the Modern Presidency*. New York: Praeger, 2001.

Linder, Laura R. *Public Access Television: America's Electronic Soapbox*. Westport, CT: Praeger, 1999.

Lippmann, Walter. *Drift and Mastery*. New York: Mitchell Kennedy, 1914.

Lippmann, Walter. *The Phantom Public*. New York: Macmillan, 1925.

Lippmann, Walter. *Public Opinion*. New York: Harcourt Brace, 1960 [1922].

Lippmann, Walter, and Charles Merz. "A Test of the News," *New Republic* 23, 4 August 1920, sup. 1–42.

Littlewood, Thomas B. *Calling Elections: The History of Horse-Race Journalism.* Notre Dame, IN: University of Notre Dame Press, 1998.

Lloyd, Clem. *Profession: Journalist. A History of the Australian Journalists' Association.* Sydney: Hale and Iremonger, 1985.

Lont, Cynthia M. (ed.). *Women and Media: Content/Careers/Criticism.* Belmont, CA: Wadsworth. 1995.

Lowenthal, Leo. "The Triumph of Mass Idols," in *Literature, Popular Culture, and Society.* Englewood Cliffs, NJ: Prentice Hall, 1961 (1944).

Lucaites, John L., and Celeste Condit. "Re-Constructing Narrative Theory: A Functional Perspective," *Journal of Communication* 35, 1985, 90–109.

Lukes, Steven. "Political Ritual and Social Integration," *Sociology* 9(2), May 1975, 289–308.

Lule, Jack. "The Political Use of Victims: The Shaping of the *Challenger* Disaster," *Political Communication and Persuasion* 7, 1989a, 115–128.

Lule, Jack. "Victimage in *Times* Coverage of the KAL Flight 007 Shooting, " *Journalism Quarterly* 66, 1989b, 615–620.

Lule, Jack. "The Rape of Mike Tyson: Race, the Press, and Symbolic Types," *Critical Studies in Mass Communication* 12, 1995, 176–195.

Lule, Jack. *Daily News, Eternal Stories: The Mythological Role of Journalism.* New York: Guilford, 2001.

Lule, Jack. "Myth and Terror on the Editorial Page: The *New York Times* Responds to September 11, 2001," *Journalism and Mass Communication Quarterly* 79(2), Summer 2002, 275–293.

Lumby, Catharine. *Gotcha: Life in a Tabloid World.* Sydney: Allen & Unwin, 1999.

Lutnick, Solomon. *The American Revolution and the British Press, 1775–1783.* Columbia: University of Missouri Press, 1967.

Magee, James. *Freedom of Expression.* Westport, CT: Greenwood, 2002.

Mancini, Paolo. "Simulated Interaction: How the Television Journalist Speaks," *European Journal of Communication* 3(2), 1988, 151–166.

Mancini, Paolo. "Old and New Contradictions in Italian Journalism," *Journal of Communication* 42(3), 1992, 42–47.

Mander, Mary. "Communication Theory and History," in Mary Mander (ed.), *Communications in Transition.* New York: Praeger, 1983, 7–19.

Mander, Mary. "Narrative Dimensions of the News: Omniscience, Prophecy, and Morality," *Communication* 10(1), 1987, 51–70.

Mander, Mary (ed.). *Framing Friction: Media and Social Conflict.* Urbana: University of Illinois Press, 1998.

Manoff, Robert. "Understanding the Soviet Other: Speculations on the End of History, the End of the Cold War, and the End of Journalism," in James W. Fernandez and Milton B. Singer (eds.), *The Conditions of Reciprocal Understanding.* Chicago: University of Chicago Press, 1995.

Manoff, Robert K., and Michael Schudson (eds.). *Reading the News.* New York: Pantheon, 1986.

Marletti, Carlo, and Franka Roncarolo. "Media Influence in the Italian Transition from a Consensual to a Majoritarian Democracy," in Richard Gunther and Anthony Mughan (eds.), *Democracy and the Media*. Cambridge, UK: Cambridge University Press, 2000.

Marlier, John. "Fifteen Minutes of Glory: A Burkean Analysis of Press Coverage of Oliver North's Testimony," *Political Communication and Persuasion* 6, 1989, 269–288.

Marques de Melo, Jose. "Communication Theory and Research in Latin America: A Preliminary Balance of the Past Twenty-five Years," *Media, Culture and Society* 10(4), 1988, 405–418.

Martin-Barbero, Jesus. *Communication, Culture and Hegemony: From the Media to Mediations*. London: Sage, 1993.

Martin-Clark, Nick. "When a Journalist Must Tell," *British Journalism Review* 14(2), 2003, 35–39.

Marvin, Carolyn. "Space, Time and Captive Communications," in Mary Mander (ed.), *Communication in Transition*. New York: Praeger, 1983, 20–38.

Marvin, Carolyn. *When Old Technologies Were New: Thinking About Communications in the Late Nineteenth Century*. New York: Oxford University Press, 1988.

Marvin, Carolyn (with David Ingle). *Blood Sacrifice and the Nation*. New York: Cambridge University Press, 1999.

Marzolf, Marian. "Operationalizing Carey: An Approach to the Cultural History of Journalism," *Journalism History* 2(2), 1975, 42–43.

Masterton, Murray. *Asian Values in Journalism*. Singapore: AMIC (Asian Media. Information and Communication Center), 1996.

Mattelart, Armand. *Mass Media, Ideologies, and the Revolutionary Movement*. Brighton, UK: Harvester, 1980.

Mattelart, Armand, and Hector Schmucler. *Communication and Information Technologies: Freedom of Choice for Latin America?* Norwood, NJ: Ablex, 1985.

Matusow, Barbara. *The Evening Stars*. Boston: Houghton Mifflin, 1983.

Mayer, Henry. *The Press in Australia*. Melbourne: Landsdowne, 1964.

Mayes, Tessa. "Privacy in the Confessional Age," *British Journalism Review* 13(4), 2002, 67–73.

Mazzoleni, Gianpetro, Julianne Stewart, and Bruce Horsfield (eds.). *The Media and Neo-Populism: A Contemporary Comparative Analysis*. Westport, CT: Praeger, 2003.

McChesney, Robert. *Telecommunications, Mass Media and Democracy: The Battle for the Control of U.S. Broadcasting, 1928–1935*. New York: Oxford University Press, 1993.

McChesney, Robert. *Rich Media, Poor Democracy*. Champaign: University of Illinois Press, 1999.

McCombs, Maxwell, and Donald Shaw. "The Agenda Setting Function of the Press," *Public Opinion Quarterly* 36(2), 1972, 176–187.

McCombs, Maxwell, Donald Shaw, and David Weaver (eds.). *Communication and Democracy: Exploring the Intellectual Frontiers in Agenda-Setting Theory*. Mahwah, NJ: Lawrence Erlbaum, 1997.

McGerr, Michael. *The Decline of Popular Politics: The American North, 1865–1928*. Bridgewater, NJ: Replica, 2001.

McKerns, Joseph. "The Limits of Progressive Journalism History," *Journalism History* 4, Autumn 1977, 88–92.

McLeod, Jack, and Searle E. Hawley. "Professionalization Among Newsmen," *Journalism Quarterly* 41(4), 1964, 529–539.

McLuhan, Marshall. *Understanding Media: The Extensions of Man*. New York: McGraw-Hill, 1964.

McManus, John. *Market Driven Journalism: Let the Citizen Beware*. Thousand Oaks, CA: Sage, 1994.

McNair, Brian. *Glasnost, Perestroika and the Soviet Media*. London: Routledge, 1991.

McNair, Brian. *The Sociology of Journalism*. London: Edward Arnold, 1998.

McNair, Brian. *Journalism and Democracy*. London: Routledge, 2000a.

McNair, Brian. "Journalism and Democracy: A Millenial Audit," *Journalism Studies*, 1(2), May 2000b, 197–212.

McNelly, John T. "Intermediary Communicators in the International Flow of News," *Journalism Quarterly* 36, 1959, 23–26.

McQuail, Denis. *Mass Communication Theory*. London: Sage, 1987.

McQuail, Denis. *Media Performance: Mass Communication and the Public Interest*. London: Sage, 1992.

McQuail, Denis, Doris Graber, and Pippa Norris. "Conclusion: Challenges for Public Policy," in Doris Graber, Denis McQuail, and Pippa Norris (eds.), *The Politics of News: The News of Politics*. Washington, DC: CQ Press, 1998, 251–257.

Meadel, Cecile. *Histoire de la radio dans les annees trente*. Paris: Anthropos/INA, 1994.

Meinhof, Ulrike, and Kay Richardson (eds.). *Text, Discourse and Context: Representations of Poverty in Britain*. Harlow, UK: Longman, 1994.

Merrill, John. *The Imperative of Freedom: A Philosophy of Journalistic Autonomy*. New York: Hastings House, 1974.

Merrill, John, and John Nerone, "The Four Theories of the Press Four and a Half Decades Later: A Retrospective," *Journalism Studies* 3(1), February 2002, 133–136.

Merritt, Davis. *Public Journalism and Public Life: Why Telling the News Is Not Enough*. Hillsdale, NJ: Lawrence Erlbaum, 1995.

Meyer, Philip. *Editors, Publishers, and Newspaper Ethics*. Washington, DC: American Society of Newspaper Editors, 1983.

Meyer, Philip. *Ethical Journalism*. New York: Longman, 1987.

Meyers, Marian. "News of Battering," *Journal of Communication* 44(2), 1994, 47–63.

Meyers, Oren. "Still Photographs, Dynamic Memories: Independence Day in Israeli Periodicals," *Communication Review* 5(3), 2002, 179–205.

Mickiewicz, Ellen. *Changing Channels: Television and the Struggle for Power in Russia*. New York: Oxford University Press, 1997.

Mickiewicz, Ellen. "Transition and Democratization: The Role of Journalists in Eastern Europe and the Former Soviet Union," in Doris Graber, Denis McQuail, and Pippa Norris (eds.), *The Politics of News: the News of Politics*. Washington, DC: CQ Press, 1998, 33–56.

Mill, John Stuart. *On Liberty*. London: J.W. Parker and Son, 1859.

Miller, David, Jenny Kitzinger, Kevin Williams, and Peter Beharrel. *The Circuit of Mass Communication*. London: Sage, 1998.

Miller, Toby. *Technologies of Truth: Cultural Citizenship and the Popular Media*. Minneapolis: University of Minnesota Press, 1998.

Miller, Toby. "Tomorrow Will be Risky . . . and Disciplined," in James Friedman (ed.), *Reality Squared: Televisual Discourse on the Real*. New Brunswick, NJ: Rutgers University Press, 2002, 203–220.

Mindich, David T.Z. *Just the Facts: How "Objectivity" Came to Define Journalism*. New York: New York University Press, 1998.

Mindich, David T.Z. *Tuned Out: Why Young People Don't Follow the News*. New York: Oxford University Press, in press.

Moeller, Susan D. *Shooting War*. New York: Basic Books, 1989.

Moffett, E. Albert. "Hometown Radio in 1942: The Role of Local Stations During the First Year of Total War," *American Journalism* 3, 1986, 87–98.

Mohammadi, Ali (ed.). *International Communication and Globalization*. Thousand Oaks, CA: Sage, 1997.

Molotch, Harvey. "Media and Movements," in John MacCarthy and Mayer N. Zald (eds.), *The Dynamics of Social Movements*. Cambridge, UK: Winthrop, 1979, 71–93.

Molotch, Harvey, and Marilyn Lester. "News as Purposive Behavior," in *American Sociological Review* 39(6), 1974, 101–112.

Monmonier, Mark. *Maps With the News: The Development of American Journalistic Cartography*. Chicago: University of Chicago Press, 1989.

Montgomery, Martin. *An Introduction to Language and Society*. London: Methuen, 1986a.

Montgomery, Martin. "DJ Talk," *Media, Culture and Society* 8(4), 1986b, 421–440.

Moore, Molly. *A Woman at War: Storming Kuwait With the U.S. Marines*. New York: Scribner, 1993.

Moriarty, Sandra E., and Mark N. Popovich, "Newsmagazine Visuals and the 1988 Presidential Election," *Journalism Quarterly* 68(3), 1991, 371–380.

Morison, Stanley. *The English Newspaper*. Cambridge, UK: Cambridge University Press, 1932.

Morley, David. *The Nationwide Audience*. London: BFI, 1980.

Morris, Nancy, and Silvio Waisbord (eds.). *Media and Globalization: Why the State Matters*. Lanham, MD: Rowman and Littlefield, 2001.

Morrison, David, and Howard Tumber. *Journalists at War: The Dynamics of News Reporting During the Falklands War*. London: Sage, 1988.

Mosco, Vincent. *The Political Economy of Communication*. Thousand Oaks, CA: Sage, 1996.

Mott, Frank Luther. *American Journalism: A History of Newspapers in the United States Through 250 Years: 1690–1940*. New York: Macmillan, 1962 (1941).

Mowlana, Hamid. *Global Communication in Transition: The End of Diversity?* Thousand Oaks, CA: Sage, 1996.

Munster, George. *Rupert Murdoch*. New York: Viking, 1985.

Murdock, Graham, and Peter Golding, "The Structure, Ownership and Control of the Press, 1914–76," in George Boyce, James Curran, and Pauline Wingate (eds.), *Newspaper History From the Seventeenth Century to the Present Day*. Beverly Hills, CA: Sage, 1978, 130–150.

Murrow, Edward R. *This Is London*. New York: Simon and Schuster, 1941.

Nasaw, David. *The Chief: The Life of William Randolph Hearst*. New York: Houghton Mifflin, 2000.

Neal, Robert Miller. *Newspaper Deskwork*. New York: D. Appleton, 1933.

Nerone, John. "The Mythology of the Penny Press," *Critical Studies in Mass Communication* 4, December 1987, 376–404.

Nerone, John. "Theory and History," *Communication Theory* 3(2), May 1993, 148–157.

Nerone, John. *Violence Against the Press*. New York: Oxford University Press, 1994.

Nerone, John (ed.). *Last Rights: Revisiting the Four Theories of the Press*. Urbana: University of Illinois Press, 1995.

Neuman, W. Russell, Marion R. Just, and Ann N. Crigler. *Common Knowledge: News and the Construction of Political Meaning*. Chicago: University of Chicago Press, 1992.

Neveu, Erik. *Sociologie des mouvements sociaux*. Paris: Editions la Decouverte, 1996.

Neveu, Erik. "Media and Politics in French Political Science," *European Journal of Political Research* 33(4), 1998, 439–458.

Neveu, Erik. "Politics on French Television: Towards a Renewal of Political Journalism and Debate Frames?" *European Journal of Communication* 14(3), 1999, 379–409.

Nevins, Alan. "American Journalism and Its Historical Treatment," *Journalism Quarterly* 36(4), 1959, 411–422, 519.

Newton, Julianne H. *The Burden of Visual Truth: The Role of Photojournalism in Mediating Reality*. Mahwah, NJ: Lawrence Erlbaum, 2001.

Nichols, Bill. *Representing Reality: Issues and Concepts in Documentary*. Bloomington: Indiana University Press, 1991.

Nimmo, Dan, and James E. Combs, *Mediated Political Realities*. New York: Longman, 1983.

Nimmo, Dan, and James E. Combs. *Nightly Horrors: Crisis Coverage in Television Network News*. Knoxville: University of Tennessee Press, 1985.

Nimmo, Dan, and James E. Combs. *Political Pundits*. New York: Praeger, 1992.

Nir, Raphael. *Lashon, medyum u-meser*. Jerusalem: Pozner, 1984.

Noelle-Neumann, Elizabeth. "Return to the Concept of Powerful Mass Media," *Studies of Broadcasting* 9, 1973, 66–112.

Nord, David Paul. "A Plea for Journalism History," *Journalism History* 15(1), Spring 1988, 8–15.

Nord, David Paul. "The Nature of Historical Research," In Guido H. Stempel and Bruce Westley (eds.), *Research Methods in Mass Communication*, Englewood Cliffs, NJ: Prentice Hall, 1989, 290–315.

Nord, David Paul. *Communities of Journalism: A History of American Newspapers and the Their Readers.* Urbana: University of Illinois Press, 2001.

Nord, David Paul. *Faith in Reading: Religious Publishing and the Birth of Mass Media in America, 1790-1860.* New York: Oxford University Press, in press.

Nordenstreng, Kaarle. "Beyond the Four Theories of the Press," in Jan Servaes and Rico Lie (eds.), *Media and Politics in Transition: Cultural Identity in the Age of Globalization.* Leuven, Belgium: Acco, 1997, 97-109.

Nordenstreng, Kaarle, and Hifzi Topuz (eds.). *Journalist: Status, Rights, and Responsibilities.* Prague: International Organization of Journalists, 1989.

Nordenstreng, Kaarle, Elena Vartanova, and Yassen Zassoursky (eds.). *Russian Media Challenge.* Helsinki, Finland: Aleksanteri Institute, 2001.

Olasky, Marvin N. *Central Ideas in the Development of American Journalism: A Narrative History.* Mahwah, NJ: Lawrence Erlbaum, 1991.

Orren, Gary R. "Thinking About the Press and Government," in Martin Linsky (ed.), *Impact: How the Press Affects Federal Policymaking.* New York: Norton, 1986, 1-20.

Orwell, George. "Why I Write," *Gangrel,* Summer 1946.

Orwell, George. *Smothered Under Journalism, 1946.* London: Martin Secker and Warburg, Ltd., 1999.

Osborne, Graeme, and Glen Lewis. *Communication Traditions in Twentieth Century Australia.* Oxford, UK: Oxford University Press, 1995.

Ouellette, Laurie. *Viewers Like You?* New York: Columbia University Press, 2002.

Paletz, David, and Robert Entman. *Media, Power, Politics.* New York: Free Press, 1982.

Paletz, David, Karol Jakubowicz, and Pavao Novosel (eds.). *Glasnost and After.* Cresskill, NJ: Hampton, 1995.

Pan, Zhongdang, and Gerald Kosicki, "Framing Analysis: An Approach to News Discourse," *Political Communication* 10, 1993, 55-75.

Parenti, Michael. *Inventing Reality: The Politics of the Mass Media.* New York: St. Martin's, 1986.

Park, Robert E. "The Natural History of the Newspaper," In Robert E. Park, Ernest W. Burgess, and Roderick D. McKenzie (eds.), *The City.* Chicago: University of Chicago Press, 1925, 80-98.

Park, Robert E. "News as a Form of Knowledge," *American Journal of Sociology* 45, March 1940, 669-686.

Park, Robert E., Ernest W. Burgess, and Roderick D. McKenzie (eds.), *The City.* Chicago: University of Chicago Press, 1925.

Parton, James. *The Life and Times of Benjamin Franklin.* Boston: Houghton Mifflin, 1864.

Pasley, Jeffrey L. *The Tyranny of Printers: Newspaper Politics in the Early American Republic.* Charlottesville: University of Virginia Press, 2003.

Patterson, Thomas. *Out of Order.* New York: Alfred A. Knopf, 1993.

Patterson, Thomas. "Political Roles of the Journalist," in Doris Graber, Denis McQuail, and Pippa Norris (eds.), *The Politics of News, the News of Politics.* Washington, DC: CQ Press, 1998, 17-32.

Patterson, Thomas, and Wolfgang Donsbach. "News Decisions: Journalists as Partisan Actors," *Political Communication* 13(4), 1996, 455–468.

Pauly, John J. "Rupert Murdoch and the Demonology of Professional Journalism," in James Carey (ed.), *Media, Myths, and Narratives*. Newbury Park, CA: Sage, 1988, 246–261.

Pauly, John J. "The Politics of the New Journalism," in Norman Sims (ed.), *Literary Journalism in the Twentieth Century*. New York: Oxford University Press, 1990, 110–129.

Pauly, John J. "Public Journalism in International Perspective," *Communication Research Trends* 19(4), 1999a, 1–47.

Pauly, John. "Journalism and the Sociology of Public Life," in Theodore L. Glasser (ed.), *The Idea of Public Journalism*. New York: Guilford, 1999b, 134–151.

Pauly, John, and Melissa Eckert, "The Myth of 'the Local' in American Journalism," *Journalism and Mass Communication Quarterly* 79(2), Summer 2002, 310–326.

Pavlik, John. *Journalism and New Media*. New York: Columbia University Press, 2001.

Payne, Jack. *This is Jack Payne*. London: Marston, 1932.

Payne, Jack. *Signature Time*. Edinburgh: Simon Paul, 1947.

Pearson, Roberta, and John Hartley (eds.). *American Cultural Studies: A Reader*. Oxford, UK: Oxford University Press, 2000.

Pedelty, Mark. *War Stories: The Culture of Foreign Correspondents*. London: Routledge, 1995.

Perlmutter, David. *Foreign Policy and Photojournalism: Icons of Outrage in International Crises*. Westport, CT: Praeger, 1998.

Perrineau, Pascal, Gerard Grunberg, and Colette Ysmal. *Europe at the Polls: The European Elections of 1999*. New York: Palgrave, 2002.

Persico, Joseph E. *Edward R. Murrow: An American Original*. New York: McGraw-Hill, 1988.

Peters, John Durham. "Public Journalism and Democratic Theory: Four Challenges," in Theodore L. Glasser (ed.), *The Idea of Public Journalism*. New York: Guilford, 1999, 99–117.

Peterson, Sophia. "Foreign News Gatekeepers and Criteria of Newsworthiness," *Journalism Quarterly* 56, 1979, 116–125.

Peterson, Sophia. "International News Selection by the Elite Press," *Public Opinion Quarterly* 45(2), 1981, 143–63.

Pfaff, Daniel W. *Joseph Pulitzer II and the Post-Dispatch: A Newspaperman's Life*. University Park: Pennsylvania State University Press, 1991.

Pfetsch, Barbara. "Government News Management," in Doris Graber, Denis McQuail, and Pippa Norris (eds.), *The Politics of News: the News of Politics*. Washington, DC: CQ Press, 1998, 70–93.

Phillips, Angela, and Ivor Gaber. "The Case for Media Degrees," *British Journalism Review* 7(3), 1996, 62–65.

Philo, Greg. *Seeing and Believing*. London: Routledge, 1990.

Philo, Greg (ed.). *Message Received: Glasgow Media Group Research, 1993-1998.* Harlow, UK: Longman, 1999.

Picard, Robert. *The Press and the Decline of Democracy.* Westport, CT: Greenwood, 1985.

Picard, Robert (ed.). *New Perspectives on Newspaper Ownership and Operation.* Norwood, NJ: Ablex, 1988.

Pilger, John. *Heroes.* London: Jonathan Cape, 1986.

Pollard, James E. *The Presidents and the Press.* New York: Macmillan, 1947.

Popkin, Jeremy. *The Right-Wing Press in France, 1792–1800.* Chapel Hill: University of North Carolina Press, 1980.

Popkin, Jeremy. *Press, Revolution, and Social Identities in France, 1830–1835.* Pennsylvania State University Press, 2001.

Popkin, Jeremy, Steven Kaplan, and Keith Baker (eds.). *Revolutionary News: The Press in France, 1789–1799.* Durham, NC: Duke University Press, 1990.

Popkin, Samuel L. *The Reasoning Voter: Communication and Persuasion in Presidential Campaigns.* Chicago: University of Chicago Press, 1991.

Postman, Neil, and Steve Powers. *How to Watch TV News.* New York: Penguin, 1992.

Potter, Jonathan. *Representing Reality: Discourse, Rhetoric and Social Construction.* Thousand Oaks, CA: Sage, 1996.

Potter, Jonathan, and Margaret Wetherell. *Discourse and Social Psychology.* Thousand Oaks, CA: Sage, 1987.

Press, Charles, and Kenneth Verburg. *American Politicians and Journalists.* Glenview, IL: Scott, Foresman, 1988.

Price, Monroe E. *Television, the Public Sphere, and National Identity.* New York: Oxford University Press, 1995.

Price, Monroe E. *Media and Sovereignty.* Cambridge: MIT Press, 2002.

Price, Vincent, and David Tewksbury. "News Values and Public Opinion: A Theoretical Account of Media Priming and Framing," in George Barnett and Franklin J. Boster (eds.), *Progress in the Communication Sciences.* Norwood, NJ: Ablex, 1997, 173–212.

Pringle, John Douglas. *Have Pen: Will Travel.* London: Chatto and Windus, 1973.

Protess, David L., Fay Lomax Cook, Margaret Gordon, and James Ettema. *The Journalism of Outrage.* New York: Guilford, 1991.

Putnam, Robert. *Bowling Alone: The Collapse and Revival of American Community.* New York: Simon and Schuster, 2001.

Pye, Lucian. *Communications and Political Development.* Princeton, NJ: Princeton University Press, 1963.

Rall, Ted (ed.). *Attitude: The New Subversive Political Cartoonists.* New York: NBM Publishing, 2002.

Ramanathan, Sankaran, and Jan Servaes. *Asia Reporting Europe and Europe Reporting Asia: A Study of News Coverage.* Singapore: AMIC (Asia Media Information and Communication Center), 1997.

Rather, Dan. *The Camera Never Blinks.* New York: Ballantine, 1977.

Reese, Stephen D. "The News Paradigm and the Ideology of Objectivity: A Socialist at the *Wall Street Journal*," *Critical Studies in Mass Communication* 7(4), 1990, 390–409.

Reese, Stephen D. "Prologue: Framing Public Life," in Stephen D. Reese, Oscar Gandy, Jr., and August Grant (eds.), *Framing Public Life*. Mahwah, NJ: Lawrence Erlbaum, 2001, 7–31.

Reese, Stephen D., Oscar Gandy, Jr., and August Grant (eds.). *Framing Public Life*. Mahwah, NJ: Lawrence Erlbaum, 2001.

Reeves, Jimmie, and Richard Campbell. *Cracked Coverage: Television News, the Anti-Cocaine Crusade, and the Reagan Legacy*. Durham: Duke University Press, 1994.

Reid, Robert D., and Curtis MacDougall. *Interpretative Reporting*. New York: Prentice Hall, 1987.

Reif, Karlheinz (ed.). *Ten European Elections: Campaigns and Results of the 1979/81 First Direct Elections to the European Parliament*. Aldershot, UK: Gower, 1985.

Reif, Karlheinz, and Hermann Schmitt. "Nine Second-Order National Elections: A Conceptual Framework for the Analysis of European Election Results," *European Journal of Political Research* 8, 1980, 3–44.

Reith, John C.W. *Into the Wind*. London: Hodder and Stoughton, 1949.

Riddell, Lord. "The Psychology of the Journalist," *Journalism By Some Masters of the Craft*, 1932, in Michael Bromley and Tom O'Malley (eds.), *A Journalism Reader*. London: Routledge, 1997, 110–117.

Riddell, Mary. "Guy Black: In the Eye of the Hurricane," *British Journalism Review* 14(1), 2003, 7–16.

Riley, Sam (ed.). *American Magazine Journalists, 1741–1900* (Vols. 1 and 2). Detroit, MI: Gale Research, 1988–1989.

Rivers, William, Wilbur Schramm, and Clifford Christians. *Responsibility in Mass Communications*. New York: Harper and Row, 1980.

Roberts, Chalmers M. *The Washington Post: The First 100 Years*. Boston: Houghton Mifflin, 1977.

Roberts, Chalmers M. *In the Shadow of Power: The Story of the Washington Post*. Cabin John, MD: Seven Locks, 1989.

Robinson, John, and Mark Levy. *The Main Source: Learning From Television News*. Beverly Hills, CA: Sage, 1986.

Robinson, Michael J., and Sheehan, Margaret A. *Over the Wire and on TV: CBS and UPI in Campaign '80*. New York: Russell Sage, 1983.

Robinson, Piers. *The CNN Effect: The Myth of News, Foreign Policy and Intervention.*, London: Routledge, 2002.

Roeh, Itzhak. *The Rhetoric of News*. Bochum: Studienverlag, 1982.

Roeh, Itzhak. "Journalism as Storytelling, Coverage as Narrative," *American Behavioral Scientist* 33(2), November/December 1989, 162–168.

Roeh, Itzhak, and Sharon Ashley. "Criticizing Press Coverage of the War in Lebanon," *Communication Yearbook 9*. Beverly Hills, CA: Sage, 1986, 117–141.

Roeh, Itzhak, and Saul Feldman. "The Rhetoric of Numbers in Front-Page Journalism: How Numbers Contribute to the Melodramatic in the Popular Press," *Text* 4(4), 1984, 347–368.

Roeh, Itzhak, Elihu Katz, Akiba A. Cohen, and Barbie Zelizer. *Almost Midnight: Reforming the Late-Night News*. Beverly Hills, CA: Sage, 1980.

Rivers, Caryl. *Slick Spins and Fractured Facts*. New York: Columbia University Press.

Rogers, Everett. *A History of Communication Study, A Biographical Approach*. New York: Free Press, 1997.

Roncarolo, Franka. "Una crisi allo specchio: Politici e giornalisti tra complicita e conflitti," *Teoria Politica* 16(3), 2000.

Rosen, Jay. "Making Things More Public: On the Political Responsibility of the Media Intellectual," *Critical Studies in Mass Communication* 11, 1994, 362–388.

Rosen, Jay. *Getting the Connections Right: Public Journalism and the Troubles in the Press*. New York: Twentieth Century Fund, 1996.

Rosen, Jay. *What Are Journalists For?* New Haven, CT: Yale University Press, 1999.

Rosenbaum, Martin. *From Soapbox to Soundbites: Party Political Campainging in Britain Since 1945*. London: Macmillan, 1997.

Rosengren, Karl. "International News: Methods, Data, Theory," *Journal of Peace Research* 11(2), 1974, 145–156.

Rosengren, Karl (ed.). *Advances in Content Analysis*. Beverly Hills, CA: Sage, 1981.

Rosenstiel, Tom. *Strange Bedfellows: How Television and the Presidential Candidates Changed American Politics, 1992*. New York: Hyperion, 1993.

Roshco, Bernard. *Newsmaking*. Chicago: University of Chicago Press, 1975.

Ross, Ishbel. *Ladies of the Press*. New York: Harper, 1936.

Rosten, Leo C. *The Washington Correspondents*. New York: Harcourt, Brace and Co., 1937.

Rovit, Earl. *Ernest Hemingway*. New York: Grove, 1961.

Rowe, Christopher. "Hacks on Film," *Washington Journalism Review*, November 1992, 27–29.

Rowe, David. *Sport, Culture and the Media*. Buckingham, UK: Open University Press, 1999.

Rudenstine, David. *The Day the Press Stopped: A History of the Pentagon Papers Case*. Berkeley: University of California Press, 1996.

Ruotolo, A.C. "Professional Orientation Among Journalists in Three Latin American Countries," *Gazette* 40(2), 1987, 131–142.

Ryan, A.P. *Lord Northcliffe*. London: Collins, 1953.

Sabato, Larry. *The Rise of Political Consultants*. New York: Basic Books, 1981.

Sabato, Larry. *Feeding Frenzy*. New York: Free Press, 1991.

Salisbury, Harrison. *A Journey for Our Times: A Memoir*. New York: Harper and Row, 1983.

Saltzman, Joe. *Frank Capra and the Image of the Journalist in American Film*. Los Angeles: Norman Lear Center at the University of Southern California, 2002.

Salwen, Michael, and Bruce Garrison. *Latin American Journalism*. Hillsdale, NJ: Lawrence Erlbaum, 1991.

Sanchez-Tabernero, Alfonso. *Media Concentration in Europe: Commercial Enterprise and the Public Interest.* London: John Libbey, 1993.

Scannell, Paddy. "The Social Eye of Television, 1946–1955," *Media, Culture and Society* 1(1), 1979, 97–106.

Scannell, Paddy. "Public Service Broadcasting and Modern Public Life," *Media, Culture and Society* 11(2), 134–166, 1989.

Scannell, Paddy (ed.). *Broadcast Talk.* London: Sage, 1991.

Scannell, Paddy. *Radio, Television and Modern Life.* Oxford, UK: Blackwell, 1996.

Scannell, Paddy. "History, Media and Communication," in Klaus Bruhn Jensen (ed.), *A Handbook of Media and Communication Research.* London: Routledge, 2002, 191–205.

Scannell, Paddy, and David Cardiff. *A Social History of British Broadcasting, 1922–1938: Serving the Nation* (Vol. 1). Oxford, UK: Blackwell, 1991.

Schaaber, Matthew. *Some Forerunners of the Newspaper in England, 1476–1622.* London: Frank Cass, 1967.

Scheufele, Dietram A. "Framing as a Theory of Media Effects," *Journal of Communication* 49(1), 1999. 103–122.

Schiller, Dan. "An Historical Approach to Objectivity and Professionalism in American News Reporting," *Journal of Communication* 29(4), 1979, 46–57.

Schiller, Dan. *Objectivity and the News: The Public and the Rise of Commercial Journalism.* Philadelphia: University of Pennsylvania Press, 1981.

Schlesinger, Philip. *Putting "Reality" Together.* London: Methuen, 1978.

Schlesinger, Philip. "Rethinking the Sociology of Journalism: Source Strategies and the Limits of Media-Centrism," in Marjorie Ferguson (ed.), *Public Communication: The New Imperatives.* Newbury Park, CA: Sage, 1990, 61–83.

Schlesinger, Philip, David Miller, and Williams Dinan. *Open Scotland? Journalists, Spin Doctors, and Lobbyists.* Edinburgh: Polygon, 2001.

Schlesinger, Philip, Graham Murdock, and Philip Elliott. *Televising Terrorism.* London: Comedia, 1983.

Schlesinger, Philip, and Howard Tumber. *Reporting Crime.* Oxford, UK: Oxford University Press, 1995.

Schmitt, Hermann, and Jacques Thomassen (eds.). *Political Representation and Legitimacy in the European Union.* Oxford, UK: Oxford University Press, 1999.

Schmitt, Hermann, and Jacques Thomassen. "Dynamic Representation: The Case of European Integration," *European Union Politics* 1, 2000, 319–340.

Schramm, Wilbur. *Communications in Modern Society.* Urbana, IL: Institute of Communications Research, 1948.

Schramm, Wilbur (ed.). *The Process and Effects of Mass Communication.* Urbana: University of Illinois Press, 1954.

Schramm, Wilbur. *One Day in the World's Press.* Stanford, CA: Stanford University Press, 1959.

Schroder, Kim Christian. "Discourses of Fact," in Klaus Bruhn Jensen (ed.), *A Handbook of Media and Communication Research.* London: Routledge, 2002, 98–116.

Schudson, Michael. *Discovering the News*. New York: Basic Books, 1978.

Schudson, Michael. "The Politics of Narrative Form: The Emergence of News Conventions in Print and Television," *Daedalus* 11(4), Fall 1982, 97–112.

Schudson, Michael. "What is a Reporter? The Private Face of Public Journalism," in James W. Carey (ed.), *Media, Myths, and Narratives: Television and the Press*. Newbury Park, CA: Sage, 1988, 228–245.

Schudson, Michael. "The Sociology of News Production, Revisited," in James Curran and Michael Gurevitch (eds.), *Mass Media and Society*. London: Edward Arnold, 1991, 141–159.

Schudson, Michael. *Watergate in American Memory: How We Remember, Forget, and Reconstruct the Past*. New York: Basic Books, 1992.

Schudson, Michael. *The Power of News*. Cambridge, MA: Harvard University Press, 1995.

Schudson, Michael. "Toward a Troubleshooting Manual for Journalism History," *Journalism and Mass Communication Quarterly* 74(3), Autumn 1997a, 463–467.

Schudson, Michael. "Paper Tigers: A Sociologist Follows Cultural Studies Into the Wilderness," *Lingua Franca* 7(6), August 1997b, 49–56.

Schudson, Michael. "What Public Journalism Knows About Journalism But Doesn't Know About 'Public,'" in Theodore L. Glasser (ed.), *The Idea of Public Journalism*. New York: Guilford, 1999, 118–133.

Schudson, Michael. *The Sociology of News*. New York: Norton, 2002.

Schultz, Julianne. *Reviving the Fourth Estate*. Cambridge, UK: Cambridge University Press, 1998.

Schulz, Winfried. *Die Konstruktion von Realtität in den Nachrichtenmedien. Analyse der aktuellen Berichterstattun*. Freiburg/Munchen: Alber, 1976.

Schulz, Winfried. "News Structure and People's Awareness of Political Events," *Gazette* 30, 1982, 139–153.

Schulz, Winfried. "Political Communication Scholarship in Germany," *Political Communication* 14(1), 1997, 113–146.

Schultz-Brooks, Terri. "Getting There: Women in the Newsroom," *Columbia Journalism Review*, March/April 1984, 25–31.

Schwartz, Dona. "To Tell the Truth—Codes of Objectivity in Photojournalism," *Communication* 13(2), 1992, 95–109.

Schwarzlose, Richard A. *The Nation's Newsbrokers* (Vols. I and II). Evanston, IL: Northwestern University Press, 1989, 1990.

Scollon, Ron. *Mediated Discourse as Social Interaction: A Study of News Discourse*. London: Longman, 1998.

Scott, C.P. "The *Manchester Guardian*'s First Hundred Years," *Manchester Guardian*, 5 May 1921; reprinted in Michael Bromley and Tom O'Malley (eds.). *A Journalism Reader*. London: Routledge, 1997, 108–109.

Seldes, George. *Freedom of the Press*. Indianapolis, IN: Bobbs-Merrill, 1935.

Servaes, Jan. "Reflections on the Differences in Asian and European Values and Communication Modes," *Asian Journal of Communication* 10(2), 2000, 53–70.

Seymour-Ure, Colin. *The Political Impact of the Mass Media*. London: Constable, 1974.

Seymour-Ure, Colin. *The British Press and Broadcasting Since 1945*. Ocford, UK:Blackwell, 1991.

Sfez, Lucien. *La politique symbolique*. Paris: P.U.F., 1993.

Shapiro, Herbert (ed.). *The Muckrakers and American Society*. Boston: Beacon, 1968.

Shattuc, Jane M. *The Talking Cure: TV Talk Shows and Women*. New York: Routledge, 1997.

Sheehan, Neil (and others). *The Pentagon Papers: The Secret History of the Vietnam War, Based on Investigative Reporting by Neil Sheehan*. New York: Bantam Books, 1971.

Shingler, Martin, and Cindy Wieringa. *On Air: Methods and Meanings of Radio*. London: Edward Arnold, 1998.

Shipler, David. "Blacks in the Newsroom: Progress? Yes, but . . . ," *Columbia Journalism Review*, May/June 1998, 26–32.

Shoemaker, Pamela. *Gatekeeping*. Newbury Park, CA: Sage: 1991.

Siebert, Frank, Theodore Peterson, and Wilbur Schramm. *Four Theories of the Press*. Urbana: University of Illinois Press, 1956.

Sigal, Leon. *Reporters and Officials*. Lexington, MA: D.C. Heath, 1973.

Sigal, Leon. "Sources Make the News," in Robert K. Manoff and Michael Schudson (eds.), *Reading the News*. New York: Pantheon, 1986, 9–37.

Sigelman, Lee. "Reporting the News: An Organizational Analysis," *American Journal of Sociology* 79(1), 1973, 132–151.

Sim, Soek-Fang. "Asian Values, Authoritarianism and Capitalism in Singapore," *Javnost—The Public* 8(2), 2000, 45–66.

Sims, Norman (ed.). *Literary Journalism in the Twentieth Century*. New York: Oxford University Press, 1990.

Sims, Norman, and Mark Kramer (eds.). *Literary Journalism*. New York: Ballantine, 1995.

Simpson, George E. *The Negro in the Philadelphia Press*, PhD dissertation, University of Pennsylvania, 1934; cited in Krippendorff 1980.

Singer, Jane. "Online Journalists: Foundations for Research Into Their Changing Role," *Journal of Computer Mediated Communication* 4(1), September 1998 (http://www.ascusc.org/jcmc/vol4/issue1/singer.html).

Skidmore, Thomas J. (ed.). *Television, Politics, and the Transition to Democracy in Latin America*. Baltimore: Johns Hopkins University Press, 1993.

Sloan, William David. *Perspectives on Mass Communication History*. Hillsdale, NJ: Lawrence Erlbaum, 1991.

Smith, Anthony. *The Shadow in the Cave*. London: Allen and Unwin, 1973.

Smith, Anthony. "The Long Road to Objectivity and Back Again: The Kinds of Truth We Get in Journalism," in George Boyce, James Curran, and Pauline Wingate (eds.), *Newspaper History from the Seventeenth Century to the Present Day*. Beverly Hills, CA: Sage, 1978, 153–171.

Smith, Anthony (ed.). *Television: An International History* (2nd ed.). Oxford, UK: Oxford University Press, 1998.

Smith, Culver. *The Press, Politics, and Patronage: The American Government's Use of Newspapers, 1789–1875.* Athens: University of Georgia Press, 1977.

Smith, Jeffery A. *Printers and Press Freedom: The Ideology of Early American Journalism.* New York: Oxford University Press, 1988.

Smith, Jeffery A. *War and Press Freedom: The Problem of Prerogative Power.* New York: Oxford University Press, 1999.

Smulyan, Susan. *Selling Radio: The Commercialization of American Broadcasting, 1920–1934.* Washington, DC: Smithsonian Institute Press, 1994.

Snider, Paul. "Mr. Gates Revisited," *Journalism Quarterly* 44, 1967, 419–427.

Sola Pool, Ithia de. *Trends in Content Analysis: Papers.* Urbana: University of Illinois Press, 1959.

Solomon, William S., and Robert W. McChesney (eds.). *Ruthless Criticism: New Perspectives in U.S. Communication History.* Minneapolis: University of Minnesota Press, 1993.

Soloski. John. "News Reporting and Professionalism: Some Constraints on the Reporting of the News," *Media, Culture, and Society* 11(4), 1989, 204–228.

Sparks, Colin. "Goodbye Hildy Johnson: The Vanishing Serious Press," in Peter Dahlgren (ed.), *Communication and Citizenship: Journalism and the Public Sphere.* London: Routledge, 1994, 58–74.

Sparks, Colin. "Concentration and Market Entry in the UK Daily National Press," *European Journal of Communication* 11(4), December 1996, 453–483.

Sparks, Colin. "Introduction: The Panic Over Tabloid News," in Colin Sparks and John Tulloch (eds.), *Tabloid Tales: Global Debates Over Media Standards.* Oxford: Rowman and Littlefield, 2000, 1–40.

Sparks, Colin, and John Tulloch (eds.). *Tabloid Tales: Global Debates Over Media Standards.* New York and Oxford: Rowman and Littlefield, 2000.

Sperber, A.M. *Murrow: His Life and Times.* New York: Freundlich, 1986.

Splichal, Slavko. *Media Beyond Socialism: Theory and Practice in East-Central Europe.* Boulder, CO: Westview, 1994.

Splichal, Slavko. *Public Opinion: Developments and Controversies in the Twentieth Century.* Lanham, MD: Rowman and Littlefield, 1999.

Splichal, Slavko, and Colin Sparks. *Journalists for the 21st Century.* Norwood, NJ: Ablex, 1994.

Sreberny-Mohammadi, Annabelle, Dwayne Winseck, Jim McKenna, and Oliver Boyd-Barrett (eds.). *Media in Global Context: A Reader.* London: Edward Arnold, 1997.

Starck, Kenneth. "What's Right/Wrong With Journalism Ethics Research?" *Journalism Studies* 2(1), 2001, 133–152.

Startt, James D., and William David Sloan. "Interpretation in History," in *Historical Methods in Mass Communication.* Hillsdale, NJ: Lawrence Erlbaum, 1989.

Steffens, Lincoln. *The Autobiography of Lincoln Steffens.* New York: Harcourt Brace, 1931.

Steiner, Linda. "Construction of Gender in News Reporting Textbooks, 1890–1990," *Journalism Monographs* 135, October 1992, 1–48.

Steiner, Linda. "Do You Belong in Journalism? Definitions of the Ideal Journalist in Career Guidance Books," *American Journalism*, Fall 1994, 11(4), 321–335.

Steiner, Linda. "Sex, Lies, and Autobiography: Contributions of Life Study to Journalism History," *American Journalism* 13(2), Spring 1996, 206–211.

Steiner, Linda. "Gender at Work: Early Accounts by Women Journalists," *Journalism History* 23(1), Spring 1997, 2–12.

Steiner, Linda. "Stories of Quitting: Why Did Women Journalists Leave the Newsroom?" *American Journalism* 15(3), Summer 1998, 89–116.

Stephens, Mitchell. *A History of News: From the Drum to the Satellite*. New York: Viking, 1988.

Stephens, Mitchell. *The Rise of the Image, the Fall of the Word*. New York: Oxford University Press, 1998.

Stephenson, Hugh. "British Press and Privacy," in Howard Tumber (ed.), *Media Power, Professionals and Policies*. London: Routledge, 2000.

Stone, Gerald, and John Lee. "Portrayal of Journalists on Prime Time Television," *Journalism Quarterly* 67(4), Winter 1990, 697–707.

Streckfuss, Richard. "News Before Newspapers," *Journalism and Mass Communication Quarterly* 75(1), 1998, 84–97.

Street, A.T. "The Truth About Newspapers," *Chicago Tribune*, 25 July 1909; cited in Krippendorff 1980.

Streitmatter, Rodger. *Mightier Than the Sword: How the News Media Have Shaped American History*. Boulder, CO: Westview, 1997.

Strentz, Herbert. *News Reporters and News Sources*. Ames: Iowa State University Press, 1989.

Stutterheim, Kurt von. *The Press in England*. London: George Allen and Unwin, 1934.

Sykes, Christopher. *Evelyn Waugh: A Biography*. New York: Penguin, 1977.

Talese, Gay. *The Kingdom and the Power*. New York: Doubleday, 1978.

Tarde, Gabriel. *L'opinion et la foule*. Paris: Alcan, 1898.

Tarde, Gabriel. *On Communication and Social Influence*. Chicago: University of Chicago Press, 1969 (1901).

Taylor, H.S. *The British Press*. London: Arthur Barker, 1961.

Taylor, John. *War Photography: Realism in the British Press*. London: Routledge, 1991.

Taylor, John. *Body Horror: Photojournalism, Catastrophe and War*. Manchester, UK: Manchester University Press, 1998.

Taylor, Paul. *See How They Run: Electing the President in an Age of Mediacracy*. New York: Alfred A. Knopf, 1990.

Taylor, Philip. *War and the Media: Propaganda and Persuasion in the Gulf War*. Manchester, UK: Manchester University Press, 1998.

Television and New Media (Special issue on September 11), 3(1), 2002.

Tester, Keith. *Media, Culture and Morality*. London: Routledge, 1994.

Thomas, Isaiah. *History of Printing in America*. Worcester, MA: Isaac Sturtevant, 1810.

Thompson, J. Lee. *Northcliffe*. London: John Murray, 2000.

Tiffen, Rodney. *News and Power*. London: Pluto, 1990.

Tifft, Susan E., and Alex S. Jones. *The Trust: The Private and Powerful Family Behind the New York Times*. Newport Beach, CA: Back Bay, 2000.

Tocqueville, Alexis de. *Democracy in America*. New York: Colonial Press, 1900.

Tomalin, Nicholas. "Stop the Press I Want to Get On," *Sunday Times Magazine*, 26 October 1969; reprinted in Michael Bromley and Tom O'Malley (eds.). *A Journalism Reader*. London: Routledge, 1997, 174–178.

Tomaselli, Keyan. "Cultural Studies as 'Psycho-babble': Post-LitCrit, Methodology and Dynamic Justice." Keynote Address, 3rd Crossroads Conference on Cultural Studies, Birmingham, U.K., June 2000.

Tomaselli, Keyan. "Journalism Education: Bridging Media and Cultural Studies," *Communication* 28(1), 2002, 22–28.

Tonnies, Ferdinand. "The Power and Value of Public Opinion," in Werner J. Cahnman and Rudolf Heberle (eds.), *Ferdinand Tonnies on Sociology: Pure, Applied and Empirical*. Chicago: University of Chicago Press, 1971 (1923), 251–265.

Tracey, Michael. *The Production of Political Television*. London: Routledge and Kegan Paul, 1977.

Trew, Tony. "Theory and Ideology at Work," in Roger Fowler, Bob Hodge, Gunther Kress, and Tony Trew (eds.), *Language and Control*. London: Routledge and Kegan Paul, 1979a, 94–116.

Trew, Tony. "What the Papers Say: Linguistic Variation and Ideological Difference," in Roger Fowler, Bob Hodge, Gunther Kress, and Tony Trew (eds.), *Language and Control*. London: Routledge and Kegan Paul, 1979b, 117–157.

Tuchman, Gaye. "Objectivity as Strategic Ritual: An Examination of Newsmen's Notions of Objectivity," *American Journal of Sociology* 77(4), 1972, 660–679.

Tuchman, Gaye. "Making News By Doing Work: Routinizing the Unexpected," *American Journal of Sociology* 79(1), 1973, 110–131.

Tuchman, Gaye. *Making News*. New York: Free Press, 1978a.

Tuchman, Gaye. "Professionalism as an Agent of Legitimation," *Journal of Communication* 28(2), 1978b, 106–113.

Tuchman, Gaye. "The Production of News," in Klaus Bruhn Jensen (ed.), *A Handbook of Media and Communication Research*. London: Routledge, 2002, 78–90.

Tufte, Edward R. *Visual Display of Quantitative Information*. Cheshire, CT: Graphics, 2001.

Tumber, Howard (ed.). *News: A Reader*. Oxford, UK: Oxford University Press, 1999.

Tumber, Howard (ed.). *Media Power, Professionals and Policies*. London: Routledge, 2000.

Tumber, Howard. "Public Relations in Media," in *The International Encyclopedia of the Social & Behavioral Sciences* (Vol. 5.2, Article 68). Oxford, UK: Elsevier Science, 2001, 12578–12581.

Tunstall, Jeremy. *The Westminster Lobby Correspondents: A Sociological Study of National Political Journalism*. London: Routledge and Kegan Paul, 1970.

Tunstall, Jeremy. *Journalists At Work*. London: Constable, 1971.

Tunstall, Jeremy. *The Media Are American*. London: Constable, 1977.

Tunstall, Jeremy. *Newspaper Power*. London: Clarendon Press, 1996.

Turner, Graeme. "Media Wars: Journalism, Cultural and Media Studies in Australia," in *Journalism: Theory, Practice and Criticism* 1(3), December 2000, 353–365.

Turner, Victor. *The Ritual Process*. London: Penguin, 1974.

Van Leeuwen, Theo. "Proxemics of the Television Interview," *Australian Journal of Screen Theory* 17/18, 1986, 125–141.

Van Leeuwen, Theo, and Adam Jaworski. "The Discourses of War Photography: Photojournalistic Representations of the Palestinian-Israeli War," *Journal of Language and Politics* 1(2), 2003, 255–275.

Van Zoonen, Lisbet. "Rethinking Women and the News," *European Journal of Communication* 3(1), 1988, 335–353.

Varis, Tapio. *Television News in Europe: A Survey of the News-Film Flow in Europe*. Tampere, Finland: Institute of Journalism and Mass Communication, 1976.

Villard, Oswald Garrison. *Some Newspapers and Newspapermen*. New York: Alfred A. Knopf, 1923.

Vincent, Richard C., Kaarle Nordenstreng, and Michael Traber (eds.). *Towards Equity in Global Communication: MacBride Update*. Cresskill, NJ: Hampton, 1999.

Volkmer, Ingrid. *CNN: News in the Global Sphere: A Study of CNN and Its Impact on Global Communication*. Luton: University of Luton Press, 1999.

Vreese, Claes de. "Frames in Television News. British, Danish and Dutch Television News Coverage of the Introduction of the Euro," in Stig Hjarvard (ed.), *News in a Globalized Society*. Goteborg, Sweden: Nordicom, 2001, 179–193.

Wahl-Jorgensen, Karin. "Letters to the Editor as a Forum for Public Deliberation, Modes of Publicity, and Democratic Debate," *Critical Studies in Media Communication* 18, 2001, 303–320.

Wahl-Jorgensen, Karin. "The Construction of the Public in Letter to the Editor: Deliberating Democracy and the Idiom of Insanity," *Journalism: Theory, Practice, and Criticism* 3(2), 2003, 183–204.

Waisbord, Silvio. *Watchdog Journalism in South America*. New York: Columbia University Press, 2000.

Walker, R.B. *Yesterday's News: A History of the Newspaper Press in New South Wales from 1920 to 1945*. Sydney: Sydney University Press, 1980.

Walton, Paul, and Howard H. Davis. *Language, Image, Media*. Oxford, UK: Blackwell, 1983.

Ward, Jean. "Interdisciplinary Research and the Journalism Historian," *Journalism History* 5, Spring 1978, front page, 17–19.

Wardle, Claire. "The 'Unabomber' Versus the "Nail Bomber": A Cross Cultural Comparison of Newspaper Coverage of Two Murder Trials," *Journalism Studies* 4(2), May 2003.

Warner, Malcolm. "Organizational Context and Control of Policy in the Television Newsroom: A Participant Observation Study," *British Journal of Sociology* 22(3), September 1971, 283–294.

Warner, Michael. "The Public Sphere and the Cultural Mediation of Print," in William S. Solomon and Robert W. McChesney (eds.), *Ruthless Criticism: New Perspectives in U.S. Communication History*. Minneapolis: University of Minnesota Press, 1993, 7–37.

Watson, Mary Ann. *The Expanding Vista: American Television in the Kennedy Years*. New York: Oxford University Press, 1990.

Waugh, Evelyn. *Scoop*. New York: Penguin, 1938.

Weaver, David (ed.). *The Global Journalist: News People Around the World*. Cresskill, NJ: Hampton, 1998.

Weaver, David, and G. Cleveland Wilhoit. *The American Journalist*. Bloomington: University of Indiana Press, 1986.

Weaver, David, and G. Cleveland Wilhoit. *The American Journalist in the 1990s*. Mahwah, NJ: Lawrence Erlbaum, 1996.

Weber, Max. "Politics as a Vocation," in *From Max Weber: Essays in Sociology*. London: Routledge and Kegan Paul, 1948.

Wesker, Arnold. *Journey Into Journalism*. London: Writers and Readers Publishing Cooperative, 1977.

Wesker, Arnold. *Journalists*. London: Chatto and Windus, 1980.

White, David Manning. "The Gate Keeper: A Case Study in the Selection of News," *Journalism Quarterly* 27(3), 1950, 383–390.

Whitney, Charles D., and Lee B. Becker. "Keeping the Gates for Gatekeepers: The Effects of Wire News," *Journalism Quarterly* 59, 1982, 60–65.

Wilke, Juergen. *Nachrichtenauswahl und Medienrealität in vier Jahrhunderten. Eine Modellstudie zur Verbindung von historischer und empirischer Publizistikwissenschaft*. Berlin: De Gruyter, 1984a.

Wilke, Juergen. "The Changing World of Media Reality," *Gazette* 34(3), 1984b, 175–190.

Wilke, Juergen, and Bernhard Rosenberger. "Importing Foreign News: A Case Study of the German Service of Associated Press," *Journalism Quarterly* 71(2), 1994, 421–432.

Wilkie, Carol. "The Scapegoating of Bruno Richard Hauptmann: The Rhetorical Process in Prejudicial Publicity," *Central States Speech Journal* 32, 1981, 100–110.

Willnat, Lars, and Weaver, David. "Through Their Eyes: The Work of Foreign Correspondents in the United States," *Journalism: Theory, Practice, and Criticism* 4(4), 2003, 403–422.

Williams, Francis. *Dangerous Estate: The Anatomy of Newspapers*. New York: Macmillan, 1958.

Williams, Harold A. *The Baltimore Sun, 1837–1987*. Baltimore: Johns Hopkins University Press, 1987.

Williams, Raymond. *Culture and Society, 1780–1950*. New York: Columbia University Press, 1958.

Williams, Raymond. "The Press and Popular Culture: An Historical Perspective," in Boyce, George, James Curran, and Pauline Wingate (eds.), *Newspaper*

History from the Seventeenth Century to the Present Day. Beverly Hills, CA: Sage, 1978, 41–50.

Williams, Raymond. *What I Came to Say*. London: Hutchinson Radius, 1989.

Wilson, Clint C., II, and Félix Gutiérrez. *Race, Multiculturalism, and the Media*. Thousand Oaks, CA: Sage, 1995.

Wilson, Tracie L. "Press Systems and Media-Government Relations in the Czech and Slovak Republics," *Gazette* 54(2), 1994, 145–161.

Windahl, Sven, and Karl Rosengren. "Newsmen's Professionalization: Some Methodological Problems," *Journalism Quarterly* 55(3), 1978, 466–473.

Windshuttle, Keith, "Cultural Studies Versus Journalism," in Miles Breen (ed.), *Journalism: Theory and Practice*. Sydney: Macleay, 1998, 17–36.

Winston, Brian. "Towards Tabloidization? Glasgow Revisited, 1975–2001," *Journalism Studies* 3(1), 2002, 5–20.

Wolfsfeld, Gadi. *Media and Political Conflict: News From the Middle East*. Cambridge, UK: Cambridge University Press, 1997.

Wolfsfeld, Gadi. *Media and the Path to Peace*. Cambridge, UK: Cambridge University Press, 2003.

Wolton, Dominique, and Jean-Louis Missika. *La folle du logis*. Paris: Gallimard, 1983.

Woodstock, Louise. "Public Journalism's Talking Cure: An Analysis of the Movement's 'Problem' and 'Solution' Narratives," *Journalism: Theory, Practice and Criticism* 3(1), 2002, 37–55.

Woodward, Julian L. "Quantitative Newspaper Analysis as a Technique of Opinion Research," *Social Forces* 12(4), 1934, 526–537.

Wright, Charles. *Mass Communication: A Sociological Perspective*. New York: Random House, 1959.

Wyatt, Clarence R. *Paper Soldiers: The American Press and the Vietnam War*. New York: Norton, 1993.

Wyndham Goldie, Grace. *Facing the Nation: Television and Politics, 1936–1976*. London: Bodley Head, 1977.

Xu, Xiaoge. "Asian Values Revisited in the Context of Intercultural News Communication," *Media Asia* 25(1), 1998, 37–41.

Zelizer, Barbie. "'Saying' as Collective Practice: Quoting and Differential Address in the News," *Text* 9 (4), 1989, 369–388.

Zelizer, Barbie. "Achieving Journalistic Authority Through Narrative," *Critical Studies in Mass Communication* 7, 1990a, 366–376.

Zelizer, Barbie. "Where is the Author in American TV News? On the Construction and Presentation of Proximity, Authorship and Journalistic Authority," *Semiotica* 80–1/2, June 1990b, 37–48.

Zelizer, Barbie. "CNN, the Gulf War, and Journalistic Practice," *Journal of Communication* 42(1), Winter 1992a, 66–81.

Zelizer, Barbie. *Covering the Body: The Kennedy Assassination, the Media, and the Shaping of Collective Memory*. Chicago: University of Chicago Press, 1992b.

Zelizer, Barbie. "Has Communication Explained Journalism?" *Journal of Communication* 43(4), 1993a, 80–88.

Zelizer, Barbie. "Journalists as Interpretive Communities," *Critical Studies in Mass Communication* 10, September 1993b, 219–237.

Zelizer, Barbie. "The Failed Adoption of Journalism Study," *Press and Public Policy* 3(1), 1998a, 118–121.

Zelizer, Barbie. *Remembering to Forget: Holocaust Memory Through the Camera's Eye*. Chicago: University of Chicago Press, 1998b.

Zelizer, Barbie. "Making the Neighborhood Work: The Improbabilities of Public Journalism," in Theodore L. Glasser (ed.), *The Idea of Public Journalism*. New York: Guilford, 1999, 152–174.

Zelizer, Barbie. "Photography, Journalism and Trauma," in Barbie Zelizer and Stuart Allan (eds.), *Journalism After September 11*. London: Routledge, 2002, 48–68.

Zelizer, Barbie, and Stuart Allan (eds.). *Journalism After September 11*. London: Routledge, 2002a.

Zelizer, Barbie, David W. Park, and David Gudelunas. "How Bias Shapes the News: Challenging the *New York Times*' Status as a Newspaper of Record on the Middle East," *Journalism: Theory, Practice and Criticism* 3(3), December 2002b, 283–308.

Zhao, Yuezhi. *Media, Market, and Democracy in China: Between the Party Line and the Bottom Line*. Urbana: University of Illinois Press, 1998.

Index